Kiumajut (Talking Back)

Peter Kulchyski and Frank James Tester

Kiumajut (Talking Back): Game Management and Inuit Rights, 1900-70

UBCPress · Vancouver · Toronto

16 15 14 13 12 11 10 09 08 07   5 4 3 2 1

Printed in Canada on ancient-forest-free paper (100% post-consumer recycled)
that is processed chlorine- and acid-free, with vegetable-based inks.

Library and Archives Canada Cataloguing in Publication

Kulchyski, Peter Keith, 1959-
    Kiumajut (talking back) : game management and Inuit rights 1900-70 /
Peter Kulchyski and Frank James Tester.

Includes bibliographical references and index.
ISBN 978-0-7748-1241-2 (bound); ISBN 978-0-7748-1242-9 (pbk.)

    1. Wildlife management – Government policy – Canada, Northern – History.
2. Inuit – Hunting – Canada – History – 20th century. 3. Inuit – Canada –
Government relations. 4. Hunting – Government policy – Canada, Northern –
History. 5. Wildlife management – Canada, Northern – History. I. Tester, Frank J.
II. Title. III. Title: Talking back.

E99.E7K95 2007   333.95'4909719   C2007-904495-6

Canadä

UBC Press gratefully acknowledges the financial support for our publishing
program of the Government of Canada through the Book Publishing Industry
Development Program (BPIDP), and of the Canada Council for the Arts, and the
British Columbia Arts Council.

This book has been published with the help of a grant from the Canadian
Federation for the Humanities and Social Sciences, through the Aid to Scholarly
Publications Programme, using funds provided by the Social Sciences and
Humanities Research Council of Canada, and with the help of the K.D. Srivastava
Fund.

UBC Press
The University of British Columbia
2029 West Mall
Vancouver, BC V6T 1Z2
604-822-5959 / Fax: 604-822-6083
www.ubcpress.ca

Contents

Maps, Figures, and Tables / vii

Preface / ix

Introduction / 5

Part I: Managing the Game

1 Trapping and Trading: The Regulation of Inuit Hunting Prior to World War II / 23

2 *Sagluniit* ("Lies"): Manufacturing a Caribou Crisis / 50

3 *Sugsaunngittugulli* ("We Are Useless"): Surveying the Animals / 82

4 Who Counts? Challenging Science and the Law / 122

Part II: Talking Back

5 Inuit Rights and Government Policy / 165

6 Baker Lake, 1957: The Eskimo Council / 204

7 Inuit Petition for Their Rights / 239

Conclusion: Contested Ground / 273

Notes / 279

Bibliography / 302

Index / 308

Maps, Figures, and Tables

Map

The Northwest Territories before division to create Nunavut / 2

Figures

1 Inuit-owned schooners trading furs at Hershel Island in the 1930s / 31

2 Moses Koihok / 33

3 Angulalik and his family / 43

4 Ikey Bolt / 45

5 John Kelsall / 54

6 Farley Mowat / 57

7 Peter Irniq / 73

8 Caribou killed by Dene hunters, Duck Lake, Manitoba / 76

9 Hunting with a musk-ox bow, 1950 / 89

10 Emik Immaroitok / 107

11 Page from the Canadian Wildlife Service booklet *How to Save the Caribou*: "Men are the main killers of caribou" / 124

12 Drawing by André Tautu, 1958 / 126

13 Moses Nargyak / 128

14 Aerial photograph of migrating caribou / 155

15 Tagak Curley / 160

16 Rachel Uyarasuk / 198

17 Doug Wilkinson / 206

18 Apex, Frobisher Bay, Baffin Island, 1957 / 207

19 Page from the Canadian Wildlife Service booklet *How to Save the Caribou*: "Employment opportunities available" / 215

20 Page from the Canadian Wildlife Service booklet *How to Save the Caribou:* "Benefits of civilization and modernization" / 216

21 Signatures on the Coppermine (Kugluktuk) petition, 6 February 1953 / 241

22 Mangitak Qilippalik / 243

23 The Coppermine (Kugluktuk) petition for a hospital, 1962 / 258

Tables

1 John Kelsall's theoretical projection of caribou decline between 1949 and 1955 / 70

2 Analysis of 502 caribou killed at Contwoyto Lake, 1960 / 78

Preface

It is commonly stated that few groups of people in the world have attracted more attention than circumpolar Inuit. Yet, in all the reading and research we have done, we have been impressed not only by what is missing from the historical record but also by the importance of intimate details about the complex movement of Inuit, as a camp-based hunting culture, to settlement living and, in Canada, a form of self-government. Perhaps of even greater significance, we are acutely aware of what the words of Inuit contribute to the record. It is not a mere addition to the record of the Inuit journey toward relations with the Canadian polity that the words of Inuit elders and others produce. Rather, it is a reinterpretation of those relations that a combined archival record and oral history create.

This book is about community development in the eastern Arctic, in the territory known as Nunavut. "Community development" is a broad and all-encompassing term, and we expand on what we mean by it in what follows. As background, *Tammarniit [Mistakes]: Inuit Relocation in the Eastern Arctic, 1939-63,* our earlier study (1994), told the story of how the government of Canada in the latter part of the 1950s suddenly shifted its policy toward Inuit from deliberate neglect – in the interest of preserving Inuit independence – to massive intervention in almost every aspect of Inuit life. Two events, the High Arctic exiles (1953) and the Kivalliq region famines (1957-58), were the core stories we used to illustrate this redirection of policy. The book was based primarily on archival research supplemented by a few interviews.

Both of us are acutely aware of the difficulties posed for collaborative intellectual work in the current institutional context of the Canadian university. Although on the surface it is often encouraged, in practice collaboration remains agonizingly difficult. To have found the degree of mutuality, different but compatible intellectual skills and temperaments, and generally agreeable personalities (at least to each other!) required to make production of this sort possible has proven, for each of us, too fortuitous to abandon. Hence, as soon as *Tammarniit* was in press, we began to conceptualize continued research and writing.

The archival material we had collected for *Tammarniit* pointed us in a number of directions. We had collected some material we were unable to use. We were also well aware of a huge amount of material yet to be perused, interesting for its volume alone. It is important to remember that the Inuit population of the Canadian eastern Arctic was in the neighbourhood of about 7,000 people in the early 1940s, rising thereafter to about 27,500 today. The effort and energy expended in attempts to incorporate Inuit into the Canadian state have been truly remarkable, and the volume of paper itself – hundreds of cases of material and tens of thousands of documents in the National Archives of Canada and the Prince of Wales Heritage Centre in Yellowknife – speaks to this commitment. Adding to our original archival record, we set about to build an oral archive that would supplement the richness of the written archive. Or would the latter come to supplement the former? Believing we knew enough to ask the right questions, we began three seasons of research, a season in each of the major regions of Nunavut. We talked to women and men, many of whom have since passed away, who were adults in the postwar period and could speak to Inuit feelings about and responses to the changes they experienced. This new work therefore includes not merely history – and even oral history as found in the written record of things done and spoken by Inuit who experienced this phenomenal transition – but also oral testimony from those who participated in the events and processes under examination. Our hope is that this combination of documentary evidence and oral testimony produces a uniquely complex, interactive, and rewarding text.

Our writing practice was similar to that deployed in *Tammarniit*. Each of us drafted particular chapters, turned them over to the other for comment and editorial support, exchanged sections, hurled delightfully whimsical one-liners at each other, in respect of Frank's Scottish heritage sometimes spiced our caustic remarks with a touch of single malt, and enjoyed watching the Stanley Cup finals with Inuit friends and from TVs in Arctic communities with more ice – and in some cases more talent – than the NHL will ever manufacture. We somehow ended up with this text, whose value will ultimately be determined by its readers.

The first four chapters were originally drafted by Tester, the latter three by Kulchyski. Since *Tammarniit* was published as a Tester and Kulchyski product, *Kiumajut (Talking Back)* is presented under the sign of Kulchyski and Tester. As with the former book, we consider this one fully a product of mutual effort, and it may properly be cited with either name first: we duck equally quickly when the criticism starts flying, and neither of us is shy about presenting himself when praise is in the air.

What remains for this preface are important words of gratitude. This study was supported by grants from the Social Sciences and Humanities Research Council of Canada at a time when funding for non-scientific research was substantially reduced. We are immensely grateful to the officials and academic referees of the council for their contribution: one cannot take for granted a state that will fund its critics and perhaps must be ever vigilant to ensure that this fundamental protocol of scholarly inquiry is maintained. Over many years of work, we have developed strong working relationships with staff at Library and Archives Canada; although all of them deserve considerable credit, the years of dedicated attention to our needs provided by Mary-Jane Jones must be recognized.

At the University of British Columbia, a fine cadre of students has worked diligently for many years to help catalogue, abstract, and sort through thousands of documents. Starting with Robert Case, now employed with a consulting firm in Guelph, Ontario; Robert Logan, working with the Ministry of Children and Families of the BC government; Kelly Wugalter, who subsequently went to work in the Philippines; Rosalind Green, now working and studying in London, England; Shabniz Kirji, who then went to work with CUSO in Tanzania; Sandra Teves, a graduate student who subsequently worked with Frank in Mozambique; and Sabah Ibrahim, our current (2007) research assistant, we have had an enormous amount of talented and committed help. It is gratifying to hear from them that the skills and sensibilities they acquired in the course of participating in this research have served them well in the occupations and interests they have pursued. At Trent University and the University of Manitoba, Aluki Kotierk, Aaron Levere, Krista Pilz, and Janet Sarson provided support in the painstaking work of transcribing audiotapes and indexing.

This work led us to many Nunavut communities in 1997, 1998, and 1999 where we were hospitably treated. We enjoyed staying with Inuit in their homes wherever possible. We found excellent interpreters and community assistants for our research. We found people, many of them elders, who were willing to talk. Their names and those of their interpreters are included in the notes. From them we learned so much; to them we say *qoyanamiik paaluk!*

Special thanks are due to our friend and frequent interlocutor Peter Irniq for his patience, interest, and support (not to mention a place to stay in Iqaluit!). Peter would like to thank his colleagues Fred Shore, Chris Trott, and Emma Larocque, the latter two for enriching his understanding, respectively, of Inuit culture and colonial processes. He also thanks Malay, whose laughter sprinkles the joy of life wherever it is heard. Frank would like to thank his Inuit friends David Ukutak, Bobby Suluk, André Tautu, and Peter Irniq (particularly for help with Inuktitut), Bill Kashla, and Pierre Karlik for insights and lots of learning. Thanks also to *Qallunaat* friends

Bob Williamson, Paule McNicoll, Doug Wilkinson (who offered invaluable comments on Chapter 6), Bob Ruttan, Otto Schaefer, Tim Tyler, Julie Cruikshank, and Hugh Shewell, with whom Frank has consulted about this text on numerous occasions. Thanks to Lana Voloshenko for gentle and thoughtful support as well as critical feedback, particularly in regard to the treatment Frank has given some of the characters in the first four chapters of the text. One other person deserves special recognition. Frank would like to acknowledge the essential role of Jean-Marie Beaulieu of the Canadian Polar Commission in this research. Archival research is prohibitively expensive for those of us not living near the national capital. Had Jean-Marie not provided Frank with a place to stay and company to enjoy when he was working in the archives for many weeks off and on over the past ten years, this text would not have been possible. Thanks for years of meaningful and deeply appreciated friendship and never-ending support. Thanks to Jean Wilson and the staff of UBC Press for their diligence and indulgence. The circles of gratitude within which we are wound do not for a moment protect us from accepting our responsibility to and for these words, constructions, opinions, arguments, reflections, and understandings.

We pointed out in *Tammarniit* that, as they published the case *Re: Eskimos* in 1939, the editors of the *Dominion Law Review* apologetically noted that the case would be of no interest except as an example of process, of how the court arrived at decisions. The editors had no idea that Inuit themselves would come to form a readership and would of course have an interest in the substance of the case (not to mention Métis, for whom it is an important precedent regarding Aboriginal status in the Constitution). Much of what was written, even up to the 1970s and later, presumed a Western audience only: the famed "we" here often assuming a white male educated reader. This includes the archival material produced in the period studied herein and the published material, including that published by anthropologists who worked with and studied Inuit. "We" – Kulchyski and Tester – are of a generation that hopefully knows better. One of the meanings of the term "postcolonial," however presumptuous the "post," points to the multifaceted manner in which the colonial "other" is looking back. We want this book to find its way to Inuit students, scholars, policy makers, and readers. To facilitate that, we have occasionally used Inuktitut words or expressions that seem apt. Although we wish that all our readers find reading this work to their benefit, we offer the particular hope that with these pages, Inuit feel rewarded for their efforts.

Kiumajut (Talking Back)

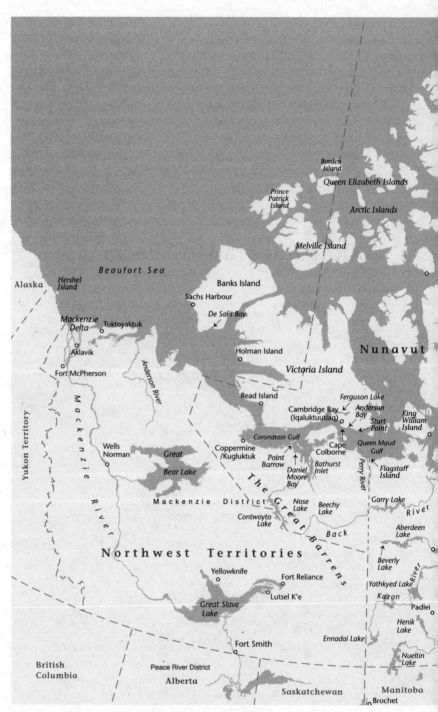

The Northwest Territories before division to create Nunavut, showing places noted in the text. Map by Eric Leinberger.

Alert

GREENLAND (Denmark)

Ellesmere Island

Alexandra
Fiord

Thule (Kanak)

Thule (Air Base)

Grise Fiord/Ausuittuq
Viks Fiord   Craig Harbour

Cape Sparbo

Devon Island

Resolute Bay/
Qausuittuq

*Bylot
Island*

*Somerset
Island*

Pond Inlet

Arctic Bay

Cape Christian
Clyde River

B a f f i n

Ekalugad Fiord

T e r r i t o r y

Cape Smith

Kivitoo   Broughton Island/Qikitarjuak
Fox 5   Padloping
Station

Fox 3
Station

*Rowley
Island*

Pangnirtung

Spence Bay/
Taloyoak

Igloolik

Hall Beach

I s l a n d

Cumberland Sound   Cape Mercy

Gjoa Haven

Hall Lake

Melville
Peninsula

Foxe Basin

Richardson Point
Starvation Cove
Chantrey Inlet

(Frobisher Bay)
Iqaluit

Repulse Bay
/Naujaat

Freuchen Bay
Palmer Bay
Blake Bay

*Cape
Dorset*

Keewatin District

Thelon River

*Southampton
Island*

Labrador

Qamanittuaq/
Baker Lake

Fullerton

Coral Harbour/Salliq

*Coats
Island*

James Bay

Fullerton Harbour

Chesterfield Inlet
/Igluligaarjuk

Rankin Inlet
Wilson River
Whale Cove/Tikiraqjuaq
Sandy Point

Povungnitu

Padlei

Maguse Lake

Arviat/
Eskimo Point

Quebec

*Nejanilini
Lake*

Hudson Bay

Churchill

0   200 miles

0   200 kilometres

Introduction

The broadest movements of history, told with relish in the inflated terms of master narratives (stories of growth, discovery, or progress, stories savoured at the tables of imperial centres), leave many marks on the values and geographic, economic, social, and cultural movements of those who have less reason to celebrate their sensibilities and outcomes. In our previous work (1994), *Tammarniit [Mistakes],* the title itself signified a departure from the common historical narratives dealing with the Arctic, where the "every day, in every way, things got better and better" content has been fed by a "tell it like it is" narrative style that could spice its overall message with a bit of tragedy from the Franklin expedition, more than a bit of adventure from the gold rush, and of course the odd bit of cultural exoticism from a passing reference to the Native occupants of northern frontiers. Coming to the study of Arctic history with the benefit of a reshaped view, that the North was a homeland as much as a frontier (in the words of Thomas Berger), we proposed a more critical view of the events and processes and of their outcomes than was common in contemporary historical accounts.

Tammarniit told three interrelated stories. One story was of the growth of the state apparatus in Arctic affairs in the postwar period. We looked at the expansion of the civil service, the growth of the Arctic branch in the south, and the associated increase in field staff in the North. From our perspective, this development had at least paradoxical results: on the one hand, it improved the ability of the state to respond to crises affecting the livelihoods of northern indigenous residents and contributed to removing the "absent-minded" relationship to northern Canada that southern decision makers evidenced; on the other hand, though, it increased the surveillance powers of the state and the ability of distant managers to interfere with the lifeways of Inuit. A second story dealt with the issue of relocation. The theme of relocation afforded us an organizing principle from which Arctic history in the 1950s and early 1960s especially could be understood, particularly in terms of its impact on Inuit. Two sets of relocations, the movement of Inuit from northern Quebec to the High Arctic (the now well-known story of the High Arctic exiles) and the relocation of inland Inuit in the Kivalliq region to coastal or community centres, provided the fodder for our reflections. Again, we attempted to show some sensitivity to how these movements of inland people to the coast and of southern Arctic dwellers to the northernmost reaches of the world may not have been entirely beneficial to those whose bodies bore the costs of what may or may not have been well-meant calculations. Finally, we dealt with the related story of how the state, somewhat under the pressure of the 1939 legal decision *Re: Eskimos,* which established federal government jurisdiction over if not responsibility for Inuit, moved from a policy of cost-motivated neglect to a policy of intensive interference and induced settlement-modernization. It was striking that no intermediate policy of support for the Inuit hunting economy was ever developed: in less than a decade, policy makers moved from the assumption that Inuit should be left on their own to fend for themselves to a policy of massive interference.

This book, *Kiumajut (Talking Back),* is not a continuation of but a companion to our earlier work. At a broad level, both deal with community development in the eastern Arctic, primarily the territory known as Nunavut. Our focus is on a geographic area now part of Nunavut, although we also include other areas historically occupied by Inuit in the western Arctic, including the Inuvialuit settlement area and the western Arctic coast. Where it serves our purpose, we make reference to territories that are part of the migration of northern caribou herds: the northern portions of the prairie provinces and the Northwest Territories. Describing our work as "about community development" may seem at first like an odd way to characterize the text, given its title. However, our research strongly suggests that community development in Nunavut was motivated by the state in multifaceted ways, from serving as a logical mechanism for the provision of social support structures to allowing for more careful surveillance of distant citizens. Similarly, community development involved attempts to regulate Inuit through management of the game upon which they depended not only for sustenance but also for personal and collective meanings and the cultural forms to which hunting gives rise. Hence, this work is related to *Tammarniit* but not as a second volume. While readers of *Tammarniit* will have a good deal of information that may illuminate this text, each can be read as a self-contained set of stories. This text concentrates on much of the same period and therefore overlaps with, rather than continues, the narrative of its predecessor. Broadly speaking, community development and community practice are areas of concern in both volumes, but this orientation has taken us here into government policy, legal history, so-called modernization, resistance, and the development of Inuit rights in areas as diverse as wildlife management and community governance, to mention a couple. One of the questions *Tammarniit* implicitly

posed – why the government did not develop a policy of strongly supporting the hunting economy – is answered in *Kiumajut* to the extent that we
demonstrate the influence of the growing science of game management on
policy makers.

Again, although we will not belabour the point, theoretical considerations
have had an impact on our framing and understanding of this material. Central to our project, the concept of totalization elaborated by Jean-Paul Sartre
(1991) in his *Critique of Dialectical Reason* continues to offer a framework
within which we can give shape to the historical material. The appearance
in English of the second volume of the *Critique* has provided a fresh set of
insights in relation to the concept. A few of our readers may understand our
surprise and delight at discovering the skeletal analysis offered there of the
impact of the fox fur trade on Inuit: "I change my hunting (walrus, seal, bear
[to] fox, formerly despised because its meat is poor). I enter the circuit for
profit; i.e. these pelts are sold not for the needs of others, which would still
have been direct, but for the profit of some people in a developed society
where the satisfaction is always indirect, as a (hidden) economic motor, and
where accumulation allows luxury (i.e. symbolic, rather than productive or
reproductive) expenditure. Who shall say if this is progress?" (409).

Beyond the coincidence of interest in and general attitude toward some of
the same material, the second volume more closely links the idea of totalization to the ideology of progress: "Progress is necessarily a totalization.
For it is the pursuit of the restoration or establishment of a totality" (Sartre
1991, 407). So much of northern history assumes the notion of progressive
improvement that when read from a critical perspective it takes the character of justificatory ideology. This is the "every day, in every way, things got
better and better" school of colonial historiography already referred to, so
deeply rooted in Canadian and especially northern history. Hence, merely
to begin with the assumption that change does not equal improvement,
particularly in the field of Aboriginal history, is to find oneself calling into
question the foundations not only of Canadian historiography but also of
the very logic upon which contemporary Western civilization has built its
many edifices.

This logic is bound up with hegemonic discourse about "need" and attempts to meet manufactured needs. Need is what Sartre identifies as the
original state of tension in regard to nature: "A need is the first totalizing
relation between the material being, man, and the material ensemble of
which he is a part" (1991, 80). Totalization of Inuit involved, for the state,
the transmutation of need away from relations to animals and toward what
so-called progress had to offer: wage employment, permanent housing, settlement living, and all that they entail. Undermining the hunting regime, as a
way of meeting culturally constructed needs, was crucial to attempts to absorb
Inuit by the Canadian state into the dominant social forms. The tension

in the movement of history is between competing forces and perceptions: the developing solidarity to resist the common deprivation threatening a collective (which develops in response to the perceived threat and which we have attempted to document in this text) and attempts by the state to replace the foundation for existing social organization (animals and hunting as *the* way of addressing need) with alternatives organized under the banner of modernization and in the name of Canadian citizenship. This process for dealing with gathering and hunting societies – as embarrassments to the machinations of modern culture – is widespread and includes state attempts to integrate people as dispersed and distinct as the Hadzabe of Tanzania and the Aborigines of Australia.

To take what is today called "globalization" as merely the latest phase – and latest fashion in language – of a process that began at least a few centuries ago, a process whose specific modality and pace have of necessity depended on the social circumstances of each new terrain it entered, is to bring to bear a measure of respect for those thinkers who become surpassed only to the extent that they are no longer widely read. The particular merit of Sartre's work in this regard is his emphasis and indeed insistence on the importance of human activity – what Sartre referred to as *praxis* in order to point to the multidimensional character of its embodiments – and resistance to our understanding of history. In *Tammarniit,* we pointed out that a critical feature missing from our account was the nature and extent of Inuit resistance. For Sartre, history itself can be constructed only from the interplay between totalization and resistance; in effect, we had concentrated on only half of the story. In *Kiumajut,* we hope to redress this omission by beginning to trace the outlines of Inuit responses to the measures being imposed, in the interest not of producing a "fuller" history but hopefully of producing a more nuanced account.

A few words regarding our view of the state may play an expedient role in our brief theoretical excursus. We contend that the concern emerging from Michel Foucault's (1979) influential work with respect to "micro politics" and the decentring of power away from the state, while evocative and in Foucault's hands deployed with a strong, critical political charge, in the hands of others has become deeply depoliticized and unsatisfactory as an approach to power relations. Certain readings of Foucault accomplish for social and political thought the same ends as those David Harvey (1990, 255) identifies with the Enlightenment's treatment of time and space: a "'pulverization' and fragmentation" that facilitated colonial control of spaces and places otherwise challenging to its logic. The uncritical use of Foucault's dictum that "power is everywhere" accomplishes similar intellectual ends with regard to state power, revealing (as if it were necessary) the profound political implications of reordering key concepts in social and political thought. Hence, in northern studies as diverse as Sherrill Grace's (2001) *Canada and the Idea of North* and Paul Nadasdy's (2003) *Hunters and Bureaucrats: Power, Knowledge, and Aboriginal-State Relations in the Southwest Yukon,* the concepts of discourse and power serve, to some extent, to muddy the political waters of what in our view is a sharp disjuncture between the colonizers and the colonized. Frantz Fanon (1966) and Albert Memmi (1972) have insisted on this distinction, which, for all the fluidity of their analyses, remains fundamental to the work of postcolonial theorists as diverse as Gayatri Spivak (1999), Edward Said (1979), and Homi Bhabha (1994). With only occasional reference to it, Grace develops an idea of "northern" identity that serves ultimately as a foundation for contemporary settler-colonial ideology; Nadasdy explicitly rejects what he takes to be a simplistic view of the state as a monolith and the notion of "colonialist and/or neo-colonial policies of exploitation" (4) in the interest of a greater "complexity" and thereby in our view undercuts the political charge of his interesting historical and contemporary analysis. In effect, the theoretical position of Foucault lends itself to co-optation by a liberal form of politics that ultimately colludes with dominating power. This is not to say that Foucault is of no use: we are clearly indebted to the concepts of surveillance and normalization developed in *Discipline and Punish;* however, we deploy his work cautiously and within the parameters of a quite different approach to questions of the state and power, domination, and colonial relations.

Drawing from the work of a twentieth-century dialectical Marxist tradition, in which Sartre is a central figure but which includes George Lukacs (1981), Walter Benjamin (1978), and Max Horkheimer and Theodor Adorno (1944) and reaches to contemporary social theorists such as Marshall Sahlins (1972), David Harvey (1990), and Fredric Jameson (1991), we are working with a notion of the state as a critical totalizing force, operating alongside the accumulation of capital and the expansion of the commodity form to establish a new social totality. This view does not presume that the state is a simple monolith; its agents work in the complex and sometimes contradictory ways to which Nadasdy, for example, pays close attention. Historical actors such as Gordon Robertson, Justice Jack Sissons, Doug Wilkinson, and John Kelsall had profoundly complex motives, made constructive contributions to the material conditions of Inuit living in Canada, and ultimately were bearers of a totalizing project that dramatically affected Inuit culture not entirely for the better. Our review of their work pays attention, we hope, to the nuances of their agency. Similarly, we should note that Inuit themselves can be and have been agents of totalization (there is, after all, a contemporary Inuit corporate elite), though in our view Inuit culture and the values enacted by those attached to Inuit culture represent the fundamental elements of resistance.

Even totalitarianism, if we read Hannah Arendt (1973) closely, operates more complexly than the caricatures of Western ideology commonly presuppose, and from the perspective of indigenous hunters the liberal-democratic state looks fundamentally totalitarian. So the point is not simple academic abstraction. Furthermore, the state (shop floorman for capital accumulation and its junior partner expansion of the commodity form) is resisted at every step of the way. Hence, for all its complexity and contradictions, the state in our view works along a multifaceted trajectory whose ultimate, over-riding objective is totalization: to incorporate by absorption or to expel by banishment any traces of social difference and social forms not ultimately conducive to the accumulation of capital. This may mean compromises but only those that can be afforded: those that do not seriously challenge or, better still, are seen to guarantee, through a delayed or alternative approach, those objectives consistent with capitalist logic or, further, that head off serious challenges to capitalist logic. We view the liberal welfare state that has had profound impacts for all Aboriginal populations in Canada in this regard: as a machine of totalization.

This approach also points to the contested construction of at least the organization of space, time (see Harvey 1990), and subjectivity along the principles of a serial logic (see Sartre 1991), the order of fragments in a linear numerical sequence, and the conjoined principles of an instrumental rationality (see Horkheimer and Adorno 1944). Certainly the historical material we have examined, both in *Tammarniit* and in this work, gives credence to such a perspective. This theoretical approach owes something to Anthony Giddens (1987) in *The Nation State and Violence* and to Nicos Poulantzas (1980) in *State. Power. Socialism,* both of which in different ways broach the notion that "liberal-democratic" states can be seen to operate with totalizing and totalitarian agendas. The fashionable view of Michael Hardt and Antonio Negri (2001) in their recent and much-read *Empire* that "there is no outside" to capital/empire is, in our view, a deeply misguided imperial conceit, constructed from thinkers operating too close to contemporary imperial centres to recognize the nature of the life-and-death struggles of those at the margins. If our theoretical impulses recall an inspiration from somewhat older theoretical reflections, Sartre and Horkheimer and Adorno, it is in part because notions of the "newness of the new" are defining features of commodity relations, a principle at the heart of the fashion system that influences the production of clothing as much as the production of ideas. In sum, theoretical considerations and influences have informed our selection and interpretation of much of the material that follows; as with our earlier work, we have preferred to keep the theoretical apparatus largely off stage and to allow the historical material its starring role.

Kiumajut is divided into two parts and tells two related stories. The first four chapters deal with the emergence and development of the science of wildlife management as it affected Inuit populations. We do not dwell on the history of science and the relationship of the science of wildlife management to this broader picture. However, the science of wildlife management does parallel other developments in scientific thought and process. In medicine, for example, the discovery of penicillin and the development of antibiotics and vaccinations, commencing in the late 1920s, moved medicine from what was in many respects a healing "art" to a scientific practice. The science of wildlife biology evolved from a naturalistic form, primarily descriptive and taxonomic (as evidenced by natural history museums, originating in the late 1880s), to a science involving observation, manipulation, and prediction. In a parallel way, wildlife biology was given impetus by refinements in the development of aircraft leading to the aerial surveying of large mammal populations, commencing in the 1930s. In the Canadian Arctic, this approach "took off" following World War II, given the experience with aviation gained during the war by some biologists and the availability of aircraft, pilots, and more sophisticated approaches to navigation over challenging terrain.

Along with the science, we trace the management regime that emerged for key species important to Inuit culture and survival. The science and regime emerged primarily in relation to a perceived crisis in the numbers and availability of wildlife. We have been heavily influenced in writing the first half of the book by Horkheimer and Adorno's (1944) assessment of Enlightenment logic, seeing in the enveloping regime of management the banishment of what they call "mythic beliefs": the supplanting of Inuit relations to animals with the logic, discourse, and machinations of science. The management regime both produced and was a product of attempts to apply science to wildlife management following World War II. This story is critical to appreciating the emergence of Inuit resistance and an Inuit concept of rights, as wildlife – for a hunting people – lie at the core of meaning, as expressed through language and culture: art, storytelling, history, interpersonal and familial relations, and day-to-day practices. In the first part of the book, we focus on attempts to manage terrestrial mammals since attempts to do the same for marine mammal populations – with the exception of walrus – did not emerge until after the period covered by our text.

We demonstrate that what would now be recognized as deeply flawed science was taken as "gospel truth" by administrators who used the information they acquired not only to interfere with Inuit hunting practices but also, in the process, to alter dramatically most other aspects of Inuit life. In fact, it is inaccurate to identify flawed science alone as the problem. A close reading of texts, combined with observations of Inuit elders who lived through this period, reveals the extent to which the attitudes and values – the ethnocentric assumptions of those playing "the science game" – drove the science itself. There are important lessons here for anyone failing to appreciate the social dimensions of scientific work and for the role of traditional knowledge in containing and redirecting what can otherwise be misdirected enquiry. There is one element of Foucault's (1979) work that conceptualizes these issues, the notion of "biopolitics" that now circulates widely in social theory, particularly in the work of Giorgio Agamben (1998). Attempts by the state to know and manage wildlife, by knowing and managing hunters, can be thought of as an element of a broader turn by the state to the definition and management of "life" as an integral element of its totalizing arsenal.

The first chapter provides the reader with historical context for what follows. We examine the early impacts of Aboriginal and non-Aboriginal activity on game populations in the Arctic. We document fledgling attempts to address them. Of significance is a cultural climate conditioned by what was understood to be the fate of North American wildlife in general and some species in particular. Dealing with the perceived "loss of game" was no easy matter. The science of game management had not yet developed. With the exception of Darwinian science, the approach taken to wildlife was that of a natural history of species and was highly taxonomic. Regulation was based primarily on perceived historical experience, heavily influenced by the fact of settlement in western Canada and the United States and the loss of species (bison, carrier pigeon, etc.). In regard to the totalizing agenda of the state, the period is illustrative of a clear ambivalence to modernity, for while increasing concern for the administration of Arctic territory is clear from the historical record (Grant 1988) the fear of creating relationships of dependency – and hence the urgent need to preserve the game populations upon which Inuit depended – are also evident. This fear gave rise to important tensions not only in the making of game laws but also, perhaps more importantly, in their application. This point is illustrated by our discussion of the state response to Angulalik, described by Dorothy Eber as "the first Inuit business tycoon" (1997, 49). Angulalik was an Inuk whose social position as trader challenged the preferred image of Inuit as hunters existing beyond the enlightened relations of commerce. While notable for the period in question, this tension carried over into the decade following World War II when the state finally concluded that Inuit hunting culture was no longer viable and attempted, as we documented in *Tammarniit,* to totalize Inuit within the Canadian state.

The second chapter documents a considerable and somewhat abrupt change in attempts to regulate Inuit hunting. The period immediately following World War II ushered in the science of game management. In this chapter, we set out to examine, in some detail, the practice of that science and to challenge its theoretical neutrality. In doing so, we read through the studies and texts that dominate the period, paying particular attention to language and difference (Derrida 1976). We find Inuit constructed not as hunters killing animals but as "primitives" involved in the "wanton slaughter" of game. This suggests a classically dialectical relationship in that the social construction, taken as "fact," gives rise to text and hence becomes embodied in the very practices – movements, designs, calculations, presentations, and so on – of scientists themselves. The science of game management is, in this way, informed by the context it generates. Our text and analysis at this point are increasingly informed by Horkheimer and Adorno's classic analysis of the concept of Enlightenment: "On the road to modern science, men renounce any claim to meaning. They substitute formula for concept, rule and probability for cause and motive" (1944, 5). We focus, of necessity, on the work of individual scientists, particularly the studies of a young John Kelsall and of A.W.F. Banfield. Our critical assessment of this work is not to be seen as a claim about personal failings. Rather, we wish to particularize the way in which Enlightenment logic expresses itself in and through those who took up the challenge of scientifically managing game in the period in question. This is a case study in the disenchantment of the world noted by Berman (1981), the attempted extirpation of Inuit animism and spiritualism that Hugh Brody visits in *The Other Side of Eden* (2000). Consistent with the observations of Horkheimer and Adorno, we work from the premise that within Enlightenment logic "what men want to learn from nature is how to use it in order wholly to dominate it and other men" (1944, 4). However, this is not a "tight vise," as they recognize (37), and we acknowledge moments of doubt expressed by our protagonists as they attempt to reconcile science and the totalizing agenda of the state with the exceptional needs of Aboriginal populations and, to some degree, the limits of scientific method itself. Thus, there is tension in their work, while the overall commitment to science and its effective use in the management of animals – and Inuit – is clear. Our focus is primarily on the developing science of caribou biology, presented and represented as "truth" to officers of the state.

Chapter 3 examines how the science discussed in Chapter 2 found its way into practice, how the logic and convictions of state wildlife officials were applied to Inuit hunters and to Inuit culture in general. We start with significant changes to the Northwest Territories game laws of 1949. In a substantial way, this event signalled the development of a tide nicely explained in *The Dialectic of Enlightenment* (Horkheimer and Adorno 1944). The machinery of domination – in this case game laws and the means by which to enforce them – gives rise to resistance, a response that must further be contained. This dialectical process – a persistent power struggle – has brought us to some interesting places: in terms of Aboriginal rights and the law, we have come to the increasing recognition and possible use of principles from Aboriginal law in the making of legal decisions (Borrows 2002). In the case of reaction to the Northwest Territories game laws, resistance came not only from Inuit – who continued to hunt, trap, and ignore the edicts of the state to a considerable degree – but also from within the state apparatus itself. In this chapter, we encounter Justice Sissons, who thwarted attempts by public servants to regulate Inuit hunting (his work is assessed in greater depth in Chapter 5). In Chapter 3, we find that state officials were relentless in their pursuit of Inuit compliance, having given them a period of grace (not to be confused with a different agenda) in which to "get the hang of it." While we focus substantially on caribou, we note the attention paid to other species – walrus and polar bear – as these species have had applied to them a management logic parallel to that developed for caribou.

In Chapter 4, the logic of the regime of management introduced in Chapter 2 and illustrated in its application in Chapter 3 starts to fall apart. We illustrate the developing conflict over musk-ox regulation as well as challenges to prevailing wisdom about caribou. Paradoxically, it was the state's abandonment of the idea of subsistence hunting as a viable alternative for Inuit that brought the hunting of musk-ox to the fore as the state considered the benefits of sport hunting and the possibility of providing a cash income to Inuit who participated. This logic encountered the ethic of species preservation, held not only by some wildlife biologists but also by many other Canadians. With respect to caribou, the population estimates generated by Kelsall and others (and the regulatory regimes they implied) have been challenged from both within the public service and by Inuit. We illustrate this challenge by focusing on the work of Robert Ruttan, a field biologist at one time employed in joint federal-provincial studies of caribou, who questions the claims made by Kelsall. Inuit resistance to the wildlife management regime – explored in more detail in Chapter 5 – is starting to grow, as can be seen by Inuit leader Tagak Curley's challenge to a prohibition against caribou hunting on Coats Island. By way of further paradox, in settings such as community councils (institutional forms seen by state actors to further the rational agenda of state management), resistance takes on new and potent forms. Inuit move to meet the state on its own terms using a combination of what Nadasdy (2003) identifies as the discursive, logical, and institutional means of the colonizing culture as well as those of a resistant and distinctive Inuit culture.

The second part of *Kiumajut* furthers our examination of Inuit responses to the colonial regime. The material is not comprehensive and, again it should be emphasized, more episodic than epic in nature. The focus of the chapters is on forms and moments of resistance and the manner in which Inuit agency or praxis began, however hesitantly, to express itself. Of necessity, the chapters deal with the manner in which the state responded to these activities. These chapters can be read in the context of an international interest in forms of resistance that itself emerged in the wake of and in reaction to a structuralist emphasis, from Louis Althusser (1971) and Nicos Poulantzas (1980) through to Michel Foucault (1979) and Jean Baudrillard (1981), on the mechanics and workings of "power" or forms of hegemony. The works of Marshall Sahlins (1972), James Scott (1985), Jean and John Comaroff

(1991), and especially Michael Taussig (1997) have been useful touchstones for us. However, given the emphasis on archival material and a historical approach, we have worked less on gestures and everyday actions that can be seen or read as resistance – the dragging of feet, petty theft, and so on that are the matter of Scott's work – and more on documentary utterances and documented actions that clearly express a contestation of the emerging hegemonic regime. Taken with the examples of Inuit resistance offered in the first part of this work, this study goes some way, we hope, toward detailing the logic of this resistance. As we noted in *Tammarniit,* "it was necessary to develop our understanding of the specific logic of totalization in this specific geographical and historical context before we could follow the logic of resistance – something that merits detailed and future consideration" (Tester and Kulchyski 1994, 8). We hope we have gone some way toward meeting this commitment.

Chapter 5, "Inuit Rights and Government Policy," details the confrontation between Inuit hunters and the state through attempts by Inuit to assert their right to continued access to land-based resources upon which their livelihood depended. The chapter begins with a discussion of a particular historical event, the smashing of a drum in Arviat, to demonstrate graphically the nature of the force Inuit confronted. The figure of Justice Sissons, who appears first in our story in Chapter 3, has some prominence in this chapter. His relatively early decisions on Inuit rights were critical in two ways: they provided strong support for Inuit "on the ground," and they demonstrated that in historical context the state's agents were capable of developing a more sympathetic position regarding Inuit rights. If Sissons, himself an agent of the state's judicial branch, could understand and make strong arguments pertaining to Inuit rights, we cannot be accused of "historical decontextualization" in suggesting that others from the state might reasonably have adopted the same attitude. The chapter demonstrates how firmly they did not. We are particularly indebted here to Dorothy Eber's (1997) remarkable *Images of Justice* and have tried to extend her work on the issue of northern justice with a stronger documentary record and additional oral history. The chapter does review the place of Inuit rights in the history of Aboriginal rights, a point we must also touch on in this introduction. It is our concern to emphasize that, while the chapter details conflicts between Sissons and other officials, Inuit hunters were primarily responsible, through their actions, for creating the conditions and the conflicts that ultimately led to recognition of Inuit rights.

Chapter 6, "Baker Lake, 1957: The Eskimo Council," involves a close reading of one set of archival documents, the record of one of the first Inuit political organizations. Although the impetus for the council came from a non-Inuk (we use the Inuit/Inuktitut word *Qallunaat* throughout the text), Doug Wilkinson, in our view creation of the council and its operation were ultimately the responsibility of Inuit, who responded to and created the conditions that precipitated its establishment and who enthusiastically supported its operation. A detailed consideration of the record of discussions of this council conveys a sense of which issues Inuit were concerned with and substantively what positions they took with regard to these issues. Hunting rights and game management played no small part in their deliberations; hence, the chapter provides another view of the Inuit response to the operation of the regime described in Part I. Of particular interest to us was the issue of how Inuit understood the Western democratic forms into which they were being inserted: their fascination with hidden ballot voting, procedural rules, and so on. This interest comes naturally to Canadian academics working in the shadow of C.B. Macpherson's (1965) scholarly studies of democratic forms. Hence, the concern in this chapter is both with the articulation of resistance and with the establishment of forms that open the space for such articulation.

"Inuit Petition for Their Rights," the seventh and final substantive chapter, reads through a selection of Inuit petitions to the government and again emphasizes an interest in the petition as a form of response along with the substance of their concerns and the state's reactions. The first of these petitions, an early 1953 land claim from Kugluktuk, in our view deserves to be seen as a document with significant heritage value and was one of our major archival "finds." We therefore read the document and the correspondence that followed it closely, particularly since Inuit were concerned here with the larger issue of land ownership – what today we would call Aboriginal title – and were not immediately deterred by the state's initial attempts to dismiss their concerns out of hand. Other petitions, made by Inuit from the 1950s and 1960s, are also examined to provide a sense of the range of issues Inuit were concerned about enough to engage in this "formal" mode of response, including a petition by the Inuit women of Cape Dorset. Our reading of these documents was partly informed by the recent, poststructural philosophical interest in writing itself and especially the signature: a significant theme in the work of Jacques Derrida (1976). Although Derrida contests the Rousseau-inspired notion that writing is one of the constitutive elements of state power, he remains a key thinker for those interested in the relation of writing to power. Nominalism, the form of naming, is virtually a theme in Inuit culture, and hence the nature of the signatures indicating the names attached to these petitions is a question of contemporary anthropological and philosophical currency.

In some respects, our text is largely about rights: the emergence of a concept of rights and rights discourse that intersected with the colonizing culture, particularly as the 1950s turned into the 1960s and 1970s. We have not dwelt extensively on theoretical aspects of this dimension of our work, believing that the text will raise in the mind of the inquisitive reader a number of questions – and hopefully provide a number of critical insights – into the emergence of this discourse, as contained in the unfolding of events and the words of Inuit themselves. From the time of Peter Cumming and Neil Mickenberg's (1971) *Native Rights in Canada,* which advanced a notion that "'Aboriginal rights' are those property rights which inure to native peoples by virtue of their occupation upon certain lands from time immemorial" (13), to Brian Slattery's (1987) postconstitutional notions of Aboriginal rights as a "hidden constitution" in Canada, through to more recent reflections from Sakej Henderson (1997), Patrick Macklem (2001), and John Borrows (2002), a body of legal scholarship has developed in close relationship to significant court decisions that has elaborated and theorized the question of Aboriginal rights. Peter Kulchyski (1994) has made a small contribution to this work, and his emphasis on characterizing Aboriginal rights as not exhausted by property rights, but also involving distinct political rights, and on articulating the value of a distinctive, *sui generis,* undefinable element of Aboriginal rights informs the approach we use here. This work, however, operates in the historical rather than the theoretical mode by studying how a distinctive though related Inuit approach emerged from their specific circumstances. Inuit resistance to the management of birds and mammals by *Qallunaat* authorities is a significant consideration in the development of Inuit rights and in the move toward Inuit self-government. It is therefore not surprising that one of the first items on the agenda of the Inuit rights organization, the Inuit Tapiriit Kanatami (formerly the Inuit Tapirisat of Canada, created in 1971), was Inuit hunting rights. The regulation of game in the eastern Arctic did not involve the "management" of birds and mammals at all but was fundamentally about the management of people – of Inuit. For this reason, the history of game management in the eastern Arctic, its implications for Inuit families and communities, and Inuit resistance to the regimes being imposed are critical considerations in any study of Inuit rights.

But looking back on our text, we see that questions emerge about the awkwardness of concepts of rights arising, of necessity, to counter the dealings of a colonial administration. Inuit take up the discourse on a playing field *theoretically* level with the administrators, politicians, and other actors whose words and deeds are aimed at them. The ensuing struggle demonstrates that the field, even once the relevant concepts have been grasped, is anything but level. However, it is interesting to note the temporal relationship of this discourse, not only among Inuit but also among Aboriginal peoples in general, following on the United Nations Declaration of Human Rights in 1949. Inuit, as collective actors, have contributed much to placing on the world stage a category of rights hitherto ill considered: the Aboriginal or indigenous rights that involve such a range of property rights, civil or political rights, and social and cultural rights. As one commentator has made clear, these comprise a special category of rights in that they focus on the collective dimension of human experience. They are "not goods belonging to specific individuals, but collective goods, that is, goods that cannot be divided, but can only be enjoyed in common. For indeed, peace, development, national self-determination, group-identity and so on, are meaningful *only in relation to communities*" (VanderWal 1990, 84; emphasis added). It is therefore appropriate – if a more in-depth appreciation of the genesis of Inuit rights is taken as one of our objectives – that our text focus on communities: those geographical communities created as part of the totalizing efforts of the state as well as communities of fraternity, mutual interest and concern, and ethical reciprocity established across Nunavut, enabled in many ways by the former.

It is important at the outset to clarify the perspective used in making the claim that racist and ethnocentric assumptions drove much of the science of game management and the development of state policy. In our view, racism needs to be sharply distinguished from ethnocentrism. The first term refers to a set of relations of domination organized around perceived skin colour or racial difference and effectively theorized by Frantz Fanon (1966); the latter term refers to a set of relations of domination organized around cultural difference and may include refusals to recognize the difference itself, theorized in a good deal of contemporary anthropology. We categorically reject the idea that racism and ethnocentrism can be muted by reference to a particular historical moment, as in "well, that's just the way folks talked back then." Although discourse we can now identify as racist may have been common – in fact institutionalized and hence normalized by the state and related social institutions – this does not counter the claim that certain acts of speech and constructed images are racist. We maintain that, while actors may unconsciously (they are supposed to be unconscious) engage in racist discourse, two things can be true at the same time: that is the way most people talked at a particular historical moment, and the discourse was often racist. We do not engage this critique from a universal vantage point: we hope those readers who find that this text deserves their attention will be as determined in their criticism of our own language and the values underlying it as we have been with our sources. This in our view is a responsibility that critical thought cannot abandon (see Howard Adams 1975, Emma LaRocque 1975, Himani Bannerji 1995, Hugh Brody 1987, and Minnie Aodla Freeman 1978).

As should be clear by now, the concept of a dialectical relation between totalization and praxis (or resistance) is the tea within which our work is steeped. For example, we discuss the development of new techniques for determining animal populations, leading to new forms of knowledge dressed up as scientific "truth." This knowledge leads to a series of policies of greater surveillance of northern Inuit practices and increased involvement in attempts to change the practices – in effect justification for increased state-sponsored interference in Inuit lives. Hence, a totalizing knowledge becomes linked to a totalizing power. Inuit respond to this intrusion in a variety of ways, from the quotidian level of "smuggling" game newly classified as illegal to the assertion of rights. What Sartre (1991) called "praxis" in his *Critique* involved a broad range of active and passive interventions – sometimes responses and sometimes autonomous developments – including forms of resistance and forms of agency, struggles and subversions, such as those indicated above.

Some understanding of this small slice from fragments of the story can perhaps facilitate our comprehension of what comes later: the struggle for Nunavut and beyond. In this, we acknowledge the contribution of George Wenzel (1991), whose study *Animal Rights, Human Rights: Ecology, Economy, and Ideology in the Canadian Arctic* resonates with the earlier period and issues documented here. We are also indebted to the strong understanding of hunting cultures that emerged in the postwar period and to which Canadian anthropology has made significant contributions. As well as Wenzel, students of Inuit culture from Jean Briggs (1967) to Asen Balicki (1970) to Hugh Brody (2000) have opened new modes of appreciation and understanding for hunters. Their work stands beside the work on hunting cultures of those who worked with other First Nations, much of which inevitably turns toward questions of rights: from Michael Asch (1984) to Robin Riddington (1990), from Julie Cruikshank (1998) to Harvey Feit (1982, 1986). Feit's work certainly broaches questions of state regulation of hunting, and his most recent coedited collection is called *In the Way of Development* (Blaser, Feit, and McRae 2004), a title that could equally characterize this work. We have also benefited from the work of students of the history of environmentalism and game management policy, an area of growing interest. In the text, we rely on a variety of scholars; here we might mention the studies of Fikret Berkes (1999) and the earlier work of Milton Freeman (1992), both of whom worked with Inuit. Certainly this particular story of an ill-advised rush to intrude on Inuit hunting practices by conservationists, in this case primarily located within the Dominion Wildlife Service created after World War II and similar bodies that predate it, is a cautionary tale to a new generation of environmentalists armed with even newer scientific "truths." Perhaps, as we study these relations and forces, we may also glimpse that which ever seems to evade the intellectual grasp: history may expose itself much more clearly on the margins – in this case the rather large fragment of Canada called "the North" – than in the epicentres of power.

Classifying this work may be a more difficult task than producing it. In the foregoing, we have treated it as history or ethnohistory, at times lapsing into what some would call psychohistorical observations as we try to make intelligible the behaviour of key actors or groups of actors. These efforts will undoubtedly raise hackles among those committed to an objectivist tradition of historical enquiry. And, of course, neither Tester nor Kulchyski is a trained "historian." Much of the material touched on involves policy analysis and politics – of the sort that appeals to Kulchyski's training in political "science." But those approaches do not exhaust the subjects we have discussed. The element of geography, foregrounded in *Tammarniit*, with its concern regarding relocation, space, and time, is less prominent here but still central to an appreciation of the attempt to manage species over a landscape immense beyond description and at a historical moment saturated with empirical certainty. Tester can claim to be a geographer with a background in environmental "science," providing us with due credentials for our claims in this area. The anthropologically inflected interpretations of the material remain a critical dimension of our practice, but we are not anthropologists, and the text is not confined to a study of cultural change. Perhaps most importantly, the work has been inspired by the sensibilities found in professional affiliations that take the problem of contested *values* and *meanings* in history and human relations seriously: Native studies, in the case of Kulchyski, and social work, in the case of Tester. Certainly the study of community development and community practice provides a broad fabric under which a good deal can be swept. The work is interdisciplinary, though to call it "interdisciplinary studies" will only satisfy the bureaucrats of knowledge and serve no purpose to those for whom thought matters. We leave it – such as it is – in the hands of our readers to determine where on their shelves it will sit, with the hope that it earns whatever space it is given.

A brief note on terms may serve to draw down the curtain on this introduction. Both Tester and Kulchyski continue to work extensively with Inuit communities and struggle to add to their limited knowledge of Inuktitut. Where appropriate, we give precedence to a few Inuit terms; while doing so may slightly estrange non-Inuit readers, we think it will help Inuit readers to find a home in this text, estranged as they will be by the many technical English-language words we have used. Hence, we use the Inuit word *Qallunaat* to describe non-Inuit; it seems appropriate to the text, it structurally positions readers on the Inuit side of the colonial divide, and it is simply less awkward than non-Native, non-Inuit, whites, and other such constructions. We have also used contemporary Inuit place names where they have been formally adopted, including older colonial place names in brackets and on the map to help situate readers. Colonial nominalism, the introduction of different manners of naming as well as different names, has never been an incidental part of the workings of totalizing power; while Inuit themselves have taken enormous strides in reversing and contesting colonial nominalism, we too may take a few baby steps in that direction.

Part I
Managing the Game

1

Trapping and Trading: The Regulation of Inuit Hunting Prior to World War II

Arctic Wildlife and "Wanton Slaughter"

This chapter examines attempts to manage northern game, primarily caribou, in the period prior to World War II. It explores the origins of the sensibilities – perhaps more accurately described as fears – that influenced these efforts. The science of game management did not develop until after World War II. Prior to the war, game management was based principally on socially and culturally constructed norms, values, and experiences. Furthermore, Canadian interest in species preservation was heavily influenced by ideas developing in the United States, where the administration of Theodore Roosevelt crystallized concerns about scarcity and the extermination of species. The inputs to management decisions and the making of game laws were anecdotal, drawing on the observations of a limited number of Arctic experts and adventurers and driven, based on historical experience, by a conviction that many species in the Northwest Territories – caribou and musk-ox in particular – were in decline and in danger of extinction. The regulation of trapping activities and hunting in relation to trapping, combined with the fear of impacting the food sources of Inuit and thereby creating dependent relations, along with the "slaughter" of wildlife by Inuit hunters, emerge as themes governing management decisions. Developing and enforcing laws affecting Inuit hunters became complicated, made all the more difficult by their questionable legal status. Were Inuit Indians? This matter would have to wait until 1939 and a decision by the Supreme Court of Canada. In the meantime, "muddling through" was the best territorial officials could achieve.

That is perhaps the most accurate way of describing the actions of officials concerned with wildlife management. The contradictions among those concerned with wildlife preservation and management were many and reflect the disparate responses of state actors to different pressures: for conservation and the management of resources with future and ongoing economic advantage in mind, and for preservation arguments of a more esoteric and philosophical nature in favour of saving species and ensuring that the fate of species such as the carrier pigeon was not repeated. The latter sensibility has recently given rise to the concept of "deep ecology" and to arguments that all species have a "right" of existence that supersedes their use value (Livingston 1981). The idea that pioneers of wildlife management were laudatory individuals championing the cause of preservation is highly questionable. This idea that a preservationist theme motivated pioneers of wildlife management in Canada, including C. Gordon Hewitt, chief negotiator of the migratory birds treaty with the United States, and the dominion parks commissioner, James Harkin, has been promoted by a number of authors celebrating the early work of wildlife officials. In *Working for Wildlife: The Beginnings of Preservation in Canada,* Janet Foster (1998) ties the work of early conservationists to the mindset of wilderness advocates such as Aldo Leopold and John Muir. In *A Passion for Wildlife: The History of the Canadian Wildlife Service,* J. Alexander Burnett (2003) does the same for officials of the Canadian Wildlife Service, formed in 1947.[1] But as the record found in this volume shows, state actors were never monochromatic in their approach to the management of game. While arguing against species extinction, they most often supported and were concerned about the ongoing commercial exploitation of wildlife. They exhibited both preservationist and conservationist sentiments, depending on the historical moment and the rhetoric called forth by different circumstances and situations. Their attitudes to Aboriginal people were most often steeped in the racist assumptions of the day, while at the same time one can find (as noted in this text) notable exceptions to the rule. The agenda we have identified (totalization or incorporation of a geographically remote region of the country, and the people who occupied it, into a Canadian polity) is not meant to imply a singular and consistent practice. The contradictions within the bureaucracy that developed in relation to Inuit hunting are many. In what follows, we note the position taken by Justice Sissons of the Northwest Territories (NWT) Court in the 1950s and 1960s in recognizing Inuit Aboriginal rights against claims by the state that they had none. While some wildlife officials promulgate the notion of the "wanton slaughter" of game by Inuit, other state officials, based on their experiences in the field, suggest otherwise. This divergence highlights a need to re-examine the colonial state and points out that more attention should be paid to the different and often contradictory behaviour of state actors, a project undertaken by Nicolas Thomas (1994) in *Colonialism's Culture: Anthropology, Travel, and Government.*

Prior to World War II, Inuit were regarded by the *Qallunaat*[2] with considerable curiosity. This was "the golden age" of modern anthropology. On the one hand, Inuit were treated by many explorers and anthropologists as a "primitive people," and studying their culture, collecting artifacts, and recording stories became part of undertakings such as the fifth Thule Expedition

(1921-24) and earlier expeditions by anthropologist Diamond Jenness and explorers such as Vilhjalmur Stefansson. Commonly, they lamented the corruption of Inuit life and practices by modern society. Consistent with the social construction of Inuit culture as primitive, they were often prone to believing that Inuit could not adapt to modern devices such as firearms and that giving Inuit increased "firepower" was bound to result in the slaughter of species they hunted. And there is no doubt that Inuit were largely ignored by federal administrators. Commencing in the late 1920s, some meagre attempt was made to provide medical services to Inuit at Pangnirtung on Baffin Island. In 1930, a Roman Catholic hospital was erected at Igluligaarjuk (Chesterfield Inlet) on the west coast of Hudson Bay, and an Anglican hospital was built at Pangnirtung on Baffin Island. These were church mission hospitals with minimal government support. Minimal expenditure on Inuit health and welfare characterized state relations with Inuit until the early 1950s, after which time the state attempted increasingly to "modernize" Inuit lifestyles. Hunting, as a traditional pursuit, was one area where the state did pay some attention to Inuit "comings and goings" prior to World War II. Administrators were concerned primarily with ensuring that Inuit did not become dependent on the state for welfare and that they continued to hunt and to trap Arctic fox for the Hudson's Bay Company.

Wildlife conservation, as part of a larger movement concerned with the efficient use of resources and scientific management, emerged in North America toward the end of the 1800s. In the United States, the unexplored western frontier, teeming with seemingly boundless resources, had all but disappeared by the turn of the century. Land speculation, characterized by a "cut and get out" attitude, left farmland throughout the western United States suffering from soil erosion and deforestation and subject to financial speculation where irrigation projects were proposed (Hays 1969). By the 1890s, unregulated mining, forest clearing, and hunting had taken their toll. The bison were gone from both the Canadian and the American plains. In Canada, the musk-ox had virtually disappeared from the Arctic mainland by 1900. From the areas around the Great Bear and Great Slave lakes in the western Arctic, the Hudson's Bay Company traded almost 9,000 musk-ox pelts between 1862 and 1885 (Tener 1965). These pelts served as blankets for those wealthy enough to be riding open horse-drawn carriages through European winters. Other animals were taken for zoos and museums. Their taking often involved the slaughter of entire herds. These observations provided clear evidence that the extermination of species was a possibility. While some attempts were made to regulate non-Aboriginal hunting and trapping, ultimately, in the public mind, Aboriginal people were to bear considerable blame for the demise of Arctic wildlife.

The fears of wildlife officials in the 1940s, 1950s, and 1960s were based, in part, on knowledge of the depletion of wildlife earlier in the century. Many of those who became involved in the Dominion Wildlife Service following World War II were early participants in efforts to deal with the depletion of wildlife, increasingly recognized toward the end of World War I. A key figure in the creation of the service in 1947 was Harrison Lewis, its first director. His unpublished "Lively: A History of the Canadian Wildlife Service" makes it clear that experiences earlier in the century guided his approach to conservation.[3] Lewis, an ornithologist, had a long and distinguished career in relation to the natural history of Canada and had been appointed chief federal migratory birds officer following ratification of the International Treaty for the Protection of Migratory Birds in 1917. He was a key participant in the first Dominion-Provincial Wildlife Conference, held in 1919. As such, he was privy to many reports about the decimation of wildlife in the western Arctic and along the Arctic coast – particularly in the vicinity of Kugluktuk (Coppermine). These reports, noted later in the chapter, dealt with the last days of whaling in the Beaufort Sea immediately prior to World War I and exploitation of the area thereafter by non-Aboriginal trappers, traders, and prospectors.

Since the turn of the century, public officials had been given many reports that, in addition to traders and trappers, Indians and Inuit were engaged in the slaughter of musk-ox and caribou and had no sense of the implications of their actions for conservation of the species. In other words, the fears held by wildlife officials in the period following World War II were based as much on socially constructed assumptions about Aboriginal hunting practices as they were on scientific data. Furthermore, as noted later in the text, these attitudes appear to have influenced how investigators interpreted what amounted in some cases to meagre data. Science, and the results of supposedly scientific investigation, were increasingly used in the 1940s, 1950s, and 1960s as evidence that, without stringent regulation of Inuit, First Nations, and Métis hunting, extinction of certain species – caribou in particular – was inevitable.

South of the border, the 1901 election that put Theodore Roosevelt in the White House was to have significant implications for a conservation movement that looked at the demise of American natural resources with alarm. It was an ethic that was soon to cross the Canada-US border. Roosevelt, governor of New York in 1899 and 1900, was an outdoorsman with a passionate interest in conservation. The newly elected president was a nostalgic conservative who longed for a simple agrarian Arcadia that, if it ever existed, could never be revived. He believed in the virtues of hard work, thrift, efficiency, and the small farmer husbanding land and resources. Growing up in the shadows of the American Civil War, he also feared social conflict and believed that it could be supplanted with a rational – a scientific – approach to social and economic matters. This approach included the efficient use of natural resources.

When Roosevelt assumed office, Gifford Pinchot, a German-trained forester and advocate of scientific management and conservation, was chief of the Bureau of Forestry in the Department of Agriculture. Across the border, Pinchot's ideas were to influence Canadian politician Clifford Sifton, who was, until his resignation in 1905 over the Manitoba schools question, minister of the interior in the Laurier administration. Before leaving office, Sifton had organized a national conference to discuss Canadian forests. When participants met in January of 1906, Pinchot was a key speaker. His ideas on forest conservation, water management, and irrigation had a profound influence on an administration that had previously shown little interest in such matters. This experience, combined with Canadian participation in a North American conference on conservation held at the White House in February of 1909, brought new ideas about conservation and scientific management to the Laurier government (D.J. Hall 1985, 237).

With control over natural resources residing with the provinces, except for the northern territories, the prairie provinces, and matters related to navigable waters, and with a prime minister little given to government regulation of private sector activities, creation of the Commission of Conservation in 1909 seems surprising.[4] That Canadian concern for the conservation of resources was growing, and that Robert Borden, leader of the Conservative opposition, had become a recent convert to the cause, may have influenced Laurier (D.J. Hall 1985, 239). Sifton, a powerful politician with western influence, often at odds with the policies of his leader, had nevertheless played a key role in the election of 1908. Laurier's attention to Sifton's interests was likely pragmatic and perhaps intended to placate someone with ongoing importance to Liberal political fortunes. In any event, Sifton drafted the act creating the commission and was appointed its first chair. The commission was to "take into consideration all questions which may be brought to its notice relating to the conservation and better utilization of the natural resources of Canada." At the inaugural address to the commission in 1910, Sifton declared that it could "exert a powerful influence in the right direction. It can strengthen the hands of all who are desirous of following progressive policies. It can help to render the labour of investigations in the various branches of scientific thought available for the service of the country. It can be the vehicle by which enlightened and educated men can bring an influence directly to bear on the administration of public affairs" (cited in D.J. Hall 1985, 244).

Sifton's wording is significant. In the case of Aboriginal people, seen as primitive, not suffering from the benefits of civilization and scientific knowledge, and, worse still, armed with modern weapons, anything but conservation was thought to be possible. In fact, the "wanton slaughter" of animal and bird species was seen as the logical and inevitable outcome of this deadly combination of factors. Nevertheless, the logic behind the idea of "wanton slaughter" was fraught with contradiction. For example, Canadian economist and social scientist Harold Innis (1962) was to speculate in the early 1930s on Aboriginal behaviour in regard to wildlife in his classic work on commodity production in Canada, *The Fur Trade in Canada*. Without any evidence to substantiate the claim, even someone as thorough as Innis was inclined to see Aboriginal people as having "an insatiable demand for the products of the more elaborate cultural development of Europeans" (388). This he attributed to their limited cultural background. The result, Innis claimed, was the rapid depletion of game, starvation, and warfare. On the other hand, Aboriginal people were also portrayed as lazy, difficult to motivate, and inclined to participate in the white man's economy only long enough to get the basics needed to enjoy life – hardly an image consistent with someone slaughtering everything in sight to live in comfort. Despite such contradictions, the image of Inuit involved in "wanton slaughter" was to have a lasting effect.

Sifton continued to chair the Commission of Conservation following Laurier's defeat in 1911 over the matter of reciprocity and free trade with the United States. The commission recommended that a federal department of health be established but was frustrated in this aim until after World War I, when the flu pandemic that killed about 50,000 Canadians pointed clearly to the need. Sifton addressed a National Conference on City Planning in May 1914. Like many social reformers at the time, he believed that crime and disease were products of the physical environment that could be addressed by scientific principles and planning. Among the legislative initiatives supported by the commission was the migratory birds treaty signed in 1916 and ratified in Canadian law as the migratory birds protection act the following year. The act was to have profound implications for Aboriginal hunting rights in the Northwest Territories and throughout the country.

The many reports of the demise of wildlife populations in the Arctic played no small role in the creation in 1916 of the Advisory Board on Wild Life Protection, a council of men chaired by Gordon Hewitt and including Duncan Campbell Scott, superintendent general of Indian affairs. Hewitt, married to the niece of Prime Minister Robert Borden, was dominion entomologist and had been the chief negotiator of the migratory birds treaty with the United States. He appears to have absorbed the many reports being circulated on the demise of northern game populations, particularly in the western Arctic. These reports included accounts from many who had sent expeditions to the Canadian North in search of species for their collections as well as from government officials. Among those reporting on the slaughter of caribou, musk-ox, and other species were Madison Grant, director of the New York Zoological Society; Thompson Seton, a well-known Manitoba author, artist, naturalist, and consultant to the Manitoba government; Maxwell Graham, from the Parks Branch of the Department of the Interior; the explorer

Vilhjalmur Stefansson; his associate on the Canadian Arctic expeditions, Dr. Rudolph Anderson; Julius Schiott, director of the Zoological Gardens of Copenhagen; as well as others (Foster 1998). It was an impressive list of experts whose observations had to be taken seriously, particularly those of Anderson, who became a member of the Advisory Board on Wild Life Protection. Stefansson, adept at making headlines, was also impossible to ignore.

Anderson accompanied Stefansson on both of his official Arctic expeditions, the first in 1908 and the second between 1913 and 1918. He was, at the time, a personal friend of Stefansson, having completed his PhD in zoology at Iowa State University in 1906, where Stefansson had also been a student. Anderson was employed as the zoologist with the Geological Survey of Canada on the second expedition. As the 1913 expedition developed, the relationship between Anderson and Stefansson deteriorated to the point where they became bitter adversaries, and the antagonism lasted until Anderson's death in 1961. Stefansson died in 1962.

During their first expedition, both Stefansson and Anderson made observations on the impact that whaling crews based at Hershel Island, and hunters working for them, were having on game populations on the Arctic coast. Their reports drew considerable attention to the problems of game management in the territories. Anderson was convinced that the introduction of firearms among the Inuit was having a devastating impact on caribou (Foster 1998, 169). In correspondence with Clifford Sifton in 1914, Stefansson offered him the following description: "Eskimos and even white men, would frequently shoot a whole herd when they knew that they would have to abandon everything to the wolves but for a single carcass or portion of one. At times bands of Eskimos would shoot down hundreds from the large herds they met, and never touched a single animal after it fell. At other times they would go so far from their homes to hunt caribou that it was impossible for them to bring back anything but the skins and the meat was abandoned as too heavy to carry" (cited in Foster 1998, 171). The comment "and even white men" is revealing.

Stefansson celebrated traditional Inuit culture in his many writings. According to Richard Diubaldo, a chronicler of Stefansson's Arctic experiences, Stefansson was also a conservationist, and this would explain his interest in communicating with Sifton. But in 1914 his perspective on Inuit life also had the net effect of recreating the idea of the "noble savage." Stefansson was therefore upset by what he saw as the corrupting influences of Western civilization, including the influence on Inuit culture in the western Arctic of the whalers and of religion.[5] The net result was that he apparently expected Inuit, armed with weapons not of their making, to behave in the manner described – but not white men. In making sense of Stefansson's observation on the shooting of "whole herds" of caribou, we should keep in mind the following account by Stefansson, dated 10 December 1909, of his own writing: "I ... have often found on belated reference to my diary that I have told to many men on many occasions ... facts and feelings which seem to have been absent at the time of an 'adventure' but which have by some mental process attached themselves to it later and have become vivid real facts, or have so overshadowed them and even obliterated the facts. Where my contemporaneous record of an event is meager, these adventitious elements are bound to remain undetected and become for me and anyone who believes me, as if they had happened" (cited in Diubaldo 1998, 27-28).

Despite good reason for skepticism over claims that Inuit were involved in the slaughter of "whole herds" of caribou, it seems likely from reports by Stefansson and others that there was a considerable overuse of wildlife along the Arctic coast to meet the needs of the whaling industry. The activities of non-Aboriginal whalers, hunters, and trappers had a significant impact on caribou and musk-ox, once found in abundance along the Arctic coast. Inuit, and the Athapaskan-speaking Dene of the Yukon and Mackenzie River Basin, were involved in the procurement of meat for non-Aboriginal whalers and traders. In some cases, Aboriginal people were employed as hunters under the supervision of non-Aboriginal hunters supplying meat to whaling crews on Hershel Island. By some accounts, a whaling ship's crew could consume more than ten tons of caribou meat and wear out a few hundred pair of mittens and skin boots in a winter (Gillies 1989).

By 1912, whaling had ceased in the Beaufort Sea. Nevertheless, extrapolating from a situation that involved considerable lawlessness, corruption, alcohol consumption, and the behaviour of whaling crews on Hershel Island and Inuit under their influence, to the behaviour of Inuit hunting to feed their families and to supply meat for their dog teams, is highly questionable. Given the images of the day – of primitive people lacking any notion of conservation and failing to appreciate the power of white man's technology – the conviction that Inuit could (and would) wreak havoc on northern wildlife was enduring.

What took place along the Arctic coast, from Hershel Island to King William Island and the Coronation Gulf area, in the period before World War I until the 1930s, had a huge impact on how game management officers subsequently understood Inuit hunting practices. A popular book written by Richard Finnie, the son of O.S. Finnie, director of the Northwest Territories and Yukon Branch of the Department of the Interior in the 1920s, and published in 1940, provides vivid verbal as well as photographic images of life along the Arctic coast at this time. It is hard to say how many people occupied Hershel Island during the heyday of the whaling trade, but it seems possible that the number of whalers and Inuit sometimes numbered over 1,000, all of whom had to be supplied with meat:

Inuit-owned schooners trading furs at Hershel Island in the 1930s. From Finnie 1940, 19.

Between 1889 and 1906, when a big bowhead was worth ten thousand dollars, [Hershel Island] was the Mecca for dozens of whaling ships. Then the invention of a commercial substitute for whalebone or baleen suddenly brought the price of that commodity down from five dollars a pound to forty cents and less, and the whalers cleared out forever.

Fur traders succeeded them, for the value of fox pelts was beginning to rise. While the whaling captains had held sway the Eskimos were encouraged to slaughter tremendous numbers of caribou to provide fresh meat for hundreds of sailors; but now they were encouraged to concentrate on trapping. (Finnie 1940, 13)

These images, combined with notions of a primitive people who did not understand white man's law, who were given to infanticide and even murder without any particular signs of remorse, and who could not appreciate ideas about conservation, were also to have a lasting impact on ideas about the relationship between Inuit and wildlife that subsequently developed in the minds of public officials.

The Legal Response
Rudolph Anderson, zoologist with the Geological Survey, joined the five-member Advisory Board on Wild Life Protection, created by order-in-council in 1916, before the Arctic expedition of Stefansson, of which he was a part, was wrapped up in 1918 (Foster 1998, 162). Tackling new legislation to regulate hunting and trapping activities in the Northwest Territories was

among the first and most important items on its agenda. Inuit hunting had never been regulated by game ordinances affecting the Northwest Territories.[6] The first ordinance of 1887 exempted Indians from its provisions where game was taken for their own use. It made no reference to Eskimos.[7] A few changes between 1887 and 1903 added seasons and quotas for some game, including caribou. An amendment in 1892 restricted the season for caribou, moose, antelope, deer, and their fawns to the period of 1 September to 31 January. The hunting of buffalo and many bird species was banned altogether.[8] In fact, apart from a major consolidation and rewrite in 1903, few changes other than details affecting seasons, permits, licensing, penalties, and the appointment of game guardians (generally the Northwest Mounted Police) were made to the legislation, with the exception that hunting on the Sabbath was prohibited.[9] Indians continued to be exempt, and no mention was made of Inuit.[10] Among the non-Aboriginal population, the provisions were barely enforced, especially recognizing that in 1903 there were only three police posts in the Arctic region of the Northwest Territories: at Hershel Island (a staging ground and home port for American whaling in the Beaufort Sea), at Fullerton (on the west coast of Hudson Bay and the wintering site of the American whaling fleet operating in the eastern Arctic), and at Fort Macpherson in the Mackenzie District (Tester and Kulchyski 1994, 15).

By 1917, in light of all the reports about the demise of wildlife in the Arctic and passage of the migratory birds protection act, the legislation was badly in need of attention. The new legislation contained a number of "first time" initiatives. Inuit and Indian hunting was regulated. The new Northwest Game Act passed by Parliament on 23 July 1917 protected musk-ox. The season for caribou was shortened by two weeks. However, despite a proposal to make Victoria, Banks, and Melville islands musk-ox preserves, nothing was done to achieve this goal. The attempt to regulate Indian and Inuit hunting was severe. Section 3 of the legislation reads as follows: "Notwithstanding anything contained in subsections one and two, the game therein mentioned may be lawfully hunted, taken or killed, and the eggs of birds therein mentioned may be lawfully taken, by Indians or Eskimos who are *bona fide* inhabitants of the Northwest Territories, or by other *bona fide* inhabitants of the said territories, and by any explorers or surveyors who are engaged in any exploration, survey or other examination of the country, *but only when such persons are actually in need of such game or eggs to prevent starvation*" (emphasis added).[11]

In other words, Indians and Inuit were subject to the seasonal restrictions on hunting caribou, ptarmigan, geese, ducks, and other species mentioned in the previous clause. According to the legislation, caribou could be hunted only from 1 August to 1 October and from 1 December until 1 April.[12] That the legislation did not exempt Inuit, and was the first attempt to restrict Inuit hunting, is made clear in a letter issued by O.S. Finnie, director of the

Northwest Territories Branch of the Department of the Interior, on 1 April 1924. However, to his credit, Finnie was inclined to seek the co-operation of Inuit rather than "laying down the law" in dealing with them. Directed at Inuit, the letter advised them against killing all the caribou they could see and went on to suggest that "a good hunter will never kill caribou in the months of April, May, June and July (except when he is very hungry and then he will only kill bulls if he can) because in those months the skins are no good" (cited in Diubaldo 1985, 55-56). The attempt to link a prohibition against hunting at a time of year when calves were vulnerable with an understanding that the skins were less than desirable during these months (which Inuit already knew) conveniently overlooked the fact that, "very hungry" or not, Inuit still had to eat:

> The regulations and restrictions shouldn't have applied to Inuit at the time when they were just more or less – well – they were still using bows and arrows at the time when I was growing up as a young man. And because Inuit didn't have rifles, whatever restrictions were put on game – even though they might have seen that game – Inuit couldn't pursue it because of the regulations. And then they might not be so lucky to get other game that they were pursuing because of not having rifles ... And then it got to the point where we came across [game], and there were regulations that we couldn't pursue it; it kind of made it a hardship for us to try and get – to provide food for the family at times ... There was a lot of dissatisfaction from the Inuit side as to some of the restrictions, so I remember there was a deal made where, if it meant life and death or if we were in dire straits, then we could pursue it. (Moses Koihok, Ikaluktutiak, 13 May 1998)

Moses Koihok.
Photo Frank Tester.

Hunting musk-ox was prohibited except in zones that the council could, from time to time, prescribe. Another significant provision relevant to understanding the forces affecting Inuit and Indian hunting practices at the time prevented anyone from contracting with Inuit, Indians, or others to procure game contrary to the provisions of the act or any regulations arising from the legislation (section 5). This provision was intended to curb what had become a disturbing practice – employing Inuit and Indian hunters, in the western Arctic, particularly along the north coast from Hershel Island as far east as Coronation Gulf, to hunt in order to supply meat to whalers, traders, surveyors, and prospectors, many of whom had their hunting rights restricted by regulations and licensing provisions affecting non-residents of the territories. While whaling had come to an end in the Beaufort Sea, the activities of prospectors, trappers, and others had not. In 1918, the act was given to the Parks Branch of the Department of the Interior to administer (Foster 1998, 176-77). It was to survive, virtually unchanged, until major revisions in 1949.

The Commission on Conservation, which had impacted all matters of conservation in the country (including concerns for northern wildlife), was dealt a fatal blow by the administration of Conservative Prime Minister Arthur Meighen in 1921 (see Foster 1998, 210-16). However, ideas generated by the commission were to grow. In 1926, by order-in-council, an Arctic Islands Game Preserve protecting musk-ox was finally created. The protection of musk-ox was only one reason for creating the preserve. The other was growing concerns about Canadian sovereignty in the High Arctic (Tester and Kulchyski 1994, 106). The following year, the Thelon Game Sanctuary, situated between Lutsel K'e and Fort Reliance in the Mackenzie District to the west, and the only inland community of Inuit in the eastern Arctic (Qamani'tuaq or Baker Lake), was also created.[13]

Despite its demise, the commission's ideas were given impetus by ongoing conservation concerns created by the industrialization of Ontario and Quebec in the 1920s, the lumbering of the Maritimes and Ontario (especially the Ottawa Valley), and the unregulated logging of coastal forests, as well as growing concerns over salmon fishing and the obstruction of the Fraser River in British Columbia.[14] The drought that accompanied the Depression on the Prairies in the 1930s renewed concerns about soil and water conservation.

In 1931, the Northwest Territories Branch of the Department of the Interior had been disbanded, a cost-saving measure introduced by the Conservative government of R.B. Bennett in the face of the persistent Depression. Finnie, director of the branch and a reform-minded civil servant concerned with matters of Inuit health, welfare, and conservation, took early retirement. Conservation and social expenditures were ill suited to a government given to parsimony and committed to any scheme – however unlikely – for using the country's resources to revive a distressed economy.

By 1932, growing concern over the need to regulate the northern fur trade, along with pressure to allow mineral exploration and once again to permit trading posts in the areas affected by the Arctic Islands Game Preserve, led officials in the Department of the Interior on a search to discover the fate of the commission and its mandate. They wanted to know whether or not, when it was dismantled, its responsibilities had been divvied up among federal departments. If so, it was reasoned, then government departments could take action in the name of conservation and the efficient use of resources. It was discovered that, while conservation would have to be a concern of the federal government, in the 1924 act creating the Dominion Research Council – which might have been expected to address ongoing matters of conservation following the demise of the Commission on Conservation – the question of conservation had been omitted from its mandate entirely.[15]

A Bit of a Mess: Inuit Status and Enforcing the Law

Revisions to the Northwest Territories Act and Privy Council Order 2033, 16 June 1921, had created a council of six appointed members to assist the commissioner of the Northwest Territories in its administration. The initiative was inspired by a renewed interest in both the mineral and the petroleum resources of the Mackenzie Basin and the discovery of oil at Norman Wells on 24 August 1920. Prior to 1921, the territories had been governed under the Northwest Territories Act of 1905, which created a commissioner and up to four councillors. In practice, the police administered the territories. Colonel F. White, financial comptroller of the Northwest Mounted Police, acted as commissioner. The council was a moribund group that hardly met. After 1921 and until 1963, the commissioner was the deputy minister of the federal department given responsibility for territorial administration.[16]

In 1918, administration of the migratory birds regulations within the wildlife division of the Parks Branch of the Ministry of the Interior had been given to Hoyes Lloyd, a chemist by profession and an ornithologist by inclination. However, his duties were quickly expanded, and he was made supervisor of wildlife protection in Canada, being responsible for both the Northwest Game Act and the Migratory Birds Convention Act. Harrison Lewis, who was to become the first director of the Dominion Wildlife Service in 1947, was hired to oversee enforcement in Ontario and Quebec (Burnett 1999, 10).

With the exception of the Maritime provinces, enforcement was not difficult since provincial governments had game officers responsible for enforcing provincial legislation that paralleled the federal migratory birds protection law. In some provinces, the RCMP became *ex officio* game officers to assist dominion wildlife officers in enforcement. Since there were no game officers in the Northwest Territories in the 1920s, enforcement was left to the RCMP, who appear, based on the number of cases and prosecutions brought to the attention of council, not to have made enforcement a priority. In territory occupied by Inuit, the RCMP had little presence, with eastern posts at Fullerton on Hudson Bay and variously, as the 1920s developed, at Craig Harbour on Ellesmere Island and at Pangnirtung on Baffin Island.

By order-in-council, October 1932, the RCMP was given sole responsibility for enforcement of the migratory birds protection act. Enforcement was, by admission of the RCMP, sporadic depending on the inclination of the officer and his perception of what was important and appropriate in the context in which he found himself (Huget 1967, cited in Burnett 2003, 21). These circumstances also help to explain why there were no prosecutions of Inuit hunters under the Northwest Game Act during the 1920s and 1930s.

In 1920, W.W. Cory, deputy minister of the Department of the Interior, became commissioner after the death of Colonel White. Cory soon became aware of problems with the status of Inuit. Were they to be treated as Indians? Were they wards of the federal government? At a council meeting in 1929, it was decided that, while it was not in the best interests of Inuit to issue them liquor permits, they did have the status of "white men" and would therefore be dealt with on a case-by-case basis.[17] The question of status was not finally answered until a case put before the Supreme Court in 1939 (Tester and Kulchyski 1994, Chapter 1).

In the meantime, whether Inuit could be regarded as Indians for the purposes of making game regulations was a moot point. The Northwest Territories and Yukon Branch of the Department of the Interior, with O.S. Finnie as director, despite legal questions, took on moral responsibility for them.[18] This moral responsibility had been interrupted on 19 July 1924 by a change to the Indian Act. Duncan Campbell Scott, superintendent of Indian affairs, had successfully argued that responsibility for Inuit should be transferred to his department. Some argued forcefully that it was an arrangement that would not work. Inuit, according to some commentators, including W.H.B. (Billy) Hoare, one of Finnie's few field personnel in the Arctic, and the first warden of the Thelon Game Sanctuary, were vastly different from (and superior to) Indians, and dealing with them in a similar manner would be ruinous to their development. Hoare wrote that "Eskimos can be developed from wards to affluent and intelligent citizens. It is the unanimous opinion of all those that have experience with Eskimos that the Northwest Territories is the proper branch to direct the Eskimos if they are to attain their highest development and to fill that place in Canada's scheme which, by nature, they are so peculiarly fitted to fill" (cited in Diubaldo 1985, 36). On 31 August 1927, responsibility was handed back to the commissioner of the Northwest Territories.

Game laws and regulations were a responsibility of the revitalized Northwest Territories Council. Roy Gibson chaired most meetings of council and was deputy commissioner until 1936, when Dr. Charles Camsell, a member of council, was made deputy minister of the Department of Mines and Resources, the newly created department responsible for Arctic administration. Camsell was also made commissioner for the Northwest Territories. Council, which met in Ottawa, relied heavily on experts and visiting dignitaries for its ideas about what needed to be done in governing a vast territory that most council members had never seen. For example, in 1925, council listened to a presentation by explorer Knud Rasmussen on his 1921-24 Arctic expedition. According to the minutes, he advised strongly against permitting traders to furnish high-power rifles to the Natives. The 40/40 Winchester, he was understood to say, would be amply sufficient for all their purposes, "the natives having no idea whatever of conservation." Furthermore, he suggested that "it was impossible to keep the natives in their original primitive state; that they had already become partially accustomed to products of civilization, and recommended that they be allowed to complete the process as soon as possible, but under supervision."[19] In the years to come, supervision would be offered in abundance to Inuit.

In 1925, Rasmussen's recommendations were of little use, responsibility for Inuit having been given to the Department of Indian Affairs. Despite the lack of jurisdiction, a year later, in July 1926, at the urging of O.S. Finnie, council took a major step in addressing matters of conservation in the Arctic by establishing the Arctic Islands Game Preserve. The Department of the Interior subsequently restricted the number of trading posts operating within the preserve, which covered not only all of the Arctic Islands but also much of the mainland between Igluligaarjuk (Chesterfield Inlet) on the west coast of Hudson Bay and north to Queen Maud Gulf and west to Coronation Gulf along the Arctic coast.

Debates that were to endure for decades about the fate of Inuit are evident from the deliberations of council during the 1920s. Should Inuit be assimilated to Canadian society, as Rasmussen suggested, or should steps be taken to preserve their traditional way of life with the idea of ensuring they did not become dependent on the state, as was seen to be increasingly true of First Nations people in the south? These debates were not likely diminished by a report presented to council in December of 1927 by well-known physician Frederick Banting. Banting had been scathing in reporting to the press what he had seen of Inuit conditions and their treatment by the Hudson's Bay Company on his trip to the eastern Arctic with painter A.Y. Jackson in the summer of 1927.[20] Perhaps contact with Canadian society was little more than a recipe for exploitation.

On 6 June 1928, Duncan Campbell Scott – deputy superintendent general of Indian affairs – was appointed to the Northwest Territories Council to fill a vacancy caused by the death of John Greenway, commissioner of dominion lands.[21] Scott's department had just lost responsibility for Inuit. Minutes of council meetings suggest that thereafter Scott played a relatively low-key role in the business of council but intervened from time to time to ensure that Indians in the territories did not get any special treatment when it came to hunting and trapping rights. For example, when asked if Indian agents had any role to play in ensuring that Indian trappers were treated fairly by traders, Scott noted that "the best type of Agent did look after the interests of Indians regularly in an advisory way, but that it must be kept in mind that he had poor material to work on."[22] He served until his retirement in March 1932.

Preventing the dependence on the state that was seen to have become the fate of southern First Nations was, in the case of Inuit, seen to be greatly related to protection of Arctic wildlife, not only, as it turned out, from non-Inuit hunters but also from Inuit themselves. Council was sensitive to criticism. An article published by the *Seattle Times* on 24 December 1928 is illustrative. Probably inspired by the release of Robert Flaherty's classic silent film, *Nanook of the North,* it suggested that Canadian Eskimos were in danger of "racial extinction" and that "the northern aborigine has been contaminated by civilization and deprived of his natural food supplies by white men, and that, as a consequence, none of his kind will be left alive on this continent within two or three generations." To add further insult, it was suggested that "Canadian and United States Eskimos are under similar conditions. The former may not have all the government care given the latter, but the one is not more easily afflicted by ailments or more seriously affected by dietary changes than the other. Alaska natives are greater in number, healthier, more intelligent and longer lived than ever before in history. If things are not exactly right for the Canadian Eskimo he ought to mush into United States territory."[23]

It is therefore not surprising that, in the face of mounting public criticism, commencing in 1929 there was a flurry of activity to introduce amendments to game laws and attention directed at means for their enforcement. At the twelfth meeting of council on 11 December 1929, Colonel Starnes, commissioner of the RCMP, asked if the provisions of the act that permitted killing moose and caribou on a large commercial scale for food meant that they could also be killed and used as dog food, to which he was opposed. It was decided that officers had enough discretion under the act to address this matter.[24] Despite evidence that caribou was not used extensively as dog food, the idea persisted to the point where T.G. Murphy, minister of the interior, felt compelled in 1935 to issue a warning to "Indians, Eskimos and half-breeds." In a public notice, he proclaimed that "All persons resident in the Northwest Territories are hereby warned of the consequences of excessive killing of caribou. The use of the meat of caribou, moose or deer for dog feed in districts where fish or other kinds of food for dogs are available is not permissible."[25] The idea that using caribou for dog food was wasteful and that fish should, wherever possible, be used instead remained an issue in the eastern Arctic until the snowmobile largely replaced dog teams in the 1960s. Conflicts between preservation and development were evident when the regulations were amended to permit prospectors access to game preserves, provided they held hunting and trapping licences.[26]

Despite questions about the authority granted to council by the Northwest Game Act, throughout the 1930s council regularly changed the quota system for different species as well as the seasons during which they could be hunted or trapped. Game management became an increasingly complicated nightmare as the decade unfolded.

Trial and Error: Regulating Trapping in the 1930s

Competing and incompatible interests collided. Fur, relative to other commodities, kept its price during much of the Depression. On the one hand, council felt pressure to create conditions that would make it possible for non-Aboriginal trappers to make a living. An increasing number of trappers, many from the Peace River District and the prairie provinces, were finding their way into the Keewatin District north of the Manitoba border and west to the Mackenzie District and Great Slave Lake. In February 1931, it was reported that 547 licences to trap were issued in the Northwest Territories (Indians and Eskimos did not require a licence), and of these 138 were issued to non-residents. It was reported to council that 74.5 percent of the fur taken in the territories was taken by "natives of the Territories," which, from the context, clearly did not mean Aboriginal people.[27] The extent to which land should be set aside to protect Aboriginal hunting and trapping interests was a topic of debate long after O.S. Finnie (who championed the idea) and his nemesis, Duncan Campbell Scott (who firmly opposed such measures), had retired from council, Finnie in 1931 and Scott in 1932.

Protecting the resource for Indians and Eskimos also meant preventing their dependence on welfare assistance. By the 1930s, the need for assistance among the Dene of the Mackenzie Basin had become desperate, with Bishop Gabriel Breyant appealing for help for people whose cash income in 1935-36 was only $110 (Zaslow 1988, 134). Of the welfare needs of Inuit in the eastern Arctic, little was known other than information provided by scattered anecdotal reports from police officers (Tester and Kulchyski 1994, 20-28). Adding to these concerns was pressure from trading companies to be allowed to reopen posts in the central and eastern Arctic that they had closed in the 1920s as game reserves were created. The Hudson's Bay Company also wanted to compete with other trading companies – particularly with the Inuk trader Angulalik – operating with the Canalaska Trading Company along the Arctic coast and with Révillon Frères Trading Company operating at different locations throughout the eastern Arctic. While reopening posts in the eastern Arctic and elsewhere to compete with rival companies and independent traders, the Hudson's Bay Company reduced its posts in

Canada from 334 in 1931 to 230 by 1937 (Zaslow 1988, 137). By the end of the decade, restrictions imposed on private traders and the fierce competition mounted by the Hudson's Bay Company had left it a virtual monopoly across the Arctic.

Violations of the game act were also of concern to council, but evidence suggests that the greatest problems with the so-called slaughter of game lay with the non-Aboriginal population. At a meeting in December 1933, council dealt with a prospector at a mining camp near Great Bear Lake who was fined $150 for killing eight caribou in one day, far beyond his personal requirements. General MacBrien, superintendent of the RCMP, noted that ice houses of exploration parties he had visited were full of caribou and that caribou was being served at restaurants in the territories.[28] When asked, restaurant owners claimed to have obtained the meat from Indian hunters, but MacBrien was skeptical. In fact, in a letter to council, the North-West Territories Prospectors Association claimed that Indian hunters "[did] not care to hunt beyond their own family requirements and point[ed] out that caribou do not migrate through the Great Bear Lake District each year."[29] Throughout the 1920s and 1930s, no evidence was brought before the Northwest Territories Council supporting claims that Aboriginal people were involved in the "wanton slaughter" of game. Regulating game and dealing with trapping were mostly a matter of trial and error.

Roy Gibson, assistant deputy minister of the Department of the Interior, sensitive to growing criticism of restrictions placed on non-Aboriginal hunting and trapping in the territories, and with a style illustrative of his meticulous and cautious manner, was wary of justifying NWT game laws and game reserves by reference to the need for conservation. In the 1930s, conservation had fallen from grace. Gibson is described by Morris Zaslow (1988, 308) as a colourless, single-minded bureaucrat given to frugality and a conscientious attention to detail. Such attention from time to time produced meticulous, if not contentless, pronouncements. At a meeting of council on 9 November 1932, "Mr. Gibson suggested that in order to facilitate disposal of many suggestions [read criticisms] made with respect to the Northwest Game Regulations that Council approve some general broad policy with respect to the relative importance of the protection of game from the standpoint of the native and white population. The Department would then be better able to deal with the details."[30] This concern followed a suggestion made by Ralph Parsons of the Hudson's Bay Company that the department create a game reserve in the Keewatin "for the exclusive use of the natives." The effect of such a reserve would have been to eliminate competition from non-Aboriginal trappers who were increasingly finding their way into the southern Keewatin, across the northern Manitoba boundary, and who were not inclined to trade their furs through the venerable company.[31]

By the late 1930s, the headache that constituted game management – particularly the regulation of trapping in the territories – had become a serious migraine. Council was severely hampered by the lack of any significant data on which to base its decisions. Pressure to liberalize regulations, in order to open opportunities for non-Aboriginal trappers faced with the economic realities of the Depression, increased. Fur prices that had remained comparatively high during the Depression increased as it abated – an indication that the Depression had different implications for those who could afford the luxury of a fur coat. As Zaslow (1988) notes, the decline in prices paid for other commodities encouraged, rather than discouraged, trapping, sending men from prairie and northern farms into the northern bush to trap from October until spring. Attempts were made to regulate "fly-by-night" trading posts by requiring licensing, specifying the locations of posts, and stipulating that they be open for a specified period of the year. On the other hand, the number of non-Aboriginal trappers and traders was growing. Regulating their activities with the Depression budgets of the Royal Canadian Mounted Police was next to impossible.

Consistent with the idea that some species were desirable while others were vicious predators capable of destroying valuable species, a bounty was placed on wolves. It was later withdrawn in the face of severe government restraint and reintroduced as economic conditions improved. Developments in aviation also played a role in the management of the fur trade in the territories. By the mid-1930s, bush planes allowed trappers to fly into remote parts of the Arctic, trap intensively from October until spring, and fly out the furs. While not initially seen as a problem, by 1939 the practice had to be regulated, and council introduced amendments to the Northwest Territories Act permitting aircraft – as well as boats, motor vehicles, and even canoes – to be searched for furs that trappers were trying to export without paying duties on them. In some cases, the use of aircraft was prohibited entirely.[32]

Evidence that the activities of non-Aboriginal trappers and hunters were affecting Inuit emerged in the eastern Arctic. In a letter dated 5 March 1938, Dr. Thomas Melling, the medical officer stationed at Igluligaarjuk (Chesterfield Inlet)[33] noted a considerable amount of relief that had to be given to Inuit in the area. This he attributed to the scarcity of game resources and the inroads made by white trappers who, presumably, were taking valuable fox pelts that Inuit would normally have traded and perhaps caribou for their dog teams. Melling suggested that the area north of the inlet to Naujaat (Repulse Bay) be set aside as a Native game preserve.

Dr. Livingston, another physician with a long history of working in the Arctic, offered an alternative explanation. He blamed the Catholic Church for promoting indigence by encouraging Inuit to leave their trap lines in early December in order to be in the settlement for Christmas celebrations and again, in April, for Easter. He added that colds and influenza, contracted when Inuit were gathered together in the settlement, further interfered with their ability to make a living by trapping.[34] While there may have been some truth to both of these explanations, it seems highly likely that non-Aboriginal trappers were having a significant impact on the number of animals left for Inuit to hunt and trap.

Challenging the Law: Resistance by, and on Behalf of, Inuit

Resistance to the regime imposed by the dominion government sometimes took unique and historically important forms. Angulalik and his struggles as a trader provided the state with perplexing problems that challenged the assumptions used to construct Inuit as subjects, defined by law, sometimes as "ordinary Canadians" and sometimes as Aboriginal people. Angulalik's case not only raised questions about his status but also did so in relation to Inuit participation in practices understood to be the purview of non-Aboriginal people. Angulalik established himself as a trader – and no ordinary one. He dared to challenge the hegemony of the Hudson's Bay Company in his own lands. Was he an Aboriginal person in the eyes of the law? Did he need or not need a licence to trade? Could he operate a post in the Arctic Islands Preserve, where all posts (operated by the Hudson's Bay Company) had been ordered closed? If he did so, then he was clearly aiding and abetting Inuit trapping (and thereby related hunting activities) in areas that the state wanted closed to such activities, paradoxically in the name of conserving game so that Inuit would not become dependent on the state for sustenance. Could Angulalik challenge the monopoly the Hudson's Bay Company believed it had when it came to operating posts in the Arctic?

The problem of jurisdiction and Inuit status continued to plague council during the 1930s, particularly in regard to the activities of Angulalik.[35] A well-known figure along the Arctic coast, he operated in the Coronation Gulf and Perry River areas, supplied with goods by the Canalaska Trading Company. The Hudson's Bay Company saw him as bleeding away their profits. Angulalik, like many Inuit trappers and traders since the turn of the century, had acquired his own boat. He used it to move freight between Aklavik in the Mackenzie Delta and trading operations at Ikaluktutiak (Cambridge Bay) and Perry River. In fact, his trading activities, which endured well into the 1960s, probably account for the fact that Inuit in the area were able to maintain their traditional lifestyles by living on the land well beyond what might otherwise have been the case. Many Inuit have clear memories of his operation and their loyalty to it:

> So Canalaska, because they were set up here [Bay Chimo, Perry River], as soon as the Hudson Bay started their trading post here, as soon as people from outpost camps came into town, uh, they were more or less met with

Angulalik and his family at his Perry River trading post. © Library and Archives
Canada, J.S. Bailey, Indian and Northern Affairs Departmental Albums, PA-175729.

gifts, like food or ammunition or things that the hunters and trappers
could use. To try and I guess, more or less, to win them over and have them
only deal with a certain company, like Canalaska. Canalaska did that, but
I know the Hudson's Bay never – yep – Canalaskans were the only ones,
the only company that did that, as far as I can remember ... People, more
or less because of the gifts they were receiving, felt obligated to only deal
with a certain group, that being the Canalaska company. (Moses Kiohok,
Ikaluktutiak, 13 May 1998)

It was only after Angulalik closed his Perry River trading post in 1967 and
retired to Ikaluktutiak that Inuit living along Coronation Gulf and Queen
Maud Sound also migrated to Kugluktuk (Coppermine) and Ikaluktutiak
(Cambridge Bay).

Angulalik got his start in the trading business by working for the Hudson's
Bay Company at Kingauk (Bathurst Inlet). The manager, a man named
Clarke, left the employ of the company and joined the rival Canalaska
Trading Company, operating a post at Perry River to the east, where the
Hudson's Bay Company also had a post. In 1928, following establishment
of the Arctic Islands Game Preserve, both posts were ordered closed. Clarke

was subsequently put in charge of a Canalaska post at Ikaluktutiak. Angulalik continued to trade and do business in the Perry River area. Over time, he in fact operated a trading post in contradiction to the order given to close operations at Perry River. Angulalik continued to do business with Canalaska, ensuring that all the furs from the Perry River area wound up in its hands.[36]

Angulalik's activities can be seen as a particularly clever act of resistance against the conservation regime imposed by the Arctic Islands Preserve. He operated not as an agent of the Canalaska Trading Company but as an independent trader, purchasing his goods from Canalaska. The distinction was important, for as an independent Inuk trader he was not an employee of Canalaska, so the company was not in violation of the order to close its post on the mainland. At the same time, by dealing with Angulalik, it derived all the same benefits from his presence. He also moved the post from the original location to Flagstaff Island, and for a while northern officials in Ottawa did not seem to know where Flagstaff Island – only a few miles from the original Perry River post – was located.

Angulalik's lifestyle – a wooden home and trading post – was likely the inspiration for other Inuit who wished to enjoy similar accommodations. A 1936 report from the RCMP at Cambridge Bay noted that the Canalaska Trading Company was supplying Inuit who could afford them with wooden houses – much to the consternation of the Catholic and Anglican bishops, who suggested that this practice would tend to hold the Eskimos in one locality and interfere with their hunting and trapping.[37] But the Hudson's Bay Company apparently was also willing to do the same for those Inuit who could afford it and had done so many years earlier. A chapter entitled "White Man's Igloo" in Richard Finnie's book *The Lure of the North* tells the story of a house transported from Vancouver aboard the HBC ship *Baychimo*. The house was erected in the fall of 1930 by Angoojuk – an Inuk headman and trapper – at Richardson Point in Starvation Cove, the last known location of the doomed crew of the Franklin expedition. Permanent dwellings for Inuit raised not only fears about the impact on their proclivity to hunt and trap but also implications for health and sanitation, as Finnie (1940, 73-74) notes in his account of the building of Angoojuk's house: "Intelligent but Naïve folk [the Inuit] would be the last to recognize [the danger in owning a house]. Had we tried to warn Angoojuk against the perils of civilization, he would have laughed at us."

Given that Angulalik was Inuk, the Northwest Territories Council was loath to shut his trading operation down, thereby raising, once again, questions about the status of Inuit that, it was elsewhere claimed, was legally no different from that of any white resident of the territories. At a council meeting considering the legality of Angulalik's operation, Roy Gibson "expressed the opinion that so long as natives were willing to operate trading posts they

Ikey Bolt in a business suit, having returned from a trip to Vancouver to purchase supplies for his trading store at Rymer Point, Victoria Island, in the summer of 1930. From Finnie 1940, 37.

should be given precedence, particularly in native preserves, and where trading companies were going to open up trading posts in Preserves [sic] they should accept responsibility for the maintenance of natives attached to their posts."[38]

At an earlier meeting of council on 15 March 1934, the legal opinion offered was that a half-breed (which both Angulalik and another trader, Ikey Bolt, were considered to be) in the employ of a trading company required a licence to trade under section 3 of the game regulations.[39] By implication, if they were not in the employment of a trading company (and both Angulalik and Bolt acted as independent traders), then no licence was required. However, trading and operating a post were two different things. The matter did not end there.

In the fall of 1934, two schooners bound for King William Island, one owned by Canalaska and the other by the Hudson's Bay Company, were trapped in the ice at Ikaluktutiak (Cambridge Bay). The Hudson's Bay Company decided to dispose of its goods by asking for permission to reopen a post at Perry River. It was given permission and paid the requisite licence fee. In the meantime, Canalaska, working with Angulalik as a trader – and without a licence – pre-empted the Hudson's Bay Company by disposing of its trade goods in the Perry River area through Angulalik. By the following year, these events had given rise to a complaint to the Northwest Territories Council, which asked its solicitor to pass an opinion on whether or not Natives and half-breeds required trading licences that could then be used to restrict their activities.[40] In the meantime, Angulalik was painted by the

HBC as someone taking advantage of his own people. Suggesting that he had no right to operate at Flagstaff Island, the Hudson's Bay Company raised questions about the Deed of Surrender – a reference to the document handing over Rupert's Land to the dominion government in 1869 – and whether it still had an exclusive right to operate trading posts in the Northwest Territories.

The question was apparently a perplexing one. In March 1936, the solicitor for the Department of the Interior again reported to council that, "under the Northwest Game Act, Eskimos, Indians and half-breeds living the lives of natives are not required to secure a license to trade. All persons, however, are required to obtain a post permit before a trading post is established."[41] The wording is significant. It is clear that, regardless of which different status was afforded Inuit, departmental solicitors could not avoid thinking as if they were dealing with people who had status akin to that afforded Indians under the Indian Act. Implicit in the opinion offered is the idea of enfranchisement: if one lived the life of a "Native," then one was a Native and had special status. However, as soon as one stopped living the life of a Native (and operating a trading post, as opposed to merely trading, qualified as a non-Native activity), one became a white person and required a licence like anyone else. Mr. Daly – a councillor and public servant with the Department of the Interior – took things one step further and suggested that next time the Northwest Game Act was revised, in order to properly control the situation, provision should be made whereby a Native would be required to take out a trading licence at a nominal fee.[42]

At the May 1936 session of council, Councillor Sir James MacBrien noted that, given the list of responsibilities of council, "not much attention had been given to Eskimos."[43] Mr. Gibson advised him that this was done deliberately since the matter of their status was before the Supreme Court. The minutes of subsequent meetings suggest that council was thoroughly confused as to the status of Inuit and consequently unclear about how to regulate Inuit hunting and trapping activities.

Enforcement of the Migratory Birds Convention Act was also of concern to council, and the treatment of Inuit under its provisions was to prove a long-standing source of conflict between them and wildlife management officials. In the summer of 1937, two missionaries in Pond Inlet – Reverend J.H. Turner and Reverend S. Flint – decided to openly break the Migratory Birds Convention Act and start a test case on behalf of Inuit. They took twenty snow goose eggs and ate them, reporting their actions to the RCMP and recommending that the act be changed to suit the needs of both whites and Natives living in the Arctic. Given that neither of them was Inuk, the strategy was ill conceived. The result was a court hearing presided over at ship time by Major McKeand of the Eastern Arctic Patrol, a conviction, and a ten-dollar fine for each of them.[44] Writing about the same incident, Graham

Rowley, travelling in the area a few years later, noted that despite losing the case the missionaries had made their point (1996, 149).

In fact, the regulations under the Migratory Birds Convention Act were loosely enforced throughout the 1930s. When Councillor Dr. H.W. McGill suggested that the regulations should be modified in the case of the Northwest Territories, Deputy Commissioner Gibson pointed out that a letter from the commissioner of national parks had been received several years earlier in which it was suggested that a general understanding existed with the United States Biological Survey that neither party to the treaty would be too harsh with the Natives or even other residents of the North in the matter of killing birds for food.[45] Inuit memories of the game regulations illustrate the capricious nature of having a law that might or might not be enforced:

> There was game laws all the time. As long as there was an RCMP, there was law all the time about game. Geese come up; who can shoot them if the RCMP was here? But again [the RCMP] are a thousand miles away. We had to [break the law]. The stores are empty and nothing else to eat, but in those days in the western Arctic, if somebody reported somebody and saw the geese, when summer came [the RCMP] went down, picked them up, and put them in jail. The government, there again, isn't using its head! A thousand miles away from a store! Inuit have nothing else except animals: caribou, seal, fish, and stuff. (George Porter, Gjoa Haven, 18 May 1998)

It is not surprising that Inuit were not prosecuted under the 1917 Northwest Game Act. Their status was anything but clear. In the 1920s, O.S. Finnie deliberately chose to treat Inuit with benevolence rather than using the "strong arm of the law." His departure from council was accompanied by a growing awareness of problems with Inuit legal status. The minutes of council from the 1930s make this – and a number of other things – clear. The "Great Barrens," in some respects, were now anything but. Mining and exploration companies embarked on detailed exploration of the interior of the Northwest Territories commencing in the late 1920s, supported by airplanes. Traders, trappers, and prospectors had arrived in force. Imperial Oil reactivated its wells and refinery at Norman Wells in 1932. Gold had been discovered at Yellowknife, and by the late 1930s exploration and development in and around Great Slave Lake had increased dramatically (see Zaslow 1988, 174-88). The bush plane had remedied problems of access. Trappers, traders, prospectors, and miners grew in number. If any impact on wildlife is worthy of note, it was the result of these activities and not hunting or trapping carried out by the Dene or Inuit. Dene hunters did supply some mining and exploration camps with meat, thereby earning much-needed cash. But records of their treatment by miners and prospectors, and the willingness of non-Aboriginal people to violate game regulations, make it clear who posed a real threat to northern wildlife.[46]

Major changes to the game management regime in the Northwest Territories were put on hold by the events of World War II, as was consideration of the implications of the 1939 Supreme Court decision making it clear that, for administrative purposes, "Inuit were Indians" and thus a federal responsibility. Policy makers had operated through the 1920s and 1930s without recourse to scientific data that might have informed their decisions. Apart from rudimentary and unreliable numbers with respect to species taken, policy makers had little to go on other than anecdotal evidence and their own "common sense." Common sense invited debate not about numbers (there were few) but about esoteric questions relevant to the regulation of hunting and trapping (should Inuit be regarded as white folk?) and questions about the images being presented to council (are Alaskan Natives more healthy, and what should be done about such a claim?). The state introduced texts and formal codes to define and regulate Inuit hunting and to establish the authority necessary to make them work. In the meantime, Inuit continued to hunt, trap, and relate to animals pretty much as they had always done. The state, unsure of its footing (having a regime based somewhat on myth and reflection), and having little means or inclination to act, declined the bold step of prosecuting Inuit hunters.

It is interesting to note that state actors, prior to the introduction of "science in the service of the state" – which we examine in the following chapters – relied heavily on legal texts to accomplish what was taken to be essential to the management and control of the economy and social conditions found in a modern state such as Canada. Where Inuit hunting practices presented a threat to this orderly development, the law was used to bring about regulation and control. However, without the backing of science, it was a tool clearly grounded in unstable assumptions and ideological convictions. It could not be applied with certainty. The science of game management was therefore looked upon as something that could bring an element of certainty to Enlightenment logic. This, as we shall see, gave the science of game management a status that it hardly deserved. The Enlightenment "logic" guiding game management included the assumption that, not unlike the armed white settlers who had decimated the wildlife of lands they had come to occupy in the 1800s, Aboriginal populations, given rifles, would do the same. That Aboriginal cultures might be guided in their experience with new technology by the norms, beliefs, and practices characteristic of their unique cultures was not considered. In the period in question, the attempt to totalize Inuit hunting practices within the logic of the modern state was met with resistance: the law was simply ignored or tied in knots by questions over the behaviour and status of Inuit such as Angulalik.

As we discover in the next chapter, this approach to management – one characterized by a degree of anguish and self-reflection in the face of mythical uncertainty – was to change. Game management was to become a very different way of understanding Inuit and wildlife, one that increasingly subjected Inuit to new attempts at totalization, efforts that cojoined legal texts with the mathematics and formalism of science, to expunge all other ways of making sense – the mythical – from debate and social action. However, the myths that constructed Inuit as "wanton slaughterers" of game were to remain an unrecognized, unexamined, and integrated element in the science of wildlife management, thereby undermining its totalizing force. Creation of the Dominion Wildlife Service in 1947 was to have profoundly different effects upon the relationship of Inuit to their lands and wildlife and, ultimately, to give rise to new forms of resistance.

2
Sagluniit ("Lies"): Manufacturing a Caribou Crisis

> In those days you don't know what would come up if you tried to
> talk against those laws – you know – or the RCMP's law. You don't
> know what could happen to you! If you talk against it, something
> might – you know – you don't know what the RCMP is going
> to do to you in those days. We didn't know anything about the
> government, about white people, what – you know – what triggers
> them and things like that. Ah, so, it was impossible for us to say
> anything bad against the government or RCMP or the law or the
> rules. And you don't know nothing about, uh, talking back, or
> having a meeting – or whatever.
>
> – Moses Nargyak, Gjoa Haven, 19 May 1998

The Dominion Wildlife Service: Science Gets off the Ground

As the 1930s drew to a close, there was considerable impetus among provincial and federal game management officers – who had been meeting regularly since the end of World War I – to create an organization to study and to influence the regulation of wildlife in Canada. The Northwest Territories Council increasingly looked to science as a basis for its decisions.[1] As noted in the previous chapter, the council was working in the dark, faced with rumours and conflicting objectives that included making sure Inuit did not become dependent on the state by maintaining a viable trapping industry. The former became all the more critical following World War II as Canada worked on the international stage and with the newly formed United Nations on community development initiatives aimed at Third World countries. Having an Inuit population that was poor and destitute would not play well on the international stage, where Canada increasingly had an important role. Making Inuit part of the Canadian polity and good Canadian citizens was progressively more important. As noted in Chapter 6, Doug Wilkinson, who was to play a prominent role in community development initiatives in

Baker Lake, was sent to the United Nations in New York between his postings at Frobisher Bay and Baker Lake in 1956 to learn principles of community work before returning north.

The collapse of the price for Arctic fox immediately after the formation of the Dominion Wildlife Service in 1947 introduced new urgencies to the problem of game management. At least until 1957-58, many state officials retained the idea of Inuit surviving by making a living as they had always done – by hunting and trapping. The modernization agenda, combined with what state officials came to believe about the status of barren ground caribou changed this idea somewhat, while it was still recognized that the demise of caribou herds would have catastrophic implications for Inuit and for the state's role in ensuring their welfare. In the face of these complex issues, it is no surprise that state officials came to rely heavily on the science of wildlife management, facilitated by the creation of the Dominion Wildlife Service. In this chapter, this science is assessed, revealing its limitations and biases. The faith of state officials was, as becomes evident, somewhat misplaced.

Some early attempts had been made at data collection. In 1934, the Department of the Interior had circulated caribou questionnaires to residents of the northern prairie provinces and the Northwest Territories in an attempt to get some indication of whether or not the number of caribou was increasing or decreasing. They clearly had some doubts, generated by conflicting reports from traders, trappers, police officers, and others. The returns, given the hundreds of questionnaires circulated, were low, ranging from 25 questionnaires in 1934 to 104 in 1940. It is highly unlikely that Aboriginal hunters completed many of them.

In 1938, when the Advisory Board on Wild Life Protection considered the content of a paper based on the research, it did not believe it had enough information on which to take definitive action. The paper noted the large number of pregnant cows being killed, that Inuit trapping required many caribou to be taken to feed dogs, that caribou skins were being sold in large numbers, and that widespread use of rifles had changed the way Aboriginal populations hunted caribou. But as one researcher has noted, "in truth, the administration lacked even the most basic data on caribou" (Clancy 1985, 440). Most of the respondents to the questionnaire blamed a decline in caribou populations on wolf predation – no surprise given that most respondents were *Qallunaat* trappers.

The questionnaire was the first attempt to gather basic data on barren ground caribou. At the time, there was also a considerable interest in getting a better grip on fluctuations in wildlife populations, particularly the valuable Arctic fox and other fur-bearing species. In the late 1930s, Charles Elton, head of Oxford University's Bureau of Animal Population Studies, suggested the establishment of research field stations across the country to study animal populations. Elton believed that natural cycles for fur-bearing animals could be predicted, thus opening the possibility of managing the industry and affecting the natural cycles to better economic advantage. The possibility of scientifically managing game in the Canadian North was on the horizon. Unfortunately, so was World War II. Pursuing these initiatives would have to wait.

Some of the chaos that had descended on game management in the North is evident from attempts to reorganize the enforcement of legislation and to give consideration to a more scientific approach to management. In 1938, C.H.D. Clarke, on the staff of the National Museum, was appointed mammalogist with the Lands, Parks, and Forests Branch of the Ministry of Mines and Resources. Clarke brought a new and scientific perspective to the job, arguing in 1943 for the creation of a wildlife management area in the Mackenzie District to integrate fur harvesting with principles of conservation that would be conveyed to Aboriginal and other trappers. Unfortunately, given the war effort, no funds were available to accommodate the scientific research required by such a management system (Clancy 1985). In the western Arctic, the department created a Forest and Game Management Service to enforce the Northwest Game Act, and wardens, many of them non-Aboriginal trappers and hunters, took over the enforcement responsibilities of the RCMP and introduced a "law and order" approach to the management problem. Contrary to what Clarke had in mind, the science introduced a few years later reinforced this approach and was ultimately to give significant impetus to Inuit resistance to the game laws and to Inuit articulation of their rights.

Others with a scientific bent on game management joined Clarke's initiative. In 1943, Hoyes Lloyd retired as federal supervisor of wildlife protection and was replaced by Dr. Harrison Lewis. As noted in Chapter 1, Lewis, an ornithologist, had been appointed chief federal migratory birds officer following ratification of the International Treaty for the Protection of Migratory Birds in 1917. In 1947, reorganization within the Department of Mines and Resources, with Hugh Keenleyside as deputy minister, included creation of the Dominion Wildlife Service – renamed the Canadian Wildlife Service (CWS) in 1950.[2] Keenleyside arrived in the post from External Affairs and had been Canadian ambassador to Mexico. A progressive humanitarian and personal friend of Lester Pearson, he accepted the post to "do something about the appauling [sic] conditions existing among Indians and Inuit" (Keenleyside 1981, 271). Harrison Lewis was appointed the first director of the Dominion Wildlife Service. He initiated the first scientific studies of northern caribou. Commenting on the role of the service, he observed that "we certainly did diligent investigation and added to human knowledge, and we had to do work of this kind more and more, as time went on, because of the great need for it and because no other part of the government service was prepared to obtain the sort of information that we required for efficient wildlife management" (cited in Burnett 2003, 23). According to Roy Gibson, director of the Lands, Parks, and Forest Branch within which the Dominion Wildlife Service was located, the service was, among other things, to carry out "scientific investigations relating to numbers, food, shelter, migrations, reproduction, diseases, parasites, predators, competitors and uses of the wild creatures that constitute the resources being managed."[3]

Lewis remained in the role of director until March 1952, when he was replaced by Winston Mair, a former military officer described by Burnett in his history of the Canadian Wildlife Service as "the charismatic wartime leader of a particularly deadly Canadian/American commando unit" (2003, 52). Mair, a zoologist and a graduate of the University of British Columbia, was to oversee the bitter struggles that broke out within the service during the 1950s over methods of surveying and studying caribou.

Lewis was a committed conservationist. One of the more interesting cases with which he dealt concerned the sale, by Indian hunters, to the Catholic Indian boarding school at Albany, Ontario, of wild geese for use as food by the young Indian and Inuit residents. While the issue was a matter for the Government of Ontario, it was of interest to the Northwest Territories Council because whether or not such practices should be allowed was seen to have implications for the provision of wild game and fowl to schools in the territories.

The game birds had been sold to the school in the open season for storage and consumption in the closed season, and while taking these birds in an open season was permitted in the Northwest Territories there was no open season in the Province of Ontario. In other words, the practice was illegal. The question was whether or not the law should be changed to allow an open season in Ontario, like the one found in the Northwest Territories. Both Hoyes Lloyd, superintendent of wildlife protection for the national parks bureau, and Dr. Lewis were consulted on the matter. Neither was in favour of making any change in the regulations. Dr. Lewis noted that "Indians in the James Bay area, when not interfered with by the white man, are natural conservationists and the children follow the example of the parents but he did not think the missions in that area [gave] practical instruction on hunting to parents or children." Furthermore, he believed that "Indians do not get the desired instruction by selling waterfowl to the missions for table use." In fairness to Dr. Lewis, he had submitted a proposal to the Government of Ontario that would have permitted the sale to the mission of 600 or 700 geese a year if the province agreed to change the regulations.[4]

The province did not, and ultimately the practice was prohibited. The coup de grace was the suggestion made by Councillor Dr. H.W. McGill at the next meeting of council that, if institutions bought from Aboriginal hunters, doing so would strain the resource and that ultimately the Indians would not be able to secure enough food for themselves.[5] The logic here, given that the birds were being used as food for First Nations and Inuit children who would otherwise be eating them in another setting, escaped other council members entirely. Fear of depleting scarce game was a consideration later applied to dealing with the question of supplying caribou meat to boarding schools for Inuit children in the eastern Arctic.

Also on staff of the Dominion Wildlife Service was A.W.F. (Frank) Banfield – Captain Banfield, as he was officially known[6] – who was to conduct the first study of northern caribou as work toward his doctoral dissertation at the School of Forestry and Conservation, University of Michigan. The school was well known for its pioneering work on the scientific management of wild game.[7] John Kelsall and John Tener, who were to continue Banfield's work on Arctic mammals, had worked as students with the Parks Branch during the war and now joined the service. Kelsall was to become a key figure in the caribou studies of the 1950s. As a young man in the Annapolis Valley, where he was born, Kelsall spent much of his free time canoeing and hunting. Too young to enlist, he had joined the air force only at the end of the war and never saw combat. Following the war, he jumped at the opportunity to turn his love of the outdoors into a full-time job.[8] He joined the Dominion Wildlife Service as a student assistant soon after it was formed, and after working on moose habitat in Cape Breton Highlands National Park he was appointed chief mammalogist for the eastern Arctic. He completed his master's degree at the University of Toronto while on leave from the Canadian Wildlife Service in 1950. Kelsall, Tener, and Banfield were to get the science of wildlife management "off the ground" with the first significant use of aircraft to survey caribou in the Canadian Arctic.[9]

Attempts to manage game after World War II were to have significant implications for Inuit rights and the genesis of Inuit resistance to the management not only of wildlife but also, by implication, of Inuit lifestyles, relationships, and material resources. The attempt to manage game, and thereby Inuit habits, relationships, and culture, was a significant – and

John Kelsall.
Courtesy Arctic Institute
of North America,
University of Calgary.

perhaps the most significant – element in the attempt to assimilate Inuit to Canadian society in the 1950s and 1960s.[10] It involved scientific research, surveillance, management, and the control not so much of wildlife as of the Inuit who depended on it. Whether the research that informed management decisions was based on "science" or prejudices common to the day is a matter of debate. The possibility that what was regarded as "factual" was driven by questionable assumptions, cultural misunderstandings, and considerable prejudices is examined in what follows.

Scarcity, Value, and the Management of Inuit Hunting

A year after the formation of the Dominion Wildlife Service, Banfield commenced his study of the barren ground caribou. The study, proposed at one of the ongoing meetings of dominion and provincial wildlife officials, was financed by the Northwest Territories administration, initially with an appropriation of $30,000 from the territorial liquor fund.[11] The image of thirsty trappers spending their money on beer in Yellowknife after a hard season in the bush, and ultimately paying for surveys of the caribou on which they depended for food while camped in the wilds, is strangely appropriate. In doing his research, Banfield set in place a number of assumptions that, as the 1950s developed, were to become "near facts." The surveys greatly influenced caribou management in the eastern Arctic. He suggested, in a 1951 departmental summary of his fieldwork and thesis research, that "it is difficult at present to estimate the number of caribou which existed upon the arrival of the first explorers. It seems probable that the population of caribou was about 1,750,000 animals in 1900. This estimate is based on the carrying capacity of the range as determined in Alaska, and must be considered to be a maximum estimate" (Banfield 1951a, 13).

Estimating the size of the barren ground caribou herds prior to the introduction of the fur trade to the eastern Arctic, the advent of whaling, and the introduction of firearms among Aboriginal people was critical to the logic used by wildlife officials in managing Inuit hunting practices. The population of caribou at the turn of the century was a central issue. It was one assumption that helped to generate a "caribou crisis" in the eastern Arctic because the estimated number of caribou in 1900 determined the degree of decline in the populations counted in the 1950s. Two other contributing factors were assumptions about the hunting practices of Inuit: that there was considerable "crippling" of animals and that the slaughter of game was common.

The crisis also involved assumptions about the role of wolves in caribou predation. In this case, Banfield and Kelsall were to have considerably different opinions. Banfield did not regard wolves as a significant threat, and at least some of his conclusions were based on fieldwork conducted by Farley Mowat, working for the Dominion Wildlife Service in the summer of 1948 near Nueltin Lake in the Keewatin District. Banfield appears to have been supported in this view by his director, Harrison Lewis. In a paper on wolf control, presented to the Northwest Territories Council for its meeting of 2 November 1944, Lewis paints an image of wolf predation that has much in common with Mowat's later observations from 1948. He notes their dietary habits and dependence on mice and other rodents and their tendency to prey only on weak or debilitated caribou and other species of big game. He makes it clear that the pressure to control the wolf populations typically originates with trappers who lose their trapped animals to wolves and who see wolves as predators of valuable game species. Lewis, in reviewing other studies and experiences, makes it clear that wolves, under normal conditions, "will not seriously reduce the population of a prey species" and that most persons of European descent have "always feared and disliked wolves, probably because they receive such prejudices at a very early stage of development through learning widespread nursery stories, such as that of Red Riding Hood and that of the Three Little Pigs."[12]

His view of wolves had some impact on the council. It is interesting to contrast their response to wolf control during his tenure with what happened thereafter. In the spring of 1946, a former RCMP officer who had taken up trapping around Arviat (Eskimo Point) found that wolves were taking half of his fur catch. He set out poison (presumably strychnine) around his traps to reduce the number of wolves. Minutes of the council meeting of January 1947 record the following:

> He was arrested and tried last summer before a Justice of the Peace. He was fined $3 but immediately wrote an appeal, his object being to force to attention the necessity of doing something to control the wolves. He wants the law modified to permit responsible trappers to poison wolves or, failing that, he wants the government to employ paid wolf exterminators. The wild life authorities were consulted and said nothing could economically be done to reduce the wolf population in such an extensive area as the cost would probably exceed the value of the fox catch. Poison cannot be permitted owing to danger to other wild life.[13]

This logic would not hold sway once the 1940s gave way to the 1950s. Lewis's conclusions about wolves were not shared by his successor, Winston Mair, who assumed the directorship of the Canadian Wildlife Service in 1952. Under his leadership, a concerted effort was made to control wolf populations by the use of strychnine-laced meat, which Lewis had condemned in his 1944 presentation to the Northwest Territories Council. Inuit hunters old enough to recall attempts to manage wolves in this way also appear to have been opposed to the idea:

Inuit people didn't favour that at all because they thought that not only the wolves would be killed but other animals too. And the carcasses that had been poisoned, like for instance wolves or foxes, during the summer they would put them in the lake in a deep area, and they would sink them. And the older Inuit people were thinking – were saying that – they may be killing our fish too. So that was one of their other concerns. They were poisoning the wolves, and that was to protect the caribou. But the mishaps that they would have is one sad thing they were having concerns about. (Barnabus Piruyeq, Baker Lake, 22 May 1997)

As a result of his 1948 studies, Banfield (1951, 41) concluded that wolves did not take more than 5 percent of the population of caribou in any given year. Kelsall, who took over Banfield's work on caribou in 1950, concluded that wolves were a significant predator. It was Kelsall's arguments that were ultimately to carry the day and lead to an extensive program of wolf baiting by the Canadian Wildlife Service.[14] Mowat's book *Never Cry Wolf,* the publication of which, it can be argued, played a pivotal role in launching the modern Canadian environmental movement in the 1960s, was to become a focus for southern Canadians opposed to the wolf kill.

To this list of factors explaining the origins of the caribou crisis, a cultural and historical context must be added. Understandably, CWS personnel were heavily influenced by what they knew of the history of other species – the buffalo, the musk-ox, the passenger pigeon, the Labrador duck, and others –

Farley Mowat. Courtesy McClelland and Stewart, Toronto.

all of which had been pushed to extinction or near extinction by the turn of the century. Wildlife officials operated with a keen sense of this history and an ethos that included the use of scientific method to ensure that this threat never happened again. That *Qallunaat* hunters and trappers contributed to these events was not entirely overlooked, and *Qallunaat* hunting was increasingly restricted in the face of the so-called crisis. In fact, in the 1930s, it was recognized that *Qallunaat* trappers were responsible for the great demise in the number of fur-bearing species available to Indian and Inuit trappers. Even Duncan Campbell Scott – not generally regarded for his progressive attitude toward First Nations – drove this point home in a 1932 letter to H.H. Rowatt, commissioner of the Northwest Territories and deputy minister of the Department of the Interior:

> Let us now look at the white trapper. While much that I will put down applies to white trappers in general, I have in mind particularly the whites found in the Territories. During my visit (in 1928) I took occasion to find board and lodging amongst them in order that I might learn more of them, and their methods. I may say, without equivocation, that I do not think I would find more red, Bolshevik sentiment had I gone to Soviet Russia. If such is the type of citizen who is being encouraged to populate the Territories, the Government is going to have a nice problem on its hands before long.
>
> The general attitude of the white trapper is that the Territories is a fur country in process of depletion and they are out after their share; a trapper is a stripper. He takes what he can and leaves nothing behind.
>
> It is my contention that the elimination of the white trapper from the Territories will materially improve the economic condition of the Indian and insure a continual source of supply of fur-bearing animals.[15]

As strange as it may seem, it was a sentiment shared by Ralph Parsons, fur trade commissioner for the Hudson's Bay Company. He joined the refrain, writing his own letter in support of Scott's ideas:

> In the matter of trapping, it is commonly recognized that the Indians or Eskimos, if left alone, will never exterminate the game or fur bearing animals in their territories. They are not the intensive trappers that the white men are and restricted, as they are, to small areas, they have every incentive to conserve the resources in them. The white man on the other hand enters the country with the fixed purpose of taking everything that he can out of it, regardless of game laws, or the consequence of his acts. When he has cleaned up one territory, he moves to another and so the unrestricted slaughter has been going on, until today, we are faced with huge territories, formerly prolific with wild life, which are now almost barren.[16]

Parsons had a vested interest, of course, in seeing trapping reserved for Indian and Eskimo people. Furs taken by white trappers did not pass through his posts in the Northwest Territories. Nevertheless, it is interesting to note that he attributes the slaughter of wildlife not to First Nations and Inuit hunters but to rogue trappers who, as he observes, acted without regard to the law. Twenty years later John Kelsall and others with the Canadian Wildlife Service were inclined to see Inuit hunters in somewhat the same light as Parsons saw trappers: slaughtering animals and acting without regard to the law.

The focus of attention in the early 1950s was Inuit and First Nations hunting. Given a rifle and the opportunity, Inuit hunters were assumed to be no different from anyone else, an assumption that others in the northern administration, with an agenda of assimilating Inuit to Canadian society, were trying to make a reality. For purposes of game management, officials in the northern administration were, paradoxically, eclipsed by wildlife officials who assumed that, in relation to animals and hunting practices, Inuit already were no different from other Canadians and subsequently needed to be regulated and controlled by the same Canadian law that governed *Qallunaat* hunting.

Kelsall, Banfield, and others within the Canadian Wildlife Service were very much products of their day. The extent to which the views they espoused have changed some fifty years later is debatable. They and others were thoroughly modern men in whom the logic of their culture was firmly – if not subliminally – entrenched. The notion of scarcity and the fear of extinction, while facts for some species, were also, even in the case of those species driven to extinction by human action, socially constructed "facts" – in this case a compilation of realities and fears originating from an economic and cultural system that depends on scarcity (for therein lies value) as much as it fears it. Scarcity is the social construction on which modernity and modern, capitalist economies are based. That which is scarce is valuable, while that which is plentiful and common is worthless. This is not to deny that the *Qallunaat* had, as already noted, driven some species to extinction. Sahlins puts it this way: "That sentence of 'life at hard labour' was passed uniquely upon us. Scarcity is the judgement decreed by our economy – so also the axiom of our Economics: the application of scarce means against alternative ends to derive the most satisfaction possible under the circumstances. But if modern man, with all his technological advantages, still hasn't got the wherewithal, what chance has this naked savage with his puny bow and arrow? Having equipped the hunter with bourgeois impulses and Palaeolithic tools, we judge his situation hopeless in advance" (1972, 4).

This hopeless situation can be overcome by sharing with hunter-gatherers modern technology, including the rifle. However, not only are Inuit equipped with the rifle but also, as Sahlins suggests, true or not, they are equipped, in the minds of game management officials (as made evident in what follows by reference to the language used), with the bourgeois mentality that goes with it. "Slaughter" must therefore be the inevitable result, not unlike the situation of the consumer confronted with an infinite number of dollars and a dealer's lot full of cars. The ensuing "slaughter" – or buying spree – is awesome to behold. For Inuit, periods of scarcity could not be helped, as revealed in this account by Monica Adjuk of two periods of starvation in her life. She survived the Garry Lake starvation in the winter of 1957-58 (see Tester and Kulchyski 1994, Chapter 6):

> We also mostly lived on caribou and fish during the winter seasons. And sometimes there would absolutely be no game available. If I were to record all the events about Garry Lake, I figure that the government would be absolutely astonished at how we survived because we were very skilful – skilful people to be able to survive up there.
>
> I will particularly highlight the trip I took from Perry River – between Garry Lake and Perry River. This occurred between the months of May and August. And because we were starving, we were eating caribou skins and lived on ptarmigan heads. At one point, we lived on lemmings for a whole month. This, what I used to work through, is totally – one would not want to experience, because it is just unheard of in today's world.
>
> We stayed in Perry River area for about two years, and then by walking back we went to Garry Lake. When we arrived back into Garry Lake, the two oldest children of ours were sent to school in Chesterfield [Inlet]. So for the children, first year they were sent out to school. Second following year, again the children went to school. And then starvation came around that period. One whole winter there was no caribou, and we survived on a small amount of fish. And sometimes you'd go a day without eating, and we also didn't have any form of fire. So there was no – there was nothing ever hot, warm, or hot to drink. And our clothing wasn't all that good either. And it was during the spring that we were taken to Baker Lake. That's when people started dying in the Garry Lake area. (Monica Adjuk, Whale Cove, 3 June 1997)

For the *Qallunaat,* scarcity was everywhere – paradoxically in the midst of relative plenty – and something to be feared. Scarce resources need managing, and the management and production of scarce commodities – be it caribou meat, university degrees, or cultural artifacts – require a temporal framework, institutions, rules, regulations, and means for their enforcement, development, and propagation.

These relationships among scarcity, value, management, and time were entirely foreign to Inuit culture at the time. Their culture prepared them for periodic times of hardship in a world that most often offered plenty. The world of Kelsall and others was upside down. Theirs was an economic and social system within which the bounty of nature was entirely dependent on human ingenuity, management, and control. The concept of scarcity – manifest through a concern with the waste of time and resources – permeates texts dealing with the game management regime introduced to the Arctic following World War II.

Conclusions, Convictions, and Cultures

Another consideration helps to explain the impact of Kelsall's work on the management regime ultimately imposed on Inuit. Kelsall was articulate. A convincing and extremely good writer, his style left little room for doubt about the correctness of his conclusions. There are many examples to be found throughout his papers and reports, of which the following, taken from a report on the resurvey of barren ground caribou in 1955, is illustrative: "In some areas the transect coverage was inadequate, or none was given because it was believed unwarranted. Estimates for these areas are given in Table 6. The estimates are believed to be reasonable and in no case significantly lower than the actual numbers of caribou present" (Kelsall and Loughrey 1955, 6).[17]

The historical record suggests that Kelsall's confidence in science and its conclusions was not altogether entrenched. As illustrated later in the text, neither were his opinions about Inuit and Indian hunters. From time to time, a modicum of doubt can be detected in his writings. Kelsall thus displays some doubts about the Enlightenment logic found within the scientific project and method and, from time to time, expresses these doubts in the form of cautions about his work and how it should be interpreted.[18] For example, in his earliest work on caribou on Baffin Island in 1949, Kelsall underlines the following: "There is the possibility of a considerable margin of error throughout this report"; "it is unwise as a general rule to base recommendations concerning management on data which are limited in scope as those above." Having underlined these cautions, Kelsall goes ahead and makes firm recommendations concerning management. Among these recommendations is the following: "Caribou hunting should be allowed on the island only during the month of August, for the purpose of procuring skins for clothing and on the condition that excess meat is either dried or otherwise utilized in a practical manner"; "the winter hunting of caribou on Baffin Island must be discontinued."[19] At the same time, he makes his motives clear: "In this case [that of more fieldwork] the matter is of vital and immediate importance. If caribou are to be saved and increased for future generations of Eskimos, action cannot be delayed. The expense involved will be considerable, and active cooperation will have to be received from all white residents of Baffin Island who are in contact with Eskimos. However, it would be much more costly to have to maintain all Eskimos on the island with imported types of clothing and with supplementary rations, which will have to be done if the caribou decrease further."[20]

Thinking outside the box of science was possible but clearly not easy. Trained as a biologist, Kelsall appears to have had little or no understanding at the time of Inuit hunting practices in relation to the environment Inuit occupied. Hunting caribou in summer is possible but, without the use of dog teams and frozen ground on which to travel, difficult and restricted primarily to areas accessible by boat – and not necessarily areas in which caribou could be found in enough quantity to feed a family for a winter. Furthermore, if caribou hunting were permitted only in August, then the supplementary rations to which Kelsall refers would be absolutely essential to avoid starvation. He suggests that white residents of Baffin Island be consulted, not Inuit. He also has some idea that Inuit produce what he calls "excess meat," clearly suggesting – without any data to substantiate it – that there is wastage in Inuit hunting practices. In other words, his science is replete with culturally based assumptions that could be understood only through self-reflection and philosophical encounter from outside the tightly knit logic of the biological science in which he had been trained. And, of course, this is precisely how Enlightenment logic, with its abstractions and compartments, works.

It is no surprise that Kelsall's commitments to the results of his work grew with the time and effort he subsequently spent in the field, to the point where, in his 1955 resurvey of barren ground caribou, no cautions parallel to those noted above can be found. As one might expect, as budgets and opportunities for research increase, so does confidence in the results: "Caribou wintering on the Anderson River were reported by a number of commercial pilots, and were seen during a resurvey flight when gasoline supplies were too low to allow extensive coverage of their range. However, the groups were evidently small and compact and the estimate of 2,100 animals from transect coverage agrees closely with visual estimates made by independent observers" (Kelsall and Loughrey 1955, 6).

In the same 1955 report, Kelsall notes that a reduction in the herd between Great Bear and Great Slave Lakes from 219,000 to 59,500, according to his 1955 resurvey, cannot be explained by either disease or overhunting (7). This reduction suggests problems with the survey results, but Kelsall is unwilling to admit this possibility. What might otherwise be seen as serious problems with the methods as well as the viability and reliability of the results are constantly swept aside. Estimates are "reasonable" and "in no case significantly lower than the actual numbers." Using actual numbers as a reference point was clearly absurd since the actual numbers were unknown and the whole purpose of the survey was to try to estimate what the actual numbers might be. If actual numbers were known, then a survey would have been unnecessary. The reference to "independent observers" – who they were and whether they knew what they were doing are unknown – lends an air of impartial reason to what was clearly mere guesswork. The impact on the naïve reader is to give credibility to methods and conclusions that were anything but.

How Far Have We Fallen? Estimating the Magnitude of the Caribou Crisis

Returning to Banfield's original survey in the late 1940s, if, as Banfield suggested, the caribou population had been 1.75 million at the turn of the century, then the population estimate he made based on research undertaken in 1948 indicated a precipitous decline. He estimated the barren ground caribou population at approximately 670,000 animals.

The caution Banfield associated with his estimate of 1.75 million caribou at the turn of the century was well deserved. For one thing, the climate of Alaska is considerably different – generally warmer – from the climate of the Northwest Territories, and consequently so is the biological productivity. Alaska also has a different history of glaciation that helps to explain its very different biological productivity. The concept of carrying capacity is often more significant for what it ignores or attempts through speculation, extrapolation, and guesswork to include than for what it considers. This is particularly relevant to understanding caribou habitat where mosquitoes, exposure to winds, protection from predators during calving season (depth of snow cover and drifting), and the suitability of local differences in terrain at different times of the year (for grazing, migration, and calving) all limit the use of terrain that might theoretically be capable of supporting a herd. This microlevel information about the vast expanse of the Northwest Territories was almost completely unknown to biologists at the time but known to Inuit hunters who had lived and walked in particular landscapes they and their ancestors had occupied for many hundreds of years. All of this suggests that the figure of 1.75 million caribou in the year 1900 was, at best, a "guesstimate." It was based on a carrying capacity of five animals per square mile over a 350,000-square-mile winter range (Kelsall 1968, 144).

Banfield was not the only one to speculate on populations at the turn of the century. Continuing his work after 1950, Kelsall was to engage in more protracted speculation about the original sizes of caribou herds. In doing so, he planted seeds of alarm, the implication being that hunting – particularly Aboriginal hunting – had a devastating effect on caribou populations in the period between the turn of the century and the end of World War II. The tone of future research and the assumptions that were to inform it were well established by Banfield: "At present caribou are becoming fewer from year to year, largely because of human wastage, which is high enough to account for annual losses being greater than production of new animals. The wastage may be comparable in numbers to the loss by predators. This wastage is due chiefly to the improvident hunting methods of the native population. Management of this resource must therefore be directed primarily towards controlling the number of caribou killed annually" (Banfield 1951a, 51).

In speculating on original numbers, Banfield cites Ernest Thompson Seton's earlier estimates of 30,000,000 barren ground caribou and notes that "modern approaches to a population estimate show this figure to be a clear impossibility" (1951a, 51). Seton arrived at this number in the following way, after a canoe trip in the central Arctic (a calculation too embarrassing even for Kelsall to explain in detail in his classic text on caribou biology published in 1968): "A year afterward, as I travelled in the fair State of Illinois, famous of its cattle, I was struck by the idea that one sees far more Caribou in the north than cattle in Illinois. This State has about 56,000 square miles of land and 3,000,000 cattle; the Arctic Plains have over 1,000,000 square miles of prairie, which, allowing for the fact that I saw the best of the range, would set the Caribou number at over 30,000,000. There is a good deal of evidence that this is not far from the truth" (Seton 1911, 220). Referring to the tundra as an "Arctic prairie" likely played no small role in encouraging this amazing comparison. In his own work, Kelsall (1968, 146) indulged in a review of estimates of carrying capacity by other biologists – all of them wildly speculative and presenting a huge range of possibilities – before settling on his own figure of 5.4 caribou per square mile of productive land and a primitive herd size of 2,395,000 animals – a number even larger than Banfield's. The net effect of such speculation was to suggest an even more dramatic decline in the number of animals and to generate even more alarm among public officials and politicians.

The problem with this "science" is that the numbers do not add up. If the herd was 2.4 million caribou, as Banfield suggested, then even the most extreme hunting by what was a small population of Inuit and First Nations hunters in the Northwest Territories and northern prairie provinces, combined with natural mortality, wolf predation, and a moderate calving rate, could not have reduced the herd from 2.4 million animals to 670,000 in fifty years. At a calving rate of 7.6 percent – an absolute minimum suggested by Banfield himself (1951a, 238) – the increment added to the herd would be 182,400 animals a year. Banfield calculated a recruitment rate over time of 15.9 percent (163),[21] and the number added to the herd using this figure would be 381,600 animals per year. Not even the most outrageous claims about the number of caribou taken by *Qallunaat*, as well as Inuit and First Nations hunters, combined with mortality from other sources, equal this number. Even assuming that the estimates of another well-respected biologist of 200,000 animals hunted per year (Clarke 1940, cited in Kelsall 1968, 278) were accurate (Banfield's estimate was 100,000 in 1948), and that wolves take about 2.5 percent[22] of the herd (a figure suggested by Banfield), and allowing for natural mortality, the numbers still do not add up to enough to reduce an original herd size of 2.4 million to 670,000. Adopting the biologists' own assumptions, the herd would have been increasing, not decreasing, in the period in question.

Making assumptions about wolf kills certainly helped to explain the apparent decline, and as previously noted Kelsall's estimates of the impact of wolf kills on herd size were considerably higher than those of Banfield. As one author explains, the reason for focusing on wolves appears to have been that it was easier to control wolf numbers than to modify harvesting methods (Urquhart 1989, 100).

If "guesstimates" of the original population's size are questionable, so was Banfield's 1948 estimate of a population of 670,000 animals. A detailed account of how this figure was determined can be found in his 1951 doctoral dissertation (1951b). Banfield includes a map of the aerial routes flown in surveying caribou in the northern parts of the three prairie provinces as well as the Northwest Territories. Caribou were counted by flying 500 feet above the ground on irregular courses over territory expected to contain caribou. How and why Banfield expected to find caribou in certain locations and not others are not explained. Experience has shown that even the idea that caribou follow more or less defined migration routes is debatable. The historical records of people travelling in the Arctic reveal that the movement and location of caribou at any given time are highly variable and not easily predicted. Furthermore, there are many technical problems associated with aerial surveys that neither Banfield nor Kelsall were aware of at the time (see Heard 1989; Nadasdy 2003, 158-73).

The extent of any grid system flown by Banfield and others in doing the population research is unclear from any available account. In fact, the map of routes flown in the course of the first survey completed, commencing in 1948, is not a grid system, despite the fact that in reporting on the research Banfield refers to the grid system flown in the process of doing his research (1951b, 16 fig. 3). Furthermore, his map of routes flown includes those flown by pilots on duty with the Royal Canadian Air Force who were asked to turn in their observations. Including them gives the impression that extensive flying was done in the service of caribou counts. Given budgets at the time and the cost of chartering planes, it is unlikely that even a minority of the flights indicated were specifically for that purpose. Which flights Banfield undertook deliberately for the purpose of counting caribou and which were RCAF flights or by commercial pilots for other reasons is not indicated. The result is a map with lots of lines criss-crossing the territories, the significance of many of them unclear.

For example, a number of flights up the west coast of Hudson Bay would likely have produced little or no results because most of these flights were made for purposes other than counting caribou (commercial or military) and at altitudes such that accurate counts when caribou were encountered would have been highly unlikely. Other routes up the Mackenzie River basin were for similar purposes and would have produced similar results. Spotting caribou from an aircraft at 500 feet flying in excess of ninety miles an hour, depending in part on the density of the vegetation, is extremely difficult, a consideration that would affect counts in the Mackenzie basin. The same is true of the northern prairies and a considerable area around and to the east of Great Slave Lake. Other methods employed are not clearly specified, as the following sentence illustrates: "Information was gathered also by means of frequent interviews, by questionnaires, and by co-operative action with other agencies" (Kelsall 1968, 3). Some of the routes included in Banfield's map were canoe trips, which could only have been made in the summer.

Since they were first introduced in the late 1940s, the aerial methods used by Banfield and other wildlife biologists have been criticized for their shortcomings.[23] They have produced results that are highly variable and that create fluctuations in total populations from year to year that cannot easily be explained by reference to calving, predation, or hunting.[24] If a review of attempts to count caribou since World War II reveals anything, it is that no one really knew the size of the barren ground herds with any degree of certainty. But despite obvious contradictions and impossibilities suggested by their data, wildlife biologists, committed to a scientific agenda, and seemingly unconscious of the cultural biases and contexts informing their work, could not stop trying.

While Banfield was pioneering aerial surveying of barren ground caribou, Kelsall was attempting to do the same on Baffin Island. If Banfield's methods were crude, Kelsall's were very much a case of "flying by the seat of his pants." Kelsall conducted a Baffin Island caribou survey in the spring of 1949 using a Dakota aircraft seconded from the RCAF. His report on this survey has been noted above in discussing the assumptions and motives informing his work. In other words, the effort was more than merely a problematic scientific study. Reporting on the survey later that year, Kelsall commences a review of his data by noting any historical report that claimed the area was once abundantly populated with caribou. He attempts to add credibility to the anecdotal evidence he cites by his choice of words: "Wright, using authoritative information from many sources, estimated the total population of the island at 25,000 animals."[25] Why the information was "authoritative" and what constituted "many" sources and whether or not they were reliable are anyone's guesses. Despite having virtually no data to support his historical claims, Kelsall concludes that "caribou are at present scarce on much, if not all, of Baffin Island in comparison with the early 1900's and before, and in some areas have disappeared completely."[26]

Kelsall bases this conclusion on a series of flights over an extremely limited portion of Baffin Island. Coverage of the southern part of the island commenced 7 April 1949 (a flight of five hours covering 750 miles at altitudes of

200-1,000 feet), continued on 9 April for eight hours, covering 1,200 miles, and concluded on 11 April for an unspecified number of hours. Kelsall was the observer. Additional flights were made on northern Baffin Island by a Norseman aircraft with S. Bailey of the NWT administration as a spotter. Bailey's regular responsibility was for the Family Allowance program, and there is no doubt that this was the first time he had ever counted caribou from an airplane. Unfortunately for Bailey, he just happened to be on Baffin Island at the time and was seconded by Kelsall, who was desperate to get on with a survey plagued by bad weather and mechanical problems with aircraft.

The results of Bailey's survey, from an aircraft often flown at 2,000 feet, were somewhat predictable. No caribou or their tracks were seen. The routes flown were, at best, over areas that were a guess as to where caribou might be wintering. According to Kelsall, "it is not believed that any significant numbers of caribou were missed during the survey flying."[27] Based on these methods and a number of incredible assumptions (that the caribou numbers and distribution noted on the survey flights were truly representative of what was to be found over the greater part of the island and that all caribou within sight range were actually seen and recorded), and by estimating the available range in the crudest manner possible, Kelsall determined the population of caribou on Baffin Island to be between 4,500 and 6,500 animals.[28] For years thereafter, the figure of 5,000 caribou was reproduced in government brochures, speeches, books, and information about the North in reference to Baffin Island and its caribou crisis.

Despite acknowledging some of the limitations of his study, Kelsall embarked on what was to become a familiar pattern. Having noted a serious decline in the number of animals from historical levels, he recommended that winter hunting of caribou be discontinued, that hunting be permitted only in the month of August, that females with fawns should not be hunted, that hunting of caribou by whites be discontinued, that the NWT administration launch a program to educate Inuit about caribou, and finally that sea mammals and other resources be used more extensively by Inuit. Unfortunately, this kind of science – combined with relocation and the move to settlements – was to have a profound impact on wildlife management policy for decades, with dramatic implications for Inuit culture, well-being, and social relations, as David Serkoak makes clear in this account of his parents' struggle, having been relocated from Ennadai Lake to the coast of Hudson Bay and urged to replace their dependence on caribou with a diet based on sea mammals:

> I think that struggling was always in [my parents' minds], because when
> you have children like my age – and we were all young – you don't want to
> give up in front of them. And I think the hardest part for them is to try to

adapt the lifestyles that were forced upon them. But they never complained. They were willing to adapt in their own way, own style. It was hard because I think that – I don't think my dad ever really accepted that he had to hunt seals, sea mammals. They were still hunting caribou in our camp in Wilson River [on the coast of Hudson Bay]. But the – like my brother who grew with watching people from the coast getting seals, he learned the skill. (David Serkoak, Iqaluit, 27 May 1999)

Kelsall's population estimates of mainland barren ground caribou were to cause alarm – and even panic – within the northern administration. After a few years of survey work, followed by statistical estimates of herd size, by 1955 Kelsall had reduced the population to only 270,569 animals. This calculation involved the application of other and even more questionable assumptions to the numbers (1968, Table 24, 201).

Kelsall's calculations amounted to a "do-loop": a year-to-year adjustment of numbers based on adding the number of calves recruited to Banfield's initial estimate and then subtracting numbers for natural mortality, hunting, and something called "crippling loss."[29] Crippling loss referred to those animals shot and wounded but not successfully pursued by hunters. Kelsall put crippling loss at 20 percent of the estimated kill. It was a guess; he conducted no research to confirm the number. However, the inclusion of 20 percent crippling loss was important in getting Banfield's original population estimate down to the point where it was continuous with the numbers generated by Kelsall's highly questionable 1955 resurvey of the herd. With a figure such as 20 percent of kill added to population losses, the crisis gets mathematically worse as time goes on. In fact, all of Kelsall's numbers are debatable, including, as we have noted, the initial herd size with which Kelsall commenced the calculations. All of this highly questionable "science" was, however, enough to suggest that by 1955, given their precipitous mathematical decline, the barren ground caribou were on their way to extinction.

The impact on officials responsible for Inuit and for policy making was considerable, as evidenced by Gordon Robertson's account of these events published in 2000. By 1954, Robertson was the deputy minister responsible for the department. In his memoirs, he makes it clear that he took the figures and accounts with which he was presented seriously and, forty-two years later, had not yet recognized the possibility that the so-called crisis was more mathematical than real (see 168-71). In fact, Robertson suggests that the reported decline in caribou was the prime reason behind relocations that took place in the 1950s, including what happened to David Serkoak and his parents. As suggested elsewhere, there are alternative explanations for the difficulties Inuit encountered in the Keewatin in the winter of 1957-58, including changes in caribou migration routes (see Tester and Kulchyski 1994).

These dramatic conclusions also contributed to the growth of the Canadian Wildlife Service's budgets at a time when budgets for matters dealing with northern affairs were expanding rapidly. Between 1952 and 1957, the CWS budget increased 50 percent, from $309,000 to $469,000 (Burnett 1999, 32).[30] The "crisis" put men like Kelsall into the field year after year to study game populations, with major implications for northern people and policies.

The "do-loop" method used by Kelsall suffered from a number of problems. The percentages used to estimate recruitment were highly variable and therefore highly questionable (see Table 1). Given that recruitment was also determined using aerial surveys, the figures are subject to all of the same problems associated with estimating total population size. The calculations are based on extrapolations, and the chances of being wrong, given the vagaries of caribou migration and territorial habits in general, are enormous. A local blizzard and very low temperatures or a few warm days at a critical moment immediately after birthing can have an impact on calf survival, while research suggests that in general calves, if they get past the period immediately after birth, are remarkably resilient to cold temperatures (Kelsall 1968, 240). Given uncertainty over the impact of weather and other considerations on calf survival, the recruitment numbers used lend an air of certainty to calculations that were anything but. Once again, a low recruitment figure used for several successive years, even holding other assumptions constant, has a dramatic impact on subsequent population estimates. Recruitment rates calculated by estimating the ratio of calves to total animals or the ratio of calves to cows for the period 1947-48 to 1960-61 vary from 6.9 percent in 1955-56 to 26.6 percent in 1952-53, and while environmental factors can explain some of the variation the high variability also suggests problems with the methods used (Kelsall 1968, 163).

The matter of crippling loss was important to these calculations and deserves further attention. Kelsall maintained that "crippling loss is high because of the hunting and shooting habits of Indians and Eskimos. Most sport hunters follow and search for wounded animals, but northern hunters do so only exceptionally. Also, hunter densities are never so high that wounded animals are frequently found and utilized by others. Twenty per cent of the known or estimated kill seems a conservative allowance for crippling loss" (1968, 202). "Conservative" was one way of putting it, but "completely unsubstantiated" would have been more accurate. As David Serkoak notes,

When the weather gets cold in the fall, most hunters would cache some [caribou], take the skin home and for later use, the food and the skin [itself]. And occasionally a hunter might kill one or two caribou on a later date, in the wintertime ... Then they would face them in a circle formation with the

Table 1

John Kelsall's theoretical projection of caribou decline between 1949 and 1955

Year	Spring population estimate	Deficit			Spring population less deficit	Increment		% deficit since previous year
		5% natural mortality	Human kill	Crippling loss		% increment after deficit	Number of animals	
1949	668,000	33,400	100,000	20,000	514,600	16.4	84,394	
1950	598,994	29,950	79,300	15,860	473,884	7.6	36,015	10.3
1951	509,899	25,495	79,300	15,860	389,244	11.0	42,817	14.9
1952	432,061	21,603	79,300	15,860	315,298	26.6	83,869	15.3
1953	399,167	19,958	65,750	13,150	300,309	15.4	46,248	7.6
1954	346,557	17,328	73,400	14,680	241,149	12.2	29,420	13.2
1955	270,569							21.9

Note: The starting point, 668,000 animals in the spring of 1949, is from Banfield (1954). Deficit and increment figures have been calculated on bases specified in the text. Increment has been added to the projected population following deficit since percent increment figures were gathered in late winter or spring of the year following the birth of calves. The terminal population, 270,569 caribou in 1955, is 3 percent lower than that determined by range-wide census (Kelsall and Loughrey 1955).

Source: Kelsall (1968, 201)

heads sticking up. So they would view it from every angle, so they would know where to look for it, without wasting too much time to find where it is. And also [they would] study what's around it: might be by the lake, by the hill, by ... (David Serkoak, Iqaluit, 27 May 1999)

No studies were ever undertaken by the Canadian Wildlife Service to verify the incredible assumptions made about losses attributable to crippling by Inuit and First Nations populations. The assumption is based on extensive use of .22 calibre rifles to hunt caribou and on anecdotal information and observations from *Qallunaat* in the field as well as Kelsall himself. This is how Peter Irniq, former commissioner of Nunavut, describes the use of a .22 calibre rifle:

One thing we have to remember is that I, like all the other boys, was taught how to shoot accurately. And to shoot a caribou, shoot exactly at the right spot. When shot properly, the caribou will die immediately. So, my father took a lot of time in showing me how to use a rifle and to shoot a caribou properly. He did this for a reason. Ammunition was very expensive, and we needed to make sure that we didn't waste the shells. He also used a .22 quite a bit for caribou. He used to say that shooting the animal at the right spot is as good as a high-powered rifle.

Also, in those days, we were taught to approach the caribou from behind a "blind" as much as possible. For example, the name Talurjuaq comes from the word *Talu,* a "blind," where a hunter always approaches the animal from behind the blind. So, when we saw a herd of caribou, my father used to be the one to approach the animals from behind a large rock used as a blind, and as the rule goes, my brother-in-law would follow directly behind him, and me from behind of my brother-in-law.

We were taught against approaching the animals side by side; otherwise, they will see us and run away. Also, we would crawl in approaching the animals if there was not enough blind between the caribou and the hunter. This is where the bow and arrow experience came in. Because Inuit did not live in the bush, they learned to approach the animals the best way they knew how. With bow and arrow, they had to get very close and hit the animal exactly at the right spot so that it died quickly. So the use of a .22 was very practical for hunting caribou. We were also taught against approaching the animal from the wind side; otherwise, it'll smell [you] and run away. That was my teaching about hunting techniques in the 1950s and 60s.

Having learned the approaching technique, we tried as much as possible not to wound the animals. When we did, we were taught to make sure that we kill them, if possible. The Inuktitut word *pinirluktuq* played a very large role among Inuit hunters. *Pinirluktuq* is when you wound an animal and the animal gets away. We were taught against *pinirluktuq* for a reason. We were taught to be good hunters. When Inuit missed the animals in those days, it was a big story told time and time again. Also, in those days, when we saw a herd of caribou of two or twenty, we used to try and kill them all.

Each summer, after fishing at the stone weir, normally early in August, we used to move to the inland – far inland – in search of caribou. The caribou in mid-August, the hair was just right for clothing, and there was lots of fat on the caribou. Inuit concentrate a lot on fat because, living in the inland, there were no seals, so we used to make candles out of fat and light the tent when the days were getting dark. Plus, fat is very good for the diet. We used to try and get enough caribou to clothe everyone in my family. There were five of us. If we caught 15 or 20 that summer, that was very good. If we caught that many caribou, then we would cache the animals. Then we would hunt a little bit in October, but the animals that we caught weren't many. Perhaps four or five, just to have some fresh caribou meat ... After the ice froze in the lakes, we are now living along the coast. And there was some hunting in December, but not much because the days were short. If we did go on the land, then if we saw a caribou, we would go after it and shoot it if we were lucky.

In those days, if I were to try to count the animals that my father and my brother-in-law took in a year, it would be around, perhaps, 70. Because, in order to clothe all the members of our family – there was six of us – the adult[s] would probably use five caribou each. Then we would catch several bull caribou for making sleeping mattresses and sleeping bags.

And don't forget, not everyone in Repulse Bay lived on the land. Only a small portion lived on the land all year round because they like the land better. Others lived on the seacoast because they preferred a diet of sea mammals such as seals, belugas, walruses, etc. The caribou clothing that Inuit women made could last for [a] couple of years at a time. So we didn't catch the 70 animals each year. (Correspondence with Peter Irniq, Iqaluit, Nunavut Territory, 14 February 2001)

The principle is clearly articulated by Joanasie Qajaarjuaq near the beginning of the compelling chapter on hunting in John Bennett and Susan Rowley's *Uqalurait: An Oral History of Nunavut*:

The boys were taught the importance of having knowledge against cruelty to animals from boyhood throughout their upbringing, as they became success-ful hunters. They were made to know that if they wounded an animal, they must make every effort to get it. Men were taught the instant kill, to make sure the animal they hunted did not suffer as a result, whether it was a land animal, a sea mammal, or any other living creature. People had to respect their existence and avoid any form of abuse or cause any kind of suffering. This is one of the ancient rules that we continue to practice. (2004, 50)

Peter Irniq. Photo Frank Tester.

Sometimes a few clear words can be far more important to our understanding than a thousand meticulously designed tables of numbers.

With this in mind, Kelsall's ethnocentric biases are obvious. Kelsall assumes that an Inuk hunting caribou is prepared to put in all the necessary time and effort planning the hunt only to lose an animal through crippling because of a badly placed shot. Removing or greatly lowering the 20 percent of estimated kill that Kelsall added to his method for calculating populations greatly affects the outcome of his calculations, even if the kill statistics – which he admits were also questionable – are assumed to be accurate.

Waste and Slaughter

Elsewhere in his 1968 classic on caribou biology, Kelsall notes the amount of ammunition issued to Aboriginal hunters and the rate at which it was used, suggesting that much of the ammunition was wasted in relation to the amount of game taken (222). The implication is that many shots were wasted and many animals likely crippled. The numbers he cites certainly suggest that a lot of ammunition was used by some hunters, but for what is unclear. Given that in the cases cited the ammunition was *given* to hunters, there is no telling whether it was used for target practice by young hunters, for hunting birds, fired in the air to greet visitors, or fired in the air to drive caribou into deeper snow, thereby making them easier to hunt. Perhaps those given so many bullets traded some of them for things they needed or stored some of them away for future use, the claim that it was all gone being one way of checking to see if more was freely available.

Kelsall provides the following example of three Inuit boys hunting with two .22 calibre rifles and one .30-30 to illustrate what he means by crippling. He notes that eight animals were killed and claims that five were seriously wounded and struggled away from the scene and that the boys made no attempt to pursue them (1968, 222-23). It is upon this type of anecdotal evidence that he bases the conclusion that 20 percent of the annual kill is not an excessive number for estimating deaths due to crippling. No mention is made of where this event took place. It is possible that the Inuit boys behaved this way, but to use the event to construct a general picture of Inuit – including adult – hunting practices is questionable. It is also likely that, had Inuit elders been made aware of such practices, the boys in question might have been dealt with appropriately.

Kelsall cites other examples that tie a high use of ammunition with crippling. He recalls his observations of a "Dogrib Indian, known to be a splendid shot," who pursued caribou on snowshoes on an open lake. He suggests that the hunter could have approached them through the woods and possibly have taken all six. However, after he failed to close in on them on the lake, the animals headed into the bush, and the hunter fired eleven shots at the fleeing animals, killing one (1968, 221). This scene can easily be reinterpreted. Who claimed that this individual was a splendid shot? Was it someone who actually knew the man or someone else – an RCMP officer – who had been in the community for two months? It is also possible that shots were fired deliberately to drive the animals into deep snow in the woods, where one would be easier to take. Perhaps the hunter was initially experimenting with techniques for approaching caribou on open ice. Strangely enough, instead of suggesting that the hunter might have taken only what he needed – one animal – Kelsall laments the fact that he did not get all six.

Finally, "waste" of ammunition is a concern for Kelsall. What he appears not to consider is the possibility that the idea of thrift, at the expense of making hunting easier while one has the resources (in this case the shot to do so), is not a cultural value held by most Aboriginal people. In fact, the virtue of thrift and what some authors have referred to as "the gospel of efficiency" are values that permeate much of the literature on game management from this and earlier periods. The origins of these *Qallunaat* values are to be found in the conservation movement that, as noted in the previous chapter, developed in the late 1800s as people began to realize that the resources of North America were not in fact limitless (Hays 1969). In turn, these values reflect values associated with the development of capitalist economic logic earlier in the century.[31]

In dealing with data generated by reports of hunter kills, Kelsall describes these data as irregular and incomplete, noting that in some cases returns from individual hunters were included in more than one report. Of particular interest is the claim that returns are particularly scanty from a number of areas where the annual kill is known to be consistently high, such as Bathurst Inlet and Coppermine in the Northwest Territories, the Brochet district of northern Manitoba, and virtually all of northern Saskatchewan (1968, 228). How Kelsall knew that the annual kill was *consistently* high in the areas in question given that, as he acknowledges, there was little data being submitted from these regions is a good question. Like many other assumptions used to generate a caribou crisis in the 1950s, his opinion seems to have been based on scattered anecdotal reports of the so-called slaughter of caribou by Aboriginal hunters. It is to these claims that we now turn our attention.

One of the photos in Kelsall's book has since become infamous. The photo in question (see Figure 9) shows caribou carcasses supposedly lying along the shore of Duck Lake in Manitoba. In the text, he reproduces an account of the sight he claims was written at the time by the game management officer aboard the flight that set down on the lake: "The sight that greeted us was something I do not believe could be seen any other place in the world. Some 400 caribou floating and lying on the shores of Duck Lake. On looking over the slaughter we discovered some caribou taken ten days or two weeks previous, apparently for hides only, and beyond any kind of use. [The Indians] did not give us any satisfactory answer to our questions why they were left to spoil" (cited in Kelsall 1968, 219). Here is the Sayisi Dene version of the kill documented by the game officer:

> As thousands of caribou made their great trek south, the Sayisi Dene would hunt them. A group of hunters would set up camp near a body of water they knew to be a caribou crossing ... They killed as many as they could. After the kill, they carefully skinned some of the carcasses and took them to their camp-sites for immediate use, but they left most of them on the shore, in heaps, for use during the brutal winter. Snow would cover the carcasses and keep them in a deep freeze. At times of need, people could find the meat by poking long, thin sticks into the snow. (Cited in Bussidor and Bilgen-Reinart 1997, 12)

As for accounts that the Sayisi Dene were starving four months later and requesting relief supplies by air, Kelsall presents no information in support of the claim. The Sayisi Dene suffered a disastrous relocation to Churchill, Manitoba, in August 1956, in large measure as an attempt to curtail their hunting practices and, as an alternative, to assimilate them to an urban culture (Bussidor and Bilgen-Reinart 1997, 12).

The photo was taken in October 1952 by Delores MacFarlane, an information officer with the Government of Manitoba. She was on a flight to the northernmost part of the province, where game officers were checking on poisonous bait that had been set out along the tree line for wolves.[32]

Caribou killed by Dene hunters, Duck Lake, Manitoba. This photo appeared in a number of publications in the 1950s and was reproduced along with other photographs on unnumbered pages at the outset of Kelsall's classic text on caribou biology. From Kelsall 1968, reproduced with permission.

MacFarlane was not even supposed to be on the flight but had been invited to come along for the ride by the Manitoba Government Air Service pilot. When their Norseman aircraft developed engine trouble, the pilot set the plane down on Nejanilini Lake. The Dene community at the southern end of the lake was known as Duck Lake. As they were landing, they noticed Dene hunters who had been hunting caribou at a crossing where a river to the south drained the lake. They apparently fled as the aircraft landed and did not return to the scene to inspect their visitors until the following day.

According to MacFarlane, once they had landed the game officer noticed the number of caribou lying along the shore (which he is reported to have counted as 2,000 in number) and was astounded, having never before seen such a scene. He noted that some of the killed caribou were pregnant cows. MacFarlane was asked to take the picture, which she did with a Rolex camera that she had never used before. And although the Dene were apparently not initially pleased to have visitors, she reports that before they left they were invited to a feast of caribou meat, one of the delicacies being a roasted head of caribou – complete with antlers.

Once the plane was repaired, they ventured on to Churchill. When Mac-Farlane returned to Winnipeg, she turned the developed photo over to the game management branch of the provincial government, thinking little of it and the use to which it might subsequently be put. According to her, she had practically forgotten about the picture until it was reproduced as the lead photo in a spring 1956 article in the *Beaver*. Written by A.W.F. Banfield, the article – headed with this dramatic photo and entitled "The Caribou Crisis" – generated a lot of attention and interest. According to MacFarlane, researchers from as far away as California got in touch with her for more information related to the picture. The caption accompanying the picture read, "A scene of carnage where swimming caribou have been speared from canoes. Each year thousands of carcasses are thus abandoned." The timing of this article and the public outrage generated over the so-called slaughter played no small role in giving government officials a rationale and motivation for relocating Sayisi Dene from their home at Duck Lake to Churchill, where they were to suffer from poverty, racism, alcoholism, and abuse before returning to Tadoule Lake, 100 kilometres southwest of the original community of Duck Lake, commencing in the early 1970s.[33] The photo and its dramatically inaccurate caption also provided the Department of Northern Affairs and National Resources with critical ammunition in its ongoing attempts to regulate Indian and Inuit hunting.

Other accounts of the "slaughter" and waste of caribou cited by Kelsall, in a section of his 1968 text entitled "The Abuse of Caribou by Man," are equally disturbing (see 216-25). In building the case that Aboriginal people are guilty of "slaughter" and waste, Kelsall cites the anecdotal reports of explorers such as Samuel Hearne. Hearne's diaries have little credibility as it has since been established that they were largely rewritten by his London-based editors to produce a dramatic text that would interest the public (see Rollason 1994). Kelsall cites others who look askance at the Indian practice of eating the fetuses from female caribou that have been killed. While the practice might have been abhorrent to *Qallunaat* observers, it was certainly no worse than many food practices that exist in *Qallunaat* culture. The language used by W.M. Pike (1892), whom Kelsall quotes (1968, 216), sets the reader up for revulsion: "the favourite dish of all, the unborn young caribou cut from its dead mother." The words "unborn," "young," and "mother," used in this context, set the *Qallunaat* reader up to see the hunters as primitive savages having no respect for life, animal or, by implication, human. No description of any ceremonies, rituals, or belief systems that might have been associated with this food are included in the text.[34] The image created embodies ethnocentric biases toward indigenous people common to the Victorian era. The problem is that such graphic misnomers were used by a wildlife biologist, writing in the 1960s about his work in the 1950s, to justify conclusions that are otherwise hard to explain.

Table 2

Analysis of 502 caribou killed at Contwoyto Lake, 1960

	Calves	1 year olds	2 year olds	Adults	Total	% of total
Total killed	61	132	122	187	502	100
Fully used*	6	22	8	44	80	16
Hide used	54	128	118	141	441	88
Tongue used[†]	54	130	101	153	438	87
Head used	53	71	33	0	157	31
Nothing used	7	2	1	20	30	6

Notes: Data from Thomas (1960)
* Meat taken to be dried, cached, eaten fresh, or fed to dogs
[†] Includes instances where the whole head was used
Source: Kelsall (1968, 217)

Similar problems exist with other and more modern field reports. Kelsall (1968) notes a report by J.H. McCauley (1960) of the Territorial Game Warden Service of hunting at Contwoyto Lake, Mackenzie District. In the report, McCauley claims that 1,000 caribou were killed by Inuit between June and September and that the actual requirements were 400 animals. Kelsall is quick to note that McCauley's estimates do not allow for crippling loss, despite the fact that there is no evidence given of any loss due to crippling.

Kelsall examines data produced by McCauley and D. Thomas in 1960. McCauley did a detailed analysis of 502 of the caribou killed. At first glance, a table compiled by Thomas and reproduced in Kelsall's text suggests that not much from the caribou killed was used (see Table 2). However, the figures in the column labelled "Total" suggest considerable overlap of categories. In other words, while the category "hide used," for instance, gives the impression that only the hide was used, it is clear that some uses were made of some animals and other uses made of others. There were possibly no animals where only the tongue or head or hide was taken, contrary to the impression created by the way the table is constructed (see Kelsall 1968, 217). In this case, 16 percent of the animals killed were fully used (but this does not imply that meat from other animals was not used at all).

Kelsall is intent on presenting a picture of waste and slaughter. What constitutes waste? He comments on McCauley's calculation that this group of twenty-nine Inuit (and we have no way of knowing if this figure is accurate) required 600 caribou hides for clothing, bedding, sled covers, et cetera and another 200 as liners for tents. This makes the killing of 1,000 animals seem not unreasonable, given that extra skins might be traded for other things needed by the group. Kelsall notes that the kill seems to have been primarily for skins and laments (and even calculates) the amount of meat not taken – which he describes as waste. Presaging the attempted assimilation of Inuit, he suggests that "all hides do not have to be replaced annually, and manufactured fabrics and clothing are used to a considerable extent" (1968, 218). The rationale – an attempt to shore up the argument that these hunting practices involve *unnecessary* waste – neglects certain realities of the late 1950s and early 1960s. Nothing by way of manufactured clothing available at the time (and, some would argue, even today) could protect Inuit from the extreme cold as efficiently and effectively as caribou-skin clothing. Being protected from the cold was a matter of life and death, and if skins were needed and available then it hardly seems unreasonable that they were taken, even if all the meat could not be used. Hunters of caribou at Contwoyto Lake were likely from the coast, where seal was the dietary staple. Caribou was prized particularly for the warmth of the hides. Meat apparently left behind may have been cached for a time when it could more easily be moved by dog team.

The word *slaughter* appears over and over in Kelsall's reports and the 1968 summary of his work. Commenting on the hunting practices of the Sayisi Dene, Kelsall attempts to substantiate his use of the term "slaughter" with facts. He turns to data from the late 1940s on the number of caribou hides traded at the Hudson's Bay Company post at Duck Lake, Manitoba. In 1948, 973 hides were traded, and in 1949 the number was 995. Kelsall attributes these kills to the work of approximately sixty hunters. He then notes that "the slaughter of caribou for trade was far beyond what the local Indians could use for meat" (1968, 228). Simple mathematics puts this conclusion to the test: 995 caribou taken by sixty hunters is 16.5 caribou per hunter per year, and, at sixty pounds of meat per animal, and assuming that each hunter had five or six people to feed, and given a diet primarily built around caribou meat, 995 caribou is about 3.7 pounds of meat per person per week – not an excessive amount by any standard, including that of Kelsall. Elsewhere in his text, he suggests that 1.5 pounds per day per person is reasonable consumption for an Aboriginal person, presumably with a diet built primarily around caribou meat (223).

The word *slaughtered,* compared with the words *hunted* or *killed,* connotes a careless and even callous disregard for the population being hunted. Its constant use in one text after another guarantees not only that others will read and cite the term but also that the image accompanying it – all that the word implies – will be reproduced. This language – and those who used it in this fashion – help to explain the prejudices and fears subsequently implanted in the minds of public officials and future civil servants, as well as the general public, about Aboriginal – including Inuit – hunting. This is not to suggest that killing in excess did not occur, but it does raise the question about what constitutes excess. The nature of the evidence Kelsall and others present suggests that this was a hand badly overplayed and driven not by science or by fact but by the culturally based prejudices and fears of those doing the research. Another way to label these prejudices would be to refer to the racist attitudes and assumptions of the proponents.

Limits to the Scientific Management of Caribou

What does the history of caribou research tell us? It suggests that the caribou crisis of the 1950s and 1960s was "manufactured," not as a deliberate attempt to be deceptive and to generate policy responses that would ultimately have tremendous implications for Inuit culture, but as a result of many prob-lematic assumptions and methods converging on questions about a species central to traditional Inuit culture. If anything, the research history of barren ground caribou is an outstanding illustration of the interplay between social assumptions and prejudices and scientific method. It points to the limits of commonly held notions about "objective" science and makes the case for what is now accepted as the importance of traditional knowledge. In these years, science established itself as the supposedly apolitical mechanism by which objective decisions could be made regarding social policy. This made science a valuable tool in the arsenal of totalizing power. But not all of its operations worked in a coherent or systematic fashion. The police officers on the ground had a different agenda, at least in this period. Meanwhile, a science developed and configured what today might be called a "biopolitical" state. As soon as the police accommodated themselves to their new function, establishing their authority as enforcers of a distant law, a new opponent within the state emerged. The legal and the scientific apparatuses of the state, both assiduously working within totalizing logics, entered a conflict to be described in the coming chapters. All along the targets of this discourse and practice, northern Inuit began to articulate their own responses.

But we cannot leave without another look at John Kelsall. In his texts – particularly his classic 1968 book on caribou biology – he comes across as a scientist who was overly sure of his methods and conclusions and as some-one insensitive to the cultures, needs, and realities of Aboriginal people. But there is some evidence to counter this image. Writing in 1964 in the journal *Oryx* – a publication of the fauna preservation society – he presents a very different picture of his appreciation of Aboriginal hunters:

> The greatest problem in reducing the loss of caribou through hunting lies with Canada's Treaty Indians. Several thousand of these people inhabit caribou ranges and depend heavily on caribou for their subsistence. These people are still following the nomadic hunting and trapping economy of their forefathers. They have inalienable rights to hunt game for food for themselves and their families, and they are not subject to hunting regula-tions that apply to non-Treaty Indians, Eskimos and white persons. Their rights were established and guaranteed by treaties signed jointly by their

forefathers and the Canadian Government ... Without the co-operation of
the Indians the enforcement of [restrictions on caribou hunting] might be
extremely difficult and meet with little success. People eking out a tenuous
subsistence in a harsh climate cannot be expected to react favourably to any
measures that make their existence more difficult. (245-46)

The idea of Inuit "eking out a tenuous subsistence" is entirely consistent with
social constructions of "primitive" people. Rather than rich, adaptive cultures,
appropriately organized in relation to the environments and ecosystems in
which they – affluent societies, as Sahlins famously pointed out – were located,
so-called primitive people (from the Arctic to Africa) were cast as miserable,
suffering, and in need of modernization. Their lands were seen as a vastly
underused and underappreciated resource. The scientific management of
game – especially caribou – was premised on four flawed assumptions: that
precontact estimates of populations were reasonably accurate; that aerial
survey methods produced reasonably accurate population estimates; that
"experts" in the field accurately interpreted what they observed by way of
Inuit behaviour in relation to wildlife populations; and that crippling loss
was a significant factor in the claimed decline of caribou herds. In addition,
they ignored two sources of information: the regular reports of RCMP officers
in the field, and reports and accounts that Inuit might have provided had
they been consulted.

Following his retirement, Kelsall moved first to Edmonton and finally to
Tsawwassen, British Columbia, where despite suffering from multiple sclero-
sis he pursued his passion for wildlife and wildlife habitat, to the point where
he was asked by dissident citizens interested in preserving agricultural land
and bird habitat from developers to run for mayor. In failing health, he declined, but the candidate who ran in his stead won a resounding victory.

How, then, do we explain Kelsall's 1968 text on caribou biology and other
writings? In Chapter 4, we document how the biology put in place by Kelsall
came under attack from inside and then from without the Canadian Wildlife
Service. The criticism of his work came at a time when Kelsall was writing
his 1968 treatise on barren ground caribou, and his defensive posture may
have had something to do with the criticism. Was this, then, a passion for
wildlife above all else? Was it a discourse that reflected the institutionalized attitudes and norms of the times? Or was this the linguistic posture of
someone located inside a male bureaucracy with a subculture of its own in
relation to the science it was attempting to practise and the direction it was
trying to give to government policy? These are all possibilities. But one thing
is evident: translated into policy, the observations of Kelsall and his colleagues
were based on assumptions and a science so questionable that in application
they could only create conditions that would make Inuit resistance necessary.
The application of science to policy is explored in the next chapter.

3

Sugsaunngittugulli ("We Are Useless"[1]): Surveying the Animals

At that time, you know, we were always out on the land, and no
RCMP came around to check on us in the summertime. When
we needed to – when we need meat for – ah – like snow geese, we
would kill a few of them. We needed them to survive! And it was
the same with the swans when we needed them to survive. We
would kill them and eat them, but we would try not to take too
many of them. The RCMP never spoke to us about why we were
not allowed to hunt musk-ox or those other three animals [swans,
geese, and caribou at certain times of the year]. But when we went
at Christmas time to the trading post, the RCMP would go to that
same trading post because everyone would get together there. And
the RCMP would ask, "how many ptarmigan did you catch this
year, and how many of whatever did you sell?" And that's all. And
nobody ever thought of why they weren't allowed to shoot those
other animals ... Before we got into communities, we didn't have
meetings like we have today. And nobody talked about why we
weren't allowed [to hunt certain species] and said things like
"no, we don't like that rule, and no, we're not going to go by it."
Nobody ever mentioned anything like that. Whatever was imposed on them, each individual person just went along with it.

– Simon Takkiruq, Uqsuqtuuq (Gjoa Haven), 20 May 1998

Attempts to manage game – caribou in particular – were met with resistance
that grew parallel to changes in Inuit social organization and the growing
awareness that talking back to *Qallunaat* was not only possible but also essential. In this chapter, we detail how the logic and convictions of state wildlife
officials, outlined previously, were applied to Inuit hunters and thus to Inuit
culture in general. In doing so, we note the emerging theme of resistance
explored in greater depth in subsequent chapters. The survey of animals – as

suggested by the above quotation from Simon Takkiruq – amounted to the surveillance of Inuit. What emerged was resistance to a regime of management not only of game but also, by implication, of culture, community, and people.

Here we document the developing regime of management and control. Following passage of the game ordinance in 1949, officials were initially willing to try education as a way of changing hunting practices. A section was added to *The Book of Wisdom for Eskimos,* a publication of the department that attempted, in the most colonial way imaginable, to educate Inuit about everything from looking after children to keeping an igloo clean and maintaining a gun (see McNicoll, Tester, and Kulchyski 2000). However, as the 1950s unfolded, this approach wore thin. The RCMP started to charge Inuit with violating game laws. Science, as noted in parts of this chapter, played no small role in these attempts. For example, prohibitions against the killing of polar bear cubs required the means to establish the exact age of a cub. Attempts to do so were fraught with impossibilities. How could anyone, with any certainty, determine if a cub was one year old, less a day, or had eclipsed its first birthday? Limits to use of the law as a way of controlling Inuit hunting soon became obvious.

This chapter establishes a clear pattern of intervention in Inuit hunting practices. The state increasingly relied on science as a backdrop to the development of measures aimed at controlling Inuit hunting and at revising and implementing new regulations. Enforcement, while difficult, and increasingly made so by the interventions of Justice Sissons, as detailed in subsequent chapters, was attempted. Caribou were an initial and substantial concern. However, other species became the focus of attention as wildlife officials increasingly realized that Inuit were not always respecting prohibitions against the killing of musk-ox. These prohibitions, as previously noted, had been in place for some time. Concern developed over the killing of walrus. Here the activities of biologists working for the Canadian Wildlife Service – Alan Loughrey in particular – were ground to a halt by jurisdictional problems, the Department of Fisheries claiming that walrus were, constitutionally, its responsibility. Henry Larson, commander of the Arctic Division of the RCMP, also clashed with CWS officials who attempted to regulate and modify Inuit hunting. Resistance therefore came not only from Inuit but also from within the bureaucracy itself. However, while differences arose over the means and approaches to be taken, the direction was clear. Inuit hunting was to be regulated.

This chapter begins with an examination of the game ordinance introduced in 1949 and informed by the fledgling science conducted by the Canadian Wildlife Service. At last, state officials had firm ground on which to base the law – or so they might have thought. Subsequent revisions reveal the persistent tension between managing game in the presence of fears about scarcity and extinction and ensuring that Inuit did not become dependent on social assistance. In the second section, we illustrate attempts to get Inuit, who, it was noted, were firmly committed to their cultural practices, to comply with the law. We note some of the conflicts arising within the administration on the best way to achieve change. In the third section, we document some of the discussions taking place about the use of surveillance and attempts to manage Inuit hunting. In the following section, we illustrate the development of Inuit resistance by discussing two cases, one involving the killing of musk-ox and another involving a charge of abandoning meat fit for human consumption. Intentions to monitor and manage Inuit hunting of walrus provide another example of surveillance and management in practice. Finally, we examine the polar bear. Unlike other species, the polar bear creates an intersection between traditional hunting practices and a market economy with which Inuit had previously, in relation to species other than Arctic fox, little experience. While not detailed at the time, issues involving the taking of polar bears raise questions about hunting, the idea of "traditional practices," changing patterns in relation to species, and Aboriginal hunting in the so-called modern world.[2]

"Going by the Book"

The game ordinance assented to 21 April 1949 reflected most of the concerns expressed by the Canadian Wildlife Service at the time. The full title was An Ordinance Respecting the Preservation of Game in the Northwest Territories (see Canada 1949). It applied to First Nations, Métis, and Inuit in the Northwest Territories, who could be granted a licence to hunt caribou to obtain meat for human consumption but not for sale (section 45[1]). The text clearly defined social relations. General hunting licences could be issued to anyone over the age of sixteen. In other words, Inuit youth under sixteen years of age could not be hunters or learn how to hunt if learning involved actually shooting an animal. Licences to hunt caribou were granted only to "a Canadian citizen who is the head of a family and resides in the Territories with his family" (section 45[1]). Heads of households were clearly male. The wording defines the nuclear Western European family and not the extended family structure – which could include son-in-laws, cousins, persons who might be single adults, and others – that constituted Inuit camps at the time.

Inuit included "a half-breed of Eskimo blood leading the life of an Eskimo" (section 1[d]). The same wording was used to include "a half-breed of Indian blood" (section 1[l]). However, while the definition of a First Nations member could be found at the time in the Indian Act, there was no definition anywhere of who was "an Eskimo." This lack illustrates the ongoing difficulty the administration was having in wanting to regulate Inuit in a manner similar to the regulation of First Nations, with special powers that would override normal rights of citizens. At the same time, officials clearly wanted to avoid what was seen as the special status granted to First Nations and subsequently treated Inuit as citizens, no different from any other Canadian. In effect, Inuit were to have the worst of both worlds: neither the designation of citizen nor Aboriginal rights were accorded to them.

The legislation prohibited hunting big game with a rifle less than .25 calibre (section 6[a]). It made it an offence for anyone "who has taken or killed a bird or animal suitable for food (to) wilfully abandon or allow the flesh thereof suitable for human food to be destroyed or spoilt" (section 9). Among other places, wild game – including caribou meat – could no longer be served in hotels, restaurants, or logging or other commercial camps. Of significance to Inuit children at boarding schools or elderly Inuit in hospitals, it could also not be served at these locations without the permission of the commissioner (section 13[3][b]). In an attempt to regulate *Qallunaat* trapping and trading operations, transporting meat, skins, or pelts by plane was prohibited (section 16[3]). Measures were included to eliminate "fly-by-night" trading operations by making eight months a year the minimum length of time that a licensed post had to be open (section 70). Penalties for violation of the ordinance included a fine not exceeding $500 and not less than $5 or imprisonment for a term not exceeding two months, or both, for all violations other than hunting, trading, or trafficking in game without a licence, possessing or using poison, or unlawfully hunting buffalo, bison, or musk-ox (section 99[a] and [b]). The RCMP and the commissioner of the Northwest Territories were recognized as game officers.

A closed season was imposed on many species, including caribou. Hunting caribou from the first day of March to the fifteenth day of September was prohibited. An Inuk hunter was permitted to hunt male caribou only during the month of March "if the meat was for the use of himself and his immediate family, but not for sale or barter" (section 33[1]). Inuit could also be granted a licence to hunt caribou from 1 August to 15 September – but only the number specified in the licence (section 33[2]). Of particular significance, the number of caribou that could be taken by the holder of a caribou licence was restricted to five. No Inuit family living on the land, as were virtually all Inuit in 1949, could survive on five caribou a year. In 1949, the price of Arctic fox pelts reached a record low of $3.50 each, down from about $20 in 1946 (Tester and Kulchyski 1994, 61). Given that this was the main source of earned cash for most Inuit at the time, and that caribou were the only "affordable" source of food, the 1949 game ordinance amounted to little more than a recipe for legislated starvation.

Modifications to the ordinance in 1950 and in 1951 did little to change the provisions affecting Inuit. The 1951 amendments did affect the Dene by making it illegal to feed caribou to dogs within a four-mile radius of the post office of any of the settlements in the Mackenzie District. Children under sixteen assisting their parents in hunting were not required to have a licence, thereby addressing the problem created by the 1949 legislation that prohibited anyone under sixteen from hunting.

By 1953, further amendments were needed to define who was Inuit. The wording of the provisions duplicated those that defined an Indian under the Indian Act. Inuit were thus located, organized, counted, and defined in a manner that could be understood by the *Qallunaat* bureaucracy. Section 2 (1)(d) of the ordinance codified the concepts of legitimate and illegitimate children – a notion completely foreign to Inuit views of the family and children. The section defined an Eskimo as "the legitimate child of someone who was a direct descendant in the male line of a male person who is or who was of the race of aborigines commonly referred to as Eskimos" (section 2[1][d][i]). An Eskimo could also be the illegitimate child of a female person who was Eskimo (but clearly not the "illegitimate" child of a male Eskimo if his partner was not Eskimo). The definition did not include the "Eskimo wife of a person other than an Eskimo, unless she had been deserted, divorced or widowed" (section 2[1][d][iv]). The definition was yet another tool in the arsenal of totalizing techniques originating with public officials in the 1950s, bringing everyone under state control by giving them an identity that suited state purposes. Lacking an "Eskimo Act" or the equivalent, officials could take heart in the fact that enfranchisement of an Inuit woman married to a non-Inuk and the "illegitimate" children of male Inuit and non-Inuit women was at least possible for purposes of the game ordinance.

The same year a section entitled "Hunting to Prevent Starvation" was added. Apparently, some public officials had come to recognize that starvation was exactly what had been prescribed by the 1949 legislation. Game and the eggs of non-migratory birds could be taken by Inuit at any time "to prevent starvation of himself and his immediate family" (section 18[1]). Heads of households were clearly males, and the net effect of restricting hunting to procuring food for the immediate family, had anyone taken it seriously, would have been to undermine the extended family and the relations within that family, characteristic of Inuit culture. The provisions made no allowance for traditional gendered roles among Inuit when it came to food procurement. The amendments had as much to do with the management of people as they did the protection of game. Resistance was the only reasonable response.

It is no surprise that the 1949 legislation was so punitive. With input from the Canadian Wildlife Service, the ordinance was a predictable text. Harrison Lewis was frank about his biases, as revealed by the following extract from a letter to Roy Gibson. The letter dealt with the service's input to changes to the Indian Act, also being considered at the time: "The rigid and ultra-generous wildlife provisions of the Indian treaties may have appeared to represent good judgement when they were first drafted, but they cannot be readily adjusted to meet changing conditions and they are calculated to prevent efficient wildlife management. Consequently, they are not in the interests of either the Indians or the whites."[3]

It was not the intention that the 1949 legislation be applied right away. Rather, a decision was made to introduce the law gradually while educating Inuit on the need for wildlife conservation. To this end, the Canadian Wildlife Service had prepared a program of education and proposed the development of an eiderdown industry and the protection of waterfowl breeding grounds to the tune of $200,000, to be spent over five years. On 14 December 1949, Henry Larson, commander of Division "G" – the Arctic division of the RCMP – wrote to the Canadian Wildlife Service to express his concerns about what the service had in mind for the education of Inuit hunters. Larson's opinion counted. Since 1932, the RCMP had been responsible for enforcement of the game ordinance of the Northwest Territories and provisions of the migratory birds protection act. It was essential that the newly created Canadian Wildlife Service get along with the RCMP.

Contrary to the results of the research being conducted by the Canadian Wildlife Service, Larson was of the opinion that the number of caribou and game birds being taken by Inuit was not a threat to conservation. He also noted that caribou were seldom found on Read and Holman Islands and that they were found only on the northern part of Victoria Island. Asked to provide his director with a response to Larson's claims, J.P. Richards, a former colonel in the Canadian Armed Forces, pointed out that caribou were scarce on these Arctic islands because "trading posts had been established on the migrational routes of the caribou and the Eskimo who had been equipped with high powered rifles had practically exterminated the herds."[4] Larson was also concerned that enforcement of the game laws would require a substantial increase in the strength of the RCMP. He remarked that many Inuit did not have enough caribou for food and clothing, thereby suggesting that enforcement would only make a situation that was destroying the health and welfare of Inuit even worse.

His logic was seized upon as yet another example of why conservation was important. Furthermore, it was suggested that, if the police could not do the job, the service might consider appointing "supervisors" for the purpose.[5] Oddly enough, despite claiming that Inuit had high-powered rifles, Richards repeated the common wisdom that had developed: that .22 calibre rifles were causing a lot of damage and that perhaps Inuit should be provided with higher-powered rifles at government expense. When it suited the service, Inuit were described as being equipped with low-powered .22 calibre rifles that mostly crippled animals. At other times, it was claimed they were equipped with high-powered ones, capable of liquidating entire herds.

Responding to Larson's concerns, J.G. Wright of the northern administration pointed out that no extra police contingent was required since there was no intention to rigidly enforce game laws as far as Inuit were concerned. In educating Inuit about conservation, Wright pointed to *The Book of Wisdom for Eskimos,* which the department was reissuing as an important tool for educating Inuit about conservation and which Inuit still remember: "I don't really remember the title of that [*Book of Wisdom*], but we used to love to read it in Inuktitut, because the only books that we read were Bibles. So we had something else to read other than the Bible. Yes [I remember that book talking about not hunting female caribou or hunting at certain times of the year]. We were 'going by the book' since we were afraid of the RCMP" (Josiah Kadlutisiaq, Iglulik, 29 May 1999). Wright noted that the schools at Tuktoyaktuk and Coppermine were going to start teaching conservation to the Inuit.[6]

"These Eskimos Are Pretty Firmly Wedded to Their Customary Life"

By August of 1950, concern was being expressed about the killing of musk-ox in the Bathurst Inlet area. It was suggested to the minister, Robert Winters, on a trip that he made to see "northern Canada," for which his department was responsible, that a warden be located near Bathurst Inlet. Winters left the matter to the squabbling officials in his ministry. A.W.J. Banfield, in a handwritten note on a memo sent to Harrison Lewis about the matter, clearly defined what he saw as an appropriate role for the service: "The whole eastern Mackenzie District and Keewatin Dist. are without Dept. Game wardens and the natives have very little supervision. I agree that there should be more local supervision and instruction."[7]

In a detailed report responding to the situation, John Kelsall indulged in his usual speculation about the dramatic impact of Inuit hunting on caribou, suggesting that, while the "Bathurst Inlet H.B.C. post traded about 2,000 caribou skins between August 1949, and August 1950, this might well represent less than one-third of the total take."[8] He went on to suggest that about thirty-six families in the area were responsible for taking about 5,000 caribou a year – a fantastic figure for which he presented no evidence. Kelsall's memo also suggested that, in the interests of protecting caribou, Inuit should rely more on seals, abundant along the coast, and fish.

Kelsall was not above proposing changes with dramatic implications for all aspects of Inuit culture. He proposed that Inuit dependent on caribou convert their lifestyle to one based on sea mammals. In suggesting a greater reliance on fish, he does not seem to have been aware of the extent to which coastal Inuit of the Coronation Gulf area already relied heavily on fish at certain times of the year. In a statement with no small hint of irony, he noted that "the caribou is an unpredictable animal and even the best of hunters will fail occasionally to make contact with them."[9] While Inuit hunters with

Hunting with a musk-ox bow, 1950. © Library and Archives Canada, Indian and Northern Affairs Departmental Albums, PA-211284.

decades of experience and guided by the wisdom of elders might have had trouble locating them, when it came to tracking them for census purposes, Kelsall himself apparently had no difficulty.

In writing in support of the appointment of a game warden to supervise hunting in the Bathurst Inlet area, Kelsall comments extensively on musk-ox in the region, citing police reports that ten of them were killed in 1947-48. He notes that barren ground grizzlies were being killed and that neither the police nor Inuit knew they were a protected species. He goes on to suggest that musk-ox are being killed because "musk-ox horn is the most suitable material available to the Eskimos for the construction of bows and many Eskimos have one or more bows each. I would also think it extremely likely that the eagerness of transient white persons to get these bows might possibly be a strong incentive to kill musk-ox."[10] He continued:

It would be absolutely essential that the man chosen be a keen traveller and sufficiently interested in Eskimos to learn something of their language and philosophy and I think that these would be difficult requirements to fulfil. At the same time, he would have to be a person who could command respect and exercise authority among the Eskimos and this is a bigger order than it sounds. The majority of persons, such as priests and H.B.C. personnel, who know Eskimos and their language, are quite frank in admitting that they have very little influence over native actions. Nearly all agree that as a general rule the R.C.M. Police are the only men whose orders or requests the natives will try to follow.[11]

Clearly, getting Inuit to change their culture and lifestyles was not going to be an easy task. With this in mind, J.G. Wright put a lid on the idea of having a game management officer in the region, noting that "these Eskimos are pretty firmly wedded to their customary life and it will require considerable time and effort to affect changes."[12] In other words, it was the strength of Inuit resistance – despite the authority of feared figures such as the RCMP and the message of church and state that *Qallunaat* authority figures were to be obeyed – that ended the matter.

Of course, any game warden travelling and living in the area would have to be dependent on the beneficence of the Inuit he was visiting and would, like them, be dependent on the resources of the land, including caribou meat. In short order, this dependence might have undermined the views of Inuit hunting and the conservation the department was trying to promote. In a memo of 25 October 1950, Henry Larson of the RCMP was quick to point this out, noting that someone who has not spent an entire season in the Bathurst region cannot appreciate how difficult it would be for Inuit to arrange their ways of living to become more dependent on seals and fish and less so on caribou. Noting that catching a seal cannot be done at any time of the year, he suggested that Kelsall's ideas were likely to cause destitution and lead to the issuing of relief.[13]

Relations between the Canadian Wildlife Service and the RCMP were on tenterhooks. A meeting between Inspector Larson and John Kelsall was arranged in an attempt to arrive at some mutual understanding. Agreeing to disagree on some points, Larson and Kelsall did conclude that more surveillance of Inuit hunting in the region would take place and that every attempt would be made to stop the killing of musk-ox.[14] Kelsall also reported to the chief of the wildlife service that Larson had agreed to consider imposing any regulations that could reasonably be enforced to cut down on the number of caribou being taken. They could not agree on the merits of sealing, Kelsall remarking that, "having seen two families of Eskimos do nothing but enjoy the weather for two months during the best fishing season, I cannot adhere to any idea that the natives cannot make a relatively large use of fish resources in particular."[15]

Larson and Kelsall were clearly at odds with one another over many matters of Inuit lifestyle and game management. Kelsall was also of the opinion that a large number of wolves were having an impact on caribou herds in the Bathurst Inlet area and that, in general, the wolves were more numerous than his colleague, Colonel Banfield, had previously indicated. Larson suggested a bounty on wolves as a way of both controlling them and providing income for Inuit hunters. Kelsall was opposed, noting that "many Indians and white men who do not need relief would also get money from bounty payments and that the total expenditure would not only be large but unwarranted."[16] He suggested a subsidy on white fox fur. Larson was not impressed by the idea.

The Canadian Wildlife Service by this time was experimenting with wolf baiting, using strychnine-laced cubes of buffalo meat to control the wolf population. Baiting was later to inspire Farley Mowat's book *Never Cry Wolf*, published in 1963. Kelsall's commitment to reason and to science comes across in the closing line of this memo to Dr. Lewis, in which Kelsall comments on the "irrational" ideas of Henry Larson: "Like so many northern residents, the Inspector has certain fixed ideas which it is very difficult to change by argument alone."[17]

The Canadian Wildlife Service was on the lookout for any bleeding hearts in the northern administration that might fail to see the seriousness of the wildlife – and especially the caribou – crisis. On 17 January 1951, the service dispatched Colonel Richards to the National Film Board theatre in Ottawa to view a slide presentation by J.S. Bailey, who had just returned from his tour of the Arctic, where he had examined the Family Allowance program to see how it was working. According to Richards, "the talk had been well-prepared but the writer felt that too much stress was given to the subject of family allowances and the resulting benefits to the native population."[18]

By late 1951, despite attempts to "patch things up," relations between Inspector Larson and the Canadian Wildlife Service remained strained. In communicating with the officer in charge at Kugluktuk (Coppermine), Larson apparently told him that he had been informed by Kelsall that Inuit in the area were killing musk-ox and making trinkets for tourists out of musk-ox horn. Kelsall, in responding to a copy of Larson's correspondence with the detachment, expressed considerable shock. He claimed he had never said such a thing, noting that musk-ox are rarely, if ever, seen by Coppermine Inuit and that, if Inuit and others believed he had said such a thing, his reputation and that of the service would be jeopardized. Almost every utterance by either party had become a source of contention, irritation, and concern.

The extent to which the game laws enacted in 1949 were enforced varied considerably from community to community across the eastern Arctic. A wildlife service memo of 19 March 1953 notes that on Baffin Island restrictions were placed on Inuit hunting. At the same time, James Houston and his wife Alma were reporting that Inuit believed the number of caribou to be increasing and that the hunting restrictions should be lifted.[19] It appears that such reports contributed to the pressure for a resurvey of both the Baffin Island and the barren ground herds in the mid-1950s. Any such suggestion seriously challenged the logic that was firmly entrenched in the Canadian Wildlife Service.

In the early 1950s, the Houstons were involved in attempts to create a "modern" economy among the Inuit that included making quilted eiderdown clothing, an idea that brought forth the following comment from Victor Solmon, the chief biologist with the Canadian Wildlife Service at the time: "It is apparently realized that one of the major obstacles in the introduction of an eiderdown industry will be the education of the natives to conserve the birds and treat them more or less as domestic animals."[20] Not only Inuit were to become part of Euro-Canadian culture in a manner conceptualized by northern officials, but also the animals on which they depended were to help make it all possible by joining them in domestic captivity.[21] Inuit were to become wildlife ranchers, not hunters, the Arctic equivalent of converting nomadic buffalo hunters or sheep and goat herders in Africa to sedentary farmers. It was a device that had been used elsewhere to clear land occupied and travelled by Aboriginal people, thus making it available for other activities. But, despite a mentality that may have wished otherwise, domestication of Arctic wildlife was not a possibility, and neither was the conversion of Inuit hunters to industrial workers. As the 1950s progressed, controversy over the killing of the musk-ox was to bring the state into open conflict with a hunting culture that refused to be domesticated.

Surveillance and Instruction: "The Tennessee Ernie Show as a Datum Point"

In 1954, reports of some seventy musk-ox killed in the Bathurst Inlet area promoted an investigation undertaken in the summer of 1955 by A.J. Boxer and John Kelsall of the Canadian Wildlife Service. Boxer was one of the first northern service officers hired by the Arctic administration in 1955.

No one at the time really knew what Inuit hunters were doing in relation to musk-ox. In reviewing Boxer's report of the investigation, dated 19 December 1955, John Tener, by now regarded as the CWS expert on musk-ox, complained that Boxer dwelt too much on questions of Inuit welfare and did not provide enough information on the musk-ox killed. The "bleeding hearts" in the northern administration were still having difficulty taking wildlife management seriously.

During the investigation, twelve musk-ox had been seen by Boxer and Kelsall in the Nose Lake area, and to Tener's relief this was an indication "that the species wasn't exterminated locally."[22] He also expressed the opinion that Inuit had simply been ignoring the game regulations and that the regular killing of musk-ox had been going on for the past decade, despite the observation by the HBC post manager that he did not think Inuit would go out of their way to hunt musk-ox. Winston Mair, the chief of the Canadian Wildlife Service, in a handwritten note, apparently chose to ignore the observations of the post manager and concurred with Tener's opinion that killings had likely taken place for the past decade. This way of operating was common to the service throughout the 1940s and 1950s and even the 1960s. Time and time again, in comments on memos, in communication with other departments, and in representations to politicians, CWS personnel emphasized what for them were worst-case scenarios, ignoring the observations of anyone who contradicted what appears to have been, for most wildlife officials, a foregone conclusion. There are dozens of documents in Library and Archives Canada that illustrate the claim that CWS officials ignored contradictory evidence. The most important of these are the many reports received from the RCMP stationed in many settlements throughout the eastern Arctic. Samples of these reports are presented in Chapter 4. On a regular basis, the RCMP was asked to report on game conditions in the areas for which it had responsibility. These reports were shared with the northern administration and CWS officials since they can be found in the records of both the Canadian Wildlife Service and the Arctic administration. As noted in Chapter 4, RCMP officers were reporting, in many situations, and at particular times, an abundance of caribou and other species, while at the same time the Canadian Wildlife Service was orchestrating shortages, scarcity, and the likelihood of extinction if drastic conservation measures were not employed. Inuit were slaughtering game, and the mandate of the service was to put a stop to this slaughter.

James Cantley, a former HBC employee and through the 1940s the proprietor of his own Arctic trading company, had been hired by the Arctic Division in 1951 to conduct a survey of the economic conditions facing Inuit as a result of the catastrophic decline in the price of fox fur in the late 1940s and early 1950s. Early in 1956, Cantley met with CWS officials in an attempt to see how its mammal research program could meet the needs of the Arctic Division. In addition to Cantley and Winston Mair, head of the Canadian Wildlife Service, the meeting was attended by Alex Stevenson of the Arctic Division and Victor Solmon, Colonel (and by now Doctor) A.W.J. Banfield, and John Tener of the service. A decision was made to study emerging Inuit communities in the eastern Arctic with a team of experts consisting of an anthropologist, a fisheries biologist, as well as marine and terrestrial mammalogists. Science was to be applied to the problems of these communities, and good data were a prerequisite to any investigation. The committee recommended that data on the use of wildlife by all Natives should be collected with the help of northern service officers, the Hudson's Bay Company, and the RCMP. Surveying animals meant surveying people, and both were important to helping Inuit. It was opined that "the use of a calendar by Eskimos to record their hunting and fishing take should be thoroughly explored."[23] The idea produced at least one cheeky response, revealing more the extremely racist attitudes held by some administrators at the time than a good sense of humour. Ward Stevens, assistant district administrator for the Mackenzie region, suggested the following:

I do not know enough about Eskimos in the eastern areas to know whether they have a definite time orientation of their own which could be fitted into our calendar to help them along. On the other hand, they may all have radios and listen to programs from Nashville so that you could use the

Tennessee Ernie show as a datum point. Or we could ask radio Moscow to keep them informed regarding the days, weeks and months. I don't know their level of knowledge in this regard, but if they are like the illiterate among the Indians, they don't know much more than their own names, which may be signed with an X.[24]

Writing a report to the chief of the Canadian Wildlife Service, John Tener noted just how far Cantley thought surveillance as well as management of Inuit should go. A people who had likely hunted the Arctic for thousands of years were to get an education from wildlife officers who were to study "the distribution and movements of wildlife resources in order to assist the natives in hunting"; the officer "should be attempting to improve hunting efficiency and to reduce the wastage in all forms and he should attempt, by example and frequent discussions, to inculcate ideas of wildlife conservation in Eskimos."[25]

Cantley was of the opinion that the Inuit of Garry Lake and the Back River areas were in particular need of instruction on the better utilization of resources and that Inuit in the Kugluktuk (Coppermine) area needed to be taught how to fish. He also pointed out that Inuit did not have access to game regulations they could read in syllabics. It appears from Tener's report this was something he had never thought of before. Tener subsequently endorsed it as a good idea – as long as the text they agreed to produce "gave the essential points in easily understood form."[26] The animals were to be surveyed. Inuit were to be surveyed. Inuit clearly were having a hard time because they did not know enough about the movements and distribution of the animals. Biologists, scientifically trained, were to help them understand not only where the animals were but also how to hunt them efficiently and how to make sure that conservation was practised. People who had hunted for thousands of years, confronted with Euro-Canadian science and scientists, had suddenly become helpless children.

One reason for wanting a closer working relationship between the Canadian Wildlife Service and the Arctic Division was related to an old and familiar problem: Arctic sovereignty and the occupation of the Arctic islands. In early 1956, Ben Sivertz, head of the Arctic Division, was still pushing for more "Arctic colonies" and wanted the Canadian Wildlife Service to undertake wildlife studies to ensure that any Inuit colonists would be able to make a living from the land.[27] By November, CWS officials had investigated the possibility of relocating Inuit families to the east coast of Banks Island. They concluded that De Salis Bay was a good spot to which four or five families could be relocated. However, it was noted that most Inuit preferred to live on the west coast of the island, where the weather was more favourable. As a consequence, it was recommended that, "prior to the establishment of Eskimos on the east coast, arrangements should be made to prevent the

Eskimos from moving to Sachs Harbour on the west coast. In the 1940s, a complex system of registering trap lines and establishing group areas for trapping had been introduced in the NWT – particularly the western Arctic. One suggestion was to register a block of land trapped by the Bankslanders on the west coast to deter encroachment by other Eskimo on their trap lines."[28] This would certainly have been an innovative way to introduce the concept of land as private property to people who had never heard of it. Both the relocation and the registered block – thankfully – never happened.

While public officials were intent on introducing Inuit to the idea of conservation gradually, and were relying on formal and informal education to "do the job," by the late 1950s they and wildlife officials had become impatient. Despite their best efforts, the evidence suggested that Inuit were inclined not to take the game laws seriously. In the presence of *Qallunaat* – and particularly the RCMP – they gave all the appearance of playing by the rules. However, in practice, Inuit had to survive, as the following observation by Doug Wilkinson (whose work as a northern service officer is the subject of Chapter 6) makes abundantly clear:

> As long as the Eskimos can remember, they have looked forward to the return of the birds to their land, to the taste of fresh eggs eaten raw or boiled. Snow geese eggs are the favourite, with murre coming a close second. Under white man's law, the gathering of these eggs is forbidden, but few Eskimos in this area [Bylot Island, northern Baffin Island] pay much attention to this. The Eskimos know it is against the law to take the eggs, but, having no clear concept of what a law is, or means, they do not pay much attention to it.
>
> "Perhaps the policeman would catch [arrest] you for taking the eggs," said one old Eskimo in answer to my query, "but then you are a white man. He would not catch me for this is my land, not the white man's. He [the policeman] does not understand geese. I do, just as my father did before me. The policeman tell me I must not take eggs. And why should I not take the eggs? Must I who am hungry for the taste of fresh eggs stand by and watch the foxes and the weasels eating eggs? No, I like eggs." (1955, 63)[29]

Inuit had to eat. They had a culture built significantly around game, hunting, meat sharing, and a technology that was significantly dependent on the eggs, meat, hides, bones, antlers – in fact every part of the animals they hunted. The many reports of violations of the game laws found in government documents throughout the 1950s make it clear that enforcement was a problem and that education was not necessarily a solution. Inuit resisted the *Qallunaat* regime of ruling over animals and, by implication, *Qallunaat* control of Inuit affairs.

By the early 1960s, many eastern Arctic settlements had RCMP officers. However, the presence of officers does not in itself indicate that there was good surveillance of Inuit hunting practices. Some officers took the job seriously, while others had other matters to contend with that limited their attention to game management. The law was difficult to enforce, and doing so would bring RCMP who in some cases were friends with local hunters into serious conflict with the community in which, after all, they had to live. In many situations, as illustrated by cases presented in this chapter, officers were reluctant to pursue charges. They understood all too well that Inuit hunting was essential and that "need" was to be taken seriously, as evidenced by the reluctant behaviour of Corporal Jones in the case of Kanoyaoyak that follows.

Prosecutions under the Law: Killing a Musk-Ox and Abandoning Caribou Meat

The history of the management of musk-ox is extremely important to understanding Inuit resistance to the management regimes increasingly imposed on their hunting practices following World War II. Some of this history has already been noted. By the summer of 1955, there were increasing reports of musk-ox killings in the high central Arctic. Father Menez at Bathurst Inlet reported to John Kelsall, who visited the post in April 1956, that three musk-ox had been killed nearby at Daniel Moore Bay the summer of 1955. The RCMP was asked to investigate. Corporal Jones visited Bathurst Inlet in the fall of 1956 but was unable to determine whether the musk-ox in question had been killed or had died of natural causes. However, in reporting on this investigation, he also noted that he had interviewed a number of Inuit, who had arrived at Ikaluktutiak (Cambridge Bay) by schooner in the summer of 1956, about other musk-ox killings. He interrogated Archie Komak and Jack Miok, both of whom had come to Ikaluktutiak to work on the Distant Early Warning (DEW) Line.

Komak denied having any knowledge of musk-ox being killed at Daniel Moore Bay. However, he had heard when he was trading at Angulalik's post at Bathurst Inlet that another Inuk, Bob Kanoyaoyak, who was residing inland from the post, had killed two musk-ox shortly before Christmas. Miok denied having any knowledge of anyone killing musk-ox.[30]

The scene is an important one. Inuit fear of and deference to the RCMP and government officials in the 1950s were considerable. Given Inuit values – including the ethic of non-interference – not to mention cultural solidarity against the regulation of hunting at the time, and given that Inuit being interrogated probably knew little of their rights in such a situation, it is not hard to imagine that such interrogations were stressful. Furthermore, Inuit culture is characterized by some very different notions of knowledge from what is commonly assumed in *Qallunaat* culture. Firsthand knowledge is real knowledge and truth. Anything else can belong to another category – something less than knowledge or knowing. In private conversations among themselves, the matter of whether or not to co-operate with the RCMP and government officials likely produced both conflict within Inuit communities and a mostly silent but growing opposition to this imposition of rule. Jones reported to Larson that he had found nothing about which he had any concern. As Kanoyaoyak planned to visit Ikaluktutiak from Anderson River after freeze-up, Jones resolved to question him on his arrival and report to Larson again thereafter.

Kanoyaoyak arrived in Ikaluktutiak and was questioned by Corporal Jones on 21 November 1956. Kanoyaoyak reported that

> Last winter I camped alone with my family on the coast near Daniel Moore Bay. The summer before, there were some caribou there but I couldn't find any when winter came. There were lots of Musk-Ox around and when I couldn't find any Caribou, I shot one of these as we had no food in camp. During all the winter I shot five Musk-Ox there, not all at one time but just one at a time when we needed food and couldn't get anything else.
>
>   Sometimes I saw around a hundred Musk-Ox in one bunch and most of the other times they were in small bunches. Some of them I saw on the sea ice and they acted just like dogs going crazy. They would turn around in circles on the ice with icicles hanging from their noses nearly to the ground. They would then stagger around for a little while and die. I think there was over ten of them that I saw do this.[31]

Was Kanoyaoyak to be taken seriously? Yes – and no. Jones took the claim that he had killed five musk-ox seriously but doubted the sighting of 100 animals, noting that "it is felt that this may be somewhat exaggerated, as from the writer's past experience with Eskimos, they have only a vague idea of numbers and generally describe things of this nature where numbers are involved by being either 'few' or 'many.'"[32] He surmised that the musk-ox in question might have had rabies. Jones also noted that Kanoyaoyak had been camped at the time about a half-day's travel by dog team from the post at Bathurst Inlet. He noted that it appeared they had been killed solely for food and as the need arose. And in addressing John Kelsall's favourite phrase, he concluded that "there are no indications of wanton slaughtering of these animals by Kanoyaoyak."[33]

What happened next illustrates the bizarre logic the Canadian Wildlife Service applied to such circumstances. It further shows the conflicts that had developed between the service and the RCMP, represented by Henry Larson, as well as the administration of conflicting policies at the time. In January 1957, an obviously exasperated Larson reported to the chief of the service on the first memo he had received from Jones prior to his interrogation of Kanoyaoyak. He noted that in 1948 there had been reports that Inuit from Beechy Lake had shot a musk-ox and that "this was investigated at the time and full reports submitted to your Department and the story has been repeated ever since."[34] He asked to know the source of Kelsall's information about the killing of musk-ox at Daniel Moore Bay that had prompted the investigation. Larson was clearly of the opinion that the Canadian Wildlife Service was wasting his officer's time.

Unfortunately, once he had received the second report from Jones, Larson had to back down from the defensive tone of his letter. Musk-ox had been killed. In further correspondence with Winston Mair, he not only backed off but also clearly set out to convince the service that the RCMP took its mandate seriously. Larson noted that Kanoyaoyak had been camped a mere fifty miles from the Bathurst Inlet Trading Post, and therefore "it is felt that no special emergency existed in this instance" and that "he could have travelled to the settlement without too much difficulty and obtained relief assistance."[35] He went on to note that any attempted prosecution would have to be by summary conviction and that the six-month limitation of action period for summary conviction had expired. Instead, he suggested that Kanoyaoyak be given a severe warning by Corporal Jones and asked if the service agreed with this action.

Inuit were constantly being encouraged to be self-supporting. In fact, as previously noted, RCMP officers were actively discouraging Inuit from camping around HBC posts in order to prevent them from becoming "post Inuit," dependent on handouts and social assistance. Inuit were to get out on the land and make a living. In this case, we have the incongruous situation of the commander of Division "G" actually prepared to prosecute an Inuk hunter because he did not "high-tail it" to the nearest post for a handout, as an alternative to hunting game available in his own backyard! If Inuit were confused and deeply upset over the apparently contradictory messages their colonizers were sending, they could easily have been forgiven. Social development policy – not to mention Inuit cultural norms and practices – were mixing badly with the conservation objectives of the Canadian Wildlife Service. Something had to change.

The following year, 1958, more musk-ox were shot in the vicinity of Ika-luktutiak. By 1959, Jameson Bond, the northern service officer in the community, was reporting a number of musk-ox sightings on Victoria Island. He suggested that, if the law prohibiting the hunting of musk-ox was to be taken seriously, wildlife officials needed to "spring into action":

I feel that it is important to make an aerial survey of this region so as to pinpoint if possible the number of animals and their distribution. Apart from any other consideration, there is a very practical one for getting this done as soon as possible. The good news will also be getting around among the Eskimos. All this adds up to the likelihood of more musk-oxen being shot by hunters and if the Eskimos don't want to tell, there is no earthly way to find out. But if an aerial survey is done right smartly, we would at least know how many there are in the area and thus be able to keep a check on numbers.[36]

Science was being called upon in the cause of social control. "Jamey," as Jameson Bond was affectionately known, got a response from the Canadian Wildlife Service. A.G. Loughrey, reporting on Bond's observations to Winston Mair, chief of the service, had no doubts about how to deal with any reports of musk-ox killings. He recommended to the chief of the Wildlife Service that charges be laid against any Eskimo killing musk-ox in the area.[37] At the same time, Loughrey advised Bond that both he and the local RCMP should inform Eskimos that musk-ox were protected throughout the season.[38] Within weeks, an Inuk hunter called Kogogolak was charged under the game ordinance with killing a musk-ox.[39] Kogogolak was not the only Inuk to have killed musk-ox in the Ikaluktutiak region. He was only the first Inuk to be prosecuted in a region where the killing of musk-ox for food had been reported for some time.

Kogogolak had hunted a musk-ox in February of 1959, and when it was discovered by the RCMP officer he was charged under the game ordinance of the Northwest Territories. His case was heard by Justice Sissons and became a landmark in Aboriginal jurisprudence. Sissons and his persistent conflicts with the Crown are detailed in Chapter 5. He found Kogogolak not guilty. The first shot had been fired in a battle over Inuit hunting rights. It was a shot that was to give impetus to a movement for Inuit hunting and land rights and the creation, in 1971, of the Inuit Tapirisat of Canada. Sissons argued that the Northwest Territories game ordinance did not apply to Inuit. He argued that the Royal Proclamation of 1763 protected Inuit hunting rights. He also noted that the Supreme Court, in its landmark decision of 1939, held that Eskimos are "Indians" and that at the time of the Royal Proclamation Inuit were also considered to be Indians, hence a federal responsibility. Parliament had done nothing to tamper with the rights granted by the proclamation, and therefore the game laws passed by the territorial council did not apply. Sissons noted that only a decision of the Parliament of Canada, rather than the Northwest Territories Council, could take away these rights. A fuller discussion of his reasoning is given in Chapter 5.

The decision was not appealed. Rather, the Department of Northern Affairs, with Deputy Minister Gordon Robertson at the helm, recommended changes to the Northwest Territories Act that made all game laws applicable to Inuit and changed the powers of the commissioner – also Robertson at the time – to make ordinances dealing with game that would apply to Indians and Eskimos. Effectively, the decision was circumvented by having the federal government devolve its responsibility to the territorial council in this area of jurisdiction. However, so as not to interfere with other rights held by Aboriginal people in general, guaranteed by the proclamation and by treaties, the amendment made it clear that Indians and Eskimos had the right to hunt for food on any unoccupied Crown land. The only exception was any species declared by the governor-in-council to be in danger of extinction. Following passage of this piece of legislation, an order-in-council (PC 1960-1256) was drawn up and stated that "His Excellency, the Governor General in Council, on the recommendation of the minister of the Department of Northern Affairs and Natural Resources, pursuant to Subsection 3 or Section 14 of the Northwest Territories Act, is pleased to hereby declare musk-ox, barren-ground caribou and polar bear as game in danger of extinction" (Sissons 1968, 121). It was a clever, if not an odious, move by Robertson (who fails to address these important events and his actions in his autobiography [2000]). The Canadian Wildlife Service was pleased indeed. It was finally in the driver's seat – or so it thought.

If Inuit could not hunt musk-ox without running the risk of heavy fines or even jail terms, the RCMP, who also depended from time to time on hunting northern game for food, appear to have been affected differently by the legislation. To the potential embarrassment of the force, an RCMP constable travelling from Qausuittuq (Resolute Bay) to Ausuittuq (Grise Fiord) shot and killed a musk-ox on Devon Island en route. The constable (unnamed in police reports but likely Corporal Sergeant, stationed at Ausuittuq at the time) and the special constable travelling with him ran out of meat for their dogs. They had anticipated shooting seals to feed their team. However, it was claimed that bad weather made this impossible, and only one seal had been shot to feed forty-one dogs. Consequently, the officer in charge located a nearby herd of musk-ox and shot two to provide feed.[40] No action was taken against the officer in question, and while this seems entirely reasonable it also seems likely that, had an Inuk encountered similar circumstances, he would have been admonished for travelling with such a large team and for not anticipating how much meat would be required to feed it. In fact, at the time, the RCMP were regularly complaining that Inuit dog teams were too large and that it took too many caribou to feed them. Furthermore, the ordinance in question made no provision for musk-ox being taken for dog food, even in an emergency. Strictly speaking, the officer appears to have been guilty of an offence. No charges were laid.[41]

Managing potential controversy in relation to this event and others was clearly a concern. At the same time Inuit hunting was being regulated, musk-ox were being removed from the High Arctic for zoos and museums. A case in point involved the Los Angeles County Museum, which had procured four musk-ox from Ellesmere Island for display purposes. The Department of Northern Affairs and National Resources went out of its way to keep the event out of the public eye. It reconsidered being involved in the publicity only once the changes to the legislation made necessary by Sissons's ruling had been completed.

In the two years following these changes, there were at least eleven convictions for the killing of musk-ox handed out by justices of the peace across the Northwest Territories (Eber 1997, 87). Other charges laid involved the abandonment of meat fit for human consumption. Sissons reversed two of them: the case of Matthew Kunangnaq and that of Frances Kallooar. The latter case deserves our attention here.

Kallooar was convicted in 1964 of abandoning meat fit for human consumption, contrary to section 15(1) of the game ordinance. The case was heard before Magistrate P.B. Parker on 2 September 1964, and Kallooar, who pleaded not guilty, was fined twenty dollars or fourteen days in prison. The decision was appealed, and Sissons heard the case. He found that Kallooar had no intention of abandoning the meat in question. It had spoiled because the engine on Kallooar's boat had broken down, and Kallooar had been forced to walk from a point about six miles east of the Kazan River to Qamani'tuaq (Baker Lake) for parts. By the time he returned, the meat had spoiled. In his judgment, Sissons, despite the change in legislation enacted in 1960 by Parliament, also maintained that the Royal Proclamation of 1763 still superseded the game ordinance of the Northwest Territories. In doing so, he was inviting an appeal to the Supreme Court. This did not happen with the Kallooar decision since another case, uncomplicated by the matter of intent, presented itself.

In the case of Sigeareak, heard 27 February 1965, the accused was found to be not guilty of violating the same section of the game ordinance that had been used to bring charges against Kallooar.[42] Sigeareak had killed three caribou while hunting along the Wilson River in July 1964. He left the area by boat, taking some of the meat and leaving the rest. He did not return to the area until September, even though many boats made the trip to the Wilson River from Tikiraqjuaq (Whale Cove) in the meantime. The Crown prosecutor, David Searle, wanted a conviction. Parker, the justice of the peace hearing the case, argued that if Sigeareak were a white man he would be found guilty but was not guilty because the game laws – by virtue of the Royal Proclamation – did not apply to an Inuk hunter. The decision was appealed to the NWT Supreme Court, where Sissons upheld the judgment. The case was then appealed by William Morrow (soon to replace Sissons as justice of the Territorial Court) in the NWT Court of Appeal. Sissons's decision was overturned, with Chief Justice Bruce Smith ruling that, as in the case of *Regina v. Sikyea,* heard in 1962, the Inuit were excluded from the provisions of the Royal Proclamation by virtue of occupying lands ceded to the Hudson's Bay Company. Therefore, they were not covered by its provisions. The case was then appealed to the Supreme Court of Canada, and the decision of the appeal court was upheld.

Despite the ultimate failure of these cases to clearly establish an Aboriginal right to hunt and fish on unoccupied Crown land, the rulings opened up troubling questions for the Canadian government. Increasingly, cases dealing with hunting and game laws raised questions about treaty rights for First Nations and the relevance of the Royal Proclamation to Inuit.

The number of prosecutions in the early 1960s makes it clear that Inuit did not stop hunting musk-ox or caribou just because of a game ordinance they had played no role in making and for which they clearly had little or no respect. Inuit resistance raised important questions about the legitimacy of the law as a mechanism for ruling in a nation where the citizens affected, contrary to the rationale behind parliamentary democracy, had no voice. Where a population has no role to play in the making of legislation and is not represented in its making, the legitimacy of the law is clearly in question. At the time, Inuit in the eastern Arctic had no voice in the federal government. Neither were they represented in the territorial government. It was not until 1965 that Abe Okpik became the first Inuk appointed to the territorial council, and in 1966 Simonie Michael became the first elected Inuit representative of the council.

A case that illustrates the limits of the law that now regulated all aspects of Inuit hunting is that of Paul Anarak, John Kuptana, and John Kohoktak. In the fall of 1962, these hunters and their relatives were camped in the vicinity of Daniel Moore Bay. The winter that followed was a poor one for hunting and trapping. In testimony given to the RCMP, Paul Anarak claimed that all winter the group got only two caribou. Every day when he went out to his trap lines, Anarak claimed he saw musk-ox, and finally, with no caribou meat available, he shot one. About a month later, Kuptana shot a caribou. He also claimed that in February Kohoktak and his wife shot nineteen musk-ox. Kuptana, in his interview with the RCMP on 3 December 1963, at Bathurst Inlet, claimed to have shot six musk-ox inland from where he was camped at the time. When asked why they had killed so many musk-ox, the respondents all claimed that they were in need of food and meat to feed their dogs. Constable Friesen, in charge of the Kugluktuk (Coppermine) detachment, who interviewed Anarak at Ikaluktutiak (Cambridge Bay), simply concluded that the Inuit in question were "hungry and in dire need of meat" and that "the natives could not have subsisted on the welfare they received at Bathurst."[43] Constable Glenn Warner, after interviewing Kuptana, suggested that commercial dog meal and tallow be made available in future to "allow the available meat and fish to stretch further for human consumption" and to "prevent such a slaughter of musk-ox as occurred here."[44] The idea of waste and slaughter had apparently become so well embedded in the lexicon of the day that even justifiable killing to prevent starvation constituted a "slaughter." In fact, the administrator of the Mackenzie District, reading the police reports, was so wedded to the idea that Inuit "slaughtered" and wasted animals whenever they encountered them that he produced the following incoherent account for his director:

> Those people seem to have been in real need during the winter months. There seems to be no doubt that the people were facing starvation conditions for themselves and the dogs. They could have done with many less musk-oxen for themselves, but felt, with reasons, that they had to feed their dogs, or the people themselves might be lost. It seems this extravagant killing of musk-oxen can be partly blamed on a lack of understanding, by the people, that they could obtain welfare assistance if they could not get fur, and were at the settlement where assistance was available.[45]

In this case, no one was charged since the six-month limitation of action under the game ordinance precluded any action. In making this clear, C.B. Macdonell, the chief superintendent who was now in charge of "G" Division of the RCMP, noted that, "had our members known of this incident earlier and laid charges, which indeed would have been justified, I have no doubt they would have been severely criticized by the courts, particularly in the light of a decision handed down by Mr. Justice Sissons in a recent case involving similar circumstances."[46]

No matter what the circumstances, Inuit were guilty of "extravagant killing" and "a lack of understanding" – apparently even while at risk of starving to death. A vicious syntactical circle had been created. Officials had been convinced by Canadian Wildlife Service reports and personnel that "wanton slaughter" was the order of the day. The language of waste and slaughter had now become the standard for a great deal of discourse – no matter how unreasonable – that involved Inuit hunting. To complete the circle, wildlife officials such as John Kelsall now relied on such reports and their wording to further substantiate their claims about Inuit hunting practices and the possible extinction of caribou, musk-ox, and polar bear.

Walrus Woes

Two species of importance to Inuit hunters were declared "endangered" with very little or no evidence that such was the case. One of these was the polar bear. However, concern for polar bears was preceded by a concern for walruses. Walrus studies were undertaken by the Canadian Wildlife Service in the late 1950s. A memo to Gordon Robertson on 27 March 1958 suggested management practices and changes in legislation, recommended by A.G.

Loughrey, to deal with walrus herds. The memo included comments received on these changes from the Arctic Division and from the Fisheries Research Board. As noted in introducing this chapter, CWS research on walruses had been truncated when the Department of Fisheries indicated that, as a marine mammal, the walrus was its responsibility. This claim did not stop the Canadian Wildlife Service from pursuing some form of regulation.

The memo makes it clear that the service had neither adequate data on populations nor adequate information about the composition of walrus herds. Having detailed all of the information the service did not have and wished to acquire by a combination of ground and aerial methods, Loughrey had recommended an intense program of education for Inuit hunters. Despite a lack of data, the service was of the opinion that the walrus, like other species, was endangered and being wasted.

The suggestion was that a general conservation education program be initiated that "must stress the simple principles of population dynamics, the necessity for conserving a renewable wildlife resource such as the walrus and the means of conserving it."[47] Inuit were to be given pamphlets, and material was to be introduced into the schools to teach Inuit about conservation. Talks were to be held with adults, and the results of the *Qallunaat*'s science – research plans, recommendations, and proposed regulations – were to be given to Inuit. And while some reference was made to discussing plans for community hunting projects with the Eskimos, it is obvious from the context that this was little more than a form of surveillance to ensure that any such plans conformed to the ideals of the Canadian Wildlife Service. Faced with all this expertise and these directives, it is little wonder that some members of a hunting population that collectively had insights and wisdom most *Qallunaat* could never acquire in a lifetime were left feeling *sugsaunngittugulli* ("useless").

In January 1959, the Arctic Division made its views on walrus management clear. It framed these views with the following statement: "Considering the fact that collection of biological information on walrus is in its preliminary stages, and considering also the fact that there has been almost no long-term experience in walrus management anywhere in the world, any administrative plan put forward must, of course, be considered tentative, and any management plan in the field, experimental."[48] This lack of management experience did not stop the deputy minister from introducing, in his role as commissioner of the Northwest Territories, new regulations governing the hunting of walrus. By Order-in-Council PC 1959-807, the new Regulations for the Protection of Walruses limited the number of walrus an Eskimo could take or kill to seven in one year. With a licence from the minister of fisheries, any person other than an Eskimo was permitted to take four walruses a year. This was a rather strange method of preserving the resource for an indigenous population, as the department had claimed to be doing on many other occasions. The RCMP was given added powers and responsibilities, something to be considered in light of the fear and deference that many Inuit had toward the force at the time: "the members of the Royal Canadian Mounted Police supervising a hunt of walrus may limit the number of walruses to be taken and limit the number of guns to be carried by the hunters."[49]

As a final recognition of the need for surveillance and control, every hunter was required to report to the RCMP on or before 31 December in each year, the number of walruses killed that year, and the date and place of killing. If Inuit had not previously lived individual and numbered lives, they were about to be reminded, in yet another way, that a command of numbers and their sequencing were absolutely essential to good relations with *Qallunaat*.[50] Like many other agendas in the attempted regulation of wildlife and of Inuit hunting practices, this one, despite appearances to the contrary, was driven more by socially constructed fear than by science – and science was definitely missing in the case of walrus management.

Polar Bear Problems: "The Ship Lands and Almost Always Another Trophy Is Collected"

Concern over the harvesting of polar bears involved wildlife researchers and policy makers in new and different problems. Commencing in the 1950s with the presence in the Arctic of *Qallunaat* involved in the building of the Distant Early Warning (DEW) Line [51] and the presence of military personnel, polar bear skins acquired a value that rose rapidly. This value offered Inuit, hard pressed for income, a new source of cash that was seen to reduce their need for social assistance. A classic tension between this new source of income and the objectives of species preservation was obvious. The matter of polar bear hunting also again raised matters of sovereignty since Greenland Inuit were hunting on Ellesmere Island.

Because the price of Arctic fox declined in the late 1940s and early 1950s (as previously noted to as low as $3.50 a pelt in 1949), and as the need for cash increased among Inuit populations, it is not difficult to understand why other strategies for making a cash income were developed. A market for seal skin that developed in the 1950s helped. Seal, always an important food source for all but the inland Inuit of the Kivalliq (Keewatin) region, emerged as a source of some cash income. Hunting a species for both food and cash was to last until the indiscriminate anti-sealing campaign of the late 1960s and 1970s created serious economic hardship for Inuit. Seals, seen to be abundant, were never regulated. In the 1950s, cash, or more credit at the Hudson's Bay Company, was needed for rifles, ammunition, and outdoor gear – including outboard motors and Peterhead boats – as well as an increasing array of household and other items. These needs arose as Inuit were relocated to settlements and, in many cases, found themselves a considerable distance from areas where they had traditionally hunted, trapped, and fished. Life in a settlement also made necessary material goods that were not part of camp life. In 1959, the Department of Northern Affairs and National Resources introduced a policy whereby Inuit who wanted a home had no alternative but to purchase one. The government shipped north what amounted to plywood boxes – affectionately known as "matchboxes." They cost Inuit about $1,200, amortized with interest over a ten-year period. For families, many with little or no access to any income, and for whom Family Allowances were often their only source of credit at the Hudson's Bay Company, it was a considerable amount. The policy ultimately failed, but in the meantime the need for income – and not just income in kind – increased further. This "necessity" into which Inuit were drawn was of no concern to the Canadian Wildlife Service in dealing with the hunting of polar bears and the sale of skins.

Attention was first given to polar bear management as the result of a report submitted by Alan Loughrey of the Canadian Wildlife Service in 1953. Loughrey observed that on Southampton Island, where polar bears were known to den, the males emerged from the dens earlier in the winter (January and February) than the females with their cubs (March and early April). Since travel in March is easier than it is in January or February, he suggested, more females and cubs were being taken by Inuit hunters than males. He opined that this imbalance in the numbers taken was not "biologically sound." His observations, for the time being, did not result in any restrictions being placed on Inuit hunting, although both James Cantley of the Department of Northern Affairs and National Resources and Inspector Dick of the RCMP did suggest a prohibition against the killing of females with cubs.[52]

Inuit, relying on their traditional knowledge, were not easily impressed with *Qallunaat* science:

> Some white people would come up to do science research – things like that. They would say that there weren't very many polar bears or whales. Because we know our environment, we knew that there were a lot of polar bears. They were even breaking things in places where there are cabins. It's like they just were there to help themselves! We have got so many bears or animals – including walruses. [And to deal with this situation] we just ... we were just doing what we were told to do ... We couldn't do anything ... We complained among ourselves and tried to talk to someone – somebody. They wouldn't listen. (Emik Immaroitok, Iglulik, 28 May 1997)

While there was growing concern expressed from a number of quarters – including RCMP officers in the field – about the killing of female polar bears

Emik Immaroitok. Photo Frank Tester.

and cubs, the data attached to Loughrey's report do not support the observation that an excess of cubs was being taken. For example, for the 1955-56 season, eighteen polar bears were taken at Craig Harbour, including one cub. At Pangnirtung, of forty-five bears killed, only twenty were female, and eight were cubs. At Mittimatalik (Pond Inlet), twenty-two polar bears were shot, of which three were cubs, and at Cape Christian fifty-two bears were killed, of which eleven were cubs. The only exception to this pattern appears to have been at Salliq (Coral Harbour), Southampton Island, where fifty-five adults and fifty cubs were killed. In fiscal year 1949-50, 191 polar bear skins were exported from the Northwest Territories. The number increased in subsequent years as follows: 1950-51 (176), 1951-52 (320), 1952-53 (387), 1953-54 (444), 1954-55 (507), and 1955-56 (417).[53]

By early 1956, the Canadian Wildlife Service had identified the polar bear as a species of concern. But a meeting to discuss the state of polar bear populations concluded that there was no obvious reason to be concerned about the number being killed. It was concluded that the situation should be carefully monitored. By late 1956, W.G. Brown, chief of the territorial division of the service, believed that a further discussion on the status of polar bears was needed. He convened a meeting of departmental officials for 3 December 1956.

Apparently, the service had tried to gauge the number of polar bears being killed by sending out a questionnaire. The results did not agree with the reported export figures. It is not hard to imagine why. Counting was difficult in a culture where numbers were typically expressed, as noted, in their English equivalents as "small," "few," "many," or "a lot," and most Inuit had no way of relating to a numerically precise record. This does not appear to have been an insight acquired by CWS officials. They preferred to believe that the discrepancy was evidence that polar bear fur was being exported illegally from the territories. Superintendent Larson of the RCMP was the only *Qallunaat* administrator to doubt this assertion.[54] Mr. Reeve of the service had calculated the number of polar bears taken in the 1955-56 season and compared it with the 417 skins exported during the same period: "Mathematical computation indicated the total kill was 454. This indicated the natives were utilizing only 8% of the polar bear skins taken."[55]

The language used here and throughout discussions held by the service is worthy of note. The deliberations are an excellent illustration of "science in the service of the state" and show how what was regarded as scientific was given the force necessary to have it taken seriously. Where the science did not exist, its effect on policy making was such that what would otherwise have been the results of scientific investigation had to be created – sometimes out of incredibly "thin air." The minutes of this meeting are illustrative of science in action. The term "mathematical computation" suggests an impressive use of numbers – something that was in fact an elementary and crude calculation. Throughout the meeting, the need for "more information," "more questionnaires," "more surveys," "more facts," and ultimately what amounted to "more monitoring" of Inuit hunters and their practices was noted.

Winston Mair, chief of the Canadian Wildlife Service, suggested that the presence of DEW Line personnel had something to do with the number of polar bears being killed. He advanced the idea that the export of skins be prohibited or that a quota system be introduced to regulate the number being taken. Concern was again expressed about the killing of females with cubs, and it was recommended that this practice be prohibited. Parallels were drawn between the fate of caribou – which the service already was convinced were on their way to extinction – and what might happen to polar bears "if action [is] not taken when [the] first signs of excessive kill appear."[56] Another participant, J.P. Richards, contributed to the developing concern by comparing what might happen to polar bears with what had already happened to musk-ox.[57]

Throughout the meeting, facts and figures were "batted about" with completely contradictory conclusions. While A.J. Reeve of the territorial division of the service had concluded that Inuit used *only* 8 percent of the pelts taken, A.G. Loughrey had calculated, based on the results of the service's questionnaire, that Inuit used *only* 20 percent of the polar bears taken. Loughrey, given to the creative use of numbers, provided an elaborate calculation in which he compared the value of polar bear skins being exported (500 a year at $25 a skin, for a total of $10,000) to the worth of caribou (30,000 a year with a meat value of $25 each, for a total of $750,000). The data were in support of his argument that it would be hard to justify a research program on polar bears equivalent to that expended in studying caribou.[58]

While attention to such details may seem trivial, it is important to note the considerable "way of making sense" dominating the thinking of those attempting, in increasing measure, to shape Inuit lives. Theirs was a serial mentality. Caribou, polar bear, and other species were commodities that could be separated out from the totality of Inuit life as a culture – counted, valued, monitored (along with those who hunted them) – and thus understood within a different totalizing logic – that of a colonizing state.

According to the minutes of the meeting, Winston Mair, chief of the service, rolled this logic into a solution: "Probably the best procedure to put the most cash into the hands of the Eskimos would be to set up a quota and allow American trophy hunters to come in. If such a system was properly organized the Eskimos could earn big money as professional guides. Mr. Mair quoted a case where it was suspected that a rich American financed a complete museum party for the express purpose of allowing the said rich American to shoot a polar bear."[59] Ultimately, while many means were discussed for regulating and decreasing the number of polar bears being hunted – including the introduction of a season, a prohibition against the killing of females with cubs, a ban on exports, a quota system, a ban on the taking of polar bears for museums and zoological gardens, and the introduction of trophy hunting – the meeting concluded that for the present discontinuing to issue scientific licences for the taking of polar bears would be the only action taken. The situation would be studied further. Concerns about the market for polar bear skins created by those involved in construction and operation of DEW Line sites remained paramount at the service.

This concern continued to grow in the minds of wildlife officials and was given impetus by a letter of 12 August 1957 addressed to A.W. Banfield in care of the "Wild Life Service" from Norman Luxton of Banff. Luxton, a well-known taxidermist who had established a highly successful wildlife museum in Banff, was not the most literate of observers. But he made his point.

The business I am in I meet many of the American flying men who are serving in the Artic.

The reports I get of the hunting class of these gentlemen, more so regarding the Polar bear is distressing to say the least.

It seems the hunting is done from the air and when a bear is found, the ship lands and almost always another trophy is collected.

Again the natives are advanced large premiums to secure skins for those who do not hunt, but wish to take a Polar home with them.

I do business with taxidermists from Winnipeg across Canada to Vancouver, the reports I hear from these men are almost unbelieveable/they tan & make the bear into rugs.

These are bouth from the Traders by the Americans, A hundred dollars is for an ordinary sized skin, a hundred and fity for large.

The Traders seldom sends any more Polars to their head offices, they find the demand right in their Posts greater than the supply.

If you are familiar with conditions in the North regarding this particular animal/I am sure you must be considering to do some thing about it.

I remain

Yours truly

Norman K. Luxton [all sic][60]

This claim was seemingly confirmed a few months later by R.N. Milmine, the RCMP constable stationed at Cambridge Bay. Milmine noted that at Holman Island the Hudson's Bay Company was selling skins locally for ninety dollars each. At the time of his writing – 14 November 1957 – there were reportedly thirty skins at the store in Holman that had been purchased by DEW Line employees. He expressed a concern that at this price Inuit would soon be killing polar bears for the price of the skin alone.[61]

The Canadian Wildlife Service was frustrated in at least one of the strategies it was trying to develop to address the problem. It had already sought a legal opinion on the option of banning the export of polar bear skins and had been advised by the legal division of the department that this could not be done.[62] On 2 December 1957, P.A.C. Nichols of the Hudson's Bay Company and Alex Stevenson of the Arctic Division of Northern Affairs and National Resources called on the Canadian Wildlife Service to indicate that neither party had any objections to the hunting of polar bears being more closely regulated. In fact, they suggested a three-year moratorium, which A.J. Reeve of the service dismissed in favour of the "application of proper management procedures."[63] Ultimately, Schedule B of the NWT game ordinance was amended to exclude the hunting of female polar bears with cubs less than a year old.

In May 1958, an issue that had been of concern to the Canadian government presented itself yet again: Greenland Inuit hunting on Canadian territory en route to, or on return from, visiting Inuit at Ausuittuq (Grise Fiord), Ellesmere Island. A.B. McIntosh, the RCMP constable stationed at Alexandra Fiord, noted that the hunting practices of these Inuit included taking polar bears. In March of that year, to the best of his knowledge, nine had been taken by Kassingwak and Kulutingwak, two Inuit from Greenland. He went on to suggest that some of the Inuit he met travelling between Ausuittuq and Alexandra Fiord, where he had gone to collect mail on 20 April, had suggested that they would like to remain permanently in the area. He suggested that perhaps there should be an immigration and trading post established at Alexandra Fiord.[64]

In response to this suggestion, Gordon Robertson sent a note to the secretary of state for external affairs on 9 May 1957, noting that there was no objection from the department to this kind of travel as long as the Inuit respected Canadian game laws. Subsequently, the Danish ambassador was advised of the same and that these Inuit were welcome to hunt seals in Canada to provide dog food while on their hunting expeditions. There was no appreciation in the correspondence that seals were as important for human consumption as they were for dog food.

The wildlife service also took note of the report that Inuit were getting as much as $300 Canadian a skin for polar bears in Greenland. This, it suggested, was motive enough for them to hunt as many polar bears as possible on the Canadian side of the border, a line of little significance to Inuit hunters who had been travelling this route for centuries. However, on 20 August 1957, in a note to the director of the Northern Administration and Lands Branch of Northern Affairs and National Resources, W.J. Fitzsimmons of the "G" Division of the RCMP indicated that the privilege was being abused. Greenland Inuit were entering Canadian territory just to hunt polar bears, and something should be done "particularly in view of the possibility of these people ... depleting the polar bear resources on Ellesmere Island and adjacent Canadian waters."[65] At the time, there were no mechanisms in place for regulating polar bear hunting by Canadian Inuit, and therefore the means for regulating hunting by Greenland Inuit, having given them permission to enter Canadian territory, were anything but clear.

Finally, in June 1960, J.R.B. Coleman, referring to a trip made by John Tener of the Canadian Wildlife Service to the RCMP detachment at Alexandra Fiord, Ellesmere Island, sent a memo to his director, Winston Mair. He recommended that the Canadian government advise the government of Denmark that Greenland Eskimos were no longer permitted to hunt in Canadian territory. In doing so, he referred to national and international pressure on the issue of hunting: "With the present concern of this Department and of national and international organizations interested in Arctic regions over the numbers of polar bears being killed annually, it would seem to us that it may be unwise to permit Greenlanders to hunt polar bears in Canadian territory, particularly as it would be difficult to exercise effective control over such hunts. The total land and sea resources available to our Eskimos are not prolific and utilization by other nationals would result ultimately in depletion of those resources."[66] Coleman also referred in his correspondence to a move by the government to place polar bears on the endangered species list. This was ultimately done even though no studies had been undertaken at the time and there was no evidence that polar bears were, in fact, an endangered species.

On receiving this advice from Coleman and Tener, Ben Sivertz, chief of the Arctic Division, wrote to the undersecretary of state for Greenland affairs in Copenhagen. His request fell far short of that suggested by Tener. Sivertz bent over backward to make his request as "soft" and reasonable as possible, noting that stories about Greenland Eskimos shooting bears had never been authenticated, that the Canadian government had absolutely no intention of charging anyone, that Greenlanders had visited Canadian Eskimos at Grise Fiord, and that the government was "naturally very pleased to know of this." He went so far as to implicate the Inuit of Grise Fiord in the matter: "You might agree that it would be helpful if your administrative representatives in northern Greenland were to draw to the attention of those concerned the necessity of not molesting polar bears on Ellesmere Island. We do not wish to suggest to the Greenlanders that there has been any accusation of illegal killing, but perhaps a gentle reminder from time to time will not only meet the needs of the Administration but avoid any cause of misunderstanding between the Canadian Eskimos and their Greenlandic neighbours."[67]

Inuit, not necessarily cognizant of the significance of international borders, were being defined, territorially, by the Canadian state. Relations between Inuit – regardless of their polar location – were irrelevant to this definition. Sivertz suggested that all he was trying to do was avoid misunderstanding between Canadian and Greenland Inuit. There was no evidence anywhere that such misunderstanding existed or was even likely to exist in the future. In fact, Sivertz, in the interests of diplomacy, appears to have deliberately misrepresented the concerns of his departmental officials. The undersecretary of state for Greenland affairs acknowledged the concerns of Sivertz that September.[68]

As the 1950s became the 1960s, the attention given to polar bears was increasingly driven by considerations additional to the survey research and data that the Canadian Wildlife Service had on hand at the time. These data, in this case, were minimal, other than RCMP reports on how many polar bears were being killed annually in each settlement.

Concern over the regulation of polar bear hunting took on yet another international dimension in the fall of 1963, and this time the matter raised questions about offshore limits and the state's jurisdiction. Bill Clarke, a pilot and trader at Tuktoyaktuk in the Mackenzie delta, announced that he was going to take his plane and fly out over the polar ice cap, beyond the three-mile limit. At the time, this was the accepted standard by which nations administered their coastal waters. He was going to shoot polar bears beyond Canadian jurisdiction. At $150 a skin, it was not hard to understand why. Since he would be beyond the three-mile limit, there was nothing that the state could do to stop him. The poor officer in charge of the RCMP at Inuvik was entirely perplexed by the matter and unable to determine whether he had any jurisdiction over this kind of hunting – musing as to whether he could seize the skin as one imported from a foreign country and seize the plane if an excise tax was not paid. He confessed that in this case his suggestions were complicated by the fact that no foreign country would be involved.

On 21 January 1964, R.A.J. Phillips, having received an opinion from his legal department that the government had no jurisdiction over such an activity, sent a letter to the director of the national parks branch asking if he had any interest in exercising federal control over the taking of polar bears outside the boundaries of the Northwest Territories. Questions about the management of polar bears were pointing to the need for an international solution, one that would of necessity involve the Soviet Union. In the meantime, the problem was solved with an amendment to the NWT game ordinance prohibiting the import of polar bear skins.[69]

As this was taking place, the northern administration had on its hands the first test of the changes it had made to the game ordinance prohibiting the shooting of cubs less than one year of age and their mothers. On or about 5 November 1963, four hunters from Naujaat (Repulse Bay), Jaki Nanordluk, Peter Katokra, Anthonase Mablik, and Kaunak, came across a polar bear while travelling along the shore northwest of the settlement. Nanordluk was the first to reach the bear and shot two younger bears travelling with the adult female. The female bear subsequently ran away. Interviewed by Corporal Knights of the RCMP, Jaki acknowledged that he had shot the cubs and that he was aware there was a prohibition against shooting cubs under one year of age. He added that he thought the bears were too large to be that young. One of the other hunters, when asked if he was aware they were not to shoot cubs under one year of age, replied "I heard but was never told myself," and the second hunter answered, "I never heard before."[70]

This response is significant. It illustrates a further problem with the law in relation to culture, a problem of which government officials and RCMP officers were largely unaware. As previously noted, "knowing" as understood in Inuit culture, means to "know directly," and knowing something as a result of hearsay is fundamentally and categorically different from knowing as a result of hearing something directly from the person or authority who has the knowledge. In Inuit culture, hearsay has a different status.[71]

This shooting of cubs called the game ordinance into question. How does one determine with any certainty whether a cub is eleven months old or, as may be the case, thirteen months old? In this case, one skin was larger than the other – the assumption being initially that therefore the bear was bigger and possibly older – that is, it was at least two years old. The skins were seized and taken to Kangiqliniq (Rankin Inlet), where not even the assistant superintendent of game could say with any certainty how old either bear might be. Corporal Knights recommended that, since not even the HBC manager and the Roman Catholic priest in Naujaat (Repulse Bay) understood the game ordinance and the prohibition against killing cubs, and because of the difficulty in determining the exact age of the cubs, no charges be laid and that the skins be returned to Nanordluk. This was done, although the Canadian Wildlife Service was further consulted about the possible age of the cubs in question.

Concerns about the conservation of polar bears continued to develop, and by 1965 some kind of watershed in their management appears to have been reached. As the demand for skins increased, so did the number of bears being taken by Inuit hunters. In June 1965, a number of reports were received from different Inuit settlements that gave some indication of the number of bears being taken. Inuit were responding to a market demand, in fact behaving as would any other player in a market. This market was one to which Inuit had been introduced, and market relations were playing an increasing role in Inuit lives.

On 4 June 1965, David Munro, chief of the Canadian Wildlife Service, received a report from E.R. Lysyk, an inspector with the Criminal Investigation Branch of the RCMP. It concerned a memo he had received from Qausuittuq (Resolute Bay) about "polar bears being *indiscriminately* shot by Eskimo hunters while travelling via ski-doo or similar tracked vehicles in the Grise Fiord-Resolute Bay areas" (emphasis added).[72] In fact, it was the number that was the problem since these hunters had succeeded in shooting ten bears.

It is not clear why their hunting of polar bears was "indiscriminate," given that there was a market for the fur and that the only prohibition in place was against killing females and their cubs when they were less than a year old. Why the Criminal Investigation Branch had received this information is unclear. Inuit, encouraged to participate in a market economy and relations not of their choosing, were now being criminalized for behaving the way that any producer behaves under conditions of increasing demand. Inuit, whose life experience was territorial, were also expected to have the global knowledge required for reasonable participation in this economy. Their failure to behave in line with the perception required of this new relationship was seen as "indiscriminate." The RCMP decided, on the basis of this communication, to request information from other detachments in the eastern Arctic.

The RCMP received a number of detailed responses. M.J. McPhee, the constable in charge at Pangnirtung, acknowledged that he did not know the exact number of bears taken by hunters in the Pangnirtung area, but he noted that the Hudson's Bay Company at both Pangnirtung and Qikitarjuak (Broughton Island) had reported a doubling of skins being traded over the previous year. He noted that the high price – $100-$200 – for green hides was an incentive. He suggested that a limit of two bears per hunter be imposed.[73]

A detailed response was received from Qausuittuq (Resolute Bay), where the officer in charge noted that hunters had taken eighty-six bears during the previous year, up from an average of fifty-five bears per year between 1958 and 1964. He noted that many of the bears were slightly older than one year and recommended that the law be amended to prohibit killing a bear less than two years of age, since a smaller bear fetched a much lower price for the skin. He also observed that, "locally, the population of the bear does not seem to have suffered from the increased harvest."[74] Mixed opinions were received from other settlements. The officer in charge at Cape Christian also noted that more bears were being hunted because the Hudson's Bay Company had doubled the price. He added that, "with all reports of sightings, and tracks in this area, there would appear to be no immediate threat to the conservation of polar bears."[75]

Nevertheless, the price paid for skins, the introduction of snowmobiles, and an increasing need for cash income were all having an impact. The two Inuit – Simonie and George – travelling between Qausuittuq (Resolute Bay) and Ausuittuq (Grise Fiord) in the late spring of 1965, who had taken ten polar bears between Viks Fiord and Cape Sparbo on the north side of Devon Island, focused the wildlife service on the relationship between hunting and the introduction of the snowmobile to Inuit hunters. Simonie and George had been hunting by snowmobile. Reporting on the incident, Constable Schollar of the Grise Fiord detachment believed that snowmobiles were the problem.

> The Eskimo people residing at Grise Fiord at present are using only dog teams for all their hunting operations. No one in this settlement owns a ski-doo at this time, and it is felt that no such purchases will be made for at least two, or possibly three years at the earliest. It is felt, however, that the apparent ease with which polar bear can be taken by this means, together with the present high price paid for the raw hide, will no doubt cause some of the people to consider the purchase of a ski-doo, with these thoughts in mind. The fact that a large number of ski-doos are owned at Resolute Bay thus creates a threat, not only to the polar bear, but also to one means of livelihood of the people from this area, who hunt by dog team only.[76]

At Kangiqliniq (Rankin Inlet), on the other hand, Corporal Andrews believed that tracked vehicles were not endangering polar bear populations in the area. Sixty-eight bears had been taken by hunters from Rankin Inlet, four had been taken at Naujaat (Repulse Bay), and sixty-three had been shot by hunters from Salliq (Coral Harbour) on Southampton Island. They had all been taken by hunters using dog teams.[77] In the central Arctic, snowmobiles were not yet being used for hunting, and the officers in charge reported that few bears had been taken. It therefore appears that the high price being offered for skins was the most significant factor in accounting for any increase in the hunting of polar bears. Inuit had learned well how to respond to a market but, based on what followed, were deemed not to be capable of dealing with the implications.

The subsequent resistance to the imposition of quotas for the killing of polar bears was not likely a reflection of Inuit unwillingness to conserve the species. As noted later in the text, once a quota system was introduced, Inuit objected to it and attempted to undermine its strict provisions by requesting of the Northwest Territories Council that they be allowed to transfer quotas by permitting their sale from one hunter to another. Inuit, at the time, were given no role in discussing the situation that involved a complex interaction between the market price for skins, technology, and changing material circumstances. In fact, the High Arctic and the north coast of Devon Island, where a high concentration of bears appeared to be located at certain times of the year, had not been home to Inuit hunters for centuries. It was the relocation of Inuit by the federal administration to the communities of Resolute Bay and Grise Fiord in 1953 that had placed Inuit in close proximity to a polar bear population with which they had had little – if any – relationship. It was also the lack of alternatives for making a living in these locations that made polar bears particularly important.

Inuit were not given any opportunity to come together and share their observations and experiences. Rather, in September 1965, wildlife experts from Canada, Denmark, Norway, the USSR, and the United States met at College, Alaska, to discuss the status of polar bears internationally. Not one Aboriginal person was in attendance.[78] The meeting concluded that "scientific knowledge of the polar bear is far from being sufficient as a foundation for sound management policies" and then stated that "all cubs and females accompanied by cubs, require protection throughout the year."[79] The latter was a strange conclusion given that participants had agreed they had insufficient knowledge to implement any management policies. In October, the Canadian Wildlife Service developed a questionnaire to obtain information about the composition and distribution of the killing of polar bears. To add force to its efforts, the service went so far as to obtain a letter from the minister, Arthur Laing, requesting co-operation in distributing, collecting, and returning the questionnaire.[80] The questionnaire was to be distributed to HBC post managers, provincial game officers, territorial game officers, and, notably, the RCMP.

A sense of crisis was to overtake these efforts. On 29 November 1965, Corporal Andrews, who had expressed little concern over the extent of hunting, developed a very different understanding of what was happening to polar bears. He filed a report indicating that, since October 1964, over 140 bears had been killed by Inuit at Salliq (Coral Harbour). He noted that the average price paid by the Hudson's Bay Company was $150 and that the price for Arctic fox pelts was very low. His superior at Kangiqliniq (Rankin Inlet) forwarded the report to the head of Division "G" in Ottawa, who in turn wrote to David Munro, head of the Canadian Wildlife Service. The suggestion was that the season for hunting be limited "before the bear population is decimated to a dangerous degree."[81]

The Canadian Wildlife Service already had this in mind. In fact, long before any research had been initiated, and even before the international conference on polar bears, the service had put together recommendations for changes in legislation governing polar bear killing and was "holding them pending receipt of supporting reports."[82] Loughrey, superintendent of the service in the eastern Arctic, in response to a request from Munro, forwarded him a lengthy and detailed paper entitled "Polar Bear Management in Canada" prepared by C.R. Harington of the service. The document followed a familiar pattern. It was introduced by the statement "we have not yet obtained firm numerical data on polar bear populations, age distribution, mobility, and productivity, and little is known of these subjects outside of Canada either."[83] These were not matters about which the service was willing to consult Inuit hunters. Nonetheless, in the same document, Harington produced figures for the total population (6,000), the number of adult females (2,100), females of breeding age (1,890), the estimated annual increase (1,008), the natural death rate (400), and the annual kill (553), thereby concluding that the population was only increasing by forty-one animals per year.[84] Where the data came from is unknown. The population estimates appear to have been "pulled out of a hat," while the annual kill data likely came from game reports submitted annually by the RCMP stationed in Arctic settlements. Harington went on to detail the use of snowmobiles by Inuit at Qausuittuq (Resolute Bay) and noted that in one case $260 was paid for a bear skin. There was no doubt about it: Inuit were under close surveillance.

Harington had a number of legislative solutions to the problem of the "local extermination of this species." He recommended that "the hunting of polar bears with the aid of any motorized vehicle be forbidden"; that "the number of polar bears taken by one hunter be limited to six per year, and that no hunter be allowed to fill the bag limit of any other hunter"; that "a closed season on polar bears be enforced from May 15 to October 1"; and "that hunting of mothers with cubs up to two years of age and cubs up to two years of age be forbidden." He also recommended that there be no exemption to the law in the western Arctic. He expressed his opposition to sport hunting but allowed that, if sport hunting were to be initiated, "guides take the hunters out after bears by dog sled." He also made suggestions about how cubs should be captured for scientific or display purposes.[85]

The memo raises no concerns about Inuit incomes. It contains no analysis of the rising cost of living in developing Inuit settlements, a housing policy that, as previously noted, required Inuit to buy a house and carry a mortgage (no rental options were yet available), and the lack of alternative means for making a living. The lead-zinc mine had closed at Rankin Inlet, and petroleum exploration had not yet been initiated in the High Arctic, to which Inuit had been relocated. The price of fox fur had not recovered significantly from the low prices of the 1950s, although a commercial market for seal pelts compensated for this loss in some locations. Living in settlements affected hunting patterns and access to traditional territory. Having cash to purchase supplies from the HBC stores in northern communities, at prices far in excess of what the same items would cost in the south, was an increasing necessity few families could avoid. For the biologists with the Canadian Wildlife Service, wildlife, an integral part of Inuit culture and essential to economic survival in the Arctic, were "a thing apart" in need of protection.

The archival record suggests that it was Ben Sivertz, former head of the Arctic Division and by this time commissioner of the Northwest Territories, who directed the service toward consultation with Inuit. On 6 February 1966, the service met with Sivertz to present him with recommended changes to the NWT game ordinance. These changes introduced the closed season previously noted, a prohibition against hunting mothers with cubs up to two years of age and the cubs, and, in the case of Victoria Island, Banks Island, and the Mackenzie District, a prohibition against the killing of cubs and the mothers of cubs up to one year of age. These changes were to go before the territorial council in the summer session of 1966. However, it appears that Sivertz was concerned both about the effectiveness of the proposed changes and about the economic implications. These concerns found their way into a briefing document on polar bear quotas prepared by Paul Kwaterowsky, the NWT superintendent of game. Kwaterowsky, located at Fort Smith since the administration had not yet been relocated from Ottawa to Yellowknife, was ultimately responsible for game management in the Northwest Territories. In practice, the Canadian Wildlife Service, while supposedly having a research function, had assumed the role of shaping both policies and practices with respect to the management of game. But as the territories moved toward the assumption of greater responsibility for governance, Kwaterowsky's role and influence were somewhat enhanced.

Kwaterowsky suggested a quota system, advancing the argument that a closed season would only concentrate hunting in the open season and would do little to reduce the number of bears taken. He also noted that "drastically restricting the take of polar bear, or in extreme cases, prohibiting its kill, will seriously affect the already depressed economic situation."[86] Ultimately, he was to prevail. Effective 1 July 1967, quotas for twenty-five Arctic settlements were used in an attempt to limit the total kill to 386 bears a year, compared with a kill for the previous year of 525 bears. It was a figure arrived at on the basis of reports, primarily from the RCMP, of the number of hunters and the number of bears being taken in each community. It was a solution, however, that did not address the problem of "the already depressed economy."

At the same time, RCMP officers in the field were starting to express concerns about provisions of the game ordinance that affected the hunting of bears and their ability to enforce the law. Of these concerns, the most interesting were about the use of dogs and snowmobiles. For example, Constable Schollar of the Grise Fiord detachment was prepared to interpret the game ordinance in the most rigid manner possible:

Regarding the use of ski-doos for hunting, according to Sec. 2(h) Game Ordinance, "hunting" is defined as "chasing, pursuing, worrying, following after, or on the trail of" game, whether or not it is taken. The definition of a motor vehicle in Sec. 2(k), describes a ski-doo. Whereas Sec. 9 states, "No person shall hunt game from a motor vehicle," it is thought that the use of a ski-doo for following the tracks of a bear, would be an offence. While it is realized that this would be difficult, if not impossible, to enforce, it is felt that Eskimo hunters could be educated as to the proper use of a ski-doo for retrieving game.[87]

But if hunting polar bears by snowmobile was illegal, so was the use of dogs:

Sec. 10 states that dogs cannot be used for hunting, and if the same interpretation is given, as is noted in para. 3, then dogs could not be used either, even for following the tracks. The natives of this area have the practice of getting as close as possible to the polar bear, and then turning some of the dogs free to run the animal down and hold it at bay. This would seem to be a definite infraction of Sec. 10, however, several of the local hunters, when advised of this, stated that without dogs being used in this manner, it is next to impossible to take a polar bear under the conditions in this area, and possibly in most areas.[88]

These were embarrassing observations from an officer in the field, whose interpretation of the law suggested that hunting by snowmobile or with dogs was illegal. In other words, for all intents and purposes, going for a long, unaccompanied (by dogs) walk across the tundra was the only legal means by which Inuit could hunt. Fortunately, no one was foolish enough to prosecute Inuit with this interpretation of the ordinance in mind. The result might have been entirely embarrassing for an administration that, in its attempts to regulate and control Inuit hunting without the wisdom, insight, and input of Inuit hunters, had codified itself into a tight – and incredibly silly – corner.

Slowly, the institutional framework within which these relations were located was changing, and with it so was the voice of Inuit. The Carrothers Report, produced as a result of investigations into the development of government in the NWT, initiated the change from administrative government

centred in Ottawa to an elected territorial government located in Yellowknife. In the years beyond 1967, the territorial government was to acquire
increasing responsibility for areas of jurisdiction that had previously been
the prerogative of the federal administration. In a by-election held in 1966,
Inuit in the Kivalliq (Keewatin) region gained representation on territorial
council for the first time. While their representative, Bob Williamson of
Rankin Inlet, was not Inuk, his command of Inuktitut and his relationships
with and commitment to the Inuit community at the time could hardly have
served them better. On 17 January 1967, Yellowknife was designated as the
capital of the Northwest Territories. In March 1967, Ben Sivertz, who had
requested a royal commission to examine the development of responsible
government for the Northwest Territories, to which the response had been
the Carrothers Commission, retired. He was replaced by Stuart Hodgson,
and in September 1967 the administration of the Northwest Territories was
relocated from Ottawa to Yellowknife.[89]

Things were also changing on other fronts. While Harington of the Canadian Wildlife Service was visiting Qausuittuq (Resolute Bay) in the summer
of 1966, he introduced to Inuit hunters the idea of a community-based quota
system. It was a sign that some community consultation was developing.
It would take much longer for the Inuit voice to actually find its way into
the making of policy. RCMP Constable Kirbyson recorded the response
of Inuit at Resolute Bay to Harington's ideas. Harington suggested that a
certain number of licences be issued to residents and non-residents of the
Northwest Territories for a large fee and suggested that, if this came about,
they would have to employ Inuit as guides at a set rate of pay per day. Inuit
hunters, independent and self-directed, were to become waged employees
of *Qallunaat* hunters. They were not impressed: "Although they realize that
this would prove to be a greater income for them there was a trend of bit-
terness towards this idea ... 'Why let us kill only a certain number of polar
bear because the white man is worried about depleting the population and
then turn around and sell licences to the white man to hunt polar bear.'"[90]
Why indeed! That Inuit were willing to express both their feelings and their
opinions to the RCMP and wildlife officials, in counterdistinction to the sage
advice being offered by the Canadian Wildlife Service, is worthy of note. It
was a clear case of "talking back":

> Inuit were given a certain amount of quotas for certain things – for certain
> animals. We finally found out that just because there's a wildlife officer –
> that, you know – we didn't need to follow that. It wasn't necessary for us
> because – ah – the caribou were almost being treated the same as polar bears.
> Polar bears have quotas and if the caribou have quotas, then the Inuit were
> afraid that they would be starving. And – um – because we have to have a
> licence – well, we were told we would have to have licences even for fishing!

And after that, well, we started – that's when we realized that we had to talk back – for our food, for the food's sake. We didn't say "How can we do it?" We just said "No!" Later on, there was no in between. It was just "No!" (Barnabus Piruyeq, Qamani'tuaq [Baker Lake], 22 May 1997)

Complaints about the quota system introduced to manage the hunting of polar bears were many. Some Inuit wanted to maximize their income under the new restrictions by creating a market for the quota itself. It was a clever move. If non-Aboriginal hunters could purchase an individual's quota, or a portion thereof, then individual incomes could be augmented considerably. By 1968, a new Liberal administration was in power, and Jean Chrétien had replaced Arthur Laing as minister. Chrétien himself got involved in the issue and in a letter to Commissioner Stuart Hodgson put the lid firmly on any such idea:

That we should institute sport hunting of any species merely for the sake of obtaining revenue seems to defeat the purpose of (maintaining meat-producing and fur-producing animals) unless it can be shown without any doubt that game stocks are not depleted by this action and that the Indian or Eskimo gains in more than only a token increase in material wealth. Now that we have been successful in instituting a quota system, which is designed to control the take, it is incumbent upon us not only to maintain it by rigid surveillance or other means, but also to be able to adjust it based on the best information available from our research and management group. To allow an individual to sell his quota is tantamount to abrogation of our responsibilities in this field.[91]

It was a paternalistic attitude that had to change. While polar bears were becoming a species of concern to the Canadian Wildlife Service – as well as Inuit hunters – parallel developments were taking place with regard to musk-ox, and the caribou "crisis" was about to be challenged from within the public service. The Inuit response to the entangled agendas of wildlife managers was also heading in a direction that few would anticipate.

4
Who Counts? Challenging Science and the Law

> Well, after I got to [work for] the RCMP, I went hunting out there, and my in-laws were out there, so him [the RCMP officer] and I come to the town. We got back to the town, and my mother-in-law was cooking, uh, swan. So we were eating there. I asked him, "What do you think you're eating?" [The RCMP officer replied,] "I don't know. I think it's seal meat." So, that was the RCMP eating it! [laughter]
>
> – John Lyall, Ikaluktutiak (Cambridge Bay), 29 May 1998

A number of Inuit interviewed in researching this book were quite open about their contravention of game laws – in the case above of the Migratory Birds Convention Act. Sometimes they had dared to bring the evidence back to town with them, not even bothering to consume it in the comparative safety of being on the land. In the story above, the RCMP officer, for whom John Lyall was working as a special constable, becomes the unwitting – and well-fed – subject of a wonderful prank.

What is interesting about this clever act of resistance are its symbolic and material forms. By unwittingly eating the forbidden meat, the RCMP officer crosses a social border, becoming one of those potentially in violation of the laws he is supposed to enforce. "Putting him in this place" may have been thought to "immunize" Inuit from prosecution. Attempts were made to affect the material base of Inuit society through education. In addition to *The Book of Wisdom for Eskimos* – discussed in the previous chapter – comic-book-style materials were produced in the 1950s and 1960s that attempted to educate Inuit about game laws, hunting practices, and the care of hunting equipment. These materials were all part of an effort to change the way in which Inuit thought about their relations to and the status of game on which they depended. These efforts are clear examples of what Italian theorist Antonio Gramsci (1971) identified as hegemonic discourse. Such texts were clear misrepresentations of Inuit material interests. However, the resistant behaviour of John Lyall used the same symbols – in this case a swan, albeit a cooked one – as counterhegemony. Such a brazen act illustrates considerable insight into the ideological relations of ruling being imposed, as suggested by the question "what do you think you are eating?"[1] Resistance therefore, while seldom organized in a co-ordinated social way during the period in question (the case of the first Inuit land claim documented later in the text being a remarkable exception), was nonetheless present and often used the same material resources as the state (game in this case) to challenge state relations of ruling. This uncoordinated but ever-present form of resistance was a precursor to more organized forms, notably the Inuit land claims that developed in the 1970s. And of significance, acts such as that documented above were not recognized as such by the state. Rather, when they were recognized at all, they were interpreted as human failings requiring first the gentle hand of education – or re-education – and when that failed, the arm of the law.

In this chapter, we continue to examine Inuit resistance to the regulation of hunting. As Doug Wilkinson – who chronicled and participated in Inuit hunting and camp life just prior to the move of most Inuit to settlements, commencing in the mid-1950s – observed, Inuit hunting was about far more than merely feeding and clothing a family:

> To the Eskimo hunting is something more than just providing the daily bread. It gives reason and meaning to his existence. How often I have seen Idlouk returning to his camp sitting atop a load of newly killed seals, head cocked jauntily to one side, faded blue beret on the back of his head, singing the ancient songs of his land. He was inook, angoteealook, a human being, a big man. Into his hunting he poured all the energy and emotion that a painter sets on his canvas, a musician brings from his instrument, a writer from his pen. He was an artist, as fine a craftsman as his land could produce, and he was happy in his knowledge. (1955, 260)

It is therefore not hard to understand why prohibitions against hunting practices that were not only essential to survival but also lay at the metaphysical heart of Inuit culture were met with persistent resistance and why the exhortations found in scripts such as *The Book of Wisdom for Eskimos* or comic-book-style educational materials, including those introduced in the 1960s and addressing Inuit hunting practices specifically, were more than merely offensive.

In the mid-1960s, parallel to the commercial hunting of polar bears, attempts were made to develop a commercial musk-ox hunt. Pressure on the state to find alternative economies for Inuit grew. As previously noted, incomes from trapping could no longer support Inuit in consolidated

Page from the Canadian Wildlife Service booklet *How to Save the Caribou,* published in the early or mid-1960s. Thousands of copies were distributed to Inuit. The title of the page declares that "men are the main killers of caribou." The text reads, "A long time ago, caribou used to be seen in somewhat many numbers, when they were migrating, and were killed with only the weapons they had when they were very close. This was when they were trading with furs. They had to have more dogs when they were pursuing trapping. They killed more caribou, for they had to have more dog food and for baits for traps. When they were killing caribou, they were being 'careless' about the meat." The illustrations down the left-hand side tell Inuit how they used to kill caribou. The text across the bottom addresses what was thought by CWS biologists to be the real problem – the indiscriminate slaughter of caribou. It reads, "When hunters were using traditional means of hunting and using traditional tools to hunt, such as bow and arrows, there were less caribou caught and lost. However, now hunters have modern rifles, and there are many more caribou caught, and all the caribou they see are shot and killed."
Canadian Wildlife Service, Ottawa (the exact date of this publication could not be determined; a memo dated 20 October 1967 notes that 6,300 copies of the booklet were still in storage with the Canadian Wildlife Service).

settlements where the need for cash – for rent, fuel, and a growing variety of store-bought goods – was growing.[2] These attempts to derive more commercial benefit from wildlife are examined in the first section of this chapter. Although Inuit hunters were responsible for the killing of polar bears and the selling of skins to *Qallunaat* working on the DEW Line and other *Qallunaat* appearing with increasing frequency in newly formed settlements of the eastern Arctic, a proposal for hunting musk-ox did not involve Inuit as hunters but as guides for sport hunters. The state response to the obviously intractable relationship of Inuit to wildlife was to move toward a redefinition of this relationship, away from one of subsistence hunting and toward the further commercialization of wildlife. While hunting polar bears and selling the skins comprised an extension of traditional hunting and trapping practices – albeit with a different species – the idea of acting as guides for sport hunting – that is, accompanying *Qallunaat* who were hunting for pleasure – was entirely new. Its ultimate impact on Inuit ideas about, and their relationships with, animals has received little attention. Inuit hunters were being redefined: first as subsistence hunters, then as commercial trappers and hunters, and finally as service providers, with some species acting as the resource for a very different (and, it can be argued, postindustrial or postmodern) economy.[3]

The second section of this chapter details contradictions emerging in the logic that informed the management regime of the 1950s and 1960s. These contradictions included observations that challenged the data being collected by wildlife biologists as well as inconsistencies in the manner in which game laws and regulations were applied. Inuit and non-Inuit were treated differently when infractions were encountered. There were obvious "cracks" in the science governing the management of game. Conflict between the state and Inuit hunters developed along a number of lines. Inuit had most often ignored the provisions of the territorial game laws and had, with some exceptions, continued to hunt as always. Attempts to educate them away from traditional practices using devices such as *The Book of Wisdom for Eskimos* had changed virtually nothing. Fear of the RCMP was one thing that restricted Inuit practices, but when they thought they could get away with it Inuit had no qualms about hunting as always – as illustrated by the quotation used to introduce this chapter.

Until the late 1950s, when Inuit increasingly moved to settlements, there were comparatively few RCMP in the eastern Arctic. They were charged with covering a territory inaccessible not merely by virtue of its size but also by formidable environmental conditions during much of the year. Inuit and *Qallunaat* had to get along, and the RCMP often depended on Inuit literally for their survival. Inuit command of the space they had occupied prior to colonization facilitated acts of resistance and ultimately the organization of collective resistance to state rule. Observations of Inuit behaviour and of game populations made by local RCMP often contradicted those of wildlife biologists, further undermining the dominant ideology. By the mid-1960s, the police force had increased, as had the opportunities for surveillance as well as the ability to enforce regulations. Furthermore, the police role had changed.

In the 1920s, 1930s, and 1940s, the police were responsible for just about everything constituting the state's relationship with Inuit. They were responsible for social assistance. They dealt with medical emergencies. They

CANADA'S FIRST WELFARE LINE

THEY CAME TO TRADE, PREACH, GOVERN AND TO PROTECT. BUT THEY WERE VERY DEPENDENCE ON THE INUIT, THEY CAME TO PROTECT!

ILLUTRATED BY: ANDRE TAUTU

Line drawing by André Tautu of Igluligaarjuk (Chesterfield Inlet), 1958. At the time, André was a fourteen-year-old student at Joseph Bernier, a residential school in Chesterfield Inlet, where many students were sexually and emotionally abused. Even at a young age, Inuit had considerable insight into the relationships developing between themselves and those sent to "modernize" them. Courtesy André Tautu.

reported extensively on hunting and trapping activities. They became responsible for the administration of Family Allowances. They were involved in the evacuation of Inuit to the south for treatment of tuberculosis. They assisted clergy and others in rounding up children from camps so they would attend school. They conducted patrols to remote hunting camps and areas far removed from their posts. They depended on Inuit, in many circumstances, for survival. This contact with almost every aspect of Inuit life, in many cases, muted application of the law to daily life. However, increasingly in the 1950s and 1960s, the RCMP were reduced to a more conventional and singular role: that of applying the law. This meant that conflict around wildlife management issues also escalated.

In the last section of this chapter, we examine these challenges in detail as the logic of game management comes apart. It is challenged on two fronts: in terms of the science underlying the management regime, and in terms of advocacy emanating from Inuit who were increasingly concerned, increasingly vocal, and about to take full advantage of the contradictions inherent in liberal democratic forms of governance introduced locally – and even nationally – as part of community development initiatives associated with the 1950s relocation of many Inuit to Arctic settlements.

The Commercial Hunting of Musk-Ox

Whereas serious doubts can be raised about the science used to determine caribou populations and whether or not the data generated were accurate, the same cannot be said for musk-ox. It appears likely that musk-ox populations were in decline commencing early in the century. The strict ban placed on hunting them may have contributed to a recovery of their numbers in the period after World War II. However, the historical record makes it difficult to determine this with any certainty. As noted in Chapter 1, musk-ox were overhunted in the 1800s and early 1900s to supply robes for the European carriage trade, but there was no serious census of musk-ox made until well after World War II.

The record also suggests that Inuit, despite the ban placed on musk-ox hunting in 1917, never really stopped hunting them. Finally, it is also true that musk-ox was never a species hunted as extensively, nor was it an animal as useful to Inuit culture, as caribou. Musk-ox were hunted when caribou were not available. Nevertheless, as Moses Nargyak of Gjoa Haven recalls, musk-ox – hunted to near extinction by *Qallunaat* entrepreneurs – had played an important role in the Inuit diet:

> The elders were not very pleased when there was a quota. I don't know if it helped or not to have the ban on hunting musk-ox in those days. The reason it really bothers me is that – uh – you know, the people count on those musk-ox or, you know, the traditional food. The elders were not very pleased at all. They were unhappy 'cause once in a while they would see a musk-ox. It's good meat, but we were not allowed to shoot them. They [the elders] would say, "Ah, I wonder how [the Qallunaat] would feel if we tell them not to pick flour – you know – wheat to make flour! They wouldn't feel too good at all." That's what they would say.
>
> When they talked about how the musk-ox meat tasted, you know, the elders would pray for it. And then, at the same time, they were afraid to shoot them. Somebody might tell on them in order to become the favourite person of the authorities. You know, if you tell the RCMP, maybe they might give you a little thing.

So, it was hard to trust any other people – hunters as well – even if they're Native people. They [the RCMP] were – ah – watching over everybody. Everybody's watching over the other person in order to keep the laws from not being broken. In those days, if you tried to talk against those laws – the RCMP's law – you don't know what could happen to you. (Moses Nargyak, Uqsuqtuuq [Gjoa Haven], 18 May 1998)

It is evident from Moses' observations that attempts to manage musk-ox had serious implications for relations among Inuit – a case of environmental regulation producing serious social side-effects. The musk-ox "problem" had been created primarily by *Qallunaat* hunters and a *Qallunaat* economy. Nevertheless, government officials reviewing the status of musk-ox in 1960 placed as much responsibility as possible for the demise of the species on Inuit. The following statement is typical of those appearing in many documents dealing with the subject: "The musk-ox was indeed greatly reduced in number by early explorers and exploiters, *perhaps most seriously by native hunters* supplying a demand for robes after the elimination of the plains bison as a commercial resource" (emphasis added).[4] By 1964, it was estimated that there were 2,500 musk-ox on the Arctic mainland and as many as 7,000 on the Queen Elizabeth Islands, with about 500 animals on the intermediate islands between Banks and Somerset Islands.[5]

Moses Nargyak.
Photo Frank Tester.

Inuit were increasingly frustrated by NWT game laws, which were consider-ably strengthened by 1965 as a result of the previously noted Supreme Court rulings. As Inuit were relocated to settlements, the need for an alternative economy in the eastern Arctic became critical. Game resources were con-ceptualized in an entirely different way.

In June 1965, following a territorial council discussion in which the difficul-ties of permitting a small annual kill of musk-ox were discussed, appointed members Vallee and Baker proposed that Inuit living on the Arctic islands be given access to the herds by becoming involved in the sport hunting of the animals by *Qallunaat* hunters.[6] The proposal received unanimous con-sent, and NWT Superintendent of Game Paul Kwaterowsky was asked to put together a paper on the topic.

Kwaterowsky took things a bit further. He travelled to Qausuittuq (Resolute Bay) and not only gathered information but also developed a plan for the sport hunting of musk-ox with the Resolute Bay Co-Operative. The meet-ing was held at the home of Joseph Idlout, 6 August 1965, and attended by thirty-five residents of the community. A similar meeting was held 11 August with members of the Grise Fiord Co-Operative. Some indication of the expectations developing among Inuit hunters is evident in the following excerpt from a report of the meeting held at Qausuittuq:

> At this point, the question was jokingly interjected whether they thought that $100 per musk-ox taken by sport hunters would be an adequate income for the co-operative. Everybody attending expressed his delight and thought that this was ample payment. It was then naturally a complete surprise when they were told that their government would not consider this amount as adequate and that each musk-ox taken should mean the better part of $1000 to them. This was accepted with real enthusiasm and the attending Eskimos went so far as to offer to refrain from polar bear hunting if more hunters would come and if they could make it more appealing to the hunters.[7]

The plan submitted to the department was detailed. It dealt with facilities, air support, accommodation, the question of a quota for the Inuit themselves, and the training of guides. The superintendent and his staff even went so far as to go on a musk-ox hunt with a number of potential guides. Using a special permit granted by the commissioner, they shot a bull in order to instruct potential guides on how to skin the animal as a sport hunter might require. A report outlining these activities and the proposal was then forwarded to the Canadian Wildlife Service for comment.

The service was less than enthusiastic about the idea but, not wanting to create undue animosity between itself and the territorial council, worded its criticisms carefully in an apparent attempt to "buy time." The comments focused on the season, suggesting that the timing would interfere with the rutting season and that "hunting activities may disrupt the social structure of herds and interfere with successful breeding."[8] The service also recommended that hunting of cows be strictly prohibited and that the program be deferred for a year. It noted that the game ordinance would have to be changed to make such a program possible.

At the thirty-second session of the territorial council, 24 January-7 February 1965, a further request was made for a detailed paper on the matter of sport hunting of musk-ox to be considered at the July 1966 meeting of council. The paper was prepared by the northern administration. It was forwarded to the Canadian Wildlife Service for comment prior to being given to Commissioner Ben Sivertz. The paper outlined growing concerns about the idea, including the possibility that other Eskimos might misinterpret the granting of hunting rights on the Queen Elizabeth Islands and commence hunting elsewhere; inadequate staff to monitor and supervise such an undertaking; a lack of data on the size and composition of musk-ox herds; the possibility that co-operatives did not represent Inuit communities and that organizing hunts through them might not be appropriate; the suggestion that Inuit were not ready to properly look after big game hunters; and an interesting concern that, if the right to kill musk-ox or to act as guides was granted only to Inuit, it "would mean building in special rights for Eskimos which would be contrary to the efforts towards integration presently being put forward."[9] The Canadian Wildlife Service had apparently loaded its guns with just about every size of ammunition it could obtain.

It is evident from the content of the document that the idea of sport hunting of musk-ox had generated considerable controversy among staff of the northern administration. It was also noted that another paper, proposing abolition of the Arctic Islands Game Preserve, had been circulated among staff and translated into syllabics and distributed to Inuit. Apart from correcting details in the report, David Munro, director of the Canadian Wildlife Service, took offence at such a paper being circulated without first consulting the service. This offence he noted in the margins of his copy and in his response to Mr. Carter, director of northern administration.[10]

Munro was not impressed by the paper on the abolishment of the Arctic Islands Game Preserve and made it clear that the service was "not in favour of such action until proper safeguards for meeting requirements for subsistence hunting by Eskimos were established, until control of hunting through enforcement and education was possible and until agreement was reached with the Eskimos on the proposed change." He also noted that, while Kwaterowsky's paper on musk-ox hunting covered the topic well, "we cannot help but observe that the emphasis is on the effects of abolishment [of the Arctic Islands Game Preserve] on people, not wildlife."[11] The preservationist as opposed to the conservationist hand was still showing itself within the service when circumstances called for it. The letter was copied to John Tener, the Canadian Wildlife Service's musk-ox expert.

The Canadian public was soon involved in the debate. That there was considerable dissent within the public administration was made more than obvious at a meeting of the Canadian Society of Zoologists held in Kingston on 18 May 1966. Dr. D.B.O. Savile of the federal agricultural department's plant research institute publicly spoke out against the proposal, noting that each caribou and musk-ox needs "hundreds of miles to support him." At the same meeting, photographer Richard Harrington raised concerns that the "motor toboggan" was a threat to polar bears, making it easier for hunters to find them too.[12]

Adding fuel to the growing fire, in July 1966 the Crown obtained two more convictions against Inuit hunters for killing musk-ox. Ivor Agak of Anderson Bay, Northwest Territories, was given a suspended sentence, fined fifty dollars, and ordered to enter into a written recognizance for one year requiring him to keep the peace and be of good behaviour.[13] The same sentence was handed out to David Ekpukuwuk. The Crown dropped charges against Joseph Elatiak of Sturt Point. Elatiak claimed that he was afraid the musk-ox he had killed would come into his camp and injure his children and that he was in need of food. The convictions did little to change the minds of those in the Canadian Wildlife Service who believed that any changes to regulations and prohibitions would have fatal implications for northern wildlife.

The territorial council continued to request information about the hunting of musk-ox and other species in order to deal with the matter of permitting sport hunting. In light of the convictions, pressure on council from Inuit communities was mounting, and Inuit discontent was growing. Writing in August 1967, biologist Milton Freeman captured interesting details of this discontent. Inuit in Ausuittuq (Grise Fiord), frustrated by the pace at which things were moving, had petitioned the council asking that it get on with approval of a musk-ox hunt: "The men at Grise Fiord have read the debates of Council regarding their petition. They now have perhaps as much idea of Council members as Council has of them! There is of course room for improvement in understanding on both sides. They were bemused and angry variously at remarks and comments made. For example, the opinion expressed by one appointee that allowing local hunters a Musk-ox quota would result in no more seal-hunting was treated with the contempt it deserved."[14]

Inuit opposition and frustration with *Qallunaat* science in relation to ideas about the hunting of caribou – as well as musk-ox – were also recorded in the minutes of meetings held the following year between hunters at Ausuittuq and the deputy commissioner of the Northwest Territories, John Parker: "The people reported that in recent years some Musk-oxen have died, but whether of starvation or old age they could not be sure. They suggested that a mixture of animals be killed, (some young, some old, some male, some female) because to kill only the old animals (who have much wisdom) would be to remove the defense of the herds. (They added that they thought the former practice of killing only male caribou had caused the decimation of caribou herds in their area by removing the protectors.)"[15] The idea of preserving the older members of a species because they have the wisdom essential to protecting younger members is not supported by the so-called logic of Western science, where the oldest members of a species should be killed since they have reduced reproductive capacity and are soon to die (and therefore "go to waste") anyway. Inuit here applied to other species the same logic underlying respect for Inuit elders. A similar view regarding the older members of mountain sheep populations is noted in Nadasdy's (2003, 127-28) account of the relations in the 1990s between state officials and Kluane First Nations people in the southwestern Yukon.

In February 1967, another paper was prepared for council that recommended a 1968 quota of sixteen musk-ox for the Resolute Bay Co-Operative and sixteen for Grise Fiord. It also detailed the season involved and outlined financing and fees for prospective hunters. It recommended that each hunter be allowed to take one caribou as well as a musk-ox and that guides receive further training.[16] This training was conducted in the summer of 1967 with permission being given for the killing of four more musk-ox. Council recommended that a hunt be permitted in 1968, subject to further surveys being conducted.

Public opposition to the proposed musk-ox hunt developed in the summer of 1967. The opposition can be seen in the context of the emergence in Canada, the United States, and Western Europe of the contemporary environmental movement and a move toward preservationist, as opposed to conservationist, sentiments. However, it is not surprising that in Canada – as elsewhere – the issues that first attracted attention were familiar to the conservation movement. It had, since the late 1800s, addressed environmental concerns primarily as a matter of species conservation and did so with nearly complete faith in the civil servants responsible. A new generation of environmentally concerned citizens – many of them young people – took up where the established conservation movement left off, inspired in large measure in Canada, as previously noted, by Farley Mowat's book *Never Cry Wolf*.

Mowat's book, in dealing with public officials, was cheeky, irreverent, entertaining, and was to sell more than 300,000 copies (King 2002). The image of the "honourable civil servant" had changed. The response of the new movement was equally brazen in its manner, tone, and tactics. It revealed itself to be a generation of people no longer content with writing "nice" letters to civil servants. It was more than willing to question authority and expertise. The "honourable civil servant" of the 1940s and 1950s was demoted to the status of "bureaucrat." Opposition to the musk-ox hunt followed outrage against using poison for wolf control in the Arctic and occurred about the same time as the first protests against the Newfoundland seal hunt that were to have disastrous implications for Inuit. Culturally, something significant was happening as Walt Disney turned animals into near people, typified by creations such as Bambi. Bears, wolves, foxes, rabbits, moose – and especially mice – became walking, talking personalities one could snuggle up to or observe parading everyday lessons on how to manage life across what was becoming in Canada a growing number of television screens. Off the coast of Newfoundland, white fluffy balls with huge sad eyes – seal pups – were embraced by environmentalists with devastating and systemic implications for Inuit hunting and the Inuit economy.

A Canadian Press story entitled "Musk-Ox Hunt Opposed" appeared in a number of Canadian newspapers in mid-July 1967. The article noted that Paul Kwaterowsky, superintendent of game for the Northwest Territories, had conceded in an interview that all one had to do to kill a musk-ox was walk up to it and shoot it. He noted that the musk-ox was an extremely rare trophy and that applications had been received from Germany by people wishing to hunt it. The article also quoted an unnamed "expert" who suggested that hunting would lead to extinction, that a hunter would be able to land and shoot one without even getting out of his plane, and that the territorial government was looking to bring in substantial revenue from the hunt. It also noted the opposition of the Canadian Wildlife Service to the plan.[17]

Opposition also came from the general public, academics, and non-governmental conservation organizations as well as from some government employees. Patrick Hardy, managing director of the Canadian Audubon Society, in a letter to David Munro, took up the theme of the "motorized toboggan" contributing to the demise of wildlife. He went on to say that,

> As for the musk-ox, I gather that to date plans are afoot only for a survey to determine population levels, but so often such announcements are only a prelude to a pre-ordained declaration of an open season. It is beyond me how anyone could take pride in displaying the head of an animal that stands perfectly still in a big group in the open; as long as the rifle will fire it's literally easier than the proverbial barn door. However, I realize that even at a cost of one or two thousand dollars (perhaps because of the cost) it could well become a prized status symbol to enough people to threaten once again its precarious survival, and I don't see how an open season can be justified.[18]

In the fall edition of *Canadian Audubon,* the publication of a news item, "Musk-Ox Hunt Opposed," that was critical of a proposed musk-ox hunt drew, in turn, considerable criticism from Douglas Clarke, chief of the Fish and Wildlife Branch of the Department of Lands and Forests, Government of Ontario. His complaints were that the news item didn't show much respect for the outcomes of scientific investigation. He suggested that, when science indicated conservation (and here he likely meant "preservation"), people such as Patrick Hardy, editor of *Canadian Audubon,* endorsed it but that if science justified some "harvest" of wildlife – meaning conservation – the science was vilified.[19] Given the science practised by the Canadian Wildlife Service at the time, this was, arguably, an astute observation.

Public controversy gave the NWT legislature second thoughts. Having initially approved for the summer of 1966 the idea of a sport hunt of musk-ox – which had been postponed – at its February 1967 meeting it decided that, in light of public opposition, it would seek the opinion of Inuit. Its reasoning was that, if Inuit approved of the hunt, many voices of opposition, not wanting to be seen to offend Inuit, would be silenced. It was a clever move, for members of the legislature knew full well that Inuit supported the hunt. By May of 1968, Inuit had voiced their support for the policy.[20] The complexity of the debate, judgment based on science versus values (a conflation of the two), and the role of Aboriginal people as allies in conservation or as part of the problem were to usher in conflicts that have dominated environmental debate ever since.

Some Canadians had difficulty with the fact that Inuit in the communities of Qausuittuq (Resolute Bay) and Ausuittuq (Grise Fiord) were enthusiastic about the sport hunting proposals. As noted, among them was Milton Freeman, at the time a professor at Memorial University of Newfoundland and well known subsequently for his authorship of the *Inuit Land Use and Occupancy Study* conducted in the 1970s as part of the Inuit Tapirisat's first attempt at a land claim settlement. Dr. Freeman was clearly opposed to the hunt under any circumstances but wished to be supportive of the community of Ausuittuq, where he was working at the same time. In a lengthy treatise on the subject, copied to John Tener and Graham Rowley, he argued that game management should be handled by "experienced management and scientific personnel" and that the Inuit of Grise Fiord enjoyed "one of the highest living and health standards in the whole Territories" and were therefore not in need of the benefits of a hunt.[21]

Opposition to the hunt did not go away. Nor was responsibility deflected away from territorial policy makers. The Victoria Natural History Society, steering carefully around any direct criticism of Inuit, suggested that, "judging from the said news release, this shooting is devised simply to release sums of money to Eskimos and trappers. The Eskimos would seem to be used as bait to ease white man's conscience in an unjustified destruction of an animal."[22] Among the dozens of letters received were many less-constrained opinions. Olive Mazuq of Toronto was blunt: "I simply cannot understand it. Canadians never miss an opportunity to cry out at the lengths the Americans will go to for dollars – yet here we say 'Come to Canada to slaughter our defenceless Musk Ox – all you need to do, is grease our palm with $4000!'"[23] Jean Trapton of Royston, Vancouver Island, simply clipped from her local paper a small news item announcing that Inuit had approved the hunt, glued it to a large sheet of paper, wrote beneath it with a thick, black pen, "This is *SPORTS HUNTING*??? Shame! Canada," and dropped her exclamation in the mail.[24]

John Tener, deputy director of the Canadian Wildlife Service, was asked to prepare a response to Trapton's outburst for the minister of Indian affairs and northern development, Arthur Laing. Tener was the author of a definitive monograph *Musk-Oxen in Canada,* first published by the Canadian Wildlife Service in 1965. Given that the service was not particularly well disposed to the sport hunting proposal, it was a difficult job. Tener attempted to shift responsibility for the decision away from the federal government to the territorial council, emphasizing the benefits accruing to the local Inuit economy. He included a paragraph acknowledging that there was not much sport in killing the animals but that this was also true for other species. He noted that the removal of "surplus animals in a population, if done properly, is sound management and is in the best interests of the species concerned."[25] The minister's final response ignored Tener's lip biting and was much more succinct. It emphasized Inuit support for the proposals and the economic benefits to local Inuit.[26]

By this time, Inuit of Ausuittuq and Qausuittuq had just about had enough of dithering, promises, and procrastination by the NWT government. They had been told that an agreement to participate in a sport hunt of musk-ox would be accompanied by a quota for their own purposes. Details of the proposed hunt – remuneration and whether guides would keep all or some of the meat of any animal shot by sport hunters – kept changing, depending on who spoke with community members. As noted, Inuit were not impressed by the debates among territorial councillors over the matter. Milton Freeman described the men at Ausuittuq as being both "bemused and angry" at what they heard. Commenting on the remark by one appointed councillor that a musk-ox quota for Inuit would divert attention away from seal hunting (the East Coast harp seal hunt – and seal hunting in general – having erupted as an environmental issue at the time[27]), Freeman noted that "a non-Eskimo must check his racist tendencies, but an Eskimo can freely libel any other Eskimos: let us remember that indulgence is as much a sign of immaturity as intolerance."[28] The possibility of matters of game management erupting into conflicts characterized by openly racist assumptions was apparent. According to Freeman, another member of council wondered how Inuit knew that musk-ox meat was not fit for consumption in summer if the fifty-year-old prohibition on killing had been respected.[29] It was a good question with an obvious answer.

Inuit were further frustrated when growing controversy prompted the territorial council to postpone the hunt for another two years. Thus, resistance was given impetus, paradoxically, by the state itself. In attempting to provide Inuit living in settlements with incomes that would lessen their dependence on the state, the state had opened a Pandora's box that gave further impetus to Inuit when ideas originating with the territorial government were not acted on. Paradoxically, the two communities most affected – and particularly incensed by the changing plans – were Qausuittuq (Resolute Bay) and Ausuittuq (Grise Fiord), both created by the federal government in 1953 in an attempt to get Inuit off the welfare rolls by providing them with an environment in which they could pursue subsistence hunting. This situation suggests that resistance to hegemonic discourse is, ironically, often given form and substance by state actors attempting to deal with contradictions commonly arising between economic and other (social and political) objectives.

In 1969, the ban on hunting musk-ox in the Northwest Territories was finally rescinded. While debate was taking place in the NWT legislature, both levels of government and responsible public officials were besieged with letters condemning any proposal to permit musk-ox hunting. The argument that a sport hunt would benefit Inuit was remarkably unpopular, as this rebuttal, sent to Minister of Indian Affairs and Northern Development Jean Chrétien, illustrates:

> Last year I wrote the Office of the Commissioner for the Northwest Territories protesting the proposal that Musk-ox hunting be allowed and received a reply that the "sports-hunting" of the musk-ox was designed to give the Eskimo co-ops guiding and tourism business. It is difficult to see how the Eskimo co-ops will benefit from such a scheme as no guide is necessary; the animals are easily spotted from the air grazing as they do on a treeless plain; it is necessary only to land and to shoot one. The charter aircraft services are not run by Eskimo and, therefore, the Eskimo would appear to benefit little if at all from such a "hunt."[30]

Chrétien's response was classically modern, full of boundless enthusiasm for Arctic development, progress, and the capacity of science:

> The increased visitation by people from the south will benefit them, notably by increasing air traffic and by encouraging rapport between the native people and the outside world. I feel this increased communication

and awareness of each other's mode of living and especially each other's problems, will serve in the best interest of the Eskimo people. Not only will the sports hunting program be restricted to carefully controlled areas but the continued advice of biologists will be a prerequisite and if it is felt that the musk-oxen population in those areas chosen for the hunt is in danger, the program will be cancelled.[31]

Finally, in 1970, Inuit were permitted to take twelve animals a year on Ellesmere Island. The quota system was extended to cover other locations. Inuit on Banks Island were given permission to take eight musk-ox a year.[32] However, these hunts were designed for local consumption, not for trophy hunting. By 1973, real concerns were being raised about the growing number of musk-ox on some Arctic islands. Paul Kwaterowsky, superintendent of game for the Northwest Territories, was clearly challenging the historical claims made by CWS biologists and others about the importance of continuing protection of the species when he suggested that "4000 musk-oxen face starvation by spring unless their numbers are depleted by at least 400."[33] Opposition to long-standing ideas about the preservation of species was now coming from within the ranks of those responsible for the scientific management of game as well as from Inuit communities.

In the process of dealing with the hunting of musk-ox, Inuit were introduced to a kind of Canadian public opinion very different from the sympathetic paternalism that had characterized the 1950s. Taken together with protests against sealing on the East Coast that were to have disastrous effects on the Inuit economy, issues such as a promised – and then withdrawn – opportunity to achieve some economic advantage by guiding the sport hunting of musk-ox made it increasingly obvious that threats to Inuit culture and well-being could originate not only with the state but also with a Canadian public ill informed about Inuit culture and interests.

Dissent from Without and Within
In the cultural context of Inuit hunters, the food sharing of illegal game illustrated by the quotation used to introduce this chapter may have created the impression of mutuality: that the hunters had gained a form of insurance against prosecution since their disciplinarians had joined them in eating the "forbidden fruits" of the hunt. This is a reverse form of the exchange of meat – with all of the concomitant obligations. Whether or not the RCMP appreciated these relationships and the implied obligations is another question. It is likely, given the close working relationship between local RCMP officers and their Inuit special constable assistants, that a good deal of meat of unspecified origin was consumed by northern police charged with the task of enforcing hunting bans. In fact, by some accounts, game shot illegally

by the RCMP was shared with Inuit: "And ... when I started working for the RCMP in the summertime – well – I didn't like it too much because I wasn't allowed to shoot swans. Eh? Well, an RCMP killed a swan, and they asked me to take it home. So, I go take it home to my house and eat it. Boy, it was in the fall [laughing]. I didn't like it all right, but I took it anyway. It was nice and fat" (Jack Alonak, Kugluktuk [Coppermine], 23 May 1998). Such stories indicate the degree to which relations in communities frequently defied colonial schemes for regulation, surveillance, and control. While the regulation of game was something the non-Inuit community might expect – and accept (albeit reluctantly in some cases) – as a legitimate role for the state, in Inuit communities such regulation was clearly an imposition on people who had never assented to it and who had no means at the time for affecting its form or content. As such, regulation directed at Inuit hunting was clearly part of colonial relations of ruling, and as noted the feeding of forbidden meat to the authorities charged with the task of enforcing regulations suggests creative, culturally significant forms of resistance.

The prosecution and increasing regulation of Inuit hunting practices described in previous chapters did not go unnoticed. Commencing in the late 1950s, settlement councils and housing associations were formed, often with the assistance of northern service officers, teachers, and clergy. Associations of hunters and trappers were also created:

[People first started to feel as if they could talk back to the Qallunaat] only after the hunters and trappers associations started forming, the hamlets started forming, and the community councils in those days and also the other committees started forming. We started learning that. Those members of – those councillors or the committees of the hunters and trappers – started planning. "This is what we should do." "This is not right for us." And all that.

And they were still quite afraid to say anything. Only the fellows who seemed to have been speaking out were from those committees. A lot of people were even still afraid to mention [in the meetings] what they didn't like about the quotas and the rules and things like that. But later on it was explained to them that they could fight back, and they could make the rules or slightly change them.

But sometimes it's impossible. So we just would follow along to see what comes out of it and – maybe next year! A few years later it might become easier to talk about it, and [we would] take a little rest from it for a while. We tried to talk about something, tried to get [the regulations] better for our own needs. (Moses Nargyak, Uqsuqtuuq [Gjoa Haven], 18 May 1998)

With characteristic patience, persistence, and a sense of time and progress that stood in sharp distinction to the colonizing culture unfolding around them, Inuit were clearly not going to be easily frustrated. The concerns brought to settlement councils and hunters and trappers associations dealt extensively with the imposed hunting regulations. They were in an awkward position. Fearing *Qallunaat* power (particularly that of the RCMP), and lacking control of the administrative mechanisms and the means for providing what had now become essential to settlement living (homes, water supplies, electricity, and other services), Inuit found themselves in dependent relations with those who claimed to be "helping Inuit to help themselves."

It took courage to confront officials with so much power. With few exceptions, confrontation was also not a characteristically Inuit way of dealing with differences of opinion.[34] The prosecutions many Inuit hunters endured between 1959 and the mid-1960s are witness to another form of resistance: refusal to behave in a manner dictated by the totalizing culture whose policies and practices, within even the most Byzantine definitions of liberal democracy, had no legitimacy. Inuit, having had no input into major policies and practices that affected their lives, were only starting to develop a role in mechanisms of ruling – and these were not of their own making.

Frank Vallee (1967), an Ottawa-based anthropologist who had researched and written about the transformation from traditional camp life to Arctic settlements, was one appointed territorial councillor sympathetic to Inuit concerns about hunting regulations. While sensitive to the need for a "new economy," he recognized the limitations of failing to connect a new economy to traditional, much-respected, and highly valued Inuit pursuits.

As noted in regard to musk-ox, Inuit resistance to the hunting regulations was growing. At the same time, doubts about the information, logic, and rationale on which the heavy-handed management of wildlife was based were also developing within the ranks of scientists responsible for the research intended to inform game management policies and regulations. Furthermore, observations of Arctic game populations by Inuit as well as the RCMP and others living in northern settlements did not correspond to the dire warnings issued by the scientists working for the Canadian Wildlife Service. The management regime imposed on Inuit started to fall apart.

Not only was the science used to establish game populations questionable, but also the Canadian Wildlife Service appears to have ignored detailed game reports submitted on a regular basis by RCMP and northern service officers stationed in northern communities. A review of these reports – which number in the hundreds for the period in question – reveals no discernible trend indicating a catastrophic decline in the number of caribou or any other species. Furthermore, while there are reported occasions when the number of caribou taken was regarded as excessive, they are few and certainly do not support the dramatic language of "wanton slaughter" and "extermination" favoured by wildlife officials. While it is impossible to reproduce all of the RCMP and northern service officer reports, the following are illustrative of what was being reported between 1955 and the mid-1960s, when, according to the Canadian Wildlife Service, there was a "caribou crisis," walrus was a species in need of protection, and polar bears were on their way to extinction.

In the Pangnirtung district caribou are found mostly on the West side of Cumberland Sound, inland a few miles between Nettling and Amadjuak lakes and Cumberland Sound. Reports from Cape Mercy and Kivitoo districts were also favourable this year, however, the herds sighted in these districts were smaller than those in the Nettling area. All reports indicate an overall increase over last year. A total of 47 walrus were taken last season compared to 64 last year. In view of last Summer's observations there is no doubt that walrus have increased during the past year. 35 polar bear were killed during the past year compared to 31 last year. There was no increase or decrease in their number during the past year. (Pangnirtung, 1955)[35]

Caribou were present in small numbers in the Padlei areas last fall, and scattered groups were present during the winter in the Padlei, Maguse Lake and Sandy Point areas, these in small numbers. The spring migration moving northward was fairly heavy. Information was lacking regarding the areas west of Padlei, however, everyone concerned seemed to think the herds were plentiful. (Eskimo Point, 1959)[36]

On recent patrols to the northeast end of Bathurst Island numerous caribou were seen scattered in small herds on the high land. At any rate, the calf crop for this year is extremely high and would indicate a great increase in the caribou population for this area. (Resolute Bay, 1960)[37]

The caribou situation in this area is much the same as last year with a slight noticeable increase in the number killed in the Pond Inlet and Igloolik districts and a decrease in the amount killed in the Arctic Bay district. It appears that the caribou have steadily been increasing in the Pond Inlet Detachment area and from all reports seem to be quite plentiful. The caribou are not extensively hunted as none of the natives in the area depend on them exclusively. There was a slight decrease in the number of bear killed in the Pond Inlet Detachment areas during the past year as compared with the previous year. From all reports the walrus are very plentiful in the Igloolik district where they are found in Foxe Basin and around Rowley Island. (Pond Inlet, 1960)[38]

Large herds ranging from 1,000 to 2,000 head were reported sighted during the fall migration period in the Padlei and Yathkyed Lake district. During the months of May and June Caribou appeared again in larger numbers.

There seems to have been a considerable increase in the number of Caribou frequenting this area. Only one Polar Bear was reported shot in this area during the 1960-1961 hunting season. (Eskimo Point, 1961)[39]

I had occasion to spend four days flying in the area bounded by Eskimo Point, Ennadai Lake, Baker Lake and Rankin Inlet, and although we did not sight the main herd which at that time was migrating north, hundreds of small herds of from 10 to 500 animals were seen and it is apparent that these animals are in huge numbers in this area. Mr. Bob RUTTAN, the Canadian Wildlife Service caribou conservationist, who I was assisting at the time felt that the caribou population was more than holding its own and no fears were felt about any decline in abundance of the animals. (Eskimo Point, 1965)[40]

Bob Ruttan, as noted later in the text, was the only CWS official who, at the time, was seriously questioning the conclusions reached by his colleagues. For daring to differ in opinion, he was to be publicly reviled by some of them. The RCMP reports, written by officers who in many cases accompanied Inuit hunters, who kept track of the number of skins traded at the HBC posts, and who could observe local conditions, were ignored.

"Do They Expect Me to Move to Coppermine and Live on Bannock and Tea and Beg This from a White Man?"

While Inuit were struggling to gain some semblance of control over musk-ox hunting, the rationale used to manage caribou was unravelling like an out-of-control school science experiment. Changes to the Northwest Territories Act appeared to have secured control over First Nations and Inuit hunting in the North. Things were not so simple in Manitoba, Saskatchewan, and Alberta, where barren ground caribou spent the winter months. CWS officials were convinced that control over First Nations hunting in the northern prairie provinces was essential to conservation.

In the 1950s, due primarily to the research and pronouncements of John Kelsall and his colleagues, the future of barren ground caribou had become the top policy issue for many Arctic officials. It is not hard to understand why. The Canadian Wildlife Service went out of its way to emphasize the importance of caribou to the northern economy. Walter Laing, a Vancouver businessman, had become minister of the Department of Northern Affairs and National Resources in the Liberal government of Lester Pearson that took office in 1963. In July 1964, Gordon Gibson, his executive assistant, asked the assistant deputy minister to report on the state of barren ground caribou since the minister was receiving correspondence and facing charges from the public that the herds were on their way to extinction. The deputy minister, after consulting with the service, reported that

The barren ground caribou of eastern and central Canada is unquestionably in danger of elimination as an economic asset, though we would hesitate to echo the hopeless attitude that the Minister heard expressed. The importance of the migrant bands to the approximately 30,000 resident humans of the barren ground range is, or has recently been, crucial. Without the caribou, life inland on the central barrens would be untenable, and the progressive decline of the herds from their primitive two or three million, to under 700,000 in 1949, less than 300,000 in 1955, and the present estimated number of 200,000 has been accompanied by starvation, misery and greatly expanded relief in the affected region, the mainland Northwest Territories and the northern parts of Manitoba and Saskatchewan.[41]

The deputy minister's memo went on to place responsibility for the situation squarely on the shoulders of Aboriginal hunters. His memo summarized nicely the figures and convictions that had been driving the Canadian Wildlife Service and government policy since the late 1940s. These convictions had become a mantra, repeated often by civil servants, deputy ministers, and politicians. They had become an indelible part of the lexicon whenever public officials were speaking about northern development. The headlines were familiar and repeated in big-city as well as small-town newspapers: "Polar Bear, Caribou Facing Extinction." The writer of the article with this as a headline went on to note that "caribou herds are shrinking with alarming rapidity. They will become extinct unless trends are reversed in two or three years."[42] The deputy minister, Gordon Robertson, also commissioner of the Northwest Territories, took up the refrain. "We are confronted with a crisis of alarming magnitude for the northlands. We must recognize that there is a distinct possibility that the caribou herds can be wiped out if the situation is not quickly changed," he was quoted as saying.[43] Everyone – including politicians, the deputy minister, government policy makers, and even the general public – had been drawn in. If there proved to be anything wrong with these convictions and prognostications, then many important people – politicians, honourable civil servants, and biologists – would look more than a little foolish.

Backed by this conviction, the government had moved to change the law affecting Aboriginal hunting rights in the Northwest Territories. It attempted to do the same in order to affect First Nations hunting rights in northern Manitoba and Saskatchewan – without success. Changes to the law affecting Aboriginal hunting had first been proposed at a 1953 federal-provincial wildlife conference and had been the subject of resolutions at conferences held thereafter. In 1957, the Administrative Committee on Caribou Preservation of the federal-provincial conference proposed changes to the Natural Resources Transfer Act of 1930 and the British North America (BNA) Act to make it possible for the three prairie provinces to regulate First

Nations hunting. Under the Diefenbaker government, first elected in 1957, the Department of Citizenship and Immigration, with Ellen Fairclough as minister, was responsible for Indian affairs.[44] Fairclough, to her credit, refused to interfere with the hunting rights of treaty Indians. Federal and provincial wildlife officials persisted and, on 15 October 1959, got agreement that certain species deemed to be in danger of extinction would be declared so by federal legislation. As previously noted, this was done by Order-in-Council PC 1960-1256 in September 1960. However, while it allowed the territorial government to restrict Aboriginal hunting, it had no effect on First Nations in the provinces.

In a sessional paper submitted 3 January 1961 to territorial council, the Canadian Wildlife Service claimed, among other things, that in the winter of 1959-60 5,000 caribou were killed in northern Saskatchewan and another 4,500 in northern Manitoba.[45] Taken with other reports and public declarations, it was evident that the service was lobbying hard for greater control of Aboriginal hunting.

In 1961, Citizenship and Immigration, and the Department of Northern Affairs and National Resources, with Gordon Robertson at the helm as deputy minister, agreed to submit to cabinet a proposal to amend the British North America Act (in effect a constitutional change) and the Indian Act so that the prairie provinces could control First Nations hunting. A memo to cabinet was submitted on 8 September 1961 with the agreement of the ministers responsible for natural resources in each of the provinces.[46] Cabinet decided not to pursue the matter. At the time, the case of Michael Sikyea, a Dene and treaty Indian from the territories, charged with shooting a duck contrary to provisions of the Migratory Birds Convention Act, was before the courts. The outcome had implications for the proposal. Apart from that, amending the British North America Act was, at the time, no minor undertaking.

The matter did not end there. Smarting over the outcome, federal wildlife officials and their provincial counterparts looked to other means for solving the caribou problem while not abandoning the legislative initiative. A meeting of the Technical Committee for Caribou Preservation held in Saskatoon on 28 and 29 November 1962 called for resource studies in Inuit and Indian communities where restrictions on caribou hunting were having or could have serious effects on the local economy. The committee encouraged the development of alternative means of livelihood as a way of reducing the pressure on caribou. Once again caribou were seen as more an economic than a cultural resource.

This view was evident from a policy statement put out by the Canadian Wildlife Service a year later in response to a call by Ben Sivertz, soon to retire as director of the Northern Administration Branch, for material to be used in a new policy statement on northern development. The service submitted a statement that identified wildlife solely as an economic resource useful as food, as income for trappers, and as revenue from recreation.[47] In fact, to emphasize the importance of management issues and the worth of its own activities, the service, in its presentations to the territorial council, constantly emphasized the economic value of the resource. For example, in 1965, in a presentation to council, it valued the barren ground caribou at a minimum of $10 million.[48]

Immediately after its November 1962 meeting, a press release was prepared for Minister of Northern Affairs and National Resources Walter Dinsdale. It dealt with the work of the technical committee and addressed the ongoing crisis in caribou management.[49] The release, prepared 11 December 1962, started with an attention-grabbing quotation from the minister: "Compared to humans, wolves are bumbling novices when it comes to killing large numbers of these animals that once numbered in the millions." The remaining text repeated the well-worn numbers used by the Canadian Wildlife Service to suggest that extinction was just around the corner. To add colour to the drama, the minister was quoted as saying "that the Central Arctic herds were once so large that the caribou were referred to by Eskimos as 'land lice'" – a phrase that was still used by Inuit hunters. Once again it was suggested that legislative changes were needed to get things under control, and, while education "to press upon Eskimos and Indians the serious consequences of taking more animals than the herds can produce" needed to be "stepped-up," "it [was] increasingly clear that hunting controls must be stiffened."[50] It was a "Canadian Wildlife Service versus Aboriginal people" announcement.

It went nowhere. A note found on the draft copy prepared by the Canadian Wildlife Service makes the reason clear: "This release was squashed because of objections by Indian Affairs."[51] A letter written by H.M. Jones, director of the Indian Affairs Branch of the Department of Citizenship and Immigration, detailed the reasons: "There is no possible objection to maintaining that there has been over-utilization by humans but I do feel that such phrases as 'wolves are bumbling novices' are not the objective type of reporting one would expect of an official departmental release."[52] Indeed – and a lucky thing for the department. Farley Mowat's book *Never Cry Wolf*, to set off a storm of protest over the poisoning of wolves in an attempt to augment caribou populations and to change long-held public images of wolves, was rolling off the presses. The ministerial release would have given the Canadian Wildlife Service publicity beyond its wildest imagination.

Whatever regulations, policies, and practices were put in place, Inuit largely ignored them. They denied the claims that caribou were on the edge of extinction and explained periodic shortages of caribou in different communities by the fact that caribou changed their migration routes and that their numbers fluctuated periodically, not unlike those of other Arctic mammals. Some RCMP officers, not unsympathetic to the hardship the management regime was causing for Inuit, and frustrated by the edicts they were asked to enforce to protect caribou herds, put pen to paper in explaining the situation. In doing so, they were going well beyond the dry, supposedly factual reporting expected of them:

> While at these Eskimo camps it was revealed that the three families from the first camp and eight families from the second camp were moving to Coppermine or Bathurst Inlet ... the reason they put forth was that a member of the Game Department who resided with the Eskimos at the second camp for a time last summer had told the Eskimos that they must cut their dog teams to seven dogs. These Eskimos feel that it is impossible for them to cut their teams to seven dogs as they have to haul their supplies from Coppermine or Bathurst Inlet a distance of close to three hundred miles. When making a trip for supplies, the whole family has to be taken along, in some cases this means seven people to one sled.
>
> The writer could feel bitterness on the part of the elder Eskimos. The older Eskimos who have lived in this area for the past forty years state that there is no decrease in the number of caribou but only a change in the migration routes. One elderly woman remarked, "do they expect me to move to Coppermine and live on bannock and tea and beg this from a white man?"[53]

But in fact the management regime had exactly this effect. Unable to survive and move about on the land with smaller dog teams, and unable to live with the constant pressure to cut down on their hunting of caribou, Inuit were forced to relocate – for this and other reasons – to settlements where, under the watchful eye of government officials and others, they could be studied, regulated, and monitored.[54] Constable Dwernichuk of the Coppermine detachment showed uncommon insight into this situation and that of Inuit from whom he was supposed to command authority and respect. He even went so far, in his report, to credit Avadluk, his special constable and interpreter, with his ability to understand the circumstances of those about whom he was writing. His observations are worth quoting at length:

> The writer spent three days and four nights at this camp, eating and staying with the Eskimos in their tents. During the second day at this camp, the Eskimos brought to my attention that a member of the game Department had told them that they must cut their teams down to seven dogs and also that they were not to kill more than forty caribou a year. The Eskimos stated that they were not too perturbed about the latter ruling. These two points were discussed with each hunter in his own tent and their views were noted. This matter was not discussed at a general public meeting, if it had been, it is certain that possibly only one Eskimo in this group would have voiced his opinion. The writer does not doubt that these people offered no objection to the seven dog limit to the Game Department officials at a public meeting

of all hunters and gave other frivolous excuses for moving away from this area. It would certainly be unethical for an Eskimo, in his way of thinking to voice an objection to a Government official and more so when they were under the impression that their supplies were brought in free of charge by this Government official. It must be borne in mind that to most Eskimos a Government official is a person to be obeyed.

In summary, six families moved from Contwoyto Lake to Coppermine to resettle. Two families returned, only after being assured that the two rulings [on the size of dog teams and the number of caribou that could be killed] were not mandatory. These people that moved to Coppermine, an area that has always been poor in fur and game, with no proper equipment to hunt and fish with, boats and nets are an absolute necessity, and in an area that already had over a 150 Eskimos scrounging and unable to obtain sufficient native food. Anyone of these people that moved will not hesitate to say and it is a well-known fact that the Contwoyto Lake area is a far better hunting and trapping area.[55]

This quotation makes it clear both that RCMP were under pressure to ensure Inuit reduced the size of their dog teams and that RCMP were reported by Inuit to have killed many sled dogs in the communities to which Inuit were relocating. While epidemics of rabies and distemper affected dog populations across the Arctic, especially in 1960, RCMP officers may have been too willing to shoot sled dogs running loose in communities, not merely because they feared for the safety of children and others – as well as being concerned about the spread of disease – but also keeping in mind the idea that Inuit dog teams were too large and needed to be reduced in size in the interest of caribou preservation.

It was also obvious to Inuit that the law did not apply equally to them and non-Inuit hunters. On 16 July 1960, Don Pruden, a technical officer with the Northern Administration Branch, shot twenty-five caribou near the east end of Baker Lake. A CWS biologist who was in the area and aware of the kill assumed that Pruden had permission to shoot the caribou and decided to do nothing. In the meantime, the same biologist warned an Inuk hunter about what he described as a "wantonly-killed caribou" he found at Aberdeen Lake.[56] It was not until Peryouar, a respected hunter from Qamani'tuaq (Baker Lake), made adverse comments about the killing by Pruden that the CWS biologist decided to pursue the matter further. Moreover, because Inuit were talking about the incident, Sergeant Auchterlonie of the RCMP detachment at Qamani'tuaq decided to investigate.

The killing was regarded as excessive because Pruden and his assistant could not have skinned and gutted twenty-five caribou at that time of year before deterioration of the meat began. The Inuit assistant had apparently advised Pruden of this. Nevertheless, Pruden was not charged. Winston Mair, head of the service, dismissed the case this way:

> Apart from Mr. Pruden's lack of qualification under the Game Ordinance to shoot that number of caribou, unless he had a special permit, the problem is that in July caribou in the area are in poor condition, blowflies are numerous and meat spoils quickly.
>
> It seems regrettable that this incident should have occurred at a time when conservation of caribou is so much to the fore, and in an area where respect for and practice of good conservation are so high. Without in any sense doubting the good motives of Mr. Pruden, one would conclude that he is perhaps not aware of the real seriousness of the caribou problem or the special circumstances surrounding killing for food in the country.[57]

Compare this *wanton slaughter* (the words were not used) of twenty-five caribou with the following case involving an Inuk hunter from the same community.

In October 1964, RCMP Inspector Lysyk, also a member of the Administrative Committee for Caribou Preservation set up between the federal and western prairie governments, sent a personal and confidential memo to David Munro.[58] Lysyk recounted the case of Kallooar, previously discussed, who was charged with abandoning meat suitable for human consumption. Lysyk's version of events was different from that determined by the court to have been true. The reader will recall that Kallooar was found not guilty because his boat had broken down and he had walked to Qamani'tuaq (Baker Lake) for parts. Lysyk's version claimed that Kallooar had killed five caribou near the mouth of the Kazan River south of Baker Lake. He had butchered two of them and loaded them into boats with about seven other hunters. They returned to Qamani'tuaq. Hugh Ungungi, working as a game officer at the time, discovered when he was tallying the caribou that Kallooar had killed five and had left three on the land after removing the tongues. Ungungi investigated, and Kallooar was charged.

Lysyk recounted this version of the case – one considerably different from the official record – to emphasize his point that legislation to control Inuit hunting was an absolute necessity. Given that Lysyk's version was distorted to suit the purposes at hand, and given the difference in treatment afforded Inuit versus *Qallunaat* offenders, it takes no imagination to appreciate the growing sense among Inuit that there was one standard for *Qallunaat* and another for themselves. New forms of the concept of justice – as well as new ideas about injustice and rights – were finding a place in Inuit conversation alongside their well-established and culturally appropriate understanding of these issues.

As noted, contrary to the dire predictions of the Canadian Wildlife Service, throughout the early 1960s field reports from the RCMP and northern service officers stationed in northern communities did not indicate a shortage of caribou, apart from seasonal and some local variations.[59] The reports of northern service officers were similar to those originating with the RCMP. In August 1957, Doug Wilkinson, northern service officer at Baker Lake, reported that "July is usually an excellent month for the Eskimos in the inland country and this year has proved to be no exception. Fish and caribou are reported to be plentiful in all areas. From the areas that we have been getting first hand reports (Kazan River, Ferguson Lake, south west Baker Lake, Aberdeen and Beverly Lake, Back River) indications are that food is abundant."[60] Report after report said the same thing: "Caribou are increasing." "Caribou are just about in the same numbers as they were last year." "There seems to be no shortage of caribou as hunters are having no difficulty finding them this year."

An August-September 1961 report from Don Bissett, a DEW Line northern service officer in the eastern sector, is typical. He noted caribou in the vicinity of Fox 3 station and that Inuit at Ekalugad Fiord were taking fair numbers of caribou. He noted that Inuit located at Fox 5 and Padloping were having no difficulty finding caribou and that an Inuk hunter had reported an abundance of caribou at Freuchen Bay, Palmer Bay, and Blake Bay on the southeastern Melville Peninsula. He did observe that a few areas had less successful hunts, hardly an indication of any "caribou crisis."[61] In the Keewatin, a report filed 5 December 1963 by J.R. Malfair, the assistant superintendent of game, stated that "caribou have, to a certain and variable extent, been available in the vicinity of all mainland settlements this year," and "the majority of hunters in camps at Baker Lake have cached sufficient meat for their winter requirements."[62]

Throughout the 1950s and early 1960s, Henry Larson, the officer commanding the Arctic Division of the RCMP, made sure that CWS officials had the detailed observations of his officers in the field. The overwhelming majority of these reports, as noted, indicated that caribou were not scarce. Commencing in the mid- to late 1950s, the observations of northern service officers corroborated their accounts. But by the early 1960s, the Canadian Wildlife Service was more adamant than ever that there was a caribou crisis. Officers in the field – as noted from the Coppermine example cited above – even went so far as suggesting to Inuit that they had to regulate their hunting and dog teams, even though no law or regulation made it mandatory for them to do so.

There are a number of possible explanations for this behaviour. They include the impact on public consciousness of the 1957-58 deaths by starvation of Inuit at Garry and Henik Lakes and the convenient explanation that a shortage of caribou was the leading cause;[63] the considerable faith placed in science and expertise in the period immediately following World War II; and the inability of wildlife biologists to recognize the severe limits to the science they were practising. Finally, they were likely skeptical about anecdotal reports originating with people in the field who were not trained as wildlife biologists – some of whom may even have been sharing illicit meat with their Inuit neighbours.

Once More Around the Block

When the Liberal government of Lester Pearson came to power in 1963, the Canadian Wildlife Service and its provincial counterparts thought they would have another try at getting in place legislation that would give the provinces control over Aboriginal hunting. C.H. Witney, minister of the Department of Mines and Natural Resources for the Province of Manitoba, approached Arthur Laing requesting the necessary legislative changes.[64] Laing made a formal request to his colleague, Guy Favreau, minister of citizenship and immigration. He sought support for a joint submission to cabinet. Favreau, a lawyer by training, and soon to be appointed minister of justice, was likely well aware of the constitutional complexities involved in the matter. He declined support. Instead, he suggested that every attempt should be made to find alternative resources for those dependent on caribou.[65] The legislative route for protecting barren ground caribou had run its course.

It is important to note, however, the extent to which bureaucrats were prepared to go in an attempt to deal with Aboriginal hunting. Changing the jurisdiction of the provinces was no small matter, requiring an amendment to the BNA Act. The proposal outlined above, as previously noted, originated with Gordon Robertson, deputy minister of the department. In the same month, Robertson was to leave as deputy to become clerk of the Privy Council. This was a repeat performance of his attempts to get around Sissons's rulings in relation to the Royal Proclamation, documented previously. Changing the BNA Act would have amounted to the ultimate use of the law to achieve the totalizing objectives of the state, and Robertson's willingness to go this far, as a senior bureaucrat, should not go unnoticed. This is particularly so in light of another initiative in the late 1960s in which, as clerk of the Privy Council, Robertson played a key role: the introduction of the infamous white paper that proposed changing the status of Aboriginal people within confederation.

Concern over the possible demise of caribou herds didn't hurt the budget of the Canadian Wildlife Service, although officials were still of the opinion that they were seriously lacking in the funds required to do the research required for proper management. Early in 1962, the service launched what was to become a critical study of barren ground caribou headed by Bob Ruttan, a management biologist who had been working for the Saskatchewan government and a member of the federal-provincial working group that met regularly to deal with mutual issues related to wildlife management. The Administrative Committee for Caribou Preservation, part of this working group, had within it a Technical Committee for Caribou Preservation. Ruttan was the CWS-provincial liaison working with this group and became co-ordinator of a new study on the size and composition of caribou herds and of hunting and its impacts. However, unlike others within the Canadian Wildlife Service, Ruttan was anything but convinced that caribou were in decline and that Inuit, Cree, and Dene hunters were guilty of "wanton slaughter." On the contrary, consistent with the observations of the RCMP and northern service officers, Ruttan believed that caribou herds were stable and even increasing in size. These convictions did not sit well with those in the Canadian Wildlife Service with whom he was now working.

To control costs, large-scale aerial surveys were to be replaced with sampling segments of the population.[66] As a tool for management, herd composition data versus total population estimates were to become a source of considerable controversy for wildlife biologists who took the science of game management seriously. In a memorandum of 4 March 1963, Ruttan defended this decision with considerable clarity and in great detail.[67] In his memo, he identified three distinct herds on which studies were to focus: the Bathurst herd, a Saskatchewan herd, and the Manitoba or Keewatin herd – later to be known as the Qamanirjuaq herd.

Criticism of Ruttan's approach to studying caribou was not long in coming. In August 1963, David Munro asked a biometrician working for the service, D.A. Benson, to provide him with a review of the barren ground caribou program. Benson was scathing in his criticisms of Ruttan, including comments on his status within the public service as someone at the "Biologist II level" rather than an experienced Biologist III. He suggested that, while Ruttan "appears to have been given a sound introduction to the Service and to the caribou problem," he then "appears to have taken the bit between his teeth and to have travelled far and wide. He has covered much ground, once-over lightly. The reins, be it emphasized, were not strongly held."[68]

Benson's memo and other documents make a number of things clear. In the first place, the tone of discussion among the men of the Canadian Wildlife Service was very "male." A lot of ego appeared to be on the table with major debates taking place over methods and approaches in which participants were mostly of the opinion that they were "right" and others "wrong." Ruttan seems to have emerged suddenly within the service and to have acquired a considerable responsibility about which others were resentful. Benson criticized him for not paying enough attention to previous work and for not detailing the methods he proposed to use in carrying out his studies.[69] Benson also quoted John Kelsall: "I do not think that any man should start other than narrowly specialized caribou studies without spending at least a year in reading and analysing our previous reports and analogous world literature."[70] Of course, much of this literature, as noted in the previous chapter, was Kelsall's, and the historical record suggests that much of it was well worth ignoring. Reading and digesting it was likely to influence the ideas of people new to the field – and that appears to have been the point. Ruttan's lack of attention to the historical literature was dangerous. It suggested that perhaps Ruttan had a mind of his own and would not be bound by the liturgy that preceded him.

Doubts were also creeping into the debate about the accuracy of aerial survey methods. Another commentator on aerial methods went so far as to state, "as you are aware game agencies throughout Canada use up a lot of aircraft time in making population estimates of large mammals from the air. With few exceptions the results are little better than an educated guess, even though they are about the best information that can be provided under the circumstances."[71]

Other developments were also starting to throw doubts on explanations for apparently low numbers of caribou. To date, Inuit hunting and predation by wolves were constantly cited as factors seriously affecting the size of herds. In November 1964, Ruttan received an interesting letter from Eric Munsternjelm, whom Ruttan had previously met and with whom he had discussed an event affecting the health of barren ground caribou in 1954. Ruttan had apparently sent Munsternjelm a letter asking him to provide more details on the topic under discussion. Munsternjelm was a trapper and a prospector and was working in the Keewatin in 1954.[72] His story went as follows:

> At Chesterfield Inlet and Baker Lake, Caribou were also scarce in June and early July. About the 15th of July they began to appear in greater numbers, though not in large herds. The biggest seen comprised 250-300 animals. Mostly they ran in groups of up to one half dozen and besides there were numerous stragglers. Some of these appeared crippled, they had difficulty in running away when approached. I also saw and smelled a few dead ones. At first I blamed this on a couple of Eskimos who were camped on Quoita River with their families. However, talking to them, they said: "Caribou sick from heat, die!" After inspecting some carcasses and finding no mark of bullets, I realized that some disease had killed the animals.[73]

Munsternjelm went on to describe a conversation with Clare Dent, the RCMP officer at Qamani'tuaq (Baker Lake), who told him of carcasses floating down the Thelon River and that he had also, initially, blamed Inuit. Sandy Lunen, manager of the HBC post, also told him that, during a hot summer in the early 1940s, there had been a similar epidemic among caribou and that thereafter herds of 2,000 to 3,000 were the biggest seen in the area. This, he claimed, compared with numbers that were perhaps ten to twenty times that when he first arrived at Baker Lake in 1926. Munsternjelm was of the opinion that about 30 percent of the caribou in the Keewatin died in the summer of 1954 from the epidemic.

What Munsternjelm described matches the symptoms of an outbreak of brucellosis. Affected animals were barely able to walk, and the disease spread rapidly in warm weather, abating when the temperature dropped. The carcasses were putrid and untouched by other animals except ravens and gulls. However, identification of what was likely brucellosis, a disease capable of reducing barren ground herds by 25 to 30 percent in a single season, had not received any serious attention from biologists with the Canadian Wildlife Service. John Kelsall, the service's caribou expert in the 1950s, paid no attention to the disease. His 1968 book on caribou, still regarded as a definitive work on the subject, dismisses observations such as Munsternjelm's:

> Between 1948 and 1959 there were two isolated instances of unexplained local but substantial caribou mortality on the tundra. Both occurred in summer, and both were reported so long after the event that investigation on the ground was not practical.
>
> Since the deaths occurred over a short period and only in a local area, insect harassment appears to be a possible explanation.
>
> Very similar reports came, from a number of sources, from the area between the lower Thelon River southward towards Padlei and the Hudson Bay coast in the summer of 1954. Again, the event coincided with the height of the fly season. It was local in occurrence and of short duration. In this case, carcasses were found floating in the Thelon and other major rivers, as well as distributed about the tundra. Questioning of white residents and Eskimos at Baker Lake suggested that up to several hundred animals died. (275)

The "several hundred animals" certainly does not sound like the 25-30 percent of the herd estimated by Munsternjelm. Thus, Kelsall dismisses what may well have been a significant factor in caribou population dynamics after World War II. He devotes half a page to the disease – which he doesn't identify – and nearly twenty-one pages to "wanton slaughter" by Aboriginal hunters. Munsternjelm's observations strongly suggested an alternative explanation for changes in herd size. Furthermore, if epidemics of brucellosis were responsible for periodic declines in population, then recovery of the herd was likely given that the disease was not an annually recurring consideration and that numbers did not go so low that removal from the population of animals for other reasons became equal to or greater than recruitment rates.

There was clearly another explanation for the decline in caribou numbers that so alarmed wildlife officials in 1955. If brucellosis was a factor affecting herd size, then the panic that ensued for the next ten years was likely unwarranted. The caribou crisis existed in the minds of those working for the Canadian Wildlife Service, not on the Arctic tundra. Backing away from the science that had defined herd dynamics and that, for decades, had identified Inuit hunting as the prime cause of herd decline would have left a great deal of "egg on the faces" of a great many biologists, not to mention policy makers and politicians. After World War II, the policy makers had placed their faith in the scientific management of game. If Inuit were skeptical, and even angry about the blame placed on them for the fate of barren ground caribou, and if they were not particularly co-operative with the management regime being imposed, they had good reasons. Inuit elders clearly had other stories to tell about the history of caribou – wisdom never sought by those who were now attempting to control what for many Inuit was the most important element of their culture.

Within the administration, a battle was brewing. In another sessional paper prepared for the Northwest Territories Council early in 1965, a titular nod was given to the role of parasites and disease in contributing to what was still regarded as a serious decline in caribou numbers. The paper maintained that "the most important, immediate, single factor contributing to the decline, however, was the excessive human kill."[74] It went on to attribute the problem to the introduction of firearms and the greater mobility of hunters brought about by an increase in dog teams. By 1965, given that dog teams were rapidly being replaced by snowmobiles, this was a curious observation. The study to be undertaken by Ruttan was described as one planned to "enable the Service to present specific management recommendations which will complement recommendations for ameliorating the social problems of caribou-dependent people."[75] The phrase "caribou-dependent" is interesting in this rendition of the problem. It can be read as if Inuit were suffering from some sort of unhealthy relationship with the species and, not unlike someone dependent on alcohol or drugs, in need of treatment.

While the proposed study was never fully carried out, some research was undertaken. The study was to prove an embarrassment to senior CWS officials and others within the northern administration. The results of fieldwork conducted in 1965 by Art Look, assistant superintendent of game, assisted by Bob Ruttan, Hugh Ungungi, an Inuk from Qamani'tuaq, and others, did not support the well-worn line that caribou were in serious decline. The census and segregation count of caribou in the Qamanirjuaq, and what were then called the Saskatchewan herds, produced surprising results. They were far larger than expected.[76]

Look's findings on the Qamanirjuaq herd were cause for concern within the Canadian Wildlife Service. David Munro, chief of the service, asked John Tener, staff mammalogist, to comment on suggestions by Look and by RCMP officers located in the field that caribou hunting restrictions be relaxed. Tener was cautious, not wanting to give too much credibility to Look and Ruttan but not wanting to summarily dismiss the findings either. He recommended that nothing be done until a study of winter range and carrying capacity was completed and that a further aerial survey be conducted the following spring. Some sense of the anxiety Ruttan's work was causing can be found in the following statements from Tener's report to Munro: "If the population is indeed greater than that figure substantially this Service should be the first to be aware of it to protect our professional integrity and to be better able to assess the significance. We must maintain the initiative in caribou research, and in management recommendations resulting therefrom, otherwise we run the risk of having our future advice ignored."[77] A "science" that was supposed to offer disinterested advice to policy makers had become an interest in its own right.

The service had already developed plans for additional studies in the following two years that, after initial conceptualization in June 1965, were further elaborated at a meeting of the Technical Committee for Caribou Preservation in February 1966. In August 1965, Ruttan, frustrated with the politics of the so-called science involved in the studies, resigned. He was replaced by CWS biologist A.H. Macpherson as project leader. Art Look, in a notice subsequently sent to Inuit communities about the research, was described as "kindly helping us when he has time."[78] The proposed studies were extensive, involving survey research, studies of habitat, age and sex composition of herds, and the nutritional and reproductive status of individual animals. The Canadian Wildlife Service approached the northern administration of Northern Affairs and National Resources with a request that information about the proposed studies be conveyed to the chairs of Eskimo councils at Eskimo Point, Rankin Inlet, Chesterfield Inlet, Baker Lake, Whale Cove, Repulse Bay, Spence Bay, Igloolik, and Southampton Island.[79]

The notice, translated into syllabics, was the first time that the Canadian Wildlife Service had bothered to communicate in any official way with Inuit about what it was doing or why. It presumed that Inuit shared the wisdom of the service: "As you know, Caribou became scarcer and scarcer in the 1940's and 1950's, and for that reason you were asked not to waste the meat of the caribou you killed, or feed it to your dogs." It avoided blaming Inuit for the supposed decline in numbers. The notice sought the co-operation of Inuit hunters and advised the reader that some caribou were going to be temporarily immobilized with a drug. It noted that a few caribou would be killed and the meat given to Inuit communities.[80] Inuit were not consulted in advance about any of the study plans, nor is it likely that they shared the wisdom of the service or were particularly interested in receiving as food caribou that had been drugged and killed.

Ruttan, although he had left the service, was not prepared to be quiet. He had taken a job as an instructor in natural resource management at the Saskatchewan Technical Institute. One of his most vocal critics was, not

An aerial photograph of migrating caribou taken by Bob Ruttan and published in the summer of 1966 in *Weekend Magazine*. The photo greatly contributed to growing controversy about the actual sizes of northern caribou herds. The caption accompanying the photograph read "After a decade of decline, Canada's caribou – the big antlered deer family that roams the far north – are reaching toward an all-time high. This photograph by Robert Ruttan, an instructor at the Saskatchewan Technical Institute, Saskatoon, and one-time biologist with the Canadian Wildlife Service, shows part of the 200,000-head Bathhurst herd, one of Canada's three major herds. Ruttan, who tagged 6,000 animals in his research, estimates the caribou population will hit 700,000 this year from 250,000 in 1956. This presents a danger to the caribou, faced with over-population and meagre food supplies. Ruttan argues that only drastic measures – immediate and large-scale reduction of the herds by systematic hunting – can save them from another decline and a big loss of food for Eskimos and Indians, whose lives very often depend on them." *Weekend Magazine* 16, 31 (July 30, 1966): 14-15.

surprisingly, John Kelsall, who, Ruttan was quick to point out, had not been involved in caribou research since 1957. Kelsall was in the process of publishing his well-known book on caribou biology. In a newspaper article published in the *Globe and Mail* on 8 August 1966, Kelsall was reported as saying that Ruttan's numbers were too high and that the population in the area was 400,000 to 500,000.[81] This was a strange response from an employee of the service given that only a few months earlier it had been advising the territorial council that the numbers were likely about 200,000. The service had clearly been "rattled" by Ruttan's research, and even Kelsall was "hedging his bets."

Publicity about Ruttan's research didn't stop there. In the summer of 1966, *Weekend Magazine* – carried in many newspapers across the country – featured a double-page aerial photograph of a densely packed herd of caribou, with a caption that quoted Ruttan as saying that the number of caribou in the territories had increased to 700,000 animals.[82] Ben Sivertz, commissioner of the Northwest Territories, wrote to David Munro asking for a brief report on caribou in light of Ruttan's claims.[83]

John Tener, the deputy director, drafted an interim reply. Tener again played it safe. He acknowledged that there had been an increase in numbers and added that this was "a situation we have all been working toward and one which we very much welcome."[84] How he could make such a statement, given that the additional work planned by the service had not been completed and that there was no data to back it up, is unclear. In fact, in the same letter, Tener notes that an aerial survey was planned for 1968. Despite spending much of the rest of the letter undermining Ruttan's conclusions, Tener nonetheless seems to have accepted that Ruttan's observations made more sense than those advanced by the service in communication with the territorial government a little more than a year earlier. Tener, in responding to Sivertz, was involved in "damage control."

In September, after the publication of his spectacular photo, Ruttan also published an article in *Country Guide* magazine.[85] He stated that even his estimate of 700,000 was conservative. While maintaining that there was a decline in population in the 1950s, he claimed that a series of mild winters between 1963 and 1966 had contributed to recovery of the herd. However, he expressed concern over the availability of food on the winter range, much of which, in the northern prairie provinces, had been destroyed by fire in the previous ten years. With it had gone the lichens on which caribou feed. Ruttan expressed fear that overgrazing could lead to another population crash. His solution? A large-scale reduction of the herds by managed hunting.

In October, David Munro provided Ben Sivertz with a more detailed response to his enquiry about the status of barren ground caribou. Munro noted that claims had been made that there were 150,000 caribou in the Keewatin District alone. In countering the claim, he noted that the work carried out by the service to date indicated that there were only 30,000 animals in the district and that calf survival was poor.[86]

Ruttan's article in *Country Guide* continued to plague the service. G.W. Malaher, director of wildlife for the Manitoba Department of Mines and Natural Resources, wrote to Munro on 8 December 1966 asking that the Canadian Wildlife Service do something to rebut the article and noting that

Dr. Joseph Showman of the National Audubon Society was using Ruttan's photos and ideas in lectures given across the country.[87] The service responded by preparing a statement to be issued by Arthur Laing, minister of Indian affairs and northern development.[88] The long and rambling release was not likely to be an attention grabber. It bent over backward to boost the credibility of the service. It went nowhere. The draft contained a statement that the Manitoba-Keewatin herd had increased little, if at all, from the late 1950s, when it was believed to number about 35,000 animals.[89] The service was again lucky. Had the statement been released, the service would soon have been forced to eat its words.

Ruttan was also speaking about caribou management. Reports of his lectures were filtering back to the service. On 14 December 1966, he spoke at the University of Saskatchewan as part of a panel discussion sponsored by the Musk-Ox Circle. Other panelists included Bob Williamson, at the time a member of the Northwest Territories Council, and CWS biologist R.S. Miller. J.B. Gollop, who reported his observations back to David Munro the next day, also attended the meeting. Ruttan argued that the estimate of three million animals in 1900 was wrong, that Banfield's estimate of about 700,000 animals in 1949 was also wrong (too high), and that Kelsall's estimate of 250,000 five years later was also incorrect.

The discussion was a good one, and even Miller admitted that the estimate of 30,000 animals for the Qamanirjuaq herd (which compared with Ruttan's 1965 estimate of 157,000) was suspect. He went on to state that "the methods were not sufficiently accurate." Ruttan made the case for a proper survey and suggested that the Canadian Wildlife Service stop trying to defend its data from the early 1950s. A member of the audience, Mr. Ziolkoski, an employee with the City of Saskatoon, suggested that, if the Canadian government could not provide resources for proper aerial surveys, perhaps the US Air Force could do the job! Ruttan argued that his management plans, "shot down by his fellow scientists and mathematicians" as not being feasible, could prevent wastage of a resource that was worth $1.5 million in meat and hides alone. While Ruttan's numbers differed from those of the service, his logic and approach to management issues were not always sharply different. The economic value of the resource and the size of the herds were his concerns on this occasion. What were different were his numbers and his willingness to pay attention to the observations of permanent residents of the territories.[90]

The idea that Inuit traditional knowledge might contribute to understanding the situation was not yet acceptable and had not even occurred to the biologists. Bob Williamson, the first person to represent Keewatin Inuit on the territorial council, made comments that reflected the frustration he had gathered from his Inuit constituents. He noted that the Inuit population at

Baker Lake and elsewhere in the eastern Arctic was increasing at three times the average Canadian rate, that half of these people were on relief, and that annually more caribou were passing nearby than they could possibly use. In another piece of correspondence reporting on the meeting to the regional superintendent of the service, Gollop suggested that Ruttan came across as sincere, knowledgeable, emotional, and having as his first interest the best use of the resource. He also suggested that the audience was left with "a very poor impression of the Wildlife Service – an agency that refused to accept new figures and was slow to do anything constructive itself."[91]

Thereafter, things got nasty. Kelsall, as the tone of his text on caribou suggests (see Chapter 2), was not a man to be wrong about anything. He'd had enough of Ruttan's criticism. In a letter to David Munro, he chastised the service for being too modest about its caribou research. He argued that there was no reason why the service should feel even slightly apologetic about things or why it should try to be so defensive in responding to Ruttan. Ruttan was quoted – or misquoted – by NWT councillor Duncan Pryde as advocating an annual harvest of caribou worth $8 million. Pryde proposed an organized hunt by Eskimos – many of whom, he observed, were living on welfare – and suggested that the meat could be frozen and sold to nearby settlements. He proposed that a freezer be installed in an Arctic coastal settlement to handle the meat. In response, Kelsall copied the article to David Munro with a memo entitled "Mush-Brush and the Caribou (Continued)." He suggested that, as an alternative to putting a man in Yellowknife (which the service was considering at the time), it should employ Ruttan as a resident wildlife watcher on Borden Island,[92] a remote and desolate island, one of the Queen Elizabeth group, in the High Arctic. This memo was followed in April by a letter to the editor of the *Drum,* published in Inuvik, and the *News of the North,* published in Yellowknife, in response to articles published in March. Kelsall was furious over remarks reported to have been made by Ruttan. He outlined the work of the "competent scientists" working for the Canadian Wildlife Service and continued that,

If, like Ruttan, you choose to ignore this source of expertise and consider it a " ... mess, of emotional fiction interwoven with just enough fact to lend it an air of authenticity," that is your privilege, but you do scant justice to the facts or to the caribou. If you read or inquire you will find that the scorned experts are genuinely interested in the maintenance of the largest possible numbers of caribou, and in their full economic use by all northerners.

I object to the personal vilification inherent in the first of Ruttan's articles which you published. He says: "Most of the information that has been made public on caribou management and research in the Northwest Territories for the past twenty years has been the work of authors who knew little or nothing about caribou." He further categorizes the work as "not worth the paper it's written on." Presumably I am the major, if not the only, target for those remarks since I have authored, or co-authored 11 publications, 13 major reports, and numerous short reports on caribou since 1949.

Kelsall went on to suggest that constructive criticism and dialogue were welcome on any aspect of his work and that Ruttan had "publicly babbled about data that shows that the experts are wrong, but he has yet to publish his methods and data in a form that will permit full and systematic judgment by his peers, or any objective person."[93]

This piece of vitriol was copied to Bob Williamson and John Parker, deputy commissioner of the Northwest Territories. Williamson, besieged with complaints from his Inuit constituents about the restrictive game laws, nevertheless responded to Kelsall with a letter of support. Meanwhile, the territorial council was growing increasingly impatient with the failure of the Canadian Wildlife Service to provide it with facts and figures useful to policy formation. Meeting at Resolute Bay in November 1967, at its thirty-third session, it passed resolutions that called deplorable the fact that after seventeen years of limited research the service was not in a position to state the condition of, extent of, and prospects for the Keewatin caribou herd; that called on the commissioner to have a game management officer in each of the administrative regions of the Arctic and that the Keewatin manager be based in the region and not in a southern province; that called on the commissioner to amend the game regulations to permit caribou hunting in the Coppermine and Bathurst Inlet areas; and that called for better co-ordination of wildlife research and management.[94]

By July 1969, the results of the two-year survey of northern caribou herds were in. They were no more conclusive than any previous survey research. In presenting them to John Tener, J.E. Bryant, director of the eastern region of the service, placed so many caveats on the results that "guesstimate" once again became the only fair way to characterize them. Bryant, without justification, suggested that the figures used for losses due to hunting of the Beverly herd be increased by 2,000 from 5,830 animals.[95] However, while the results did not correspond with Ruttan's figure of a total population of 700,000, they moved significantly in his direction. They suggested a population almost double that of the figure used by the service in its brief to the territorial council in 1965. The total of all herds – the Qamanirjuaq, Bluenose, Bathurst, and Beverly – was estimated at 385,872 animals. If the herd had indeed increased from 200,000 to almost 400,000 animals in three years, the recruitment rates suggested by the latest research made little sense. Wildlife officials continued to insist that mortality, including that from hunting, particularly in the case of the Qamanirjuaq herd, was so severe that the incremental increase was negative. Yet, if the increment was negative, how did this herd double in size from the estimated 30,000 animals determined as a result of fieldwork in 1966 to 63,372 animals by 1969? It was a question that conveniently went unanswered. Counting caribou was clearly a fool's game in which Inuit had no part and the results of which they were no longer willing to tolerate.

On 3 October 1966, a young Inuk from Coral Harbour, Southampton Island, visited John Tener at the Canadian Wildlife Service. In his own words,

They were trying – you know – Coral Harbour – my hometown was [trying to get the game laws changed] every year. I remember my uncle, Sandy Sateena – he has another big boat too – a Peterhead boat, based in Rankin – on the beach now. He used to – he believed the government. "Next year the wildlife regulation for prevent[ing] ... hunting is going to be lifted at Coats Island." Every year, every summer, he heard that. Every summer he waits for the wildlife regulation to lift on Coats Island. And every end of the fall – he's my favourite uncle – he's a guy much younger than my father. He's a guy I would ask questions directly, which I won't ask to my father. He'd say, "They said they were going to lift the caribou regulations. It still didn't happen!"

So that's when I went to Ottawa, I mentioned that to Ralph Ritcey, you know. This is a genuine concern of my people! I went in to see the director of wildlife. He [Ritcey] arranged it. I remember talking to him – the wildlife director. His name was Mr. Tener ... I went to see him in his office. That was my first political mission. Literally. And I told him about it, and the

Tagak Curley.
Photo Frank Tester.

following – I think it was right at the following fall session up in Resolute – the caribou hunting was lifted finally ... Here they didn't know – they didn't know how to consult with the people. (Tagak Curley, Iqaluit, 14 May 1999)

"They didn't know how to consult with the people." But Inuit such as Tagak Curley were about to make sure that *Qallunaat* learned how to consult with Inuit. The content of this exchange was passed on to the director of the Canadian Wildlife Service, David Munro. In a letter to Ben Sivertz, Munro acknowledged that the issue of caribou hunting on Coats Island had been raised with the service since 1961 and that, given the growth in the population, the service had recommended to the territorial council on a number of occasions that some hunting be allowed.[96] However, it appears that the northern administration had advised council against this as it planned to move caribou from Coats Island to Southampton Island, where herds had long since been depleted. This, however, had not happened. In the meantime, hunters such as Sandy Sateena were constantly frustrated – a caribou herd that had overpopulated Coats Island offshore from Southampton Island and the community of Salliq (Coral Harbour), boats to get there, and limited recognition by state actors that they had a right to hunt. Articulating this as a *right* was just beginning to happen.

Salliq was not the only community to have requested that changes be made to game regulations. Tagak Curley was not the first Inuk to place a community's concerns before government officials. In fact, Curley, the son of a well-known Inuk, Joe Curley (Kayakjuak), and part of a family with a history dating back to the days of whaling at Fullerton Harbour, had listened to a growing chorus of complaints from Inuit hunters throughout the Kivalliq region (Tagak Curley, Iqaluit, 14 May 1999).[97] Since the court cases of the late 1950s and early 1960s, Inuit – as well as First Nations across the country – had increasingly focused on hunting rights. These rights and relations with animals were, for Inuit, not just a matter of access to a "resource" with – as the CWS biologists understood it – economic value.

What most Canadians failed to appreciate in the 1950s and 1960s was that the relationship Inuit had with animals was the "glue" of Inuit culture and not something that could easily be replaced by a different set of institutions. Changing the relationship between Inuit and animals and supplanting this relationship with one that used Western science to manage them as an economic asset posed a threat to Inuit culture that struck at the core of Inuit existence.

But at the same time, many other changes were taking place that posed threats to and opportunities for Inuit culture and traditional ways of living, including the move to settlements; the introduction of formal, Western education; the fact of living in a house; and the organization of settlement councils, hunters and trappers associations, and co-operatives. Attempts by the state to change the relationship of Inuit to wildlife played a critical role and to some degree provided a foundation for many of the other changes. It was a relationship that was instrumental in defining what it meant to be Inuit. It is therefore not surprising that anything that challenged Inuit relationships with animals and the land on which they depended was likely to be met with original and passionate responses. It is to some of those responses that we now turn.

Part II
Talking Back

5
Inuit Rights and Government Policy

From Game Management to Inuit Rights

The officials whose job it was to put into policy and practice whatever implications emerged from the information provided by scientists acted as if they were operating in a constitutional *terra nullius* with respect to Inuit. They ignored the possibility that Inuit may have possessed Aboriginal rights. The doctrine of Aboriginal rights in Canada has a venerable lineage, though in recent years, especially after entrenchment of Aboriginal rights in the Canadian Constitution of 1982, it has gained significant new attention from scholars (see Borrows 2002; Macklem 2001). It is not our intention to review this well-trod ground, but a few words are in order. The notion of Aboriginal ownership of land is often thought of as the foundation of Aboriginal rights.[1] This notion can be traced as far back as the writings of Spanish theologian Francisco de Vitoria (1532) and the Papal Bull of Pope Paul III, *Sublimis Deus* (1537), which acknowledged Aboriginal land ownership.[2] Early land purchases between settlers and Indians in the seventeenth and eighteenth centuries confirmed the notion that Aboriginal peoples had land ownership, but these sales were often fraudulent, leading to a British attempt to regulate them through the Royal Proclamation of 1763, which established that Aboriginal title to land could only be surrendered to the Crown. The proclamation is referred to in Canada as an Aboriginal Magna Carta and is reaffirmed in section 25 of the Constitution Act, 1982. Although there is much debate about the meaning of the proclamation, it clearly acknowledged Aboriginal land ownership, established the notion that the highest level of government should be responsible for dealing with Aboriginal issues, and in limited ways acknowledged that Aboriginal peoples (at least "the several Nations ... of Indians, with whom we are connected") were sovereign nations.[3]

At least the first two, though arguably all three, of these principles were reaffirmed at the moment of confederation through the British North America Act of 1867, section 91(24), which said that "Indians and lands reserved for

Indians" were a federal responsibility. Whether such responsibility implied a trust-like obligation or simply a matter of jurisdictional authority was arguable until the Supreme Court of Canada determined the former view in 1984.[4] Although in the first six decades following confederation the notion of Aboriginal rights was a fixture of Canadian law – leading to the negotiation of the western Canadian treaties, clauses in the Rupert's Land purchase (1870), and the various provincial boundary extension acts and Natural Resources Transfer Acts that acknowledged a need to protect Aboriginal rights, titles, or interests – from the 1930s on support for Aboriginal rights waned. Using its jurisdictional authority, the state passed an Indian Act that became the critical tool for Indian policy making; although some early Indian legislation contained protective measures that reflected a notion of Aboriginal rights, these measures were increasingly ignored or dropped from the Indian Act as it evolved into a dramatically repressive piece of legislation in the late nineteenth and early twentieth centuries.[5] The treaty process stopped short of completing the surrender of Aboriginal title in Canada, particularly in the Far North and British Columbia.[6] Talk of Aboriginal rights ceased to play a significant role among government officials until four decades later when the confrontation over the white paper of 1969 and the *Calder* case in the Supreme Court of Canada forcefully brought the question back to the forefront of policy making.[7]

Inuit were in the unusual position of having been excluded from the Indian Act and of being constructed as subjects of government policy at the low point of recognition of Aboriginal rights. As we documented in *Tammarniit* (Tester and Kulchyski 1994, Chapter 1), their status in confederation was a question that reached the Supreme Court of Canada, which, in a 1939 decision, determined that Inuit were Indians within the meaning of section 91(24) of the BNA Act (see Kulchyski 1994). Hence, after 1939 responsible civil servants could have asked logical questions about who owned the land in the Arctic, which rights the Inuit had as its original occupants, and which policy alternatives such a view might have generated. Instead, in keeping with officials working with Indians, the tendency was to insist on Inuit status as Canadian citizens and attempt not to repeat the perceived mistakes that had been made with Indians by separating Inuit from the mainstream. Yet Inuit had to be regulated, and to do so they had to be singled out: the position was contradictory and unstable. As knowledgeable an individual as Dominion Anthropologist Diamond Jenness, whose first fieldwork had been with Inuit, favoured a range of policies that ignored or utterly dismissed Inuit rights,[8] so it is perhaps not surprising that most government officials did the same.

This chapter reviews the struggle over the emergence of Inuit rights. A regime had been established that had little compunction about its ability to regulate hunters as if they were entirely subject to common law. Its confidence was underwritten by the authority of a science that was not as disinterested as the policy makers presumed. Much of the Aboriginal rights jurisprudence in the middle of the twentieth century dealt with hunting rights and particularly the ability of provinces to limit Aboriginal hunting rights in the face of treaties designed in large part to protect them. The regime was established and pushing ahead with increasing steam, as the first episode in this chapter, regarding the suppression of cultural practices, documents. The emerging regime did not have an empty playing field to work with, however: it was briefly derailed by a judge who, as a loyal subject of the Crown, had happened to read the Royal Proclamation of 1763, likely in a search to find any support in law that would give him sufficient reasons to side with Inuit in the cases brought before him. The two chapters that follow this one focus more directly on Inuit articulations of their concerns at the time: Chapter 6 reads closely the minutes of the first Inuit community council in Baker Lake, while Chapter 7 examines a variety of Inuit petitions to government, from a number of communities, also in the 1950s and 1960s. While the issue of hunting rights is a thread that weaves its way through these chapters, of necessity we have widened the perspective somewhat to look at Inuit rights more broadly and Inuit concerns more generally.

Arviat: Outlawing the Drum

On 6 January 1958, Farley Mowat wrote to the commissioner of the RCMP because he had "encountered reports and rumours concerning the RCMP detachment staying at Eskimo Point which, to say the least, were most disturbing." Mowat believed that "the reputation and standing of the Force in the vicinity of Eskimo Point and Padlei had suffered severely." He also noted that "the informants – and they were numerous – unanimously insisted on anonymity on the grounds that they feared reprisals" and that, since he had "satisfied [him]self that these fears were perfectly genuine," he would "respect their desires." Mowat copied his letter to Ben Sivertz of the Department of Northern Affairs and Natural Resources. Among the serious complaints listed, the following appeared as the third of five: "During the summer of 1958 a drum dance was being held in a tent occupied by a family of the [names withheld] who were then at Eskimo Point under the direction of the RCMP. The Cpl. i/c the detachment had apparently warned the [name withheld] that drum-dancing must cease. When his order was not obeyed he entered the Eskimo tent, without permission, seized the drum from an old person and broke it over his knee."[9] The "old person" from whom the drum was "seized" would today be called an elder. The story told by Mowat is still remembered vividly by members of the community and remains well known in the region.

For example, Guy Alikut, who still lives in Arviat, while speaking about Corporal Gallagher, told the story as an illustration of how poorly Gallagher treated Inuit:

Bill Gallagher, he was the officer here. He used to treat, like, Inuit like dogs! Dogs! ... Like, uh, there, there was one time, a drum dance with, just, uh, down from the RCMP, where they are right now. Down on the beach? Apparently, he didn't like the beat of a drum or something like that. He didn't want people to gather in one place, do [a] ceremonial thing or something. He went down to try to rip our drum. Everybody was just scared like, so they, and, so that, that's Inuit's way. Even, uh, we were afraid of, uh, Hudson's Bay clerks, like eighteen-year-old clerks. We thought they are all big [leaders], eh? ... He tried to rip the skins. Couldn't do that, so somebody gave him a knife. He started, he used the knife to rip the skins. Every, by that time, somebody blew out ..., somebody blew out the candle. It was dark now, so everybody just went out, uh, where, where the, like, just lift the tent, eh? Never mind the entrance! Everybody just took off, eh? (Guy Alikut, Arviat, 29 May 1997)

David Serkoak, now living in Iqaluit, is the son of the man who was drumming that night (Mickey) and still has vivid memories of the event, which we asked him about directly:

I think it was just like he [played] in the drum dance organized by the community elders who wanted [to] share with the new people, make friends, learn their songs, etc. ... [It took place] the following spring or summer [after the relocation to Arviat], because we arrived not in midwinter or for spring ... Yeah, it was just a regular drum dance ... We were allowed to [meet] other Inuit in Arviat ... They ... also like to drum dance, so they organize to have a drum dance. I don't know if that was their first time or second time. Nothing went wrong; either [there was a] complaint to the police, or the police got tired of hearing music, chanting, sounds of drums, I guess. Only the police can tell that ... He come, stop the dance, and break the drum. And also injured my father, who was standing at the time, a very tiny man ... Some of the men, who were in a traditional formation to dance, were in the background. The lady singers in the front were like a [round] shape or a circle. When the incident happened, the men at the back ... left at the back of the tent ... The people who were there left the tent that way. Some went to [another place on the land]. I remember that time, people hide behind the rocks. I remember my mom and dad, anyone with clothes on, in case they had to go out again ... People from Arviat still remember the incident ... I guess I know how I felt at the time. I guess probably scared. The way that my dad was scared. My mother was scared too. But you cannot hear a complaint from my dad. He's very quiet. He was not, he never tells stories about it in public ... [After that, it was] just business as usual. Every day dealing. Because we were still under the care of the RCMP, government ... (David Serkoak, Iqaluit, 27 May 1999)

And what interesting "care" it was. Although Inuit were not subject to the Indian Act (which only applied to status Indians), a piece of legislation that in earlier form deliberately banned two prominent cultural practices (the sun dance of the plains and the potlatch of the Pacific coast), Inuit on the ground were nevertheless faced with a variety of assaults on their culture that had much the same effect.[10] In Arviat, that meant practising the drum dance far enough away from the community so that the local government officials would not know it was taking place. This tactic created a somewhat paradoxical situation since part of the meaning of the drum dance is its celebration of the bond of community itself. Having to leave the community to "follow the drum" can be seen as a difficult and contradictory practice, especially since on some level the drum speaks to the fact of community. In this instance, Inuit culture went underground to preserve itself. The state had a measure of success in driving the drum dance underground not because it had established legislation that deliberately and explicitly attacked Inuit cultural practices but because it had a whole series of policies, policy objectives, plans, personnel, structures, materials, and forces whose overall effect was to attempt to displace or marginalize Inuit culture and to replace it with the dominant culture. A key weapon in that arsenal was the "scientific" knowledge regarding animal populations that, as we have seen, justified the state in constraining Inuit hunting practices. It could do so with impunity to the extent that, in the period in question, in spite of knowledge to the contrary, it acted as if the Inuit did not enjoy any Aboriginal rights, which might have acted as a legal ground to protect their economic strategies as much as their cultural and spiritual practices.

The emergence of Inuit rights was an Inuit response, a ground from which Inuit could take back some of the power over their lives that the state had assumed or at least limit the application of state power. Tracing the emergence of these rights through the 1950s and 1960s is therefore critical in showing how Inuit responded to the regime that had, particularly through management of hunting practices in the name of wildlife conservation, come to position itself as all powerful in the North – so powerful that one of its minor officials felt free to defend his sleep by attacking and insulting a whole community. What follows traces the legal discussion that took place through the late 1950s and 1960s regarding Inuit rights. In many of these instances, it was an Inuk whose actions, violating this or that regulation and putting herself or himself at risk, provoked the discussion.

Inuit Citizens: "The Drinking of Beer Commends Itself to Us"

As noted earlier, Inuit had legally been recognized as Aboriginal peoples who were a federal responsibility since 1939 as a result of a Supreme Court of Canada case known as *Re: Eskimos* (see Tester and Kulchyski 1994, Chapter 1). Although the government planned to appeal the decision to the Judicial Committee of the Privy Council in England, the war intervened; in the postwar period, it could not reassemble the federal legal team familiar with the case. After 1949, the Supreme Court of Canada became the highest arbiter of legal matters, making an appeal untenable. However, it is clear that officials with responsibility for Inuit were not inclined to see them as Aboriginal peoples with special rights and did not want to apply to Inuit the policies that seemingly had failed Indians. Hence, Inuit were not included in and indeed specifically excluded from the Indian Act when it went through a critical revision in 1951. The implications of *Re: Eskimos* were narrowly interpreted in an administrative sense to mean that the federal government had jurisdiction over Inuit, with carte blanche over how that jurisdiction was applied. Yet the issue of Inuit rights continued to emerge through the late 1950s and 1960s, particularly around hunting issues but also in relation to liquor consumption, land rights, and a broader range of rights that might be associated with Inuit as Aboriginal people. Government officials deliberately blinded themselves to the notion of Inuit rights, dealing with specific issues as they arose and trying, with decreasing success, to keep Inuit leaders away from the idea.

The general formula or approach that was used is articulated in a letter of 11 June 1956 from Frank Cunningham, then director of Arctic affairs, to R.H. Chesshire of the Hudson's Bay Company. Chesshire had been concerned about five Inuit from Cambridge Bay who had died as a result of drinking methyl hydrate (used as fuel for primus stoves). He reasoned that if they had had legal access to alcohol they would not have been making "home brew," and hence the tragedy could have been avoided. Cunningham noted that "the Council [of the Northwest Territories] favoured the removal of discriminatory legislation and regulations in matters of this kind." Their reasoning was that, "while it is true that a primitive people may suffer disadvantages and even injury because they have access to liquor, it is more of a disadvantage to them to be denied the opportunity to learn responsibility for their own conduct both as individuals and as groups." In effect, some of the paternalistic reasoning that partly influenced the broader establishment of Aboriginal rights, as vehicles to protect Aboriginal peoples, was being deployed here. And the archival record shows a consistent concern in this period with the removal of discriminatory barriers that impeded Inuit equality rights. In that context, there could hardly be much sympathy for a notion of positive discriminatory rights such as Aboriginal or Inuit rights. Cunningham also noted that, "constitutionally, it is within the power of the Northwest Territories Council to give full liquor privileges to Eskimos, but insofar as Indians are concerned, any action must be initiated by the Department of Citizenship and Immigration under the Indian Act."[11] There was concern that removing barriers for one group in communities where there were both Indians and Inuit would create special difficulties. But Cunningham's statement is a bit disingenuous: the territorial council had powers respecting Inuit because it was a federal creation, and in fact it was up to the federal government to deal with both Inuit and Indian liquor privileges. It could choose to deal with one group through the Indian Act and the other through territorial legislation, but that was a matter of its own administrative choice, not a matter of constitutionally specified devolutions of power. The *Drybones* case, which reached the Supreme Court of Canada in 1969, dealt with this issue as it pertained to Indians by determining that the provisions in the Indian Act were discriminatory (see Eber 1997, 155).[12]

It would take more than two years for the issue to be resolved. On 5 November 1958, Ben Sivertz, director of the Northern Administration and Lands Branch, wrote to the deputy minister an extensive and broad-ranging memorandum under the heading "Eskimos and Liquor." The memo is interesting because it involves a substantive argument around Inuit equality rights and is clearly directed toward ending social discrimination: "The greatest objection to the present regime is the social distinctions which it creates." Sivertz had his eye on the broad, critical question of Inuit social status:

> The next few years are crucial in fixing the position of the Eskimos in the new social patterns in the Arctic. They can become accepted socially and work towards a position of easy equality with whites, both learning from them and educating them. On the other hand, they can become, like the Indians, or native peoples elsewhere in the world, a second-class race in the eyes of the whites. In these circumstances they might be well treated, but never equally treated ... There is all too great a possibility that the Eskimos will unconsciously be regarded as very decent people but a race apart, a race whose aspirations no one treats seriously.[13]

The memo draws on the historical experience of Greenland in trying to legislatively contain Inuit alcohol consumption and of South Africa in establishing an apartheid regime that legislatively discriminated against a majority of its citizens. Sivertz proposed "that all Eskimos in the NWT be permitted to consume beer in public taverns and that all restrictions governing their use of beer, in private messes or in clubs licensed for the purpose, or at home, be removed," and he took the ethical high road in doing so, arguing both that "we do not think we are morally justified in permitting the continued deterioration of the present social situation" and that "the drinking of beer commends itself to us, particularly because it is a relatively temperance [sic] drink."[14] The proposal involved a continued ban on Inuit consumption of "spirits," and lifting the ban on beer was seen as an intermediate step. The concluding paragraph is particularly telling:

> This proposal is with regard to Eskimos, and it leaves the status of Indians unchanged. There is no way of accomplishing the objectives I have described under the Indian Act. I do not think we should delay this desirable action with respect to Eskimos on account of the arguments that may apply in a similar way to Indians, but about which we are unable to do anything. Parliament has not passed an Eskimo Act, – presumably because they think none is needed. I agree, and hope there will never be an Eskimo Act. By the same token, I believe there is no reason for any discriminatory legislation pointed at Eskimos on liquor or any other subject by any level of government.[15]

Well-intentioned as this approach was, it nevertheless left little room for the possibility of positive discriminations of the sort embodied in the concept of Aboriginal rights. More troubling, the movement away from social distinctions could also be part of the process of moving away from social differentiation, from the continued existence of a distinct culture: Sivertz was squarely in the camp of those who would promote the wholesale assimilation of Inuit. That approach is even more starkly revealed by a handwritten note and drawing at the end of the memo, agreed to with a check mark and signature by none other than Gordon Robertson, at that time also acting as commissioner of the Northwest Territories. The note read, "I am in complete agreement with this memo. I know Council wants to see no discrimination between Eskimos and Indians, but if we must have a fence, I prefer to see it thus." The note goes on to represent Inuit-Indian-white relations through two drawings, each with two columns, one a "wet side" and one a "dry side," separated by a barbed wire fence. The first drawing shows "Whites and Eskimos" on the wet side, "Indians" on the dry, as preferred to a second drawing showing "Whites" only on the wet side and "Indians and Eskimos" on the dry side.[16] Inuit might be an Aboriginal people, but the consensus among senior officials in the Department of Northern Affairs and Natural Resources was that they would be brought onto the non-Aboriginal side of the divide: legally, socially, and presumably culturally.

The issue of alcohol consumption is of interest in itself (see Brody 1983, 61, 196; Eber 1997, 153-54). Many of the Inuit we talked to for this study made comments about the problems alcohol abuse had created in their communities and about their efforts to deal with it. For example, Aime Ahegona described how having money as a young man created opportunities: "Money makes big changes. Some people, they use it wisely. Some people use it the other way. And, um, so 'it's up to you now to do what you want to do in your life.' And even worse, when I turned twenty-one, I was allowed to drink. 'Now you can drink if you want. Now it's up to you. It's legal now.' You know? So when you're told again by the same people that taught you English, English had to be it. You're told again about the legal rights that enforces your power. Power!" (Aime Ahegona, Kugluktuk, 27 May 1998). It is of some interest that Ahegona made the connection between alcohol consumption, rights, and power. Simonie Michael, whose name appears later in this chapter as the first Inuk elected to the territorial assembly, said that,

> When there were more white people coming into the town, that's when there was more alcohol and even before 1961, well before that date. But in 1966, '67, '68, um, since I was the local Inuit leader, I did write to the commissioner and did want the commissioner to start closing down the liquor store ... In the year 1966 and [1960], that liquor store had closed because there were a lot of problems that were arising from alcohol. So I did write to the commissioner, and the people decided to have a vote on this, and the majority won. And so since the majority decided that the liquor store should be closed, [ever since] it has been closed. But it was open to the other communities, not Iqaluit. (Simonie Michael, Iqaluit, 14 May 1999)

No sooner had Inuit received the "right" to drink than at least some of the leaders appear to have agitated to have the "right" restricted.

The follow-up memorandum from Deputy Commissioner Brown to Robertson as commissioner was written on 21 February 1958, just a few months later. The issue of separate provisions governing Inuit and Indian drinking was about to be resolved by amendments to the Indian Act. If the territorial government could pass matching legislation respecting Inuit, then a coherent regime would remain in place, with both Inuit and Indians gaining the "right" to drink through the appropriate, different legislative mechanisms. The concern expressed in this memo is that the whole section purporting to regulate Inuit drinking might be legally challenged: "Recently we received an opinion from the Department of Justice to the effect that the amendments to the Liquor Ordinance which were intended to restrict the privileges granted by Section 95 (2) of the *Indian Act* are *ultra vires*. As I recall, the Justice opinion is based upon the view that the Council does not have power to enact legislation dealing specifically with Indians and Eskimos, and I may say that I am in agreement."[17] That is, any legislation or legislative regulation would be seen as legally discriminatory and could be challenged. The recommendation made by Brown was to pass the law, which reduced discrimination by allowing beer consumption but not consumption of "spirits," and wait for the outcome of any legal challenges that might appear. This was the approach taken. In effect, the administrators placed themselves in a contradictory position. They were in favour of removing discrimination against Inuit and clearly in favour of establishing a regime that did not follow the legislative approach taken to Indians. But they wanted legislation to regulate Inuit and did not want to remove that legislation all at once. The perspective became clearer when other issues became threatened by the spectre of rights.

In general, where the notion of special rights was raised, officials moved quickly to suppress it. A letter from C.K. LeCapelain, then chief of the Mining and Lands Division, to R.A.J. Phillips is a telling case in point. The letter concerned the issue of Inuit as employees of prospectors – that is, not their Aboriginal rights but their citizen rights. Yet LeCapelain, in a memorandum of 29 August 1957, wrote to "suggest that you do not use the word 'rights' in the phrase 'to safeguard the rights of the Eskimos' in the second last line of your draft letter. The word 'rights' is liable to misinterpretation as meaning the rights which the Eskimos may have to mining land. I believe it is the opinion of some people that the Eskimos have special rights to mineralized areas in the Arctic somewhat along the lines which the Indians would have to similar rights on Indian reserves. Actually, the Eskimo has no such right." LeCapelain gave no basis for the claim that "the Eskimo has no such right," a view that history has proven wrong. He went on to "suggest that you use some other word such as 'safeguard the interests' or 'welfare' or 'wellbeing' of the Eskimos."[18] The word *right* was itself to be banned from the lexicon of administrators, a dangerous concept that would potentially lead them down a slippery slope.

The issue of mining and potential Inuit ownership – the slippage between Inuit employee or citizen rights on the one hand and Inuit ownership, land, or Aboriginal rights on the other – continued to confuse administrators. It was also a source of confusion for Inuit: how could it be that the land they had lived on for so long was in some way no longer theirs?

> We have the [Chantrey] Inlet, Back River area, I was raised in that area. I thought it belongs to our group of people. That, that's our tribe, if we were tribes, I guess. But, yeah, that's our own area, that's our own land. And then Gjoa Haven, that's where Netsilik people are living, so it belongs to Netsilik people. Not to anybody else, but to, uh, the, uh, you know, each an individual person, not just one person owns the land, but those groups of people own that area. That's their own territory. That's what I thought. I didn't know it ... belonged to somebody else [laughter] ... Like the queen [laughter] ... In those days, I thought the people ... owned that area, ... their territory. That Back River area belongs to the people, the [Chantrey] people, the [Chantrey] Inlet people! I didn't know anybody else from outside the country owns the land [laughter] ... Now, I don't think about that. I don't think like that anymore. I know I don't own the land now [laughter]. I'm, I'm told. (Moses Nargyak, Gjoa Haven, 18 May 1998)

A memorandum from Commander Henry Larson of the RCMP dated 12 September 1957, less than two weeks after LeCapelain's, was titled "Rights of Eskimos, Employed by Prospectors and Others in the North" and noted that "the rights of Eskimos in regard to mineral discoveries that they may make, constitutes quite a problem." Larson argued that, since prospecting was liable to increase, some kind of a plan would be necessary to deal with Inuit employment in the sector. He thought that "the most that could be expected for the Eskimos employed by them to stake claims, is a percentage of the subsequent value of the claims."[19] But he thought of this as an arrangement that would take place because the companies usually could not afford wages – that is, it indicated compensation for their work, not a belief that Inuit were entitled to a percentage of ownership on a claim because of their land title. The boundary between the two became difficult to sustain. Larson's memo provoked a small flurry of activity in the Northern Administration and Lands Branch, with Phillips writing a memo of 24 September to the director that began, "we have been giving considerable thought to the problem of the protection of the interests of Eskimos who stake claims on behalf of prospectors," adding that "the basic question is whether they should be given some pay other than their hourly or daily wage." After some consultation of a "guidance paper" prepared by the Mining and Lands Division for northern service officers (hardly a division that could be expected to have insight into the legal status and rights of Inuit), Phillips concluded that "Eskimos cannot expect to benefit from the claims other than by the immediate payment for services rendered, or by the eventual benefit which comes from the opportunities created by mining."[20]

However, concerned that this was not enough, Phillips left an opening: "Before I resign myself to that conclusion, I would like to be certain that we have explored every possible avenue for a workable arrangement of Eskimo benefit sharing," calling for a meeting on the subject. A handwritten response in the margin of the original document (the response dated 25 September) from Sivertz quickly closed the door on other possible benefits to Inuit: "I do not feel hopeful of any result such as you have in mind and I must confess that I cannot see a very strong case for such a result on any grounds of equity and just dealing in the eyes of the law of this land, – and no special case that appeals strongly to me. However, if you wish such a meeting I shall be glad to attend."[21]

Whether or not the meeting took place, the tone was quickly and clearly established and the policy of suppressing or ignoring the possibility of Inuit rights reaffirmed by the time Phillips replied to Larson, on 31 October 1957, a reply that reveals the general approach to Inuit rights taken at the time:

> We have given this problem a good deal more study. We have been conscious of the fact that probably in no other part of Canada are the local residents

at such a disadvantage in participating in local staking ... It is unfortunately true that much land will be staked in the Arctic before the Eskimos are able to take a genuine part in this activity. On the other hand, it would be very difficult to apply some special regime for Eskimos while resisting claims for particular treatment for residents of other remote areas in different parts of Canada. We have also concluded that quite apart from the extremely complicated administrative considerations a system of special Eskimo rights in claims might be a real discouragement to prospectors whom we are seeking to attract. A final point is that if an Eskimo were to gain some right in a claim, there might well be a good deal of sharp practice in obtaining these Eskimo rights. In conclusion then, we have decided that the benefit which the Eskimo gains from staking activity must be restricted to the wages which he is given at the time, and to the economic advantages which flow from the development of the area concerned.[22]

This is a striking set of admissions. Phillips clearly had a general sense of state responsibility for Inuit (a responsibility that had a legal basis in the fact that Inuit were constitutionally in the same position as Indians, a fact well known to all since the 1939 decision) and certainly evidenced genuine concern for their well-being. He also demonstrated an intricate understanding of the issues on the table: the whole of the North would likely be claimed by newcomers, leaving Inuit without ownership interest in the mineral wealth of their homelands. Yet Phillips refused to distinguish between Inuit and other isolated, rural Canadians. That Inuit are original occupants did not seem to occur to him or, if it did, could not be articulated because it put one on the terrain of special status that officials had a paramount concern to suppress.

At virtually the same time as these discussions were going on around mineral rights, Percy Moore, director of Indian and Northern Health Services, was also writing to Sivertz, as director of the Northern Administration and Lands Branch, to express concern over escalating Inuit demands for health services. Moore wrote on 29 October 1957: "As you know, one of our difficulties is the widespread but completely false belief among most Indians, from the needy to the well-to-do, that they have a statutory right to free medical and hospital care and can therefore demand service. It will take a great deal of patient explanation over many years to correct this misunderstanding. Naturally we are anxious that this misunderstanding of our position should never gain a foothold with the Eskimos. Medical and hospital care is not something they can demand as a right." Moore noted that the various ways in which health services were paid for could certainly lead to confusion among Inuit: "With Indian Health Services providing free medical care for Eskimos leading the native way of life and with the employed Eskimos getting medical care for 'camps' and the DEW Line – either in exchange for monthly 'insurance' deductions at source (that they may not understand) or perhaps free of charge, I would not be surprised if most of them honestly believe that medical and hospital care is FREE to all Canadians." The danger that seemed to present itself to Moore was a desire among Inuit to wantonly avail themselves of the comforts offered through health services. He wrote that the Inuit "sees aircraft whisk his sick relatives off into the skies. He hears tales of the soft beds, white man's food, gadgets, medicines and personal service." Moore proposed that a pamphlet, with appropriate Inuktitut translation, be prepared and distributed to explain that Inuit did not have a right to health care, thereby catching any misapprehensions before they could spread and become a movement. Once again, the categorical certainty – "medical and hospital care is not something they can demand as a right" – and the emphasis on refusal were positioned as a bulwark in a complicated and confusing situation. Health care was provided through a number of avenues, but something had to be done to ensure that people did not come to expect it as their right: that avenue was unacceptable. Interestingly, in Moore's account, other First Nations were equally without such a right, whatever their views on the matter.[23]

A document dealing with the provision of welfare, titled "Eskimo Welfare" and dated 21 March 1958 (on another page, the document is dated 24 March 1958), appears to have been written by Walter Rudnicki. This document is striking because it contains something slightly less than the categorical denials of the existence of Inuit rights of the sort that were becoming a litany. Rather, the strategy deployed in this account is to indicate the source of welfare relief through one or another legislative authority that would apply to Canadians in general. The document also shows that officials were well aware of the 1939 legal decision:

> Although it has been ruled by the Supreme Court of Canada that the term "Indians" was intended to include Eskimos under the British North America Act, the subsequent Indian Act expressly excluded Eskimos from its provisions. The Eskimos, therefore, are not legally wards of the Federal Government, although this Department and its predecessors in the administration of northern affairs has assumed a broad, ever-increasing responsibility for Eskimo Welfare. In the Northwest Territories the various social security programmes, to which Eskimos are entitled as other Canadians, are administered by the Federal and Territorial Governments ... An important objective in the rehabilitation programme is the encouragement of self-help and self-support among Eskimos in hospitals whose conditions prevent them from taking up the rigorous life of the Arctic again.[24]

The general thrust of this perspective was, again, to emphasize that there were no special programs being developed on the basis of special rights. The categorical or definitive denial of rights discourse here was deployed in a more limited, but still firm, fashion – "the Eskimos ... are not legally wards of the Federal Government" – though it is possible to detect some uneasiness, an opening perhaps, in the end of the same sentence – "this Department ... has assumed a broad, ever-increasing responsibility for Eskimo Welfare." Perhaps this is why the statement on promoting self-support concluded the section, to mitigate the concern that "a broad, ever-increasing responsibility for Eskimo Welfare" would likely provoke. But the intervening, seemingly benign, sentence is also critical, referring as it does to "the various social security programmes, *to which Eskimos are entitled as other Canadians*, ... administered by the Federal and Territorial Governments" (emphasis added). Again, here, the attempt was to ensure that social assistance and welfare services were not offered because they were owed, were not a response to constitutional rights, but were provided as they would have been to any other Canadian through the normal channels.

In the waning years of the 1950s, in the areas of land (mineral) rights, health care services, and welfare services, there was an attempt to articulate a position that ensured Inuit were treated as citizens without any special rights. But the position was incoherent and unstable. Inuit at the time were discriminated against through a number of federal and territorial provisions: they were marked out legally as Aboriginal peoples. Hence, for example, they did not have access to alcohol even when their non-Inuit neighbours had such access. They did not have the same voting rights as non-Inuit. Certainly, officials were concerned about this discrimination, and a serious effort developed in the next decade to end it.

More problematically, no less a body than the Supreme Court of Canada had already clearly established that Inuit were in the same constitutional position as "Indians." Officials scrambled to interpret the judgment in as narrow a fashion as possible, but it lurked on the horizon as a threat that had to be countered at every turn. The word *rights* itself was banned from their lexicon. It could not be casually used for fear that it would be misinterpreted. For fear that their actions would be similarly misinterpreted, Inuit had to be educated about their lack of (medical) rights. The strength of the categorical statements on an issue of law made by administrative, medical, and social work authorities betrayed the strength of the concern among these authorities to repress, suppress, deny, ignore, or contain any claim that Inuit might have special rights as first occupants that would match their special status as Aboriginal people. This became a litany, a mantra, to be repeated with a degree of stridency that came to match the degree to which the position became increasingly untenable. This position fully accorded with the idea that Inuit hunting practices could be controlled because they had no special rights even in that arena. The notion of an undifferentiated equality was deployed here as a powerful totalizing tool.

Inuit Rights: "Tread Softly, for This Is Dedicated Ground"

In the decade between 1959 and 1969, the problem became more complex. Inuit began taking advantage of their rights to protect themselves when charged with hunting offences. Officials struggled to remove any form of discrimination as on the ground the varieties of discriminatory practice expanded. This proved to be a particularly vexing problem when it came to the issue of alcohol consumption. Meanwhile, in other regions, the talk of Aboriginal rights was growing, and officials understood that it would soon spread to Canadian Inuit but worked to contain and delay it. Finally, non-governmental organizations began to use the language of Aboriginal rights more forcefully just as the federal government, at the end of the decade, proposed a final termination of rights through the infamous 1969 white paper. Inuit leaders from Canada ultimately became increasingly forceful and began to rely on the language of rights as officials made last-ditch stands to defend the position that there were only equality rights for Inuit. The irony, of course, is that the state did have a special responsibility to Inuit and should have been the one institution that took Inuit rights seriously. Officials had known about the parameters of that responsibility since 1939. Instead of fulfilling its constitutional mandate to protect Inuit rights, it worked ceaselessly though increasingly against the historical grain to be the key institution that denied rights. As early as 1959, it began to encounter serious opposition.

A draft article by Bill Willmott, an anthropologist under contract with the Department of Northern Affairs and Natural Resources, attached to a letter he wrote to Graham Rowley on 17 January 1959, clearly expressed the contradictory nature of the policy on Inuit rights: "NANR policy is neither consistent nor clear. This is probably due to a contradiction within the terms of the Department itself. On the one hand, Northern Affairs considers the Eskimo as equal to other Canadians in every way and therefore deserving everything that other Canadians have access to. On the other hand, the Department was established on the assumption that the Eskimos are not equal, but need special protection which other Canadians do not receive – protection from social and health problems that might destroy them because of their isolation and underdeveloped technological condition."[25] Willmott wrote that "it is not my purpose to argue this policy. Obviously there is truth on both sides and their resolution will always be a problem," and he went on to show how it was confusing at the ground level, in the communities, by using the example of minimum wages applied to Inuit. His point in the latter regard was again conveyed using an "on the one hand ... on the other" approach: "On the one hand, Eskimo have a right to a wage in line with other Canadians; on the other, they need special privileges no other group of Canadians gets: preferential hiring," which created problems, not least of which because "agents felt that Eskimo labour, which is not as yet motivated or controlled by the same cultural conventions as workers in the south, was not worth $1.45 an hour, and also that wages at that rate would cause problems among the Eskimo themselves." Willmott did not specify what those latter problems were. But the clear problem he did specify among the "agents" was that "they also felt that if they were to pay that high they should have the right to hire whomever they chose, such as white men who were willing to work in their spare time, or workers from the south."[26]

The general tone of Willmott's essay is interesting. Much of the paper involves a call for an attitude of humility among government workers: "Humility in relation to the Eskimo means being willing to learn from them. It means showing respect for their culture, which is indeed a wonderful thing. It means, as an important beginning, learning the language as quickly as possible and using it as often as possible instead of an interpreter."[27] Certainly, this was an appropriate message for an anthropologist to deliver to civil servants. The comments on the contradictory nature of the policies themselves seem to go as far as permitted: it would have been hard to find an ear had Willmott advocated for Inuit rights, but he could get some attention by showing the incoherence of the dominant approach. His plea for cross-cultural understanding was timely. Many a human misery might have been avoided had it been given greater attention at the time it was made. If his essay lifted the lid a crack to expose a problem with government policy in January 1959, within a few months Justice John H. Sissons would blow the lid off entirely.

As noted in Chapter 3, on 20 April 1959 Justice Sissons rendered a decision in the NWT Supreme Court in the case of *R. v. Kogogolak.* There we touched on the case and on several of Sissons's other decisions because of the roadblock they represented to the emerging set of wildlife and hunter management policies. Our concern here is with the manner in which the decision also opened up the broader question of Inuit legal status in Canada. The decision, which quickly received attention from the media, reads like a manifesto on Inuit rights. Sissons began by noting that, "traditionally, this is the land of the Eskimos – the Innuit, i.e., – the People (par excellence) – and from time immemorial they have lived by hunting and fishing."[28] This is one of the few places where the term "Inuit" is used in official records prior to 1970. Noting that the *Re: Eskimos* decision "was a unanimous decision of a strong court headed by the Right Honourable Sir Lyman Duff, Chief Justice," Sissons understood that "the Supreme Court of Canada has held that Eskimos are 'Indians' within the contemplation of Section 91 (24) of the British North America Act ... and under the exclusive legislative jurisdiction of the Dominion."[29] Sissons also quoted the Royal Proclamation of 1763 extensively, arguing that "this Proclamation conserving the hunting rights of the Indians has been spoken of as the Charter of Indian Rights. It is the *Magna Carta* of the Eskimos. Indians have their Treaties. Eskimos have none. Indians have the Indian Act. This Act does not apply to Eskimos. There is no Eskimo Act. This Proclamation is the only Bill of Rights the Eskimos have as Eskimos. They seem to have nothing else. What they have is extremely important and far reaching, and must be guarded and upheld by the Court."[30]

Among the most wide ranging of Sissons's arguments, somewhat beyond the boundaries of the case at hand but certainly compelling when read in historical context, was the following:

> I think the Royal Proclamation of 1763 is still in full force and effect as to the lands of the Eskimos. The Queen has sovereignty and the Queen's Writ runs in these Arctic "lands and territories." This is the Queen's Court and it needs must be observant of the "Royal will and pleasure" expressed two hundred years ago and of the rights Royally proclaimed. The Queen's Justice is a "loving subject" and would not wish to incur "the pain of the Queen's displeasure." The lands of the Eskimos are reserved to them as their hunting grounds. It is the Royal will that the Eskimos "should not be molested or disturbed in the possession of these lands." Others should tread softly, for this is dedicated ground.[31]

The conclusion of the decision makes for equally compelling reading:

> There has been no Treaty with the Eskimos and the Eskimo title does not appear to have been surrendered or extinguished by Treaty or by legislation of the Parliament of Canada. The Eskimos have the right of hunting, trapping, and fishing, game and fish of all kinds, and at all times, on all unoccupied Crown lands in the Arctic. This right could be extinguished or abridged and the Eskimos could be prohibited from shooting Musk-Ox or Polar Bear or Caribou but this would have to be by legislation of the Parliament of Canada. The Game Ordinance of the Northwest Territories cannot and does not apply to the Eskimos. I find the accused Not Guilty.[32]

It was as if a group of seals that had been happily basking in the sun on an isolated ice floe suddenly found a polar bear in their midst. The 1959 decision presented a clear, well-argued position that was entirely opposed to the policy of the government and to the predisposition of the policy makers. Moreover, the repeated claims documented above that Inuit had no rights were made by administrators, medical officials, and welfare officials, without formal legal training. Their opposition was a lawyer and judge. And the words of the lawyer and judge were quoted extensively by newspapers, including an *Edmonton Journal* front-page article headlined "Judge Says Eskimos Not Bound by Laws Protecting Musk Ox."[33] Furthermore, the suggestion that we, Kulchyski and Tester, are holding officials to a standard around Aboriginal rights common in the later twentieth century but not widely held in the middle part of the century is entirely belied by Sissons's work: a clearer articulation of the legal source and value of Inuit rights was forcefully made in 1959.

Close attention to the reasoning behind the state's response is also warranted here. Within two months (18 June 1959), a meeting of the key players in northern administration – Sivertz, Phillips, Stevenson, Hunt, Bolger, Mitchell, Bennett, Loughrey, Rudnicki, and Tener – was held to discuss "what steps the Department should take with respect to Judge Sissons's ruling that the Northwest Territories Game Ordinance does not apply to Eskimos."[34] Needless to say, there was not much interest in letting Inuit know about the decision and the possibility that they might have unceded Aboriginal title to their traditional lands. The meeting was chaired by Ben Sivertz but appears to have been dominated by the only key administrator not present, Gordon Robertson, who wrote a memorandum for the meeting that was read to all present by Hunt. Clearly, the administration was not going to change course:

> Mr. Robertson stated that it was the opinion of the Justice Department that an appeal would probably not be upheld by the Supreme Court. In Mr. Robertson's words, the Department "will have to muddle through" until an amendment to the Northwest Territories act can be passed by the Federal Government, the amendment to allow the Territorial Government's game and other legislation to be applicable to all Eskimos. It was pointed out that at present all game laws in the Northwest Territories are inapplicable to Eskimos. The question of Eskimo entry into the Thelon Game Sanctuary was raised and it was concluded that it is doubtful if Eskimos can be prevented from entering the Sanctuary and shooting muskoxen.[35]

The fact that the decision raised some fundamental questions about the department's whole policy respecting Inuit does not seem to have been discussed, even though officials recognized that Sissons's decision was legally accurate and not likely to be overturned. The minutes of the meeting do not record any attempt by any of the participants to consider how a policy could be crafted that would be based on the legal position Sissons had articulated – a policy, that is, based on affirmation of and respect for Aboriginal rights of Inuit in Canada. Instead, it was business as usual: find some technical way to get around the roadblock in their path. If Sissons insisted that only the federal government could legislate hunting restrictions for Inuit, then get the federal government to use its powers to grant the territorial government jurisdiction, and hopefully Parliament would pass these amendments within a year. Problem solved. Except that the problem lingered, and the threat posed by Inuit rights continued to grow. But now they grew in a context where the actors had access to a clear, articulate, legally binding statement of Inuit rights. In Chapter 4, we followed the cat and mouse game played by the department in relation to Sissons's attempts to legally protect Inuit hunting rights. Here we follow the work of the administrators who tried to contain the damage.

The next day Alvin Hamilton, minister of the Department of Northern Affairs and Natural Resources, wrote to Ellen Fairclough, the minister of citizenship and immigration, the departmental home of the Indian affairs branch, "to discuss control of Indian hunting by legislative means."[36] The concern in this memorandum was with caribou hunting and with Indians rather than Inuit, but the sweep of the changes contemplated would clearly affect Inuit hunting and fishing rights. Near the outset, Hamilton "took cognizance of the fact that a Joint Committee has been established to review the whole problem of Indian rights in Canada," which meant that any immediate action would have to be co-ordinated with the expected broader policy. After outlining three alternatives, all involving changes to Natural Resources Transfer Agreements that had been negotiated with provincial governments, Hamilton concluded that "it would seem a waste of our deliberations if we did not endeavour to make our decisions respecting the hunting of caribou as wide in their application as is possible."[37] No comprehensive strategy emerged in the immediate years, though the eventual white paper ("Statement of the Government of Canada on Indian Policy, 1969") certainly made recommendations in line with those contemplated in this exchange (see Weaver 1981).

By early 1960, the broader implications of Sissons's ruling had sunk in. A 13 January 1960 package of materials relating to meetings between Northern Affairs and the Federal Electric Corporation included a letter from Alex Stevenson to John J. Navin, the secretary and counsel of that body, which referred to a parallel ruling and noted that "the decision was not appealed and this now means that an Eskimo in the Northwest Territories is entitled to the same privileges under the Liquor Ordinance as a non-Eskimo,"[38] spelling out in some detail what this meant in terms of alcohol purchase and use. Stevenson also mentioned that "the special references to Eskimos in the Ordinance will eventually be removed by an amending Ordinance."[39] What is striking about this correspondence is the manner in which officials appear to have taken Sissons's judgment and turned it on its head. Instead of moving more forcefully in the direction of recognition and enactment of Aboriginal rights for Inuit, the senior administrators accepted the narrow logic that the Northwest Territories Council could not develop separate legislation for Inuit unless enabled by federal devolution of powers. Therefore, any territorial legislative provisions that discriminated for or against Inuit would be removed. Effectively, the administration would continue along the path it had charted, except that, prodded by judicial obstacles, it would move more quickly to remove any legislation at the territorial level that specifically and exclusively applied to Inuit. And, where Inuit may have had special hunting rights, they would be denied those rights through federal legislation and specific federal empowerments of territorial legislation (see the discussion in Chapter 3).

Sissons himself, in his memoirs published in the late 1960s, had a clear sense of what was at stake and how the government attempted to work around his ruling. He noted that "Section 17 of the Northwest Territories Act was amended by adding this: 'All laws of general application in force in the territories are, except where otherwise provided, applicable in respect of Eskimos in the territories'" (1968, 121). He also observed that section 14 of the same act had been amended to ensure that the commissioner could not "make ordinances restricting Indians or Eskimos from hunting for food ... other than game declared by the Governor-in-Council to be game in danger of becoming extinct" and further that, within a short time of the amendment having been passed, the governor general through an order-in-council was "pleased to hereby declare musk-ox, barren-ground caribou and polar bear as game in danger of extinction" (121). In Sissons's view, this effectively meant that Parliament was "seduced into repealing" the Royal Proclamation of 1763. Dorothy Eber notes that Sissons was "furious" about the amendments, which, "he later contended, were slipped through a sleepy Parliament in the dog days of summer" (1997, 86). But Sissons was not deterred and took every opportunity at his disposal to use his court to advocate for and protect the Aboriginal rights of Inuit. And the issue of rights could not be so easily legislated into oblivion. It continued to haunt the policy makers. Robertson's statements to Eber to the effect that "I don't remember any difficulties or problems with Judge Sissons. It's a long time ago and it may be that my memory is faulty. I'm not saying there weren't any but I don't remember them" (13) cannot help but strike us as somewhat disingenuous.

Business as Usual: The "Alleviation of Social and Economical Equality"

In late 1961, the Committee on Social Adjustment in the Arctic met for the second time, and among the issues it discussed, according to the minutes, was "Alleviation of Social and Economical Equality [sic]."[40] The typographical error in this heading is telling: no doubt the committee wanted to "alleviate inequality," though in this context it may well have served Inuit better, given the way equality rights were being deployed, had officials actually looked for ways to "alleviate equality." The extensive discussion at this 27 December 1961 meeting particularly involved Neville, Phillips, Doctors Willis, Mooney, and Wiebe, as well as a few others. The discussion was opened by Willis, then general superintendent of Northern Health Services, who "painted a word picture of the Eskimo being waited on at the bar and restaurant at a place like Inuvik. This, he submitted, was one of the few chances the local residents had to feel equal. He stated that these premises were in contrast to the shack-town conditions where the local residents lived. He thought that anything which tended to bring two cultures together was a mark of progress. Differences in the level of housing [were] an indication of a lack of progress."[41]

There seems to have been no reflection on the fact that this divided world had been created by the colonial practices of the state itself, in the name of that same "progress." There was no real effort, of course, to bring "two cultures together"; rather, the process that would be "progress" in that realm involved repression of one culture, that of Inuit, so they could be absorbed into another, that of the administrators. Equality was still going to be the basis of policy making and was still the underlying value of the policy makers.

Tracing the lineaments of the conversation at this meeting is revealing. After this opening "word picture," Neville, the superintendent of welfare, "stated that there were a number of concrete inequalities such as housing, the inability to compete for better jobs because of the lack of education and the consequent lack of equal opportunities. He submitted that these were the types of inequalities which contributed to excessive drinking." Both Willis and Neville began by referring to a series of inequalities but tended to bring the discussion around to the problem of alcohol consumption. This quickly became the focus of the conversation: thirteen of the twenty minuted entries deal with drinking. Willis replied to Neville by suggesting that "drinking was an indication of status seeking"; then a concerted effort was made to turn away from the topic of drinking, with Neville suggesting that "the causes were inseparable and that we should be concerned with listing inequalities to determine how they applied and attempt to suggest what could be done about them," which would seem to be the purpose of having the item on the agenda. After a few more comments, Mooney, a consultant in psychology, noted that "the problem being discussed was a classic problem confronting social scientists" and went on to suggest "that alcohol was perhaps not the problem but rather one of the symptoms of deeper emotional disturbances. He thought that we might recognize other symptoms if we diverted our attention from alcohol for a while."[42] His suggestion was not heeded; the conversation quickly devolved back to the issue of drinking among Inuit.

Soon after Mooney's intervention, Wiebe, a regional superintendent with Northern Health Services, argued that there was a "breakdown of community structure forcing people to function in a cultural vacuum. Stratification was not peculiar to the north but it was equally real in more advanced cultures,"[43] with Vic Valentine and Staff Sergeant Coombs challenging the notion that social stratification was the main source of alcohol abuse by referring to other jurisdictions, the latter noting that "stratification was a fact in rural and urban society." Wiebe eventually clarified his position: "Problems had arisen not so much as the result of social differences or repression as to the current breakdown of Eskimo society," though there was no reason for him to point out that the "current breakdown" was a direct result of the whole administrative approach or policy trajectory at the time. The discussion then turned to questions about the high incidence of alcohol offences in the community of Frobisher Bay before the following statement closed discussion of this item: "The Committee agreed that a sense of inequality appeared to have been a factor in causing people of the North to resort to the excessive use of alcohol, but that the change in society was a more important factor than the character of the society itself. The problem would be solved by economic betterment from which would flow social equality and stability."[44] This attempt to tie together the two opposing strains of argument – was excessive drinking by Inuit a result of their being at the bottom of a new social hierarchy, or was it a result of the disintegration of their culture? – with the compromise that both were factors, though cultural change more so, could become sensible only by attaching the final, inevitable statement that would resolve all contradictions: "The problem would be solved by economic betterment." Every day, in every way, things will get better and better.

The discussion is useful because it illustrates how, after Sissons's decision, the department was able to maintain a "business as usual" approach. Obviously, there were real problems emerging in northern communities around the social divisions created in part by the presence of non-Inuit administrators and others in the "helping" professions. The administrators and medical personnel who were making decisions chose to see "cultural disintegration" as an inevitable process beyond their control rather than as something they were actively contributing to. There would be no thought given to using Aboriginal rights as a vehicle for cultural revitalization. Rather, attention would continue to focus on ensuring the greatest degree of equalization between Inuit and *Qallunaat* possible, of finding a way to reduce social difference. Struggling to achieve an equality that many of their own policies and practices strongly mitigated against – after all, many of those at the top of the hierarchy in northern communities worked for the same departments – had established itself firmly as the basis, incoherent as it was, of policy.

Toward Political Agency: "This Is Something We Should Watch Very Closely"

The situation, from the perspective of officials trying to contain the talk of Aboriginal rights, continued to deteriorate. The December 1961 issue of the newsletter of the Association on American Indian Affairs featured a story called "The Eskimos Speak," basically a report on a conference held in Point Barrow, Alaska, planned and conducted by "Eskimo leaders" "on Native rights" a month earlier. The "Statement of Policy and Recommendations" coming from the conference was basically a manifesto of Inupiat rights, called Inupiat Paitot. It began, "we the Inupiat have come together for the first time ever in all the years of our history."[45] Among the passages underlined by Northern Affairs officials who read the newsletter were several that pertained to Aboriginal rights. The Inupiat stated that "we found that we have two problems with our rights, which are special. One is the Migratory Bird Treaty with Canada and Mexico." The policy statement made consistent, forceful mention of Aboriginal rights, many of which were underlined by Canadian officials who read the report closely, as in "our Inupiat right to own the land and minerals of our ancestors, to hunt and fish without restrictions over this land and the sea."[46] And the statement includes a section on building the capacity to defend Inupiat rights; the last section is called "Organization" and suggests (again underlined) "that a self-supporting organization be recognized by this conference and pay small dues toward the cost of another conference ... This organization should be well established, not to be allowed to die."[47]

Gordon Robertson passed the report of the conference on to Graham Rowley, who gave it wide circulation. In the 29 January 1962 covering memo sent by Robertson, he said, "the views being expressed here are probably the sort of views the Canadian Eskimos will be putting forward within the next few years."[48] It was certainly a prescient comment, though Robertson was far from urging that these "views" be supported, and his staff held similar predispositions. Vic Valentine, a researcher with the department, had already, three days earlier, written to Rowley about the report: "You may recall that I sent you a copy of the last issue of this newsletter some time ago. I think it extremely significant that the Eskimos held this kind of conference to discuss their grievances. I was aware that many of the Indian groups in Canada and the United States are trying to form national movements but did not realize the Eskimos in Alaska were attempting to do the same thing. This is something we should watch very closely."[49] Inuit in Alaska who started organizing themselves to protect and promote their Aboriginal rights would be among the signatories to the Alaska Native land claim ten years later. Canadian Inuit in the eastern Arctic would have to wait until the 1990s for a comprehensive land claim settlement.

One of the more thoughtful responses to the newsletter report is contained in a letter that Sivertz wrote to Professor F.C. Toombs, of the Ontario Hospital Department of Psychiatry, on 20 February 1962. Toombs had sent a book to Sivertz on community development issues among Pueblo peoples in the American southwest. After an extended commentary on the book, in praiseworthy terms, Sivertz "was interested to note the small and virtually insignificant degree of hostility encountered." He added, "the kind of hostility that I think remarkably absent is the 'aboriginal rights' cry which we hear nowadays from leaders of Indian people and which is encouraged by some of their white advisors in schools of anthropology here and there."[50] Far from feeling any responsibility as a government agent to fulfill the constitutional mandate of protecting Aboriginal rights, Sivertz and his colleagues clearly thought that those who even mentioned the concept were "hostile." The sentence above helped Sivertz to launch into an extended review and critique of the Point Barrow "Statement of Policy," worth following in detail for a strong articulation of the position and reasoning that underlie Canadian policy toward Inuit.

After a brief review of the report – "I have just been reading in the News-letter of the Association on American Indian Affairs, a Bulletin ... entitled 'The Eskimo Speak'" – Sivertz moves quickly into his criticisms. The confer-ence, he argues,

> is "on the themes of aboriginal rights to hunting, to land, to minerals, and other resources." This sort of thing seems to bring pleasure to some people and they spur on this supra-nationalistic fragmentation of society. It is a short step from this to the assertion we hear from the spokesmen for the Caughnawaga Indians down near Montreal, who talk of taking a minor dispute with the Government not to the Exchequer Court of Canada but to the United Nations, on the grounds that they are a separate nation. Actually, this sort of thing saddens me. I can get nostalgic and maudlin about the Icelandic heritage which is mine and which is being lost, – but I don't ... I really have no objection to being one of the ingredients in a melting pot. Integration followed by assimilation has been the pattern of human cultural relationships ever since the race began and it is going to continue.[51]

That other people might not legitimately feel differently about their herit-age is not on the table. That Icelandic culture might have a different legal and cultural position in Canada from the cultures of original occupants – that is, if Icelandic Canadians lose their culture it will continue to thrive elsewhere, in Iceland, whereas if Inuit culture in Canada were to disappear those forms of Inuit culture would disappear from the world – does not seem to have played any role in Sivertz's analysis. And the broad claim that "assimilation has been the pattern of human cultural relationships ever since the race began" is as defensible as the contrary claim that "cultural differentiation has been the pattern of human cultural relationships ever since the race began." As important as the substantive argument, however, is the general attitude that this analysis betrays: a philosophical predisposition against special status, linked to a hostility to those who advocate it, whether Mohawk militants or the "white advisors" referred to above or even the Inuit leaders or community members who would agitate for or assert their rights.

But the extended discourse by Sivertz did not end there. In reading this letter, one gets the sense of a certain defensiveness, as if Sivertz knows his "wards" may soon be turning on him, as if he has to remind himself of the "first principles" that ground the policy trajectory he supports and helps to invent, as if perhaps some small glimmer that a profound challenge to that policy is in the works and he needs to buttress his own actions by restating his ideals. The letter moves to a discussion of Sierra Leone, where thirteen tribes "are rapidly learning to work together and live together and talk together" as a more positive example. And then the following, which moves from reasoned articulation of principles to an impassioned stand:

> What is the intelligent approach to culture preservation? Language is the chief among cultural attributes, – but there are some other things. Are all to be preserved? If so, what will society be like in such a regime? I cannot even imagine it. Extreme fragmentation was at one time the rule rather than the exception. It worked too, – but acceptably to people with aspirations above animal existence? Tribe against tribe, town against town, nation against nation? Developing concepts of human dignity and compassion give us sights of something better. The price is surrender of some of the jealousies and fears that have been the basis of an awful lot of man's little fence-building efforts. I find it hard to see any real difference between those who fight for Indian and other aboriginal rights separately from their white neighbors of this Continent and the posturing of the white trash of the southern States or of South Africa, who demand separatism. Both are for selfish ends and to obtain a preferred position. Both are denials of the principles which I think have tested out to best advantage, namely the principles of equality of opportunity.[52]

Here the notion of a "civilizing mission" is the effective basis of the argument. The reference to "people with aspirations above animal existence" is telling as a description of so-called primitive cultures. And the deliberate attempt to confuse those who advocate for positive discrimination for a marginalized people – Aboriginal rights – with those who advocate for negative discrimination against those they want to marginalize – racists in the southern United States and South Africa – is again an almost personal attack on the emerging critics of the state. The "principles of equality of opportunity" that Sivertz assumes have "tested out to best advantage" came out of and operated constructively within a particular (Western) history and culture; the test of those principles as applied to other cultures could in fact be seen as one of the great challenges of the twentieth century, and the jury is still out on how well the principle did, though in Canada the alternative doctrine of Aboriginal rights has clearly established itself.

Consistent through this letter is an attack on those who would advocate for Aboriginal rights, usually represented as misguided non-Aboriginal peoples, an unsavory lot of unscrupulous and irresponsible outsiders. A common theme in colonial history is the attempt to attribute forces of change to outside "troublemakers," and this seems to be reflected in Sivertz's attitude. The last substantive part of this letter reiterates this theme:

> I often wonder if one or another of the people who make an avocation of this kind of thing have considered carefully the responsibility he assumed in promoting Indianishness ... The end of it may well be a destruction of the normal capacity human beings have for adjustment ... Are people to be advised that their reaction to anything in the way of change to their environment should be a hot hostility and automatic protest? A lot of this is happening these days, and all in the name of human rights. I am one who had a deep respect for human rights and the principles of freedom, but that does not mean I accept everything so labelled, – and I have the conviction that aboriginal people at least on this continent have some doubtful voices nagging at them and reiterating that the palefaces, – (yes they use that word too) mean no good to us redskins.[53]

This was written on the verge of a period of history that would be characterized by intense social activism. The rhetorical strategy deployed here is telling: Sivertz recognizes that those he opposes use the same rallying cries, freedom, and human rights, so he has to challenge those who want to adopt the labels. He clearly implies that the "nagging voices" in favour of Aboriginal rights are from outside the Aboriginal communities, neglecting to mention at any point that the newsletter on the Point Barrow conference specifically states that "the Eskimo leaders whose names appear in this newsletter conceived the Conference, planned it, conducted it in their own way and largely in their own language, and wrote the historic statement that is presented here."[54] And perhaps to help clear the reputation of the Aboriginal "innocent" leaders seduced by the language of rights, he puts himself in their position – "the palefaces ... mean no good to us redskins." Sivertz was no "redskin" but rhetorically positioned himself that way in order to distinguish between the outside agitators who advocated rights and the Aboriginal leaders who in his view were basically good-hearted and easily misled.

Sivertz was, beyond a doubt, not the only one who held these views. They were a forceful expression of the thinking of senior administrators in his time. A handwritten note at the bottom says, simply and tellingly, "a marvelous letter!" Obviously, Sivertz articulated the principles behind a position that was increasingly under attack. The defence of those principles was, by early 1962, strident and defensive. Sivertz's letter does articulate a set of principles diametrically opposed to those advocated by Justice Sissons in *Kogogolak* and other cases. While in the 1950s policy makers could operate largely in a vacuum, developing policies for the most part free of criticisms and without strong alternatives, by the early 1960s the notion of Inuit having Aboriginal rights was underwriting the possibility of an entirely different policy trajectory and implicitly criticizing the direction taken by northern administrators. They did not react generously. They did not seriously re-evaluate their principles and directions. They did not recognize a legal responsibility to protect rights that Inuit arguably may have had. They moved, rather, in a variety of areas to circumvent or shut down the dissent they knew would be growing in the coming years.

This is not to say that Sivertz, Robertson, Phillips, and the administrators they led were ill intended. With the benefit of historical hindsight, one cannot help but be struck by the passion of Sivertz's argument, its depth of thought and seriousness. As in *Tammarniit,* we emphasize that these officials were not a group of castoffs but in many ways the leaders of their generation in Canada. There can be no doubt that they were doing what they thought was in the best interests of Inuit. But the principles they enunciated were particularly useful to a totalizing regime. Our point, then, is that, beyond the personalities, the modernist, universal principles they were attached to that led them to rely heavily on the truths of science, and the structure wherein a few men (and they were all men) had decision-making powers over many people of a different culture, were all, tragically, of a piece that led straight to Corporal Gallagher on the beach in Arviat.

Confusion and Debate

Sivertz's memorandum expressed the attitude that allowed administrators over the greater part of the decade to "muddle through." They knew there was a problem. They knew they themselves recommended legislation and policies that at times discriminated against Inuit in the name of protecting Inuit, as was the case with special legislation governing drinking. At the same time, they avoided any attempt to develop any positive legislation that would come to be the basis of special status or special rights for Inuit. The problem was not theirs alone. By the mid-1960s, the federal government was re-evaluating its broader commitment (which had always been half-hearted at best) to the concept of special status in light of the emerging activism of First Nations and Métis communities. This would eventually culminate in the historic struggle around the 1969 "Statement of the Government of Canada on Indian Policy," which gave way slowly to the notion that Aboriginal rights were here to stay (a notion finally solidified in the Constitution Act, 1982). Activities regarding Inuit here and there had a special flavour: for example, in the late 1960s, officials seriously began trying to decide once again the legal status of Inuit, given the 1939 decision and the policies and legislative regime established in the decades that followed the decision. By 1969, the lines of debate were drawn as sharply in Inuit country as they were in Indian country.

A confidential letter from J.R.B. Coleman, a director in the Department of Indian Affairs, to his deputy minister on 11 December 1964 noted that the federal cabinet was considering that "a full enquiry be made into the inconsistencies between Indian treaties and existing legislation with the object of working out a realistic and appropriate way of carrying out our commitment to the Indian people."[55] The enquiry had been prompted by the *Sikyea* decision on Dene duck-hunting rights at the Supreme Court of Canada, which supported an appeal court overturning of Sissons's decision in lower court (see Eber 1997, 117-23). Lest anyone have doubts about where Coleman stood on the issue, he noted that "Indian privileges in regard to the taking of fish and wildlife have been a matter of controversy for decades"; the "privileges" were a matter of conflict rather than attempts to deny commitments made through treaties. Coleman then goes on to summarize in broad strokes "the position of the Indian Affairs Branch," noting that "the treaties are inconsistent and ambiguous," that some would like to see "legislation which would clearly convey to Indians an unfettered right to hunt and fish on unoccupied Crown lands and Indian reserves," while others, especially "fish and game administrators, ... claim that special rights for Indians in regard to the taking of fish and game reduces the effectiveness of management of game and fish populations." The approach suggested, underlined in the letter, was to "continue to compromise while moving toward the situation where there is no longer any need for special rights."[56] Coleman raised the possibility of some form of "special compensation" that would be paid in order to "extinguish Indian rights to game and fish" and argued that "the special needs of those Indians, and of Eskimos as well, who continue to live off the land can be set by exercising discretion in enforcement."[57] Coleman's letter illustrates that by 1964 the notion of Aboriginal rights was seen to be a problem in both Indian and Inuit affairs, and the emerging problem in the latter area would be solved by a global policy being developed to deal with the former. R.A.J. Phillips of the Northern Administration Branch noted on the last page of the letter, "I concur."

In mid-January of the next year, the minutes of the Northern Policy Co-Ordinating Committee reveal that senior administrators were again having to deal with Sissons, though it is not clear from the record which of his decisions concerned them. As his memoirs reveal, Sissons had a passionate concern to protect Aboriginal rights. He was sorely disappointed by the Supreme Court decision in *Sikyea* and other cases at the time, and he would not live long enough to see its reasoning come to accord with his (as in Justice Hall's famous and influential dissenting opinion in the *Calder* case of 1973). Several of Sissons's decisions at the time directly challenged departmental orthodoxy on Aboriginal rights, as noted in Chapter 4. At the 18 January 1965 meeting, although "the Commissioner pointed out that some of the points made by the Judge were of a positive nature and should be recognized as such," for the most part "the consensus of the meeting was that the Judge had gone beyond his duty and that the decision to appeal his judgement should be proceeded with." In particular, "the Commissioner noted his own points of issue with the Judge, he felt the latter was extremely paternalistic and that his views on game conservation were at odds with basic national policy."[58] The minutes reveal that the administrators were not sitting on the fence as a huge debate raged around them about the question of Aboriginal rights for Indians, which they would wait out and then apply the results to Inuit. They were aligned with their colleagues in Indian Affairs and actively worked to obstruct the emergence of a regime based on Aboriginal rights – in this instance by appealing legal decisions that went against them. Hunting rights were at the forefront of the legal battles, and any moral uneasiness could therefore be settled with reference to scientists' concern over species extinction.

On 11 February 1965, a lengthy memorandum for cabinet, which proposed establishing an Indian Claims Commission, summed up the official position on Inuit status in a concluding section called "Exclusion of Eskimos." The "question of including Eskimos in the proposed claims legislation was formally raised by the Commissioner for the Northwest Territories," according to the minister of citizenship and immigration, who submitted the memorandum. The minister went on to explain that

> The proposed legislation has been drafted within the framework of Indians as defined by the Indian Act, and accordingly excludes Eskimos, even though Eskimos are Indians for the purpose of the British North America Act. The terms of reference of the Commission for the most part have to do with the reserve system, treaty obligations, and trust fund administration which are peculiar to Indians and have no parallel in the administration of Eskimo affairs. In addition, the organization of Indians into bands with a statutory definition as to membership, with band councils and operating under special legislation, has no counterpart among the Eskimos. There are also other points of difference arising out of historical development and environment. For these reasons it is not considered practical to combine the situation respecting Eskimos and Indians in the same claims legislation. In addition, there are no known claims that have been raised by the Eskimos.[59]

This shows a grasp of the different legal positions of status Indians and Inuit but does not address the fact that Inuit might have the same rights respecting Aboriginal title as Indians who had not negotiated treaties. However, the minister left open the possibility of a need to deal with Inuit claims that might arise from Inuit: "While Eskimo claims are not provided for, if at some time in the future a sufficient volume of Eskimo claims should arise which cannot be resolved through the ordinary courts, the Government would be prepared to give consideration to appropriate legislation to ensure equitable treatment for the Eskimo people."[60] There appears to have been a sense that Inuit land claims might be coming, though for the moment they would be left to the courts to deal with. And there certainly was not going to be an attempt to educate Inuit that they might have Aboriginal title and other land-related rights. For all the understanding it shows of the legal situation of Inuit, the document basically advocated a "do nothing for now" position respecting Aboriginal rights of Inuit, which in the case of land title actually rested on much the same legal ground as the title of other First Peoples.

The forces coalescing to defend Aboriginal rights were beginning to include Inuit in the broader picture. A brief of the Indian-Eskimo Association of Canada submitted in July 1967 made a strong case for the government, in response to Supreme Court decisions such as that in *Sikyea*, "to enact remedial legislation to restore to Indians of Canada their historic and basic right to hunt for food at any time on reservation lands and unoccupied Crown lands."[61] The brief made a strong case in defence of Aboriginal rights, expressing a view diametrically opposed to that of Sivertz in the hope that "we express the desire of all Canadians for justice and the vindication of the nation's honour."[62] For the most part, the document deals exclusively with Indian legal cases and topics (treaty rights) but notes in relation to the Migratory Birds Convention Act that "Indians and Eskimos are exempted from provisions of the Convention so far as certain migratory non-game birds are covered,"[63] indicating some awareness that the issues may have been as relevant to Inuit as to Indians. The name Indian-Eskimo Association itself raised the profile of Inuit nationally and helped to ensure that the phrase "Indians and Eskimos" would be used extensively in the documents of the period. That formula was also promoted through moving the Indian Affairs and Northern Affairs branches into the same department, Indian Affairs and Northern Development, in 1967, which placed administrators responsible for Indians and Inuit in a closer working arrangement.

Similarly, on the other side of the issue, an awareness that Inuit were involved in the questions began to emerge. A few months later, on 10 November 1967, a letter to "voting delegates" of the Canadian Wildlife Federation raised the issue in relation to legislation proposed by Member of Parliament R.J. "Bud" Orange "in connection with the rights of Indians and Eskimos under the *Migratory Birds Convention Act*." The letter "assured" members that "the bill gives no cause for alarm" in part because "he [Orange] does not want the bill to be passed but does want its content discussed"; then, in two brief paragraphs, it sums up the degree of confusion that seemed to exist around the issue:

> Mr. Orange believes that native people still living off the land should be able to use migratory birds for food without regard for seasons or bag limits ...

Mr. Orange believes that native people living off the land should not have to break the law when they use migratory birds for food ... Mr. Orange does agree, however, that Indians or Eskimos who have become fully integrated into white society should be bound by the same laws as the rest of us. The question of establishing the status of individual Indians or Eskimos, or determining when they might revert from one status back to another, is a complex matter for which Mr. Orange claims to have no pat answers. As a matter of fact, I can find no one in the Ottawa area who does claim to have the answers.[64]

This section of the letter concludes with a call for advice. If it was true that the executive director could not find anyone "in the Ottawa area who does claim to have the answers," then this was a telling statement. He would have had extensive contacts with all the key players in Arctic administration and many in Indian Affairs; if they claimed not to have answers, then it would have been a change from their earlier, seemingly secure, position that Inuit did not have rights and that Indian rights should be extinguished. In this letter, "Indians or Eskimos" became a stock phrase, and Inuit were seen as players in the emerging debates over Aboriginal rights.

Four months later the minister, Arthur Laing, was using the same phrase as a matter of course in a letter to the president of the Quebec Wildlife Federation: "I want to extend to Indians and Eskimos, as an evidence of good faith, the opportunity within the law to take migratory birds as they need them for food." The reasoning rewards our attention:

I want to do that because, quite apart from legal arguments based on variations in wording in the various Indian treaties, it is generally believed by Indians and accepted by the government that Indians have a special claim on fish and game. However, in view of my responsibility for migratory bird conservation, I do not feel that under present day circumstances I can properly relinquish all control over Indian and Eskimo hunting of migratory birds. I therefore propose that Indians and Eskimos should be required to observe a shorter closed season covering the breeding periods in different parts of the country. I propose also that Indians and Eskimos be encouraged to impose needed restrictions on migratory bird hunting on themselves of their own volition, and I will see that the necessary administrative machinery is available.[65]

Laing also wrote that some form of "free hunting permit" would be used as a device to educate "Indian and Eskimo hunters" so as to aid "the progress of our native people toward economic and social equality with other Canadians."[66] His proposal could be seen as balanced and moderate or as incoherent, depending on one's perspective. Certainly, he was trying to balance conservation interests with subsistence needs. Just as certainly, he was leaving aside the question of rights: it was needs, not rights, that would govern Inuit subsistence hunting of migratory birds. Although he was trying to enforce the Migratory Birds Convention Act in a less restrictive manner, he would also not "relinquish all control over Indian and Eskimo hunting of migratory birds," proposing a form of self-regulation that, in the hothouse political climate of the time, was probably not workable.

As this proposal worked its way forward, it too received criticism. David Munro, chief of the Canadian Wildlife Service, wrote to the deputy minister, saying "I will do what I have to do to implement that course of action, if that is what I am directed to do. However, I would hope that you and the Minister would give further thought to a major disadvantage that I think might result,"[67] and once again the issue of special rights impeding assimilation was raised:

> The point I have in mind is that the establishment of special regulations – the enshrinement of particular privileges in current legislation and regulations – would be additional evidence of discriminatory treatment. This, it would seem to me, is something we are trying to avoid, for example, by the integration of certain Indian and Eskimo educational and welfare programs with similar programs directed toward other Canadians. I suggest that formalization of privileges beyond the level that now exists would tend to harden relationships between Indians and Eskimos and other Canadians ... It seems to me that an essential approach to solving the many little problems that combine to make the larger "Indian problem" is to meet them in a practical manner without resort to any measure that could be construed as discriminatory in terms of race, or that could be said to set Indians and Eskimos apart from other Canadians because of their race.[68]

The "no special rights" position continued to attract strong support within the Canadian Wildlife Service as well as within the department throughout this period, and every opportunity was made to defend it. Munro suggested "continuation of the policy of leniency in enforcement of the Migratory Birds Convention Act and Regulations as it applies to Indians and Eskimos who need migratory birds for food" because "that policy meets the practical needs of Indians and Eskimos," noting that this approach had been applied "on several occasions ... for the benefit of white residents of some isolated settlements in Labrador, so it is possible to say it is purely a response to need." Finally, Munro argued that, if "the formal extension of special privileges to Indians and Eskimos by regulations" were to take place, "it would be useful to state clearly that it is an interim measure designed to meet a need that is expected to disappear." An abrupt, handwritten note on the front page responded with "we have had this discussion before. There is a difference between discriminating positively and negatively and the Indians with some justice now feel they have lost something which should be restored,"[69] betraying some sense of exhaustion over the debate and perhaps a feeling that the political "masters" were being frustrated by the entrenched views of their bureaucratic "servants."

"A Person Claims Eskimo Status Because He Believes Himself to Be an Eskimo"

In the period between mid-1968 and late 1969, the specific problem of how to understand Inuit legal status had reached the point where some resolution was critical. A draft document, apparently not used, on "The Constitutional Position of Eskimos," dated 13 May 1968, illustrates that the issue needed explanation in both government circles and legal circles. Reference was made to the 1939 decision, which was interpreted by the Department of Justice to mean "that, as with the Indians, the BNA Act gives Parliament exclusive legislative jurisdiction in respect to Eskimos, but that provincial laws of general application apply to Eskimos when not in conflict with federal law." There was no mention that an implication of the decision was that Inuit may have had Aboriginal rights, and the decision was still construed in the narrowest of interpretations to mean a simple statement of jurisdictional position. The exclusion of Inuit from the Indian Act was noted, and "various Appropriation Acts of the Parliament of Canada have, over a period of years, authorized expenditures for programs of health care, education, welfare, and economic development for Eskimos." The draft also stated that, "since there is no legislation qualifying their rights, Eskimos are full citizens of Canada. All federal, provincial or territorial legislation of general application applies to them." This was a remarkable statement though in line with the direction taken after and in reaction to Sissons's 1959 decision. The draft added, "they are eligible to vote in federal, provincial and territorial elections. Those earning sufficient income pay income taxes, and all pay the normal provincial taxes. The special federal responsibility represents an extra service and not an alternative to normal citizenship."[70] For some incomprehensible reason, it seems, the constitution marked Inuit as an Aboriginal people under federal jurisdiction. This pesky piece of Supreme Court thinking, however, need not have interfered with taking a "business as usual" approach to Inuit: in spite of a distinct constitutional legal status, they could be treated with impunity exactly as other Canadians.

Problems were emerging that could not be so easily glossed over, for the government was treating Inuit differently. It had a whole regime of laws, rules, and practices that marked Inuit out. One of those was the use of e-numbers and identification discs, in circulation since the 1940s. Inuit often treasured the identification discs as something that the government had given to them, but equally often the "gift" appears to have imposed a fearful burden: "We were told by the RCMP not to lose those discs that time, so we were fearful that, uh, if we ever lose them, because that, those days, the RCMP were really bossy, and, you know, so we feared them. So we were told not to lose those discs" (John Arnalukjuak, 27 May 1997, Arviat). The fear of losing them could become nearly overwhelming, as was the case when Rachel Uyarasuk actually lost her family's discs:

> I was scared to lose mine ... We were told not to lose them ... I didn't wear it around my neck. I put all my children's and mine, tied them, tied them together, so they wouldn't get lost. And I lost them! I was ever scared [laughter] ... It was on the sea [ice] that we were camping, the dogs didn't have very much to eat. That's when they got lost ... We went to camp, move onto the [land], and I, I missed them. So we went back to that camp looking for them. We even picked on the ice, looking for them ... We couldn't find them, so we just moved back to where we were, and I had to tell someone because we lost, I lost them, and I was very scared ... I thought I was going to be arrested. I told the Hudson's Bay manager that I lost them, and he just told me that they can be replaced [laughter]. That's how it went. (Rachel Uyarasuk, 28 May 1999, Iglulik)

Uyarasuk, now a respected elder, never had doubts about her status as an Inuk. Her story reveals how seemingly simple administrative solutions created significant pressures and burdens on Inuit.

Within a year, the legal gloss produced in the spring of 1968 was clearly not helping on the ground. In response to a question about whether a young child should be issued a disc and an e-number, an assistant director

Rachel Uyarasuk.
Photo Frank Tester.

in the Territorial Relations Branch, A.B. Yates, wrote to the administrator of the Arctic under the heading "Eskimo Status – Disc Numbers": "As you are aware, there is no legal definition of the term 'Eskimo' per se. Eskimos have been defined specifically for purposes of identification in legislation and administrative policies; however, these definitions are related to specific situations and are not consistent with one another." His admission regarding the inconsistencies in policy, practice, and law was a far clearer statement of the situation than the Department of Justice's continual legal glosses. Yates noted that "there is no final authority on Eskimo status. Any person who considers himself to be an Eskimo and is regarded as such by a community in which he lives may be said to have Eskimo status."[71] Use of the term "status" here is significant, implying a parallel with the more legally established framework of Indian status. But the admission that "any person" who wanted to and was "regarded as such by a community" could be considered Inuit was the sort of opening to uncertainty that lawyers and administrators alike were deeply uncomfortable with: not an ideal situation for a totalizing force, which was assiduously working to construct social homogeneity.

In the case at hand, Yates recommended that only after the adopting Inuit couple had secured a legal adoption order could their new child be issued a disc and legally considered an Inuk. Yates noted that "the questions of Eskimo status and Eskimo disc numbers have been debated for many years, yet no firm legal definition of an Eskimo has been made." In fact, for over a decade, the department, with the help of the Department of Justice, had insisted on a consistent legal approach and articulated it clearly as recently as the year before. The problem was that the Inuit themselves had begun to rely on a different interpretation of their status and were, with mixed success, using that interpretation to defend themselves in court. And the government was consistently forgetting its own principles and legislating measures for Inuit that marked them out, most frequently to discriminate against them though supposedly in their interest. Hence, the clear and consistent policy, especially when connected to practice, was incoherent at best. At worst, it underwrote systematic attempts to undermine Inuit distinctiveness. Yates, in conclusion, stated the case for a "confusing" policy quite well: "Although this may be confusing in certain instances, I feel that the advantages of the present system outweigh the disadvantages. A strict legal definition would tend to segregate Eskimo persons from other Canadians. Such segregation would present another barrier to their participation in Canadian society. Programs for persons with Eskimo status may in time become a part of broader programs for Canadians. To insist on a legal definition of Eskimos because of existing programs would, in my view, be an error."[72] In the name of equality, a little inconsistency, a small bit of trouble that seemed to pop up here and there, was of little account.

The troubling inconsistency would not go away. By the fall of 1969, a legal adviser named Hugo Fischer was consulted on "how, in fact, the Federal Government and, in particular, this Department and the Government of the Northwest Territories determines Eskimo status and to evaluate this determination from a constitutional and legal point of view." Fischer noted that the disc system "is carried out as part of the process of gathering vital statistics" and asked "if the disc system is the sole criterion in use for determining Eskimo status for the purposes of social assistance, child welfare, the Community Development Fund, the care of the aged and infirm and the repatriation of Eskimo patients, and the Indian Off-Reserve and Eskimo Re-Establishment Housing Program." This was quite a list of special services for ordinary Canadians with no special rights. Fischer also wanted to know "how Eskimo status is determined for the purposes of the Game Ordinance, the Liquor Ordinance, and the Fisheries Regulations" – also good questions.[73]

Another acting director of the Territorial Relations Branch, D.A. Davidson, attempted to answer these questions in a reply dated 15 October 1969. The letter started off relatively clearly but quickly sank into a quagmire: "The disc system is not the sole criterion in use for determining Eskimo status for such purposes as social assistance, child welfare, housing, etc. From the administrative viewpoint, it is regarded only as a system of identification and should not be confused with 'Eskimo status,' as a person of Eskimo status may not possess a disc number." Striking here is the admission or assumption that the notion of "Eskimo status" seems to have taken hold and appears to be separate from the administrative procedures. Davidson then made another interesting admission: "One might say that a person claims Eskimo status because he believes himself to be an Eskimo and is commonly considered to be an Eskimo in the community in which he lives." There does not seem to be any instance where any official actually tested the latter part of this definition by asking a community if an individual who claimed to be was in fact Inuk. Legal status could not be allowed to rest solely on self-identification. Finally, in this review, Davidson noted that "Eskimos who reside in Labrador, for example, come within the administrative jurisdiction of the Province of Newfoundland and are not issued discs. Those in Quebec may not be issued discs when that province eventually assumes administrative responsibility for them."[74] While it was clear that "status" could not be linked to the discs, it was not at all clear what "status" could be linked to, and no one seemed to be asking the question of what such "status" could mean.

Davidson then pointed out that "the Commissioner of the Northwest Territories has proposed the elimination of the disc system ... To this end he plans to institute a program to encourage Eskimos to select and use family or surnames. Additional identification is planned through the use of social security numbers." Wholesale changes were coming. Government officials had little if any idea of the extent to which the use of "surnames" was not merely a development that would be administratively convenient but also a dramatic imposition on intricate Inuit cultural processes involving naming (see Alia 1994). But for the moment, it was clear that such a change would mean that Inuit "status" was entirely separate from the disc number system. So Davidson turned to the other fashion in which Inuit were legally defined: "With regard to the definition of 'Eskimo' in legislation, the one common description which seems to be used when 'Eskimo' is defined, whether in federal acts or territorial ordinances, is 'the race of aborigines commonly referred to as 'Eskimos.'" He cited several pieces of federal and territorial legislation, which used that definition, and then referred to Sissons's 1959 decisions. Finally, Davidson concluded that "a person is determined to have Eskimo status or to be an Eskimo administratively for whatever purpose necessary based on good judgment and common acceptance of the individual's status in his community."[75] In fact, this is what the growing mountain of documentation amounted to: on-the-ground judgment. If a person dressed in the manner of an Inuk and spoke Inuktitut and came asking for relief rations, then the RCMP or area administrator gave that person the rations and listed him or her as one of the Inuit. But why list that person at all?

1969

As the above letters and reports suggest, by 1969 the whole regime was coming unravelled. Within a few years, there would be a transition toward acknowledgment of Inuit special rights, that Inuit did indeed have Aboriginal rights to hunt and fish and perhaps had Aboriginal title to lands. Some of that struggle goes beyond the bounds of this book – for example, the well-known Baker Lake case of 1978. But 1969 is an appropriate place to draw this part of the narrative to a close. Inuit leaders themselves, in a variety of ways and forums, were starting to make their views known on what it meant to be an Inuk. And the language of Aboriginal rights was very much a part of their discourse.

A brief example helps us to draw this chapter to a close. On 1 February 1969, the Northwest Territories Council sat and discussed a motion by Simonie Michael. The presence of Michael itself marks the transition, as for two years Inuit politicians had been sitting on the council. Michael recalled a variety of struggles he engaged in on behalf of Inuit during those early years:

> It was 1966 [when I was first elected]. The good thing that came out of this, when I was first elected, I wanted to represent the Inuit people properly. There were some, C.D. Howe was the ship that came here to check some patients who had TB. And [the] same day there were some families who had lost relatives because they had to leave with the C.D. Howe. And ... they were gone for like three, four, five years, and the families who were left behind were very – they missed our relatives. And I started talking about this at the

NWT Council, and that's when they stopped bringing the C.D. Howe up here, 1969 ... When I was first elected, I started talking to the council about having new airports or new runways and new nursing facilities. That's the time when they [were longing] for their relatives, when I was representing [Avalu] ... In 1966, it was in Resolute Bay, for the first meeting. (Simonie Michael, Iqaluit, 14 May 1999)

Simonie's motion in early 1969, seconded by Bob Williamson (as mentioned earlier, a strong advocate for Inuit), noted that "still many of the people of the Eastern Arctic are expecting to hear more about their land rights and revenues from mineral development" and moved that "the Commissioner have prepared for the next Session a paper explaining the law as it stands in the NWT and elsewhere in Canada regarding the rights of the native people."[76] Hence a legal opinion on the question was sought, which led to the correspondence later that fall, discussed above.

Simonie explained his motion in part by reference to the confusion that reigned: "So far I understand we have no information for the Council. I think people know about this information and where they are going to get it." The latter statement conveys a sense of distrust, that there are those who know about Inuit rights and have not been forthcoming. Simonie also noted that "the Alaskan Government has been governing the people in a different way than Canada is doing today," a pointed reference to the Alaska land claims process. The commissioner responded by admitting that "this is a very deep and involved issue that you are asking for, and I think what you are asking for here is something far outside the scope of the Northwest Territories Council," suggesting he would have to contact "federal authorities" to prepare the paper. A lengthy statement by another councillor, Trimble, followed; he argued that "the Government of Canada can no longer drag its feet and procrastinate but has to determine the legality of the aboriginal claims of the Indians and the Eskimos, and, for that matter, of the Métis people and develop a suitable policy of compensation to the original races."[77] The motion was carried.

Legal obstacles had emerged to the science-based policy makers' attempts at totalization. A legal response was developed: the principle of equality would be deployed to justify their treatment of Inuit. In essence, while in the immediate postwar period the police had been responsible for dragging their feet when it came to enforcing game regulations and thereby acted as a brake on totalizing power, by the 1960s police opposition had almost disappeared. Acts of resistance were prosecuted by police (some of whom deployed their power with relish), but another level of the justice system afforded shelter to those Inuit who insisted on continuing to practise their hunting culture. The notion of equality that underwrote totalizing policies and practices was belied by the necessity of marking out those at whom its dictates were aimed: a legal instability developed and was exploited both by those in power and by those who resisted its exercise.

The late 1950s and 1960s were a striking period in terms of government policy regarding Inuit. A fully modernist regime with a determined agenda of directed cultural change was operating in high gear. The regimental commanders knew that they had a problem with the likelihood that Inuit had special rights to match their special constitutional status but ignored, repressed, and suppressed the possibility. Doing so allowed them to continue to develop their programs unrestrained by the legal checks that a system of rights involved. The statement of philosopher Levinas that "we need rights because we cannot have justice" seems to be entirely appropriate to this historical moment. Although suppression of the discourse of rights is a story in itself, as this chapter makes evident, more critical is the manner in which that suppression opened a space for the state to have a legally clear field of action. The situation would change dramatically in the next decade, but through the 1960s officials could and did apply their modernist agenda almost unchecked or checked only by a disarmed but still growing powerful set of voices. It is to the early articulation of those voices that we now turn. When a police officer who worked for the state deliberately smashed a drum in Arviat in the summer of 1958, he was giving full expression to the policy trajectory that dominated government circles. By the late 1960s, the police would no longer be in a position to smash drums.

6
Baker Lake, 1957:
The Eskimo Council

While at the higher levels of policy making a debate of varying intensity and practical significance took place regarding Inuit rights, in the relatively newly formed Arctic communities the debate took a range of local forms. It was at this level that Inuit responses to these issues could have been sought but generally were not. As noted with respect to game management, until Ben Sivertz insisted in 1966 that a consultation with Inuit on proposed changes to the game laws regarding the hunting of polar bears take place before they were enacted (see Chapter 3), Inuit were not often consulted about policies affecting their culture and their lives. A parallel refusal to consult significantly with First Nations had come to characterize Indian policy development. It can be argued that this had been a foundation for Indian policy since the early years of confederation (see Brownlee 2003; Shewell 2004). The refusal to engage in meaningful consultation with those who would feel the effects of these decisions also came to characterize the development of Inuit policy.

The establishment of a council at Baker Lake in 1957 was thus a signifi-cant moment in Arctic history. While attempts to start councils in other communities had already taken place (Doug Wilkinson had made such an attempt in Frobisher Bay), the Baker Lake council was among the most sus-tained of the early ventures, leaving a detailed record of its workings. Close attention to this record reveals which concerns were emerging among Inuit at the local level. The council was supported by higher-level administrators, who appeared to desire mechanisms of consultation but had little idea of how to develop them. The council that emerged was the brainchild of Wil-kinson and male Inuit leaders in the community of Baker Lake. Our interest in the record of this council has also been piqued by the great excitement that Western democratic forms seem to have elicited from Inuit. Although arguably they had developed deeply democratic decision-making forms that became embedded in their culture, the new forms appropriate to a repre-sentative rather than participatory democracy appear to have fascinated them.[1] Close attention in the manner of an intensive rather than extensive reading is therefore drawn to this set of records for what it can tell us about Inuit responses to the regime that was forming.

"Never Have I Seen Eskimos Toss Ideas and Suggestions Back and Forth as Did This Group"

In the spring of 1957, Doug Wilkinson, in his capacity as northern service officer for the community of Baker Lake, helped to establish what was called an Eskimo council. That it was an "Eskimo" council is worthy of note. Later attempts to organize a residents' association led to the creation of a body dominated by *Qallunaat,* with minority Inuit participation. Likely, a "community council" in 1957 would have attracted the interest and participation of *Qallunaat,* which in turn undoubtedly would have detracted from Inuit involvement.[2] When the peculiarly divisive relations between *Qallunaat* in Baker Lake are recalled (see Tester and Kulchyski 1994, 245-49),[3] one can appreciate why such a move would not have been seen by Wilkinson as constructive. He had spent half a year in Baker Lake in 1950, returning in 1957 as the northern service officer, a position with a broad range of responsibilities and considerable importance. The officer did not have the same defined statutory role of the Indian agent. If on anything, the position was modelled on that of a diplomatic ambassador, the result of some of the senior officials in the Arctic branch applying their previous experience in the Department of Foreign Affairs (see Tester and Kulchyski 1994, 330). Consequently, they acted somewhat as community development workers and administrators, taking responsibility for steering economic development, ascertaining local infrastructure needs, and managing paperwork.[4] The Baker Lake Eskimo Council, for a few years in the late 1950s, was a vehicle for Inuit in the area to express concerns and in a limited way take some responsibility for their affairs. Although Inuit undoubtedly expressed opinions and engaged in discussions and democratic forms of decision making that were an intricate aspect of their customary cultural life, the council provided a different form for such discussions and promised different kinds of outcomes. The discussions of this council represent one of the first times Inuit were systematically consulted over a lengthy period. The records of those discussions therefore represent a vital articulation of Inuit concerns about and responses to the developments taking place and the policies guiding those developments. It was a modest beginning to the movement for Inuit governance that would lead to the creation of Nunavut. The development of this council, as revealed primarily through the minutes of its meetings, but also through some of Wilkinson's official correspondence, provides insight into local social and political dynamics as well as into Inuit strategies for dealing with the emerging order.

Doug Wilkinson.
Photo Frank Tester.

A few words about Doug Wilkinson are in order. He came from a white, working-class background and had grown up in Toronto. Through his service in the army, he came in contact with the National Film Board and with a wider world where, as he describes it, "ideas mattered." He eventually became a filmmaker and made two very successful films about the Arctic – *Land of the Long Day* and *Angotee*. He also published a book in 1955 with the same title – *Land of the Long Day* – a remarkable work that centred on the notion of hunting as key to Inuit identity and was prescient regarding the value of the hunting economy to Inuit. This work eventually led to his recruitment by the Arctic branch. Prior to his posting in Baker Lake, he served in Iqaluit (then Frobisher Bay), where in 1955 he had "tried to start at APEX/Frobisher ... the first Eskimo council." In correspondence with us regarding the earlier experience, Wilkinson reported that, "in a similar manner to the process I would follow later at Baker Lake, I had meetings with individuals, the 'get togethers' with groups of Inuit. We met at the ex-Airforce Jamesway shelter that served as a kind of community hall to the original Iqaluit townsite, or garbage heap next to the base. My memory is that we held at least four meetings at which we discussed many things. But I didn't have time to record minutes or to write reports to Ottawa. When we knew we would be leaving Apex, the meetings were discontinued and promptly forgotten."[5]

Apex, Frobisher Bay, Baffin Island, 1957. The photograph shows "512" housing in the background and high-wall tents in the foreground. The 512 was the first housing provided to Inuit at Apex. The community is now a "suburb" of Iqaluit, the capital of Nunavut. Courtesy Doug Wilkinson.

Although Wilkinson had no formal training, he had something of the right temperament for Arctic service – at least the dimension that involved working with Inuit – and had the benefit of spending time between the Iqaluit and Baker Lake postings at the United Nations, where he "worked long hours talking with former field officers who had worked with communities in India, Africa, South America. Some were former 'Colonel Blimp' types but many were not and I began to get an understanding of just what good community development was all about – process rather than progress alone."[6] In effect, Wilkinson was well positioned to facilitate an inspired group of community leaders in taking a new approach to local-level decision making. In *Land of the Long Day*, he reported on the impact of his first stay in the Arctic in 1951: "In that fifteen-month period I came to know individual Eskimos as friends and neighbors. For the first time I stopped thinking in terms of 'Eskimos,' and thought of my friends, Sengeetuk, Aliuk, Idlouk and Kadluk" (1955, 21). While this might imply a view conducive to thinking of Inuit as "ordinary" Canadian citizens in the manner that policy makers desired, it is clear that for Wilkinson the gesture of treating Inuit in a face-to-face manner, a key element of Inuit culture, opened the way for him to "hear" what they had to say.[7] This in turn meant he was in a position to find or help invent vehicles for them to speak. In other words, the attitude or temperament was a critical precondition for the kind of consultation that might give rise to a discourse of Inuit rights.

On 27 February 1957, Wilkinson wrote to the chief of the Arctic Division under the heading "Baker Lake Eskimo Council," noting at the outset that he had "postponed" his "early field trip so as to interest local Eskimos in the formation of an advisory group or council that would meet regularly to discuss Eskimo affairs in the Baker Lake district."[8] The letter is compelling reading. The steps that Wilkinson took to reach the goal of a functioning council could today make a manual on community development. It began with individual and small group meetings designed to boost confidence among Inuit in their own decision-making abilities, and it likely had the additional effect of building a relationship of trust between Wilkinson and local Inuit:

> During February I had many informal talks with individual Eskimos, and with small groups, getting information on their life and their region. At each of these talks the main emphasis was placed, not so much on the information the Eskimos gave although it was invaluable, but on the fact that they had this information and were, therefore, knowledgeable persons in the area. I tried to gradually introduce the feeling that the Eskimos themselves, because of their intimate knowledge of the area and its peoples, were in by far the best position to find answers to the problems that crop up in their lives.[9]

That Inuit might not have had such feelings was no accident: they had experienced decades of *Qallunaat* who were not interested in their opinions and a distant government that was uninhibited in making decisions that would affect their lives with no thought given to consultation. In such a context, it is clear that simply calling Inuit together to a meeting to create an advisory body was not likely to meet with much success. A more gradual process such as that pursued by Wilkinson made much more sense. Without stating it directly, he was aware that the colonial pattern of decision making had left its imprint:

> Very rarely was anything said outright about this, but at the conclusion of each talk I hoped the Eskimo, or Eskimos, would go away feeling that he had contributed, had been a part of the evening discussion rather than a spectator or a pupil. At first it was difficult to ascertain if this feeling was there. The Eskimos here are not used to the idea of their being sought out for advice, rather it has been the reverse that has been true ... I have attempted to go deeper than this in my questioning: "what do you think" instead of "what do you do."[10]

"What do you think?" was not a question on the list of Inuktitut phrases that had been provided to government staff in the Arctic. As we noted in *Tammarniit* (1994, 337), northern staff had been furnished with a list of Inuktitut phrases to help them in their work; almost all of these phrases were direct commands, many relating to the tasks of menial labour. Wilkinson was leaving the beaten path when he began to seriously pose a question such as "what do you think?"

When a council was finally established, it was comprised entirely of male Inuit. This was likely not an accident since Wilkinson only approached men to sit on it, though he retrospectively noted that "no female ever suggested or hinted to ... us that she felt left-out by not taking an active and visible role in the council. And no male Inuk ever expressed a desire to have women with them at the meetings."[11] Although there is considerable debate about the place of women in traditional Inuit culture,[12] certainly the strong separation of gendered roles among Inuit (if not equally among *Qallunaat*, given the predominance of males in the roles of trader, missionary, and police officer) led to a situation where Inuit men were positioned to negotiate with *Qallunaat* men. Inasmuch as the latter began to set up public institutions, the situation appears to have created a bias that may or may not have existed earlier.

In terms of establishing a council, the approach worked, and it worked more quickly than anticipated, indicating that Inuit had been waiting for such an opportunity. Wilkinson wrote that "after three weeks of this form of discussion a good many of the Eskimos were losing a lot of their early reticence, and their somewhat non-committal attitude. They began to come to me with suggestions and ideas."[13] He believed that their desire to speak for themselves and have a role in decision making had always been present, only needing someone to "unlock the gates":

> I was quite surprised to find them doing this so quickly. I had thought that, in view of their previous dependence on the advice of missionary and trader ... it might prove to be a difficult job to get them started expressing opinions of their own. However this has not been the case; rather the reverse has been true. I now believe that my questions probing for their thoughts and feelings have released a flood of repressed desire on the part of the Eskimos to participate more fully in the life of the settlement and the area. I suspect that this desire has been smothered or has lain dormant over the years, losing none of its potency in the process.[14]

This eagerness caused Wilkinson to move more quickly than he had planned: "It was necessary for me to revise my thinking and plan for an early get together of all the Eskimo men in the settlement." In this statement, as in the one below, emphasis on the fact that the meetings were called with "the men" implies that the gender constitution of the council came more from Wilkinson's predispositions and presuppositions than from Inuit, although no doubt it all seemed entirely "normal" at the time. "I began casting about for topical and interesting matters that could be discussed at such a meeting. Out of the informal talks with the Eskimos a number of such topics presented themselves. In addition there were quite a number of welfare cases at Baker Lake with which the Eskimos themselves should be more concerned ... I suggested to the Eskimos that it might be as well if we were to have a meeting of all the men to talk about some of the matters we had discussed in our informal, private talks."[15] It is clear from this that he carefully and sensitively worked toward having a meeting, building on the earlier conversations in a step-by-step, progressive fashion. It is notable that the agenda of the meeting was partly set by Inuit inasmuch as they had raised issues in conversation with Wilkinson – though he did not specify what they were – and that his own agenda was directed toward "welfare issues."

A meeting was scheduled for 27 February at the school. Wilkinson "asked two Eskimo men to make sure that all Eskimo males over the age of fifteen should know of the meeting and that they were welcome to attend." Corporal Wilson of the RCMP was in Chesterfield Inlet and "because of his long, unforeseen, absence I have been unable to include him in this new development."[16] Although Wilkinson wrote that the absence was "unfortunate," likely the reverse was true, as can be seen from the role Wilson did play when he attended a meeting later that spring. The meeting date was changed to 26 February because

> there occurred a small event that was to do much toward making the first meeting an outstanding success. On Sunday morning, February 24, I received word that Canon James was confined to his house with the latest in a series of boils that had plagued him since Christmas. He would be unable to take the church service for at least a week. This meant that the church services ... would be conducted by the Eskimos themselves. This was too good an opportunity to miss. I contacted some of the men and suggested that it might be better if we held our meeting right after the church service on Tuesday evening rather than the following evening.[17]

Both Wilson and James, by coincidence, would be unable to attend the meeting. Wilkinson thus had a freer hand in the formative stage of the Eskimo council.

His report on the meeting is worth following in full before we turn to the minutes themselves:

On Tuesday evening, all the Eskimo males in the settlement came to the school directly from the church service. As I had hoped they came in a group and there was no awkward pause between time of arrival of the first and the beginning of the meeting. I had set the tables up in a row, but not the chairs, so everyone picked out a chair he liked best, at the same time indulging in a little horseplay to see who got the best ones, and then all sat down around the table. There was a good deal of laughing and joking among the group as they took up their places, particularly when old Kanayuk, the school janitor, got squeezed out of all the good chairs and had to sit at a desk. The atmosphere of the group was jovial and relaxed. Although I have no way of actually knowing if my feelings are correct, I feel this was because the group had just come from the church where they had been in complete charge of the evening service. This is not a new thing for this group, but I am sure that every time they do it, their self esteem is boosted quite high. I hoped the meeting would catch them at this high point and carry it over into the discussion of community affairs.[18]

The celebratory mood is striking. That "self esteem" gets "boosted" in the absence of *Qallunaat* direction does not in retrospect seem surprising and is a quiet testament to the reverse process. Every time a *Qallunaat* was "helping" Inuit by making a decision for them, he or she was doing damage to their sense of self. Wilkinson himself, more sensitive than most to this dynamic, could not help in some instances repeating the pattern, though to his credit he was one of those who early on made a sustained attempt to break it. The report continued:

As soon as we were settled around the table, I spoke briefly about the reasons for holding the meeting. I suggested that if the Eskimos could handle their own affairs in the sphere of religion, there should be no reason why they couldn't do the same thing in the social and economic spheres as well. Following this the meeting proceeded with the business at hand ... The meeting lasted from nine p.m. until after midnight, and it was necessary to defer discussion on two listed items. Never have I seen Eskimos toss ideas and suggestions back and forth as did this group. It was a pleasure to be sitting at the same table with them. I've conducted many a meeting with Eskimo groups, but never one in which so little of the customary reticence was displayed. I suggest that the main reasons for this are as follows: 1. Timing 2. Discussion of both local and national topics 3. Sense of participation felt by each person.[19]

Reading through the triumphal tone, we can emphasize a few points. The meeting was called and steered by Wilkinson. It took place in a jovial atmosphere, it appears to have been quite lively, and time seems to have flown by. Inuit in attendance did not appear awkward or reticent, did not need to be coached or encouraged to speak, but managed to "toss ideas and suggestions back and forth." The "timing" to which Wilkinson referred as a reason for success involved Inuit who had come from a church service that they had conducted, but implicitly the "timing" also involved the absence of two important *Qallunaat* authority figures whose presence might well have stifled discussion.

Inuit recollections provide some additional support for the notion that development of the council played an important political role. James Ukpagaq from Baker Lake reported that Inuit believed that the council started to give them an opportunity to speak up or even "talk back" to *Qallunaat*:

When we, when the Inuit, started talking back, about the time we started talking back was when there was a council formed, and that's when we finally started talking back. Then, ever since then, since our council is forming, since the council was formed, that's when Inuit started letting the council know, know about their concerns ... Seems to be a little bit different than talking back directly, but letting the council know about our concerns.

Then, during the meetings, when they are meeting, Inuit people used to look at the future, what we, what's going to hold ahead, what's going to be ahead in the, in the future, rather than the present. There are some councils would, used to, uh, when we know or have an idea of how the future is going to be, and that's when we used to start letting our concerns or talking back ...

Sometimes, I guess, the majority of the time, our concerns have been, they've listened, but it, sometimes I, Inuit know too that it takes time to get what they want done or our concerns to be enacted. Like it doesn't take right away but then later on, ... then that's when they started listening more often. But then when it first started, it took a lot, it took a long time. Although it wasn't, it wasn't immediate.

I can, for instance, I can use the example of the dogs, that they were not allowed to eat certain things. At that time, when they enforced it, it was, there was no way that you could feed your dogs, but when later on, when they knew people started being more concerned, it took a while. And now it's not even, nobody's feeling that way now. (James Ukpagaq, Baker Lake, 25 May 1997)

Although there can be no doubt that Wilkinson himself deserves a great deal of the credit for inspiring and organizing the council, it was also the creation of Baker Lake Inuit who supported the venture with such willingness and enthusiasm. Many attempts to organize consultative bodies die on the vine for lack of interest, and self-evidently there can be no such "voice of the people" without interest among and participation of the people themselves.

The First Meeting: "So Other Eskimos Have Our Troubles, Too"

The 26 February 1957 meeting of the Baker Lake Eskimo Council was attended by fifteen people, all males, all Inuit except for one *Qallunaat,* Wilkinson. Inuit attendees are identified in the minutes with the organizations they worked for – RCMP, Department of Transport, the missions – or as "trappers" or "school pupils." For example, the minutes record a "Kaneeyuk" as "DNA (Department of Northern Affairs), Education"; he was likely the "Kanayuk" identified in the report above as the school janitor. Clearly, he spoke as little for the education branch of the department as "Iyago," to borrow another example, may have spoken on behalf of the RCMP. Inuit attendees were present to speak for themselves and their community. Wilkinson chaired the meeting and took quite detailed minutes (six single-spaced pages, a significant effort for a field worker at this time) but was also at pains to ensure that Inuit at this meeting would feel uninhibited, able to speak their minds freely, and that Inuit would organize future meetings.

The meeting began with Wilkinson "explaining the reasons behind the group coming together." They were fourfold and revealed a somewhat contradictory role: "1. To provide a forum for discussion on problems in the area and to give all Eskimos the opportunity of participating in the handling of their own affairs. 2. To assist the NSO and RCMP in their job of helping the Eskimos in the area to live a better life. 3. To give Eskimos the chance to meet as a group with the NSO, RCMP, Nurse, Teacher and others, in order to make known their opinions on the problems within the community. 4. To provide an opportunity for dissemination of news of local and national interest."[20] Making "known their opinions" and assisting "the NSO and RCMP" may at times have been contradictory, particularly where an NSO or RCMP was responsible for a variety of social-control-style initiatives, as in the extensive caribou conservation efforts under way at the time. In fact, the council came together at the same time as government officials had decided that education wasn't working and that Inuit would be prosecuted for violating the game laws. As noted in previous chapters, by the early 1960s, particularly with respect to hunting practices, there is reason to believe that the goodwill Wilkinson had tried to foster through the council was severely stressed. However, this tension was already developing as the council was forming, as the minutes of this and other meetings reveal.

The agenda, which had been developed in conversations with individual Inuit, began with discussion of a government booklet on caribou, moved on to the role of the northern service officer, a particular child welfare case, future meetings of the council itself, and finally an opportunity for members to raise their own issues. The discussion of the booklet is of obvious interest to us. While the initial response to Wilkinson's request for their opinions about it was that it was "excellent" – "of all the books he had seen put out for the Eskimos, this was the best of them all,"[21] slowly, hesitantly, a number of critical comments also emerged.

"Tagoonak" (later known as Armand Tagoona) was the first who "brought forward one criticism"; he noted "that the syllabic character writing of the booklet was without 'finals' and this made it difficult for Eskimos who spoke and wrote a different dialect of the language than that in which the book was written to understand many parts of it." According to Tagoonak, this was a particular problem for inland Inuit, though for him "the language used seemed like that spoken by children. Others agreed with this." Interestingly, handwritten in the margin, presumably by one of the southern readers of the minutes, is a telling response: "Finals make no difference. Most Eskimos don't use them." Apparently, southern administrators knew more than Inuit about the latter's language. The brevity and finality of the statement betray a general attitude much less conducive to consultation than that evidenced by Wilkinson, and illustrate the general defensiveness that characterized the Arctic administration. That the use of finals may have helped to overcome dialect difference was not a consideration. Wilkinson himself expressed sympathy for the position enunciated at the meeting, though he noted that "it would be impossible to print material in all dialects."[22] That Inuit noticed the "childish" nature of the language used was insightful: the writers of this material deliberately "pitched" it at a children's level, in part because of their assumptions regarding the child-like nature of Inuit.[23]

The next important comment on the booklet was also from Tagoonak, who "went on to say that not all Eskimos seemed to understand the things they read; they read, and then went on their way as before."[24] Taken with the earlier comment, and bearing in mind that the purpose of the booklet was to promote caribou conservation, it is possible to trace a subtle line of resistance here, as if Tagoonak were implying that Inuit might not follow the pamphlet, good as it was, because they did not properly understand it, and others did not seem to follow it in any event (perhaps, more subtly, he may have been trying with the latter comment to determine the consequences of ignoring the pamphlet's suggestions). Wilkinson responded by suggesting that they not only read but also discuss the booklet and happily reported through a note in the minutes that the next day he had "found two Eskimos discussing the booklet with the HBC clerk."[25]

In discussing and explaining his own role, Wilkinson focused on his work with other *Qallunaat,* likely emphasizing the importance of working together with them to present a common front. He made some important suggestions about the council itself at that point in the meeting:

> He stressed that, although he was meeting with the Eskimos alone, this was not because he worked alone, rather it was because he felt that Eskimos would

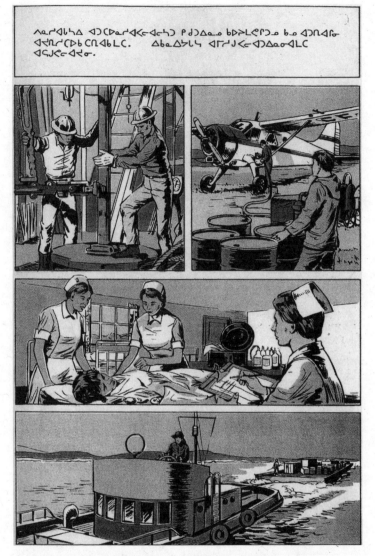

On this page from the Canadian Wildlife Service booklet *How to Save the Caribou*, the text conveys the message that for a long time there was a lot of trapping, but now more people are learning new things and new ways to lead new lives. The text states, "employment opportunities available to anyone will be increased and coached/taught by people knowledgeable about the job. Jobs will increase yearly." The illustrations show some of the possible jobs available. The intent was to encourage Inuit to embrace wage employment and move away from trapping and killing caribou to feed dog teams and, presumably, themselves. Canadian Wildlife Service, Ottawa.

Page from the Canadian Wildlife Service booklet *How to Save the Caribou*. The illustrations show all the benefits of civilization and modernization, including a store and health centre. While noting that some people are still living traditionally and hunting caribou, the text extols the virtues of modern living, noting that employment is available, that Inuit communities have social and health services so that people won't get sick as often, and that there are radios, schools for children, and airplanes for people who want to go south. The intent was to encourage Inuit to modernize. Hopefully, they would be less dependent on caribou, work for a wage, and buy their food at the store. Canadian Wildlife Service, Ottawa.

feel less shy without too many of the whites present at their first meetings. Being alone he represented all the other whites present in the settlement, as he had informed them of the meeting and they were all interested in it. Later on the Eskimos might want to have others present. Perhaps it would be better to have the meetings of the combined groups of Eskimos and whites. This would be up to us to decide.[26]

A clearer example of words and actions belying each other would be hard to find, though no doubt Inuit from Baker Lake knew full well how "shy" the presence of some of the more domineering local *Qallunaat* would make them and appreciated the absence as fully as Wilkinson. Interestingly, Wilkinson's own subject position in this meeting slid between that of a personally involved individual and that of a detached, "objective" observer. Most commonly, Wilkinson reported on himself in the third person as "he" and "Mr. Wilkinson," but in the report about reading the booklet and discussing it, for example, he wrote, "I pointed out that they often discussed and annotated the texts in the New Testament,"[27] and above there is the use of "us" in the final sentence. He thereby moved from the impersonal bearer of state sanction, to the personal reporter of the meetings, to a member of the council – the narrative instability here standing in for the peculiar and ambiguous position of someone who conscientiously adopted the role of a state employee determined to improve the position of Inuit subjects.

The discussion of a particular child welfare case involving a deaf-mute orphan boy, which did not lead to resolution, afforded Wilkinson an opening to suggest continuing to meet as a council: "There were bound to be more matters such as this. Perhaps it would be best if we could arrange to meet once every week at the same time and the same place, in order to take care of all such problems that might arise in the community."[28] This suggestion provoked an interesting discussion:

> This idea met with an enthusiastic response. Questions were asked about the conduct of such weekly meetings. Mr. Wilkinson suggested that it would be better if he were not chairman of the meetings but rather he should be an advisor to the group. It would be better if they could choose one of their own members as chairman with perhaps two assistants. It was decided that, at the close of the next meeting which would be held one week from that date, they would choose one of their members as chairman, voting by secret ballot, plus two men to assist the chairman. The chairman would act in this capacity for four meetings and then step down, to be replaced by his first assistant, and a new assistant would be chosen. The idea of monthly replacement was suggested by the Eskimos as they felt it would be unfair to ask one man to do such a job for too long a time.[29]

The notion of rotating the chair may also have accorded more closely with Inuit egalitarian practices and beliefs, not as a practice Inuit engaged in but as one that resonated with their values. To some extent, the form that council meetings took was inspired by Wilkinson's initiatives, including the idea of a "secret ballot," but other aspects were clearly determined by Inuit. Although Wilkinson himself appears to have provided the impetus for meeting and continuing to meet, the "enthusiastic response" of Inuit played as prominent a role.

At this point, the agenda had been completed, it was becoming late, and Wilkinson could have been fully justified in calling proceedings to a close. Instead, he "asked if there were any matters that anyone present would like to bring before the meeting for discussion. This brought a few minutes silence." The uncomfortable silence could easily have been interpreted as a refusal to speak further and a pretense to quickly end the meeting. Many of the better facilitators working with Aboriginal communities today would recognize this silence as a pause, a hesitation. Wilkinson, in 1957, saw it as an opening (not for the self but for the other). The minutes record the fact of hesitation, then move briskly on: "Then Tagoonak spoke out with a problem. Some of the Eskimos at the settlement were having difficulty with mail order buying." Apparently, the HBC manager "didn't have enough cash in the store to give them any. At other times he was annoyed with them for buying through the catalogue and wouldn't give them the money but would try to persuade them to order the same items through his store, which usually cost more."[30] This presented a sticky problem for Wilkinson. Was it a test to see in which direction his loyalties lay or an immediate, practical problem?

The discussion was extensive and involved articulating the concepts of "banking," price differentials, and consumers' rights. Wilkinson's initial response, though, was among the most interesting aspects of the discussion: "Mr. Wilkinson said that this was a problem which not only the Baker Lake Eskimos were having; Eskimos all across the Arctic were having it as well. (I noticed a new idea strike the group at this moment; some turned to one another and murmured, 'so other Eskimos have our troubles, too')."[31] The "I" here seems to represent a more engaged observer, one fascinated with, appreciative of, and drawn to the Inuit. This position contrasts with the role of a more formal and impersonal onlooker, required to make the state-mandated observations of a "Mr. Wilkinson." The moment of recognition recorded – "some turned to one another and murmured, 'so other Eskimos have our troubles, too'" – was significant. It was the first vital step taken independently in each distinct Inuit community, in what would ultimately lead to extensions of Inuit alliances, to organizations that would reach beyond and back to community needs, to new levels and dynamics of Inuit politics. While this was not the first time for such recognition – Inuit travelled widely in the early historical period and passed information across vast swaths of the Arctic, from Greenland to Alaska – it was, in Inuit history, an early moment in the emergence of a broader commonality. And, if it spoke to the fact that Inuit were becoming aware that other Inuit were having troubles with *Qallunaat*, underlying that awareness was the fact that the new regime was creating difficulties.

Most of the response to Tagoonak's question came from Wilkinson, as if having allowed for a silence he felt compelled to compensate for it at the first opportunity. At one point, though, "Thomas Tapati then asked if Eskimos trading foxes at the store were required to spend the money so earned at the store,"[32] a question that revealed the local dynamics taking place. Wilkinson noted that "the Eskimo could spend his money where he wished" and turned the conversation to a suggestion that he collect the "counter slips" in order to "better advise Eskimos when they came to him with problems connected with the spending of money."[33] Again interesting in terms of local dynamics, "Naigo asked if the NSO would ask the post manager to tell all the Eskimos to bring their slips. Mr. Wilkinson replied that he felt it would be better if this were not done. Rather the Eskimos themselves should undertake this job," although earlier in the minutes he noted that "I had already talked about this matter with the post manager and he felt it to be an excellent idea as he said most of the Eskimos just threw away the counter slips."[34] It appears that Inuit were having difficulties with the post manager and that a degree of diplomacy had been demanded of Wilkinson to ensure that their consumer rights, and to a lesser degree their interests, were taken into account.

The minutes record that, "at this point, Mr. Wilkinson suggested that the meeting should be brought to a close. It was getting late and everyone had to be at work the following morning," though he went on to outline a topic for the next meeting ("Eskimo identification and the use of names"), and he "gave a short summary of news of local interest ... and screened a selection of colour slides from the new development at Frobisher Bay," noting that "the Eskimos were intensely interested in the Frobisher Bay town, and the lives of Eskimos at that point."[35] Although his report indicated that the meeting went on until after midnight, the minutes record it closing at 11:45 p.m.

An Inuk who was present at early council meetings and who recalled them years later was Harold Etegoyak:

Yes, I remember [the Baker Lake Eskimo Council], but not that much anymore. When they start [forming], they are in a big ... associations when they start that one ... I was [from the Garry Lake group] ... Well, we starting, we starting like, small practice committees to start to say what our people like to have, our community in Baker Lake here ... I don't really remember the year ... [Although there were some people from outpost camps], some, but it was [actually] more who were here from here ... All I remember is I was on that committee, so I don't remember who were on the first committees too ... We can decide how the things should be running better. (Harold Etegoyak, Baker Lake, 21 May 1997)

Like James Ukpagaq, quoted above, Etegoyak stressed the role of the council as a vehicle for Inuit voice – "to start to say what our people like to have." This first meeting of the council was one of the starting points for Inuit to develop political organizations that would be recognized by the state. As tentative a start as it was, the discussion had some forceful resonance. Inuit seemed to be concerned about the form of the council and played a critical role in determining its structure. They raised questions about the language of the state and about relations with local *Qallunaat* (the post manager in this instance). Their interest in Iqaluit (Frobisher Bay) and in the problems that other Inuit faced was the first flickering of the need for a pan-Inuit agenda that would quickly develop over the next decade into a movement.

"To Give Everyone a Chance to Conduct a Meeting"
The first flush of organizing and creating the council gave it an energy and momentum. The council met weekly through the spring until mid-April, when land-based activities led to a reduced level of participation. Monthly meetings were held over the summer. Wilkinson was out of the community for much of the summer and fall that year. The pace picked up somewhat in the fall of 1957 with monthly or biweekly meetings and trailed off again to a more infrequent – monthly or less – pattern thereafter. Wilkinson left Baker Lake in 1958, and it appears that the council met without him, though meetings do not seem to have been minuted. Although it is not possible here to read the minutes of each meeting with as much attention as we paid to the first meeting, it is worthwhile to pay some attention to this rich record of Inuit concerns and discussions, particularly from the detailed minutes of the well-attended meetings in the spring of 1957. During one of these meetings, the council met with officials travelling with the Eastern Arctic Patrol.

Attendance at the second meeting, held on 5 March, a week after the first, was larger at twenty-one people. This number included the orphan boy discussed at the previous meeting and five "hunter-trappers" who had just returned from being on the land. As with the first meeting, it was an all-male attendance. Under the "set" agenda, two items of particular note were the discussion of Inuit naming systems and the election of "officers" of the council. These items were preceded by discussion of two particular child welfare cases.

The discussion on naming began with Wilkinson, at the request of Tagoonak and Louis Tapati, explaining "the system using his own and his wife's family names as a start and following this by taking some of the names of the local Eskimos." Simple as the idea appeared to Wilkinson, it was not easily absorbed by Inuit: "As a few of the Eskimos present could not grasp the system too clearly, it was decided that some of the Eskimos who did understand the system well would explain it further in private discussions over the next few days."[36] Given that the "family names" Wilkinson used were patronyms, in hindsight it is easy to understand confusion over the notion of the marriage partner adopt the Inuit man's name. The minutes nevertheless report the Inuit response to "a better method for Eskimo identification" as "enthusiastic."[37] Interestingly, the comment was also made that "this matter would not be one that would be settled easily and quickly, it might be that the recommendations made by the Baker Lake group would be the guiding factor for a plan to establish a system of identification through name only for all Eskimos in Canada."[38] No specific mention of the e-number system in use at the time, and Inuit views of it, is recorded. In Wilkinson's view, this "was definitely not an issue in the Inuit community at that time. Inuit took to e-numbers the way that servicemen did in the Second World War ... It wasn't a pressing issue in the Arctic world in the mid 50s."[39] That Inuit in Baker Lake could make suggestions that might lead to changes in policy affecting all Inuit may have seemed like an unusual and powerful promise.

The election of a chair and two assistants, in accordance with Inuit notions that the positions should be rotated, immediately followed the discussion on naming. Wilkinson noted in careful detail the procedure used: "Slips of paper were passed around to all present and each person wrote on his slip the name of the Eskimo he would like to see conduct the meetings. All Eskimos present went to elaborate lengths to make sure no one else saw the name of the man on his slip. The slips were then tabulated by Tapati and Attungala. The results were as follows: Tagoona[k] 13 slips; Tapati, Thomas 3 slips; Tapati, Louis 2 slips; Attungala 1 slip."[40] The "elaborate lengths" that Inuit went through to "make sure no one else saw the name of the man on his slip" are retrospectively as interesting as Wilkinson must have found them. In a culture where alternative, perhaps secret, names were used, the notion of hiding a name must have resonated, and the "game" of hiding the name one writes may have been appealing. Curiously, although the minutes of the first meeting indicate that the chair would be rotated to minimize the work placed on one individual, at the second meeting the rationale for the system was "to give everyone a chance to conduct a meeting."[41] That is, letting everyone be chair was specifically linked to an egalitarian notion of leadership. Compared with the election that followed four meetings later, the result here was one sided. It was also noted that the three who had been elected would meet with Wilkinson and plan the agenda, which ensured that he would have a continuing role on the council.

The set agenda for the second meeting concluded with Wilkinson relating local news. That was followed by questions or other business, and, as if they had been testing the waters and were now ready to plunge in, a serious issue was immediately broached:

> Louis Tapati then raised a problem that was troubling the Eskimos who lived at the settlement. Last year these Eskimos had not been allowed to hunt caribou in August and because of this they had no skins for clothing, either for themselves or their children, or for slippers etc. that whites in the settlement asked them to make. Early August is the only time that caribou pass close to Baker Lake, and it is also the time when the skins are at their best for clothing. He would like to know if anything could be done so that they could hunt at that time to get the skins.[42]

Inuit were running up against the game management regime described in the earlier chapters of this book. Wilkinson responded by saying that this was a matter that he would "take up with Cpl. Wilson on his return from Chesterfield," but the issue was too important to be summarily brushed off. In fact, as noted in Chapters 1-4, game management was one of the most vexing issues in northern administration and one of the main fracture lines of state relations with Inuit. While it was unusual for Inuit at the time to push issues that might bring them into conflict with state authorities – particularly the RCMP – they pressed ahead with this one: "Thomas Tapati said that they all understood that caribou were getting fewer and this was the reason they were not allowed to hunt, but they still needed the skins. If they couldn't hunt themselves perhaps they could get skins from friends who were on the land."[43] This statement shows that Inuit understood the conservation goals of game management regulations. However, this gesture of understanding may have been part of a negotiating strategy: if what the *Qallunaat* claimed to be true of caribou numbers were to be acknowledged (even though hunters likely were skeptical), then perhaps this "goodwill gesture" would have led to negotiations around the prohibition against hunting caribou in August.[44] In any event, Inuit were at an impasse because their subsistence was threatened: unspoken here was the necessity of having caribou skin clothing to support subsistence activities in the winter months. Tapati's insistence provoked a longer response from Wilkinson, who "felt this matter could be straightened out quite easily once Cpl. Wilson returned from Chesterfield, at which time we could all meet together and discuss the problem ... This was agreeable to all present."[45] A land mine had been set: local Inuit were determined to use their council to actually raise issues that concerned them. The discussion would not disappear. The meeting ended at midnight after another slide show, this one on Aklavik and reindeer herding in that region.

The importance of this issue raised in this manner cannot be overstated. After "testing the waters" to determine whether they really could speak their minds, really could raise issues of concern, the Inuit first brought to the table the question of caribou hunting. They stressed their need for caribou skin to make clothing, belying the officials' stress on caribou meat. Repeatedly told not to waste meat, Inuit here emphasized that they needed the caribou for their skins. The statements provide clear evidence that the wildlife and hunter management regimes had provoked justifiable resentments.

The third meeting, also attended by twenty-one people, though with some changes in terms of which individuals were present, was held a week later, on 12 March 1957, and was chaired by Tagoonak. Comparatively, he had extensive experience with *Qallunaat*, having driven heavy equipment for them as early as the mid-1940s, and according to Wilkinson "he seemed to be a natural leader with a lot of drive to succeed. He was elected chairman of the council at Baker Lake (as opposed to older men) largely because of his personality and ability to communicate (in English and Inuktitut)."[46] The issue of language barriers, touched on in Chapter 7, clearly played a role in how meetings were run and who was involved in them:

When we, when there's first, had the council, during that time, until 1960s, it was kind of difficult to get interpreters for them too, even to that, it wasn't easy, [reliable] interpreters for, experienced interpreters ... Back in 1940 and 30s, there was hardly any white people here, and the only time they would see them was when they would go out trading. Hardly any Qallunaat at that time ... [Sandy Lunen] was the Hudson's Bay manager there, and [Canon] James was the minister, and both of those two were fluent in [Inuktitut], so there was no reason to have interpreters at that time. (Barnabus Piruyeq, Baker Lake, 22 May 1997)

The reliance on somewhat younger, bilingual Inuit to fill leadership positions appears to have been one result.

This meeting seems to have had a more flexible agenda. The meeting began with a discussion of the form of the meeting itself, went on to deal with the specific child welfare cases, and then was dominated by a lengthy discussion of Family Allowances. Tagoonak's opening and the discussion that followed are noteworthy:

Tagoona[k] commenced the meeting by outlining his position as chairman of the group. It was his job to bring before the council such matters that he, or other council members, felt should be discussed by the group as a whole. He would make sure that everyone who wanted to speak on any subject had the chance to be heard and he would keep a record of the proceedings. His two assistants would help him in these tasks, and if he should be absent from a meeting one of them would act in his place. The entire proceedings would be in the Eskimo language. If Mr. Wilkinson, or any other of the whites who might be present, required translation into English they would ask for a translation.[47]

That proceedings would be in Inuktitut obviously increased Inuit comfort with the meetings and control over them. Inuit appear to have been quite interested in the formalities of this approach to decision making and absolutely careful to understand the protocols, as the following indicates: "Ameetenak then asked if more than one person could speak at once. The chairman said it would be better if only one person spoke at a time so that all could here [sic] what was said. If two people started to speak at once, he would indicate which should be heard first. All agreed this was good."[48] One has a feeling, reading these minutes nearly half a century later, of the tentativeness and caution with which Inuit approached this new form of discussion, while at the same time their good humour alleviated any discomfort, and their "enthusiasm" marked the importance of the venture.

After the discussion of the two orphan boys, "Tagoona[k] ... introduced the subject of Family Allowances,"[49] which came to dominate the meeting. While Family Allowances had been established by the Canadian government as part of the postwar welfare state's limited attempts at wealth redistribution and social programs, in this case designed to support families with children by making universal payments on a per child basis, the program was applied to Inuit in many Arctic regions on a needs basis. The small sums of money involved in Family Allowances were significant to poorer families in the south and of great value to cash-starved Inuit families in the Far North. Controlling and distributing payments became a source of power for northern field staff, especially the RCMP (see Tester and Kulchyski, 1994, Chapter 8). The problem as Tagoonak explained it was that the RCMP officer acted as a mediator: Inuit had to provide him with a verbal list of what they wanted, he recorded it, they took a slip over to the store manager, who then filled it. Unfortunately, "many of the Eskimos from the land only come to the settlement two or three times a year and only know goods in the store if they see them on the shelves or can handle them." They had to guess what they wanted, which was then put on the form: "The store manager can only give them what it says on the form and if they have made a mistake, they have to abide by it." Interestingly, the minutes record that "Ammetenak, Angnaryouweega, and Attungala all agreed with this. There was general agreement among the group."[50] It appears that community Inuit were prepared to use the council to raise issues for those of their relatives who lived out on the land. That along with Tagoonak three other Inuit were willing to note their agreement with his statement of the problem, supported then by the group, is significant as well; some importance was attached to this issue. There can be no doubt that issuing Family Allowance purchase forms was a source of the local RCMP officer's power. Local Inuit seemed to be trying to find a way to circumvent and reduce that power, though this was not stated explicitly.

Wilkinson responded carefully, noting that "on all matters pertaining to Family Allowance he worked very closely with the RCMP and with the nurse. Corporal Wilson and he had already discussed the issue of Family Allowance and had agreed that they felt some change was necessary."[51] He then explained the cheque system used across Canada and noted that in some places it was being used by Inuit who were wage earners "accustomed to handling money in cash or cheque,"[52] clearly a reference to employees of the DEW Line, then being constructed. He suggested that in Baker Lake some Inuit were in such a position and could be paid by cheque while "part of the group would carry on as at present."[53] This latter notion was strongly rejected by Inuit at the meeting, clearly showing that by this point they were comfortable speaking their own minds and disagreeing with Wilkinson:

> Tapati said that he thought the cheque system would be best and he would like to see it installed; but he would not want to see the Eskimos at Baker Lake divided in the way they received the Family Allowance. Such divisions in the group, he felt, would not be good for the group as some of the Eskimos who did not receive cheques might be jealous of those who did. There was unanimous agreement on this point. Mr. Wilkinson said that he agreed with this himself, and he felt it was praiseworthy that the Eskimos should put thoughts of themselves as a group ahead of thoughts of themselves as individuals.[54]

It appears that Inuit had something to teach their *Qallunaat* counterparts about collective responsibility and equitable treatment. The meeting closed with the nurse, Lang, dropping in to play tape-recorded greetings from Inuit in southern hospitals – "quite a good number of the messages were for Baker Lake and vicinity Eskimos"[55] – followed by Tagoonak and Wilkinson relating local and national news and the regular slide show, this one of the icebreaker *Labrador*'s summer 1955 journey through Foxe Basin.

The Fourth Meeting of the Council: "It Didn't Seem Right"
On 19 March, as well as twenty local people (all Inuit save Wilkinson), the meeting was joined by Corporal Wilson, back from his extended trip. He was in time to greet visitors: the Central Arctic Patrol and five civil servants from the northern affairs branch (four from Ottawa and one, Jameson Bond, an NSO at Cambridge Bay at the time). The last portion of the meeting consisted of brief speeches by the visiting dignitaries, outlining their work

and congratulating the council on its progress. However, the meeting itself was by no stretch a mere formality: Inuit used the opportunity to raise the problems that concerned them and to push for accommodations.

After a round of introductions (Tagoonak chaired and introduced the visitors, while Wilkinson introduced the councillors), the "first topic of discussion" was raised by Tagoonak: the inadequate rations provided by employers of Inuit: "They received no fresh meat, no fresh vegetables or fruits, no canned fruits, no cheese, to name some items. If they were not able to obtain fresh meat from the land, they went for months with only canned meat.[56] He felt that this was not good for the health of the Eskimos. Besides they all saw the large quantities of fresh foodstuffs that were shipped in for 'white' DOT employees. It didn't seem right for them to get such rations and not the Eskimos."[57]

This complaint produced a rash of suggestions by Harry Wilson, Don Snowden, Corporal Wilson, and "Jamie" Bond, none of whom addressed the basic question of unfair treatment. Rather, they tended to suggest that the wage-earning Inuit "trade the canned meat they received for fresh meat from other Eskimos." There was some back-and-forth conversation with Louie Tapati and Tagoonak regarding this option; the former thought "the idea might work except that in recent years the Eskimos on the land have had trouble getting sufficient meat for themselves," though it is hard to know if this comment refers to lack of game or problems with game regulation (the latter interpretation seems likely given that the issue of restrictions on caribou hunting had been raised by council). Snowden, the most senior official present, noted that "the problem raised was a vital one" and that Inuit had two choices: "a direct approach to the employer, man to his boss," and "a direct recommendation of the council."[58]

However, the issue of getting fresh meat from employers was only an opening onto the larger issue of game management itself, as the next Inuk speaker made clear: "Angnaryouweenga said that even for those Eskimos who worked for whites but could still get out after caribou, they still did not get enough fresh meat. He felt that the need for fresh meat was strong in the spring, but the season on caribou was closed at that time and they could not hunt. He went on to say he did not understand why it was that an Eskimo living on the land could hunt caribou in the spring, while Eskimos living and working at the settlement could not."[59] The administrators had avoided the question of discriminatory treatment by employers who provided their *Qallunaat* workers with foods not being supplied to Inuit by focusing on ways for wage-earning and hunting Inuit to co-operate. This approach allowed Angnaryouweenga to raise the more vexing and important question of game regulations and put the administrators into a more difficult bind. In response, "[Corporal] Wilson gave a quick run down on the game regulations concerning the killing of caribou and the reasons why such regulations are needed." Wilkinson entered the discussion at this point (presumably to calm things down) by first talking about an exchange program – fresh meat for fresh store-bought foods – in Iqaluit and then suggesting that "a number of ideas had come from the discussion and the Eskimos might want to talk them over during the next week. At the next meeting of the council, the question could be raised again and possible courses of action agreed upon."[60]

However, Inuit were not content to let the issue rest – evidence of how crucial the issues surrounding game management had become. The next portion of the meeting involved sharp exchanges between Corporal Wilson and the Inuit present around a number of subjects, with Wilkinson occasionally stepping in to mediate. It must have made for some uncomfortable moments for the visitors, but they had an opportunity to see firsthand how their policies were aggravating the people who lived with them and how the particular dynamic between *Qallunaat* and Inuit in Baker Lake was playing out. Having spoken up once, it appears that Angnaryouweenga felt comfortable to lead the charge a second time: "Angnaryouweenga then raised the next topic for discussion: the eating of eggs from nests in the summer and the killing of geese in the summer. All Eskimos looked forward to eating fresh eggs in the summer and eating fresh goose. He felt that they didn't eat many but they really enjoyed what they ate. Why was it that they were now not allowed to gather eggs in the summer, and the only time they could kill geese was when the geese had left their land?" Again Corporal Wilson of the RCMP took the bait, using "a map to explain the migration routes the birds take" and explaining that, "if there was unrestricted killing of geese in the Arctic in the summer, and unrestricted killing in the south in the winter there would perhaps come a time when the geese would no longer come to the Arctic each summer."[61]

At this point, an unusual – for Inuit almost unprecedented – event took place. The corporal was "interrupted," and a rather wry but truthful point was made: "Tagoona interrupted to say that this would not matter as the Eskimos could not kill them when they did come, therefore it didn't matter whether they came or not."[62] Wilson fell back on the fact that the law was the law: "It would be impossible to make any change in the open season on the taking of geese due to the pressures exerted on the governments by the sportsmen's groups in the United States and Canada."[63] Wilkinson then tried to smooth things over by suggesting, again, further study and discussion of the problem, noting that "the job would probably be a formidable one, but we should not be discouraged."[64]

Although the council then moved on from the issue of game management, Wilson still found himself in the hot seat: "Thomas Tapati said he would like to raise a question on the issue of Family Allowance. He would like to know why it was not possible to get flour on Family Allowance." To this, Wilson – responsible for allocating Family Allowance "rations" – responded that "usually the Eskimos did not have sufficient money to get flour after they had received items such as ammunition, clothing and milk." He thought the first and last mentioned items were most important, thereby revealing that he also thought he was the one who should be deciding. Speaking "for others who lived on the land," Tapati "agreed with this but said that Eskimos liked to have some flour for bannock and if they have no income, then Family Allowance is the only way they can buy flour," and he added that "he knew Family Allowance was for the children, but children liked bannock now and again, particularly when on a diet of fish for fish is a monotonous food."[65] Tapati clearly knew the purposes of Family Allowance and wanted Inuit to have more choice in how they used it in order to achieve those purposes. Wilson's behaviour was representative of the draconian approach of a generation involved in northern service who thought they knew better than Inuit families what was best for them. Wilson responded by saying that "often Eskimos did not know what they wanted and the RCMP Corporal has to suggest items to them," which produced an immediate riposte: "Tagoona then recommended that this would not be so if the Eskimo could order his Family Allowance goods while he was in the store where he could see the goods rather than at the RCMP detachment where he could see nothing."[66] This was thought a "good suggestion" by Wilson, who agreed to speak to the HBC post manager. The council had actually effected a change in the way local Family Allowance was managed. It also demonstrated to senior officials some of the problems that concerned them and, more subtly, the problems they were having with some of the local officials.

Wilson must have decided that enough was enough and interrupted proceedings to introduce his own agenda item. Wilkinson's minutes indicate the strain obviously present: "At this point, [Corporal] Wilson broke into the agenda of the meeting to introduce a subject ... He did not realize that subjects for discussion must first be presented to the chairman." The issue was the predictable concern of most officials involved in northern administration: Wilson was looking for "suggestions from the Eskimos as to how many of the Eskimos presently receiving relief issues of food should not be on relief." Inuit present "agreed that it would be better if relatives could assist in the support of such people and mentioned one or two persons who might fit into this category"; the subject was held over "until a further meeting."[67]

From this point, the meeting turned to the speeches from the visiting officials. While they frequently asked for advice from the Inuit, none is recorded in the minutes, though when Bill Edwards, the northern service officer posted to Iqaluit, discussed "what good use of fish products and other marine products can accomplish in the cutting down of killing of excessive numbers of caribou" this "made most of the Inuit make their distaste for moving to an increase in fish in their diets known." Edwards seemed to have little idea of the different resources available to Inuit in coastal communities as contrasted to the inland Inuit of Baker Lake. The meeting ended at 11:30 – not as late as many of the other meetings – after which "members of the Central Arctic Patrol talked privately for a short period with individual Eskimos," though there is no record of what was said.[68]

Interestingly, Barnabus Piruyek later recalled how Inuit initially thought their relations with government would unfold: "When we were working, we were requesting and trying to get the Inuit to form councilors, so that when Inuit want something then that person would write what the council would want ... At that time when the first few councilors were formed, we thought whatever we met about, whatever our concerns are, when we want something from the federal government, we would get it right away! [laughter]" (Barnabus Piruyeq, Baker Lake, 22 May 1997). The laughter here perhaps stands for a sense of irony in someone who, by painful experience, learned that things would not operate that way. Possibly, the 19 March 1957 meeting was one such experience.

More Meetings: "The Eskimos Greatly Enjoy the Suspense of the Secret Ballot"

The meeting on 26 March (in correspondence referred to as 27 March) involved an extended discussion of changing fox behaviours (comments of Inuit hunters were duly excerpted and passed around in the south to the Canadian Wildlife Service as well as relevant officials) and an explanation of savings accounts (Wilkinson compared them to food caches). There was some follow-up from the previous meeting. Several Inuit had asked their employers about fresh meat and had received responses ranging from one employer who agreed to "take the matter up with his department" to another, predictably the employer of the RCMP Inuit constables, who "had been told that fresh meat shipped in for them was impossible, they would have to find other means of getting it."[69] Off the hot seat, Wilson appears to have reverted to his normal behaviour. A final interesting point about this meeting: at the beginning, Tagoonak "welcomed the new people" (there were twenty-one present, with a number of different "hunter-trappers" at their first meeting), explained how the council operated and what it did, and "as an example of what the council could accomplish he gave a review of the changed system of issuing Family Allowance at Baker Lake and how this had been brought about largely by the suggestions of the members of the council."[70] Local Inuit were thus aware that they could make a difference.

The 2 April meeting was the last at which Tagoonak was chair. It was attended by nineteen people, including two Inuit who were at their first meeting. The bulk of the meeting was taken up with a discussion of caribou numbers, migration patterns, and behaviours (an excerpt from this discussion was passed around in the south; it contained the interesting information that Inuit had tried to help dying caribou by bringing them water, cited and discussed in Chapter 4). At the outset, a "secret ballot" was held for the new "second assistant": this time seven individuals received votes, which were distributed much more evenly, with Iyago winning on five votes, while two other candidates had three, two had two, and two had a single vote each. Wilkinson added the following note to the election: "The Eskimos greatly enjoy the suspense of the secret ballot. They go to great lengths to make sure no one sees their slip of paper and the name written on it." As with the earlier meeting, the drama of the election was an occasion for excitement and humour, Tagoonak was appointed "permanent recording secretary" to ensure his continued presence.[71]

Thomas Tapati chaired the meeting held on 9 April, at which there were sixteen people, including only one listed as a "hunter-trapper" because "all others were out on the land tending trap lines during the last weeks of the open season."[72] The meeting primarily involved an extensive discussion of fish, with Inuit reporting on their increasing use of nets, fish depletion in specific areas, areas that were good fishing sites, storage techniques, and so on, while Wilkinson diligently talked about the life cycles and movements of Arctic fish. At the beginning of the meeting, interestingly, Tagoonak "asked to speak to the Council" and "showed the members a small piece of aluminum tubing"; every month, in small numbers, such tubing was discarded from the radio station. He had collected quite a few pieces, and it "occurred to him that the cores might be useful to Eskimos in some way. He asked for opinions."[73] A lively discussion with several suggestions ensued – handles for fish gaffs, tent poles, and canoe rollers were ideas recorded – deserving our notice because, at a time when no one in the Arctic service was thinking about waste and recycling issues, they appear to have been of some importance to Inuit. In this way, they clearly had something to teach the southern administrators about environmentally supportive approaches. This approach to what today is called recycling reflects a well-established Inuit cultural pattern of inventively taking and using whatever materials are at hand, including much of what was left behind by *Qallunaat* traders, whalers, missionaries, explorers, soldiers, police officers, and even government officials. Wilkinson seems to have been one of the few who listened at least enough to record their views.

On 16 April, Thomas Tapati was "absent on a trip to his trap line," so Louis Tapati chaired the meeting, attended by fifteen people. The reduced number and the absence of the normal chair "led to a discussion of the pattern of the summer meetings," which were obviously affected by the fact that "many of the Eskimos were roaming farther afield than during the winter months"; as a result "it was decided to hold only one regular council meeting per month during May, June, July and August, and to resume the weekly meetings in September."[74] Immediately after this discussion, an Inuk named Parker "brought up the subject of the aluminum cores introduced at the last meeting."[75] He had tried "various ideas," but "the best one he had come up with was a pump for pressure gasoline lamps." After he showed his model, "all agreed that the pump was far superior to the ones sold at the Hudson's Bay Company store," and "it was suggested that Parker should make a few more pumps as some of the local Eskimos would buy them from him." This provided an opening for Tagoonak to suggest that "it might be possible for an Eskimo to start a small business at Baker Lake, making such articles as the pump mentioned above, the small tent poles, possibly fish nets as well." Wilkinson, likely enthusiastically, "agreed that such a business proposition was quite sound if operated in the beginning as a cottage type industry" and promised to assist in drawing "up plans for such a business enterprise."[76] Apparently, Inuit were giving some thought to local economic development.

This meeting also appears to have had a more open agenda. Tagoonak followed the discussion of small business by asking about radio, which led to an extensive discussion with explanations from Wilkinson about "how radio broadcasting in Canada operates" (all this about ten years before the petition for Inuit radio discussed in Chapter 7). The discussion eventually focused on the possibility of Inuktitut-language broadcasting – Louis Tapati had apparently picked up some Greenland broadcasts during the war years – though Wilkinson turned this issue to a lecture on the merits of learning English. Interestingly, Iyago, perhaps taking a more prominent role because of his new position, made more far-reaching comments during this discussion, noting "that most Eskimos at the settlement understood that their way of life was changing and they must change with it. The Eskimos on the land were different and it would be a long time before they spoke anything but their own language."[77] Throughout the meetings, Inuit showed great sensitivity to the differences among themselves, particularly between those who lived in the community and those still based "on the land." It is also possible to read a trace of political leverage in their references to more land-based Inuit, who gave Inuit present at meetings a set of "principles" they could ostensibly speak for in the name of their own hunting and cultural rights. In this instance, instead of contradicting Wilkinson directly and stating "we don't want to have to learn to speak English," Iyago could note that there were some Inuit who were not in a position to learn it. Similarly, with hunting out of season or having direct access to Family Allowances, it was the land-based Inuit who gave council members a reason – or excuse – to broach their dissent. And in this manner, the council acted as a voice for all hunting families, including those who were not living in the settlement at the time.

The meeting ended with extended discussion on the quality of rifles being made available to Inuit and construction of nylon fish nets. Wilkinson noted during the former discussion that "he had seen a few caribou hunts in the interior, and noted the amount of ammunition used to bring down each caribou. The caribou was one of the easiest animals to hunt in the Arctic, he felt, and with modern high power weapons that had been well kept, plus a better understanding of what the more modern rifle could do, the Eskimos could get far more caribou with less effort than they could with older type weapons."[78] At a time when other officials were claiming that the number of caribou was declining and that Inuit overhunting was the main cause, and a concerted effort was being made to impose regulatory schemes, Wilkinson's statement indicates at a minimum that mixed messages were being delivered. At the time, the Canadian Wildlife Service was producing propaganda designed to encourage Inuit to reduce their dependence on caribou. One cannot help but wonder how CWS officials felt on reading these minutes and discovering that other agents of the state were helping Inuit to increase their caribou-hunting abilities.

"The Local People Were Thinking of Their People's Problems and Thinking Up Ways to Solve Them"

The presence of six "hunter-trappers" boosted attendance at the 7 May meeting back to twenty, with Thomas Tapati present and in the chair. The meeting date had been moved up for a week to allow Wilkinson to be present. This meeting appears to have been less planned, with a somewhat "looser" agenda, since much of the discussion pertained to issues brought up at the meeting. "One of the new members" asked for information on the trial of Angulalik, who had been acquitted, though that was not known at the time. Wilkinson used the opportunity "to outline legal procedure as it related to cases such as that of Angulalik."[79]

Tagoonak then "gave an outline of the new camp that is to be set up by a group of Eskimos in the area of the Kazan River mouth," and "everyone listened to the account with interest and, although few of the Eskimos committed themselves to opinions on the concept of the camp idea, they all felt it might be an excellent idea for this area." Unfortunately, the minutes do not record what the "idea" comprised, though interestingly Tagoonak referred to "the elected head man, Ookpuga," who was in attendance and had been at the second meeting of the council. It appears as if Inuit were interested in establishing a community at a site of their own choosing. That they had elected a leader and had "been at the settlement over the past week or so and had talked with the local Eskimos on this project" imply that the council meeting was a formal opportunity for one group of Inuit to gain support from another. That is, Inuit may have been using the council as a vehicle not just to represent their views to *Qallunaat* but also to negotiate among themselves. Wilkinson "suggested that the members of the camp meet in the same way as the Baker Lake Council meets to discuss their life and problems," and "Ookpuga agreed."[80]

Louis Tapati, who would be travelling to Rankin Inlet, indicated one of two interesting issues raised when he noted that "he would like to bring to Baker Lake some of the Eskimo children of people working in the mine in order that these children could go to school at Baker Lake. There was no school for these children at Rankin Inlet. He asked Mr. Wilkinson if he could do this, and asked other Eskimos if they could board children brought from Rankin to attend school at Baker Lake."[81] It appears that some Inuit had their own solution to the problem of distance education and a way of avoiding the use of residential schools. Wilkinson "thanked Louis for his suggestion," which he thought "excellent," particularly because "it showed how the local people were thinking of their people's problems and thinking up ways to solve them."[82]

The second issue of note had to do with Inuit art: "Wilkinson displayed a bleached caribou antler that he had picked up on the land on one of his short trips out of Baker Lake. He asked if any of the inland Eskimos had ever carved on such antlers." In response, he was told that "no one present knew of any local Eskimo carvings or making items from antler, but many of them had seen carvings from other areas."[83] Wilkinson then showed "illustrations of carving on caribou antlers," and "this resulted in a long discussion on Eskimo carving with local materials. A number of Eskimos expressed interest in carving and said that they would talk about this between themselves."[84] From such humble beginnings, which included the initiatives of James and Alma Houston in Kinngait (Cape Dorset), would come one of the finest forms of internationally recognized art in the world: Inuit sculpture. That "they would talk about this between themselves" was a common notion and indicated that Inuit would discuss issues at their leisure and use the meetings as a formal opportunity to present their ideas to Wilkinson for action.

A letter to Wilkinson from R.A.J. Phillips, as a result of the meeting, conveyed the news that Angulalik had been acquitted and asked, "when you next submit minutes of a Council meeting, you might like to tell us a little bit about the attitude of the Eskimos towards these meetings. Are you finding for example that more of them are participating in discussions than did so in the first few meetings?"[85] This letter illustrates the interest of at least one senior southern-based official in the Baker Lake Eskimo Council and that, if Wilkinson had by implication reported somewhere that few Inuit were speaking up at meetings, perhaps Inuit were attending as "witnesses" and supports to those whom they thought could best represent their views. Wilkinson responded in his cover letter to the 25 June council meeting by suggesting that he "prepare a paper on this subject as one of my contributions at the coming conference of Northern Service Officers," which he indeed did.[86] In the same letter, while noting that "it is not expected that important items will come up for discussion at the summer meetings of the Council" because of reduced attendance, Wilkinson reported that, "despite the increased activity and the difficulty of finding time to attend meetings, a suggestion that the meetings be postponed altogether until the fall was emphatically rejected by a majority vote of the local Eskimos. The emphatic nature of this rejection seemed to indicate that the discussions at the Council meetings are filling an important need in the life of the people – they are creating a 'felt need' in the people for self expression and participation in the affairs of the area."[87] The council had established a momentum of its own.

There were only fourteen people in attendance at the 25 June meeting – still a significant presence, with all the elected officers and Tagoonak in attendance. No "majority vote of the local Eskimos" in favour of continuing the meetings is recorded, though the minutes do state that "it was decided to hold a meeting of the Council for those available" during the summer months. It was also decided that Thomas Tapati would remain as chair "because of the small turn out, and the very informal nature of discussions with the small turn out."[88] Interestingly, at this meeting, Iyago, Tapati, Seetenak, Attungala, Parker, and Tagoonak are all recorded as having spoken, though whether Wilkinson was more sensitive to recording additional speakers because of Phillips' inquiry or whether the more informal nature of the meeting helped them to feel comfortable is unclear. Discussion focused on caribou, wolf, fox, and lemming movements. Wilkinson also passed on information he had received about Angulalik and indicated that there was "interest" in Inuit information about diseased caribou[89] and in the meetings themselves. At that point, near the end of the meeting,

> Tagoonak asked for information on the recent general election in Canada. He had heard bits of information about it but did not understand just what had taken place. Mr. Wilkinson told of the election and what it would mean to the people of Canada in so far as their governing body was concerned. A great deal of interest was shown in the fact that many of the leaders in the government had been discarded and new ones elected by the people. (I think what aroused their interest was the fact that people in such high positions could be removed from their jobs by the simple expedient of votes from private citizens, people such as themselves).[90]

One wonders whether this was of such interest because there were a few particular officials Inuit would have liked to have seen replaced! Certainly, every step of their own and other democratic processes appears to have been the subject of intense curiosity among these Inuit.

The meeting on 30 July was chaired by Thomas Tapati, with all officials except Iyago present and an attendance of fifteen in all. The most interesting discussion occurred near the beginning of the meeting. Apparently, in response to the discussion at earlier meetings regarding the lack of fresh meat, community caribou hunts had been conducted that summer: "A number of Eskimos spoke out in approval of the summer hunts for caribou by settlement people by which all the local Eskimos share in the proceeds of the hunt thus giving them fresh meat during the summer months. This sharing of proceeds also helps to cut down on meat loss in the hot weather as the meat is eaten quickly by a lot of people. Suggestions were made as to where caribou would most likely be found over the period of the next few months and who would be most able to go after them."[91] The minutes are unclear as to whether it was Wilkinson or local Inuit who thought that "meat loss" had normally been a problem. No doubt the community hunt was of great benefit to those Inuit who were employed at wage labour: "A number of Eskimos spoke out in approval" is a significant statement in the context of these minutes.

A second issue was raised by the presence in the community of Dr. Fitzgerald, a wildlife biologist apparently working on lemmings. It was suggested that she come to a council meeting to give a briefing ("the Eskimos thought this to be a good idea") but also noted in the discussion that Wilkinson "would ask the Wildlife Service biologists to speak to the Council if the visitors could afford the time. Usually they were in and out again in an hour or so but it might be possible to ask them to stay for a few hours in order to speak to the Council."[92] That wildlife biologists "were in and out again in an hour or so" is revealing of the degree to which they sought out Inuit knowledge and of the growing "gap" between their analyses and forms of knowledge regarding wildlife and those of the Inuit – an issue discussed in earlier chapters.

Other issues at this meeting included a review of who had opened savings accounts at the local store (by that date, six had, with three more committed to the idea), a discussion of caribou movements, a request to the council "for assistance in procuring articles for exhibit in southern Canada as part of government displays on life in the Arctic"[93] (which the members readily agreed to do), a discussion of the summer building program, a discussion of the national flag, and a screening of slides from Wilkinson's field trip to Aberdeen Lake.

Later Years

Although the Eskimo council continued to meet, the record of meetings grew sparse. There do not appear to have been minutes of meetings in the fall of 1957 (for some of the period Wilkinson was not in town). Minutes were kept by Wilkinson in the winter and spring of 1958; the last minutes on record are from 9 April 1958.[94] At that meeting, attended by twenty-seven people, officers for a full year were elected (Armand Tagoona, Thomas Tapati, and

Francis Iyago). Wilkinson left the community and northern service soon after: this was also the time of the Garry Lake and Henik Lake famines, so no doubt he was preoccupied with these matters in the last few months of his tenure. Although Tagoona apparently kept a syllabic record, and certainly meetings continued, no minutes are extant in the archival record. A 1962 report on the establishment of a Baker Lake Residents Association noted that "the Eskimo Council has continued to function to this day and even now plays an important part in local affairs"[95] – this in spite of the fact that an attempt had been made to form a "community council" with *Qallunaat* and Inuit representation. The community council had quickly withered. The Eskimo council appears to have had greater durability, though a memorandum from Superintendent of Welfare J.M. Saulnier to Alex Stevenson, 29 May 1963, states that the northern service officer, Gunn, "should be complimented on having reactivated the Eskimo Council."[96] In November 1966, P.J. Green, the area administrator, reporting on "organizations" in Baker Lake, listed an Eskimo council with a president (T. Seeteenak), a vice president (N. Attungala), and a secretary (M. Ookowleaga),[97] the first two of whom had been involved in the 1957-58 council. It appears that, perhaps with an interruption in 1962 (which may have been related to the creation of the residents' association), the Eskimo council remained in existence until a formal municipal body, the Hamlet Council of Baker Lake, was created in 1967 with the devolution of the territorial government to Yellowknife.

A close reading of the Baker Lake Eskimo Council minutes from its earliest years provides a remarkable insight into relations between Inuit and the state. The range of issues raised, usually at the initiative of Inuit members, is remarkable and covers the gamut of northern concerns: game regulations, distribution of Family Allowances, food distribution, child welfare, naming practices, arts, small business development, the form of decision making, and democratic practice at the local level. As we have shown here and in *Tammarniit* (Tester and Kulchyski 1994), these were issues grappled with at the highest levels. In Baker Lake, Inuit had a good deal to say about these problems and issues and had very good ideas about how to deal with them. While much was presented to them in the form of *fait accompli* (or more appropriately *ayunarmut*[98]) – for example, this is the housing allocation for this year, this is what the laws say – the council accepted responsibility for the problems Inuit faced and with characteristically Inuit ingenuity drew on local resources to develop local solutions. As in the case of the aluminum pipes, in many instances Inuit were thinking far ahead of their *Qallunaat* counterparts.

Equally interesting about this record is the degree to which Inuit were clearly engaged in and enthusiastic about forms of democratic decision making. The novelty of secret ballot voting aside, Inuit had their own ideas about democratic decision making consistent with their own tradition of recognizing different people as having different expertise and therefore playing leadership roles in different circumstances. Adapting this idea to an elected council was not easy, and the idea of a rotating chair was likely as close as they could come, given that many different topics that required different expertise and insight were presented at each meeting of the council. To some degree, the council appears to have been a vehicle for local Inuit to speak through representatives, in the presence of supporters and witnesses, to Wilkinson and other officials. The record clearly indicates that Inuit met among themselves apart from Wilkinson to clarify issues and to further discuss them. When he left the community, attempts were made to develop other community organizations. While Inuit were willing to be involved in these organizations, they also continued to meet among themselves, the Eskimo council being their vehicle for doing so. It also became, apparently, the most consistent and longest lasting organization in the community.

As an exercise in community development, the formation of this council and its successful operation were a testament to the energies of local Inuit and to the aptitude of Wilkinson. His willingness to invest the time neces- sary, beginning with individual and small group consultations, and building toward a carefully timed meeting, his willingness to allow silences at meet- ings, and his willingness to trust the decision-making abilities and actual decisions of Inuit were all significant contributing factors to the success of this venture. He helped to ensure that early on in the process practical decisions made by the council were carried out so that it was clear to all that the discussions would be meaningful. That the council allowed for the release of pent-up energies that, in Wilkinson's view, appear to have been "repressed" is equally significant. It implies that Inuit had been looking for just this kind of consultative, decision-making body; they were certainly eager to participate in it. Inuit lent the council their attendance, their thoughts, their votes, their participation, without which it obviously would not have functioned. This council was a model of community consultation as a basis for community development.

Clearly, the council was a learning experience for Inuit, though one in which they nevertheless exercised a significant degree of initiative:

> It was kind of difficult for us for a while, but once we start finding out what we really need from the government, and we started [having] a little bit more [impact] ... We weren't really sure what we would need until the – what do you call that again? – area ... administrators would teach us at that time. At the same time we weren't, we weren't even aware that there would be, there were sewage trucks and garbage trucks and this kind of things. We weren't aware of these kind of things, we had to be told and taught by the area ad- ministrator, and then from there we would – you know, we were learning at the same time. (Barnabus Piruyeq, Baker Lake, 22 May 1997)

In the context of the times, this council was an extraordinary development. It illustrated that Inuit were prepared to speak up about problems, to offer solutions, to participate in planning, to question officials, to take part in forms of democratic decision making different from those embedded in their own culture. With careful preparation, they were eager for the opportunity to do so. That so little consultation took place, that Inuit voices were paid such little attention, often begrudged, was not due to a lack of interest or ability among Inuit. In the right circumstances, where they would be heard, they were happy to speak. They had important, insightful things to say. For the most part, though, no one really wanted to hear them, so there was little reason to speak.

7
Inuit Petition for Their Rights

Actions that contradicted the law and the newly constituted order were one form of resistance. Sometimes these gestures provoked state attempts to discipline and repress, and even less frequently the repressive activities were challenged in court. This dynamic fed the conflict between the legal arm of the state and the scientific apparatus that grounded policy making. The whole sequence was started, though, by an Inuk or group of Inuit engaging in an activity they had likely engaged in for the better part of their lives, following ancient customs. This form of response, discussed in Chapter 5, was one of the most direct manners in which totalization was challenged. A second challenge could be posed by newly emerging organizations or bodies that encouraged or made space for Inuit views to be expressed. The Baker Lake Eskimo Council, discussed in Chapter 6, was one such body. The records of this council represent another manner in which Inuit could "talk back" to the state – not so much through bodies and actions as through recorded words. Through this vehicle, frustrations could be expressed, and changes could occur at the local level. Furthermore, Inuit learned about the forms of Western democratic decision making and began to see a solidarity among themselves. Both of these elements can be understood as generative moments in the construction of a broader movement for Inuit governance of Inuit affairs.

A third form of response, of resistance to totalizing power, came in writing. Although Inuit were not without their own forms of writing, just as they were not without their own forms of democracy, the linear, phonetic notation engaged in by the machinery of the state was largely alien to them.[1] In this chapter, we turn our attention to a variety of Inuit petitions. While we are again not comprehensive, we look at what were certainly some of the key documents in Inuit attempts to "write back" to the state. The petitions represent a collective form of written response, and their creation can be seen as a coalescing moment in the establishment of new democratic modalities for Inuit as much as new written modalities. A close reading of the language used is therefore necessary. The chapter is organized temporally, dealing with each petition in the order of historical appearance. By working through these documents, we call attention to the emergence and development of another form of Inuit "voice," another manner in which Inuit found a form to address the state. The first petition, though, is not first merely because it appeared first; it also happens to raise some broad questions and to offer a rich field of interpretive possibilities. As in other chapters, our examinations deal with both the moments of resistance and the reactions of the state.

Kugluktuk 1953: "Our Signatures Will Tell You that We All Agree on Those Points"

On 6 February 1953, about thirty Inuit from the community of Kugluktuk (then Coppermine), using marks and Roman orthography, wrote their names on a piece of paper to indicate their support for demands expressed in a letter directed to the Government of Canada. It was perhaps the first time[2] Inuit as a group in the Canadian Arctic formally petitioned the government. The paper, which today rests quietly in an obscure file in the National Archives of Canada, is a historic document of powerful resonance. It indicates that at least some Inuit in one region of the Arctic had developed a consciousness of two things: that they had a grievance of a critical and particular kind with the emerging social order, and that the appropriate way to respond was in writing and by marking the paper as individuals to indicate their affirmation of what was written on it. The paper inaugurated a whole new field of social action in which Inuit deployed the tools of the state to address it in a manner that demanded a response.

The primary objective of the petition was to secure Inuit mineral rights. Given the importance of the document, the importance of the issue it addressed, and the importance of the actual words used, we cite it in full (all sic):

Dear Sir,

Father Adam asked you what was our position regarding the copper deposits some of our boys have found around Coppermine.
You said that we had to follow the same laws as the whites regarding the staking and holding of the claims. We feel such a law is not right, because,
(1). The land is ours and we never gave it or sold it away and never will.
(2). We are one of the poorest people in the world; we have no money to buy a licence or to register a claim.
(3). We are too ignorant to steak a claim according to the regulations.
(4). We Eskimo feel we should be given a chance.
Therefore we send you a petition requesting that any Eskimo finding ore deposit will have the right to steak it, and hold it free of taxes, and hold it

free of taxes, and that he may sell it to any Company free of taxes whenever he wants to do so.

Although we have no leader amongst us our signatures will tell you that we all agree on those points.

'Hoping that we find the Government most co-operative we sign:

The Eskimos of Coppermine.[3]

Signatures on the Coppermine (Kugluktuk) petition, 6 February 1953.
NAC, RG 85, vol. 41, file R-1875-2-4, Acc. 95-96/310.

For some time, the Coppermine River area had been a lure to *Qallunaat* in search of the metal that the river was named for and for its more valuable yellow relative. It was therefore one of the Arctic regions that had seen a number of prospectors. The concern of the petitioners with mineral rights was significant, for they were seeing their land, which they themselves had in earlier years quarried, being taken from under their feet. Prospecting activity the previous year by an American company, as well as local knowledge and discoveries of potentially precious metals, seem to have pushed them to act. They decided that something had to be said. Something had to be done.

Some of the context was remembered almost fifty years later by Nellie Hikok when we asked her about the petition:

> What I heard about it, this one territory, not too far from here, about forty miles, that's the only one spot that, I don't think that the people, I think people doesn't want that area to be touched because it's a hunting route for the community. I think he [Father Adam] was involved in that one ... Ah, it must be somewhere around 1962 or sometime in that ... Yeah, I was, ah, there was a public meeting, I think. There's a, there's some prospectors are, what do you call them anyway? The people who was involved with, ah, taking the meeting, like, ah, I don't know how you ... like you two come here to talk to the people. And those, well, they could be explorers or prospectors set up and had talks with the Natives, not the Inuit alone, but the prospector ... Alright, like, you know, Inuit people didn't know nothing of what's happening with, ah, some white person approach the community and start talking about something ... Yeah, sometimes you never notice prospectors are there doing prospecting before they even let the people know. Unexpected visitors, like [laughter]. (Nellie Hikok, Kugluktuk, 26 May 1998)

The document is in both English and Inuktitut, though the Inuktitut uses Roman orthography rather than syllabics. The signatures, most of which are in Roman orthography, though a few use an "X" or "+" mark, are on a separate sheet of paper. It is notable that both women and men signed the document. At this distance of temporal and cultural difference, it is likely difficult to grasp the degree of emotional stress that engaging in an unprecedented activity of this sort – signing a petition of protest – may have caused for the signatories. They were speaking up; they were "talking back" to a figure – the government – with a power they had already experienced as nearly absolute. It was in the same region that three decades earlier two of their number had been taken south to trial for murder and ultimately convicted to demonstrate the power of the sovereign. To sign a document of this sort, directed toward a strange, distant, unpredictable power, must have caused concern.

The language of the petition rewards close reading. Near the outset, the extraordinary statement "we feel such a law is not right" signals the profound degree to which these Inuit were opposed to the established order: not policies, not particular officials, but the law itself is put into question here. The signatories were willing to draw a distinction between what was law and what was just or right. The numbered statements are manifesto-like, invoking land ownership, pointing out their humble circumstances and lack of knowledge, and modestly asking "for a chance." Of those four points, the first burns with clarity: "The land is ours and we never gave it or sold it away and never will." These lines recall the sentiments of plains chiefs eighty years earlier when they heard about the Rupert's Land purchase.[4] At that time, the sentiments gave rise to a treaty process and the development of solemn, binding, nation-to-nation agreements. The first point that these petitioners insisted on is simple, elegant, and powerful: "The land is ours." Many Inuit whom we spoke to expressed their concern or confusion over this issue: how government had somehow come to have control and ownership over the land.

When I was a young boy, and this person that I saw for the very first time tells the Inuit, "This is government land." So because this is government land, if you were told to move from here, you would have to move. And if you were told that you have to live here or there, you have to do it. Because this is government land. That was for me very hurtful ... For somebody to say

Mangitak Qilippalik.
Photo Frank Tester.

that this belongs to the government, the land belongs to the government, animals belong to the government, it's very painful, because I thought the land was there for my, my – I've even lived up here for all, for a long, long time, a long time. (Mangitak Qilippalik, Cape Dorset, 22 May 1999)

As much as questioning the law, it was the most politically radical statement they could make. But they made it not to be radical or to challenge the existing order; they made it as a statement of self-evident fact. They then asked for the right to stake a claim – a citizen and not an Aboriginal right, hence a right even government officials should have been prepared to acknowledge – and to hold and sell it free of taxes – this latter clearly within the parameters of Aboriginal rights.

The last two statements of the petition are telling. The signatories point to their signatures, to the act of signing as signifying assent. While the "although we have no leaders" betrays a sense of insufficiency (perhaps a worry that *Qallunaat* may see an insufficiency here), it is overcome by "our signatures will tell you that we all agree on these points": the act of signing to signify assent is understood by the signatories and fully compensates for any lack of a leader. The "we all agree" emphasizes the unanimity of the people, while "on those points" stresses full agreement with the entire text. Something unique was etched into the pages of history here, an Inuit *écriture* or inscription, *titigakman,* "a new writing."

The letter can be said to have three signatures. First, the text is signed in print "The Eskimos of Coppermine," a collective inscription marking a community identity. The letter was authored by this particular Inuit collective identified with a particular place. They thereby carefully delimited their petition as representing themselves only. Underneath, in handwriting, is "Paulette Anerodluk (Typist and Interpretor)": that is, the individual who translated and typed the letter, who bore direct responsibility for putting the words of the petition on paper, is marked out. Interestingly, in the Inuktitut version in Roman orthography, Anerodluk's name is not added in handwriting but simply "Kokloktokmiun" (today we might write Kugluktukmiut: "The Inuit of Kugluktuk"). Where Anerodluk typed and interpreted, in the English version, it was thought that her name must sit beneath the words, that she must claim a measure of individual responsibility for them. Where the words are in Inuktitut and her role was presumably limited to typing, they stand as the direct words of Kokloktokmiun, and her name did not have to be added. The third signature consists of the approximately thirty names that stand on the attached page, the names of those who agree: Elizabeth Niak, Robert Noyakik, Georgina Niptanakiak, George Evaglok, William Kakolak, Hikomak, Jems Hala, Bob Kapapok, Alodik Jahn, Etokana Horice, Mallee Kanivak, Susie Kigolo, Effie Kakaiak, Edward Nigan, Frank Aklok, Edward Naviuyaw, Alek Tatona, Bissis Kodla, Ohoilak, Edie Alkolon, David

Kayogana, Bessie Kakago, Dick Kilikavioyak, with marks for Friday Hakiak, Peter Aivgak, June Uliguna, Winnie Tupektak, and Bennett. The names appear in various sizes and hands, carefully traced, though it is difficult in a few cases to determine a clear boundary: for example, how Bissis Kodla Ohoilak is to be read, as one, two, or three people, and if one or two which two go together. Here and there one also finds difficulties sorting out letters: is it Bob Kapapok or Bob Kakakok or Bob Kararok? Perhaps this ambiguity can stand in for the other forms of naming represented in this group, for the cultural divide being crossed. This third signature represents a gesture of unusual power: these individuals will not hide behind the collective representation they have given themselves – Kokloktokmiun – but will as individuals take responsibility for constituting the collective. They will stand behind the words that have been written as both a community and the individuals who collectively found it. As the act of petitioning was understood by some of the Inuit of Kugluktuk in 1953 (the use of Father Adam's name suggests the Catholic portion of a community to this day somewhat divided along denominational boundaries), it involved a cautious, deliberate, precise action. In the measured tones of this form, they addressed the Government of Canada, at the end of their petition expressing the hope "that we find the Government most co-operative." It was not to be.

"The Petition Concerns Top Level Policy"

The response of government officials in the early 1950s is of nearly equal interest and occupies a much greater space in the archival record than the petition itself. The first response was from the mining recorder in the Northern Administration and Lands Branch, R.A. Bishop, who wrote on 23 February to his superior, C.K. LeCapelain, chief of the Lands Division, enclosed the petition, and noted that "some time ago" officials had become aware "that the Coppermine Eskimoes were becoming increasingly interested in the mineral deposits in that part of the country but had no idea of the action they should take to protect their interests in any discoveries which they might make." Bishop suggested in response that "some steps should be taken to instruct them in the procedure of staking and recording claims and in the identification of minerals," with most of his response directed toward the mechanics of accomplishing this aim: he and another official could travel there and instruct the teacher, who could then pass the information on to local people. He made specific reference to items two and three on the petition, ignoring one and four. Regarding item two, he noted that "this has been a very bad year for the Coppermine Eskimos and that they are in fact extremely bad off financially." Although "it would be a simple matter to make provision for reduced or nominal fees for the recording and dealing with claims for these people," Bishop was against the idea "because we would immediately be pressed to grant the same privileges to the Indians."

Regarding item three, he was more succinct: "If we are to maintain orderly staking I can see no means by which the natives could be permitted to ignore the Regulations." The capitalization of the final term is telling – as if more force needs to be given to the rules within his grammatical structure in order to shore up their force over Inuit. The memorandum concludes with an admission that something more is "at stake" in the questions raised: "I have not yet replied to this petition as policy is involved and I would appreciate your instructions."[5]

LeCapelain's response to Bishop a few days later was brief and pointed: "It is felt here that the petition concerns top level policy and I am forwarding it to the Deputy Minister for consideration."[6] Clearly, LeCapelain could hear the warning bells ringing. It is also striking that officials at the highest level were made aware of the petition and given an opportunity to assess its significance. LeCapelain went as far as to tell Bishop that he supported the latter's educational approach and would recommend it.

The issues were discussed at least at the deputy minister level and with some alacrity. By 4 March, Frank Cunningham, the deputy commissioner of the Northwest Territories, wrote to the deputy minister and enclosed the petition, which he summarized as follows: "A petition ... requesting the right to stake mineral claims free of fees and taxes and without the necessity of having a valid miner's licence, and the right to sell any such claims to anyone free of taxes. The petition also claims that the land and mineral deposits around Coppermine belong to the Eskimos and that they are among the poorest people in the world and have no money to buy a miner's licence or to register a claim, and are also too ignorant to know how to stake a claim according to the regulations."[7] As a summary, this was a curious reordering of the demands of the petition, placing the unnumbered point about taxes from the final paragraph first and burying the demand about land ownership as the beginning of one long summary sentence relating all the other points on the petition. Nevertheless, senior officials in the northern administration clearly knew in the early 1950s that Inuit were claiming land ownership and mineral rights. Cunningham's suggestion in response to the petition was that "it would be a bad precedent to grant the Eskimos exemption from the provisions of the Quartz Mining Regulations because they are poor," noting that Indians, "half-breeds," and even whites "who are without adequate financial means" would "claim the same concessions." The conscience-saving straw of responding to the petition by providing some education on mineral identification and regulations was grasped as firmly by Cunningham as it had been by Bishop and LeCapelain; Cunningham went so far as to note that "this trip would cost $1000." Curiously, at the end of his memo on this subject, as an afterthought, he referred to staking activity of the American Metal Company in the area "in 1945 and again in 1952," which had likely triggered the petition, suggesting on no basis from the extant record that "apparently the Eskimos would like to have the area placed somewhat in the position of an Indian Reserve for their benefit. I do not think we should accept such a proposal."[8] Coming at the end, it indicated that the petition had created an uneasiness, perhaps because its logic, if accepted, threatened the basis of the established regime.

On 9 March – again with remarkable speed – LeCapelain wrote back to Bishop with a copy of a letter to be forwarded to Anerodluk. To Bishop he wrote that "we agree with you that it would be unwise to grant the Eskimos any special privileges under the Quartz Mining Regulations," citing the same reasoning as Cunningham that others might want "similar privileges" and adding that "the situation could get too complicated and it is considered much better not to grant any deviations from the regulations." While Bishop's "suggestion" regarding education "had been considered favourably," Bishop was not to be given the chance to make the trip: "This was turned down because of the estimated cost."[9]

Bishop protested this last point in a response dated 16 March, but the plan was firmly rejected on 25 March by LeCapelain, who noted that "the Deputy Minister is taking a keen interest in all departmental estimates," and "in view of this I do not feel like re-opening the subject of your proposed visit to Coppermine for this purpose. We will all have to carry on and do the best we can under the conditions laid down by the Director."[10] While at the lower levels administrators clearly wanted to have a positive response to the petition, a modest salve to their consciences perhaps, even a substantive version was rejected by their superiors. Educational workshops would be tacked on to trips made for other, more important, purposes: no funds would be allocated for even the most modest of substantive responses to the petition. That message came from on high, at the most senior levels of northern administration.

More importantly, LeCapelain's letter of the same date to "Miss Paulette Anerodluk" and "The Eskimos of Coppermine" contained a full expression of the policy. After acknowledging receipt of the petition, LeCapelain hastened to assure the Inuit that "a great deal of thought has been given to the well-being of the Eskimo people and we are constantly seeking ways in which to assist them in improving their standard of living." He then added a lengthy paragraph noting that "the copper deposits in the Coppermine area have been known for many years," commenting on the distance of the deposits from markets, referring to world copper supplies, and adding, "I can well understand the desire of the Eskimo people to benefit from this development." Some of this may have been deliberately designed to confuse the Inuit recipients of the letter, to let them know that LeCapelain and the government he represented knew about a wider world they could not hope to comprehend, and to use a language barely capable of being interpreted. The next two paragraphs convey the official response to the petition:

I would like to suggest that your people look upon themselves as Canadian citizens as well as Eskimos and as being subject to the same laws by which all Canadians are governed. It is the view of the Government that all land in the Northwest Territories and all minerals which lie on or under it, except such land as has been granted by the Government to individuals and corporations, belongs to all the people of Canada in common. The Government has passed laws and regulations under which the rights to land and minerals are administered and it is the duty of this Department to see that these laws and regulations are administered with equal fairness to all Canadians.

I do not think it would be fair to other Canadians to grant the special privileges for staking mineral claims and exemptions from fees and taxes which you have asked for the Eskimos who live near Coppermine. However, it is felt that your people can be helped to take part in the development of the minerals which lie in the area in which they live by explaining to them the regulations and by teaching them how to stake claims and recognize mineral deposits.[11]

That the land belonged to "the people of Canada" was an interesting way of expressing the issue, correct in the legal sense that courts had determined Aboriginal title was a burden on underlying Crown title, but hiding the fact that such a view left the land available to ownership and exploitation by private parties. As with the phrase "equality rights," tossed around so frequently when Inuit legal status was discussed, here "the people of Canada" is a code phrase for "available for private ownership" – in both cases, the logic of totalization is well served.

The final paragraph dealt with using the upcoming visit of various officials and later the mining inspector as an opportunity for educational work. The letter is an almost classic bureaucratic response to threat. Ensure that the language of rights is treated exclusively – translated, in effect – in terms of a language of privilege to ensure that "fairness" is the prerogative of the state. Use as much legal-administrative language as possible ("except such land as has been granted") to emphasize the superiority of the regime. Direct the discussion as much as possible to the administrative nuts and bolts of how the meagre response ("teaching them how to stake claims") will be implemented to exhaust energies in more technical, less threatening, discussions while giving every appearance of sympathy and doing as much as one can. There is nothing in the petition that indicates the signatories did not "look upon themselves as Canadian citizens as well as Eskimos." Indeed, to a certain extent, the paternalism evidenced here could not be so easily directed to *Qallunaat* citizens and itself marks a particular status and place for Inuit: as marginal, colonial subjects. The Kokloktokmiun were not about to let the matter rest there.

Writing Back: "I Do Not Think ... You Understood the Full Meaning of Our Petition"

On 13 April, Anerodluk, on behalf of the petitioners, replied directly to Le-Capelain. The opening of her letter represents a study in contrast, on the one hand a frank expression of gratitude for the response, on the other questioning whether the respondent understood the questions posed: "Thanks a lot for your nice letter. I do not think however that you understood the full meaning of our petition."[12] Half a century later, once again across the enormous gulf of temporality and cultural difference that divides the writers of these lines from the writers of this petition, these words still resonate: "I do not think however that you understood the full meaning of our petition." Resolute. Insistent. Determined. The words forcefully impress themselves upon us. A statement of bare fact, an expression of the feelings or perceptions of the Inuit signatories, it opens up to something more: part plea, part condemnation, part call. In the language of a phenomenologically oriented philosophy, it could be characterized as the call of the other. It was not heard.

Picking up on the notion that LeCapelain had insinuated into his response, to the effect that by thinking of their own claims Inuit may not have been acting or thinking of themselves as Canadians, Anerodluk continued, "indeed, we are glad to be looked upon as Canadian citizens by Ottawa; but we feel that we cannot play our part in a satisfactory way if we are let alone to do it. We appreciate very much what the government is doing in the field of Education and Health etc, but still on account of our ignorance and poverty we believe it is the duty of the government to give us assistance in order that we may not be deprived from what rightly belongs to us. This is what we meant when we sent you our petition."[13]

While markedly respectful in tone, and concerned to express appreciation for existing services, the letter contains several notes of dissent. There is "we are glad to be looked upon as Canadian; but we feel that we cannot play our part" – being happy to be looked upon as Canadian by Ottawa can hardly be thought of as a ringing endorsement of citizenship, nor can playing the part be thought of as an enthusiastic adoption of that role. While it would have been easier to write "we are happy to be Canadian," the careful avoidance of a locution of that sort is significant, implying that Inuit felt differently about their status as Canadians than LeCapelain and his superiors seem to have wanted and expected them to feel. The sentence "it is the duty of the government to give us assistance in order that we may not be deprived from what rightly belongs to us" similarly registers a dissident note. The concept of rights again makes a forceful appearance, insists that it be recognized: "This is what we meant when we sent you our petition." The emphasis is on the broader issues – "that we may not be deprived from what rightly belongs to us" – rather than on the technical details.

The next, short paragraph and the rest of the letter may be read as muting the dissonance somewhat: "We do not claim a right to all the land and minerals in our area; but we feel that when we find something we should be protected through coaching and financial support until we are able to take care of ourselves as any Canadian citizen." This opinion provides an opening for the discussion to be diverted entirely from questions of rights to questions of educational and financial support, an opening that would be eagerly grasped. The next paragraph indicates that it is not "big Companies" that local people are concerned about but "claim jumpers with whom [we] would have no chance whatsoever because we have no money to buy a licence and register a claim." What follows conveys a note of pathos: "We do not think that a little financial assistance in the form of a loan would be unfair to the other Canadians. Is there anything in the law against this? We would be glad if you could find a way to solve this problem."[14] The last substantive paragraph is interesting in light of contemporary legal discussions about Aboriginal rights, wherein the Supreme Court of Canada has emphasized the degree to which early – Aboriginal – use of a resource is a key factor in determining whether an Aboriginal people have a right to continued use:[15] "In your letter you said that copper deposits have been found many years ago. That is true, but new copper deposits have been found and the stuff is much better and much closer to the sea. This would cut down a lot of the expense to get this metal to the market. This is where our people used to go looking for [n]ative copper before the coming of the white man." The letter concludes by asking that "the R.C.M.P. take charge of our interest in that field. They have always been fair and square with us" and by offering, poignantly, "thanks again for what you have already done for us."[16]

On historical reflection, more was done to the Inuit of the region than for them. No one with whom they corresponded for a moment contemplated taking the role that arguably was constitutionally mandated of protecting their rights and looking after their interests. While in historical context it might be said that few at the time understood things in this way, other individuals – such as Justice Sissons – did open themselves up enough to hear what Inuit were saying, in words and deeds, to realize that more thought on these issues was warranted. Sissons did begin to follow the trail of documents that led to the Royal Proclamation of 1763 and the notion of Aboriginal rights. LeCapelain, not inclined to work in a similar fashion and supported by his superiors, again forwarded the letter, noting that a loan was being asked for and suggesting, "I do not recommend the acceptance of Miss Anerodluk's suggestion as this would establish a precedent which could be extended to Indians, Half-breeds and whites who were or claimed to be without adequate financial means."[17] He had found the formula he could faithfully apply to requests of this sort. In response, Cunningham first – going through the motions – asked whether "this is a case for assistance from the Eskimo Loan

Fund."[18] He was told that "any staking of claims is a gamble and not a good loan risk. I do not think we could lend money from the Eskimo Loan Fund without some reasonable prospect of getting it back and I do not think those prospects exist when a novice does the staking." The costs of licensing and working a claim were noted to be modest, and again it was emphasized that "I don't think [the Eskimo] should be assisted to hold claims as a speculative venture."[19]

That those claims might be on land that in some form belonged to the same Inuit, that they were trying to ensure they could gain advantages from developments on their ancestral and contemporary lands, were no longer on the table for consideration. Clearly, the Eskimo Loan Fund, initiated in 1952, was to be a political tool (see Tester and Kulchyski 1994, 136-38, 165-67). It would be used for projects that officials endorsed, such as the relocation of Inuit to the High Arctic that year (surely a project that was equally a gamble), but Inuit who had their own ideas of economic development, which involved finding ways to ensure they would benefit from the natural resources of their own lands (certainly a much more reasonable and, over the long term, viable economic strategy), would not be supported.

On 22 April, Cunningham wrote a short note by hand to LeCapelain: "I think we must send Miss Anerodluk a polite reply, turning down her request. We might say that there are no funds available to the fed[eral] gov[ernmen]t for such assistance, and also tell her what the out of pocket costs to stakers are."[20] The polite reply was duly sent out on 24 April. Following the lines suggested by Cunningham, much of the letter dealt with the costs of a licence and administrative costs and rules associated with staking a claim, though in response to the question about whether there were laws preventing the government from loaning funds to Inuit in Anerodluk's second letter LeCapelain noted that, "while there is nothing in the law against it, there is also nothing in the law for it. In other words, no funds have been provided by Parliament for this purpose."[21] No mention was made of the Eskimo Loan Fund established to promote economic ventures among the Inuit, which did exist at the time. The only economic ventures that it would support were those approved by department officials, but it would have been inconvenient to let Anerodluk and the Inuit of Kugluktuk know that. On 29 June of the same year, James Cantley reported on his trip through Kugluktuk, where he held an instructional meeting about mineral rights with Anerodluk as an interpreter, noting that "one of the main questions asked was 'how much will we make out of our mining claim when we sell it' and 'the name and the address of the prospective buyer?' Needless to say, these were two questions which were impossible to answer."[22]

A final few pieces of correspondence related to this story dealt with setting up the local RCMP officer as a "sub-mining recorder," at Henry Larson's suggestion, so that Inuit would be spared the cost of travelling to Yellowknife to record their claims. Larson at least found some small but important way to help Inuit in the area participate in mineral development. This may have represented a response to the last request made in the second letter from the Inuit of Kugluktuk.

The petition represented exactly the form of interrogation government officials at the time were most concerned to prevent. They wrote with all the assurance that their cultural biases and bureaucratic positions of power gave them; they pretended they knew more about the law than they actually knew; they deployed reason within the narrow compass that their instrumental rationalities allowed. They deliberately did not lift their gaze to the broader horizon of rights (not to say justice). The documentary record indicates that they did not for a moment search their souls and wonder whether in fact their presuppositions might be flawed. Instead, when confronted with this document, which destabilized the foundations of their practice, they repressed, dismissed, and ignored it: they ultimately put it in a file and buried it. Even those aspects of what Inuit were looking for that fit squarely within the existing official policy trajectory – finding some mechanisms to help Inuit participate in the potentially wealthier side of economic development – were rejected, as if on the premise that anything the Inuit themselves proposed was not worth supporting.

But it would not stay buried. Over the next twenty years, as more Inuit found the appropriate forms to deploy in addressing the state, they did so with increasing urgency. A mere two decades later Inuit would be in a position to firmly and clearly make a case for their rights and make suggestions about how those rights should be handled. By the early 1970s, the state had to listen whether it wanted to or not. In the intervening period, it is possible to trace the lineaments of an Inuit "voice." There were other courageous *arnaq* ("women") and *anguti* ("men") who put their names to documents or whose voices were recorded in the minutes of meetings, names that stood for a different policy path through the difficult questions that needed to be negotiated. In petitions, in community council meetings, in consultative processes – which appear in a vast ocean of archival documents as if they are solitary, unpredictable, ringed seals bobbing for a breath – it is possible to trace a history of dissent to the totalizing machinery of a state-constructed, -sanctioned, and -enforced policy trajectory. The mechanisms used to repress these efforts ripple through the archival record and sometimes leave more of an impression than the gestures that provoked them, as the ripples left by the seal catch our eye soon after it has slipped back beneath the surface. But the story of forms of repression must be treated as a footnote in the history of this resistance, the main lines of which follow something of far greater interest.

Paulette Anerodluk did something extraordinary for her times. She put the skills she had likely learned from *Qallunaat* at the service of her elders. How many elders must have asked their children about such service as they sent them (or were forced to send them) off to learn the *Qallunaat* ways, to learn to speak and write *Qallunaatitut* ("English"), so that finally Inuit would have a way of properly explaining what was being done to them, what needed to be done? How bitter was the disappointment when so many returned from those schools no longer able to speak Inuktitut, emotionally scarred, unable to function well in either *Qallunaat* or Inuit worlds, and clearly unprepared for the role upon which so many hopes may have rested? No doubt Father Adam, whose name touches down here and there in this record, played a part in encouraging and facilitating this petition, perhaps even in making the petition form known to Inuit as a vehicle of expression. As was the case with Wilkinson, who worked for the state but in some modalities and on some issues opened a space for Inuit to gain power, Father Adam's name here reminds us that being a missionary (or a police officer or a trader) did not exhaustively define one's role as a bearer of totalizing power. Particular individuals in specific ways could play roles as facilitators of resistance in the manner Father Adam did here. However, it should be emphasized that Inuit were the main signatories. And Anerodluk's name was attached to the correspondence. Anerodluk effectively subverted her training in Western forms of literacy directed at assimilating Inuit, at creating a class of Inuit who would carry the "burden" of civilization more effectively to their own people. She used her skills in the opposite fashion. She took the literacy and linguistic abilities she had gained and used them to express dissent, to begin to trace an argument for the rights that would support continued cultural difference.

Many other Inuit began to play the same role, and through the 1950s and 1960s a generation of young people became engaged in politics at an early age. John Amagoalic spoke about this process: "You know, when I learned to speak English, or when my generation learned to speak English, we became the communicators between our parents and the *Qallunaat*. I think as a result of that we were just sort of forced into this political situation. I can't really pinpoint my first political thought or my first political act, but I've always been involved in people politics ever since I was very young" (John Amagoalik, Iqaluit, 18 May 1999). Anerodluk wrote in *Qallunaatitut* what Inuit leaders and elders wanted her to say. In doing so, she played a subversive role. In the context of her time, with very little precedent or support, it must have taken great courage. It is the spirit of that courage – whose traces are discussed in what follows – that forms the story that deserves to occupy our abiding interest.

"Eskimo Citizens ... Have the Right in Our Society to Give Expression to Dissatisfactions"

Petitioning became a tool that Inuit from Kugluktuk would remember in the years to come. In the fall of 1957, Inuit from Kugluktuk wrote letters to complain about their treatment – the "conduct and attitudes" – at the hands of the local RCMP officer and nurse (his wife).[23] In early 1962, the Eskimo Advisory Council of Kugluktuk apparently petitioned for a hospital to be built in the community.[24] Other Inuit also used the petition form. John Ayaruak, the well-known leader from the Kivalliq (then called Keewa-tin) region, soon after attending the tenth meeting of the Committee on Eskimo Affairs, petitioned the government in the fall of 1960.[25] There were two other petitions to go along with Kugluktuk's in 1962, separate petitions from the Inuit women and men of Cape Dorset. In the latter part of the 1960s, there were petitions from Pond Inlet, for a licence for the local radio station in 1967, and from Iglulik to prevent sending their children to the residential school in Iqaluit in 1968, while in 1972 there was a petition from a group of Inuit in Povungnituk who wanted to return to their homes in Cape Smith. While we did not find some of these petitions in the archival search we conducted, we found traces of all of them, certainly enough of a record that something can be said about each. Undoubtedly, there were others, but this selection is enough to indicate the manner in which the form was used, to provide a sense of what Inuit at the community level were concerned enough about to take the risk of writing, to follow the pattern in which the state acknowledged them and responded to them, and in some small way to reflect on this sketch of the spirit of resistance among Inuit in northern Canada in the period from the early 1950s to the early 1970s, a spirit that would be foundational in inspiring much greater activity in the decades that followed. The above petitions, with their more modest claims and immediate objectives, call attention to the singular character of the Kugluktuk petition of 1953. It stands out among these documents and in this history as a unique call for respect and attention.

On 25 October 1957, R.A.J. Phillips, in his capacity as acting director of the Arctic Division, wrote an extensive memo to the deputy minister that dealt with a serious conflict – a "crisis" in the words of the document – that had taken place in Kugluktuk. The series of epidemics that the community experienced between 1949 and 1962 – measles, chicken pox, meningitis, flu, and tuberculosis – had put enough strain on already bad relations between *Qallunaat* and Inuit that the latter had engaged in a letter-writing campaign directing criticisms at the RCMP officer and nurse, who were married. The epidemics experienced by this community were not unique. Throughout this period, from 1940 to the 1960s, the fledgling Inuit communities experienced one epidemic after another, sometimes resulting in tragic deaths, particularly of infants and elderly residents. Inuit had no natural immunity to many diseases common in the western European population, with the result that epidemics of measles, flu, chicken pox, and so on hit them particularly hard. This problem was not addressed until widespread vaccinations were introduced as nursing stations were constructed and health care improved in the 1960s.[26] The letters appear to have been directed to Leo Manning, who worked as an interpreter for the government, spoke and wrote excellently in several dialects of Inuktitut, and frequently helped Inuit in contacting and corresponding with hospitalized relatives. Manning, as someone who, Inuit knew, would understand their concerns, was a logical place for them to direct their complaints, though it was not any part of his official position, and he had no capacity in which he could adequately respond. Unfortunately, Phillips did not cite any of the Inuit letters directly, though he referred to them and, in the passage that follows, dealt somewhat with their right to write them:

> Perhaps more important now are the basic principles involved. I refer to the Eskimo citizens of Coppermine who, though they as yet cannot speak with the voice of elected representatives, nevertheless have the right in our society to give expression to dissatisfactions, real or imagined. There can, therefore, be no criticism of the practice of Eskimos airing alleged wrongs in letters to a department which is specifically concerned with their welfare. Next to Gorlick and Sperry, Superintendent Larson has vented his main rage on "them bums of Eskimos who think they can criticise our man."
>
> If the right of Eskimos to have a higher court of appeal is to have any meaning, then that high authority must be prepared to exert the necessary pressures to bring about any changes locally that seem justified. I believe that at Coppermine, the evidence is overwhelmingly in favour of such changes.[27]

Since in other contexts we have tended to cite Phillips critically, it may provide those readers who pay attention to the personalities of the era with some measure of balance to know that he also advocated for Inuit to have the right of freedom of expression, in this case in the face of apparently heated opposition. Moreover, he appears to have evidenced a genuine concern to deal with the issues Inuit raised and to try to protect them – unsuccessfully in the event – from reprisals. His sense that his department was "specifically concerned with their welfare" indicates some level of awareness of responsibility though perhaps short of a constitutional mandate. Phillips' position here certainly marks a change in the approach from the attitudes and responses expressed four years earlier.

At least one of the events that gave rise to the letters is conveyed in the memorandum. Phillips quotes the welfare principal (a teacher who was given responsibility for working with RCMP officers in the administration of social assistance), Donald Green: "All were deeply shocked to have Connie Halvana and her son John row in from a distant island with the body of her husband and also to report the death of the baby which they had left at their camp ... Ice had stopped all attempts to reach the island earlier but I feel the disaster might have been avoided if one of the planes that were in had been asked to check the camp. This was suggested to the RCMP but was apparently forgotten."[28]

Allegations from a Dr. Kelly, who apparently "resigned from Health and Welfare after the Coppermine episode," and from "others who were witnesses" also criticized "the conduct and attitudes of the nurse and policeman during their regime at Coppermine." That the tenure of these individuals is characterized as a "regime" gives some indication of the power they held, in this instance apparently with something like a tyrannical impact. Interestingly, though not untypically, it appears that one response in a report on the events by another doctor who also worked for Indian and Northern Health Services, Falconer, was to suggest that a northern service officer with the department – Gorlick – had been responsible for generating the Inuit complaints. Phillips firmly rejected the suggestion: "Not only do I doubt that he became an agent provocateur, but I do not think that in the time available it was possible for him to become one."[29] Blaming outsiders – in this instance non-Inuit – for "stirring up trouble" has been a common response of the state, which likes to deny that the conditions it creates are the source of criticism; it was also an important mechanism for denying the validity of the "voices" raised in the Canadian Arctic, though one finds the same ideological mechanism at work in other colonial contexts.[30]

As well as Green, Phillips quoted three other *Qallunaat*. A Dr. Davies from Camsell Hospital was most neutral of the four, simply noting of the nurse that after "two excellent years of work" in the Arctic "she be replaced at an early date." This "early date" suggests that her service was no longer so "excellent." C.L. Merrill, who worked with the branch, wrote simply that "it does appear in the interest of Eskimo welfare at Coppermine that Cpl. McDougall be sent elsewhere." Canon Sperry was most pointed, referring to the letters of local Inuit: "The words of the sufferers themselves and their simple conclusions are more than enough to demand that this situation is immediately rectified by restaffing Coppermine Nursing Station with competent and sympathetic personnel,"[31] throwing into question the competence as well as the attitude of the nurse.

Phillips' memorandum betrays significant empathy with the Inuit letter writers, noting the difficulty of their circumstances with some clarity: "It is unfortunately true that most Eskimos are reluctant to make statements under oath to white men who are strangers to them about other white men in the community. There is a deeply ingrained fear of retaliation that can be overcome only by winning their complete confidence." The statement is all the more striking when placed next to his comment on the RCMP reaction to the letters: "Every Eskimo who dared to write a letter to Leo Manning was subjected to a police interrogation, and Superintendent Larson boasted to me – 'You don't have to tell us who wrote those letters. We have ways of finding out, and I have a stack of affidavits that high on my desk.'"[32] Here is plain evidence of the courage of those Inuit who spoke up. Being "subjected to a police interrogation" from those "who have ways of finding out" means that those who wrote paid a price in time and anxiety.

Their writing did have an impact, though whether they were aware of it or not remains in question. Phillips noted that, with departmental staff, where they became a "storm center," it was a "cardinal part of our staff policy" to remove them (though "without prejudice" to the individual, who was presumed "innocent until there is evidence to the contrary"). This was a firm and, for the most part, sensible policy in the circumstances. However, Phillips reported that "the RCMP, on the other hand, has an equally firm policy that it will not move one of its men when under criticism. It is the people of Coppermine and many other Coppermines who pay the cost." It appears that, while Phillips had the ability to convince Percy Moore, head of Indian and Northern Health Services, to replace the nurse, he could not do much about the RCMP officer. One can imagine what relations were like in the community during the remaining part of that officer's tenure. But the events and the letters did provoke a change in policy, in part as a result of changing Phillips' views. His letter ends on an eloquent note, suggesting that the branch would have to

> Accept as temporary the present RCMP role in the administration of Eskimo affairs, and to take it over ourselves as soon as possible. It is a recommendation I make with the greatest regret after years of opposition to it. While the present responsibilities and attitudes remain, the Northern Service Officer or Welfare Worker can be of only limited effectiveness. In the eyes of the Eskimo, the RCMP, the man who hands out relief, and is responsible for family allowances and so many purse strings, is still boss. If, as in Coppermine, he says "Bite the dust," then the dust will be bitten while we confine ourselves to quiet moral indignation.[33]

At the community level, Inuit could not have known that their letters helped to lead to a policy change: the administrative role of the RCMP in the Arctic would be increasingly curtailed and ultimately disappear as northern service officers, welfare workers, area administrators, and other officials took on the role. Even if they had known, it may have afforded small consolation to Inuit in Kugluktuk who had to rely on the same RCMP officer – who knew they had complained about him and his wife, who knew they were responsible for transferring his wife from her position as nurse, and who knew they would have had him transferred if his superior had not stood behind him – for welfare cheques, Family Allowances, and various other kinds of critical support.

Kugluktuk Hospital, 1962

Early 1962 found the Inuit of Kugluktuk once again concerned about health care in the community: they petitioned to have a hospital built there. The wave of epidemics experienced by the community had clearly challenged the capacities of the Indian and Northern Health Service, with communication and transportation being particular problems. Additionally, local Inuit no doubt were interested in a hospital so they could stop sending relatives to southern sanitariums for tuberculosis care. Correspondence surrounding this is sparse but reveals that the state's "surveillance" apparatus was operating

The Coppermine (Kugluktuk) petition for a hospital, 1962.
NAC, RG 85, vol. 1347, file 1000/147 (part 7).

more effectively – on this occasion, officials knew the petition was coming in advance – and again evidences concern over "agent provocateurs." In mid-February 1962, C.L. Merrill, as administrator of the Mackenzie District, wrote to P. Templeton, a regional administrator in Yellowknife, to instruct him that "the area administrator at Coppermine should not become identified in a public petition protesting the activity or lack of activity of some agency of Government. He should not take any official action in support of the mechanics of this petition, nor should advise strategies in the matter of such a public petition."[34] This is a carefully worded instruction, obviously designed to severely restrict on-the-ground support from officials for expressions of dissent. Given the job of such officials – to "help Inuit to help themselves" – such an instruction placed them in a contradictory situation because Inuit would obviously be inclined to look to northern service officers, especially those who had established strong relationships of trust, for assistance in these kinds of matters. Nevertheless, they made sound administrative sense since one would not want various government agents on the ground deploying Inuit dissent against others in the field with whom they may have been in conflict, especially since such conflicts appear to have been common. The comments above obviously also seem to have been designed to discourage petitioning as a form of achieving desirable changes.

The contradictory nature of the northern service officer's role emerges in the explanation that follows the instruction: "He can be helpful, and he should be helpful to the Eskimo Advisory Council, in bringing to the attention of the Federal authorities the wishes of the Eskimo people at Coppermine. As I see it, all that is necessary is for Mr. O'Brien to pass along the fact that the Eskimo people feel very strongly that the hospital should be built at Coppermine, giving the reasons which they list in support of this. The Area Administrator could then add his comments or advice." The officers were allowed and encouraged to pass on the views of Inuit, but they were not allowed to encourage or assist Inuit in presenting their own views. Their participation, it was thought, would throw into question the authenticity of any petition so developed: "If such a petition does go directly to some higher authority it is more than likely that some of our officers will be given the credit for having put the people up to the tactics employed."[35]

Inuit in Kugluktuk appear to have so closely followed this advice – made to the area administrator – that one assumes their area administrator did play a role, though from our position and perspective that role in no way undermines the significance or legitimacy of their views and demands. On 9 November, Merrill wrote a memorandum for the director, attaching "a petition addressed to the Area Administrator at Coppermine. This petition asks that a hospital be built at Coppermine. Also attached is Mr. O'Brien's covering memorandum." Merrill "would have preferred" that the area administrator had followed his advice even more closely and "forwarded reports to us explaining the way the people felt about hospital facilities and possibly adding how he felt," but in the absence of such reports and with a petition in hand, the government would have to respond: "In the lack of other types of advice we do now have this petition and I am passing it along to you for discussion." Merrill also forwarded his earlier memorandum with a note that "your comments on this subject and on our approach to it would be much appreciated."[36]

This abbreviated correspondence reveals that northern service officers and area administrators were in a delicate position: they were to "help Inuit help themselves," but not to the point of helping them represent themselves to the government, yet this representation was one of the most critical tools they needed in helping themselves. No hospital was built as a result of the petition (we have neither the petition nor the official response on file). The area administrator in this instance appears to have subverted his superior's instructions by having local Inuit petition directly to him as a government agent (though it is also possible that Kugluktuk Inuit adopted this strategy without his assistance); this approach in turn allowed him to pass on their petition and make his own supportive comments on it. We must also emphasize that almost ten years later Inuit in Kugluktuk were still attempting to use the petition form, for at least a third time, to effect change – in spite of the generally dismissive response to the first petition and the harmful consequences for at least some individuals (if not the community) of the second.

The first of the Kugluktuk complaints was sent to the mining recorder, the second to an interpreter, the third to the area administrator. The pattern seems to have been to write to officials close to (or situated at) the community level rather than to high-ranking officials or politicians with either level of government. Inuit were still developing an awareness of the petition as a political tool, how and when to use it, and where to direct it.

"The Mothers of Cape Dorset Who Have Signed the Attached Paper"

On 31 July 1962, two meetings were held in Cape Dorset, leading to two separate petitions being sent to the "Commissioner and Council of the Northwest Territories." The first meeting was held by the "eskimo mothers" in the school during the day. The petition dealt with four issues that led to four requests: "A. Permanent Home Economics Teacher in Cape Dorset. B. What will our children do after they are 16??? C. Can we have a Kindergarten with permanent staff??? D. Have a properly trained interpreter in town." A list of thirty-three names was attached, all clearly Inuit except possibly the last name, "Mrs. J.R. Pederson." The petition ended with the words "the above questions and problems are presented by the mothers of Cape Dorset who have signed the attached paper and we sincerely hope for the advice and assistance from the Commissioner and Council for the Northwest

Territories." Although the presence of Pederson's name here (and the fact that two of the demands, if favourably responded to, would have created local job opportunities for someone in her position) at the end of the list suggests a degree of non-Inuit assistance that may have been motivated by self-interest, the demands were directed as well to serious local concerns. For example, the kindergarten request was supported by the comment that "we would very much like to have a Kindergarten so they may learn some english before they start school so they can better understand the subjects when they do start school. This is needed because the education is only in english, not in our own language." The interpreter was needed "especially for medical problems"; here the petitioners showed some foresight since community health worker programs would eventually be established partly to fill this precise need.[37]

The second demand related to the fact that, "according to school regulations children leave school at 16 years of age. Then our problem is, what will our children do after they reach 16. This is a big problem for us." The language here is very much that of local Inuit women concerned about the future. In fact, the wording used to justify the request for a home economics teacher is telling of community politics: "Some [of] us eskimos now live in wooden houses rather than tents which were very unhealthy and as time goes more and more white people come here to work for the eskimos. Almost all the whites want to have an eskimo girl helping in their houses, but we feel we know too little about housework and this sometimes makes it difficult for both sides."[38] There is something disingenuous about noting that the "white people" who "come here to work for the eskimos" – already a politically loaded statement – cannot find well-enough-trained Inuit staff for their home care needs. Although Pederson's voice arguably may be detected in the note that "this sometimes makes it difficult for both sides," the overall effect produced here is along the lines of "*Qallunaat* who come to work for Inuit cannot find the Inuit they need to work for them." The petition is a remarkable testament to the problems that Inuit women faced at the community level, including issues related to what today might be called early childhood education, youth development, and health care.

A second petition, also addressed to the "Commissioner and Council" of the NWT government, may have been inspired by the first. It begins with the sentence "on the evening of July 31st, 1962, the undersigned men of Cape Dorset held a meeting and discussion concerning problems of Cape Dorset." That is, the women's meeting took place first, perhaps earlier in the day, while the men met later that evening. Hence, it is possible that the first meeting inspired the second, as if the men, having seen that the women were determined to petition the government, decided they should do so as well. The language here is hardly untutored and indeed can be characterized as bureaucratic in tone: "It was unanimously decided, except where otherwise noted, to present [the] following points for the consideration and advice of the Commissioner and Council."[39] There are eight demands listed, also by letter rather than number, in the same type as the women's petition though likely by a different writer. Taken together they amount to a fairly comprehensive list of community concerns.

The first of the eight demands dealt with the need for a senior's home: "We all feel that a home for our aged senior citizens is greatly needed, we have in previous years and especially last winter seen cases where our old people suffered great hardships due to extremely poor housing and no one to look after them." The request was for much of the cost of building and operating the facility, while the men proposed "to pay [one-quarter] of the cost of the building ourselves, also to staff the building at the expense of the community." The men also wanted "a detachment of the RCMP established in Cape Dorset" because "it is felt a representative of Law and Order should be present to assist and teach our young people about these matters." That is, the police presence was not asked for to enforce laws but to educate young people about the law. The third issue dealt with the need for better forms of housing, not prefabricated houses, to "be made available to everybody, very soonest, even those not employed as wage earners."[40] There can be no doubt that this was a critical need in the community at the time. That such housing should be supplied to "even those not employed as wage earners" implied the influence of more traditional Inuit in the construction of these demands.

The fourth request was the one not "unanimously decided," as the second sentence of the petition (cited above) indicated: "It was decided by a vote of 46 for and 10 against with 6 abstaining to ask the Council for a community controlled Liquor bar outlet in Cape Dorset." This makes it clear that sixty-two men were involved in the petition – a substantial number for an Inuit community at this time – and clearly the alcohol recommendation was controversial. Fifth, the petition stated that "all fully support the requests made by our women in their petition." Perhaps the men's meeting was held because the women requested it, looking for a statement from them of this sort. The phrase "all fully support" certainly leaves no question about, in fact emphasizes, the unanimous and informed nature of the men's support for the women's issues. The sixth request was for "a better reporting system about our sick people in hospitals," and it was noted that "there are some cases now when we don't even know which hospitals they are in." As well, under this heading, the men asked for "regular progress reports and also advice about possible discharge dates." In this period, many Inuit had been relocated south for tuberculosis treatment and convalescence. Seventh, the men asked "to see better playground and recreational equipment for our children and young people." Finally, the petition asked the council "to ensure that even if a new system of writing is adopted for the Canadian Eskimo, that the syllabic system will still be kept alive." The petition closed with "we sincerely request the Commissioner and Council for the Northwest Territories to reply to these problems soonest. Signed by men of Cape Dorset."[41]

These are remarkable documents. Whatever degree of *Qallunaat* influence in their construction – certainly much of the language of the latter petition was unique for local Inuit of the era – some degree of Inuit influence is evident. There were very articulate Inuit in the region (e.g., Peter Pitseolak), so Inuit may well have played a greater role in determining the grammatical structure than might otherwise be supposed. That the men's petition expressed support for the women and contained separate clauses expressing concern for elders and youth may reflect Inuit values. One expression that does stand out in these documents is "our old people suffered great hardships," which, given the context and the standards of the time, deserves underlining: these Inuit wanted to ensure, as a first priority, that their elders were not left shivering and forgotten in substandard houses and were willing to devote community resources and their own labour to improve the situation. The petitions taken together deal with housing, health, education, and justice: issues that continue to be touchstones in Aboriginal affairs and that were critical at the community level at this time. The emphasis on housing also stands out: the demand of the women for educational support – "we know too little about housework" – here links with the men's request for better housing for elders and better-quality housing "made available to everybody, very soonest, even those not employed as wage earners," and marks this area as a continued trouble spot in community development. The request for better communication with relatives taken south to hospitals reflects a consistent and reasonable concern among Inuit in this period, given the extensive use of southern sanitarium facilities in the treatment of tuberculosis. Notably, the one issue that did not enjoy unanimous support was the request for a liquor outlet. The final request of the men, involving the continued use of syllabics, can be read as a curious kind of plea for cultural protection. It was critical, if other orthographies were going to be taught, that syllabics not disappear so that elders would continue to be linked to youth. In the statement in the women's petition that "education is only in english, not in our own language," one can detect the trace of a similar concern.

These petitions represent another sort of Inuit manifesto, though it is unfortunate that so much of the language of these petitions was palpably *Qallunaat* (i.e., the demands particularly in the second petition were translated into a "proper" administrative grammar and out of the likely forms of address used more commonly by the petitioners). Nevertheless, the demands and issues were clearly inspired by Inuit, and many remain of concern to this day. These petitions were sent to the politician-administrators (i.e., with some elected though a majority appointed, administrators playing a nascent political role alongside a small number of political colleagues) who ran the government of the territories: the petitioners understood that their demands needed to be directed to government at its higher level rather than to local or regional officials. This set of demands was clearly sparked by the women of the community. That two separate but interrelated sets of demands were drawn up by the women and the men also recalls and inscribes Inuit practices regarding gender roles. The petitions amount to an early, community-based version of what would become the most striking – and ultimately unsuccessful – proposal of the Nunavut Implementation Commission three decades later for a gender-balanced territorial assembly. It appears that in Cape Dorset in 1962 women and men as *arnaq* and *anguti* saw themselves with distinct and separate, though mutually supportive and interrelated, roles in the political development and indeed in the very construction or constitution of their community.

"The Voice of the Arctic"

On 12 October 1967, Joop Sanders, an equipment mechanic working for the department at Pond Inlet, wrote to two ministers – Arthur Laing of the Department of Indian Affairs and Northern Development (DIAND) and Jack Pickersgill, the secretary of state – as well as Alex Stevenson, the administrator of the Arctic, and the Board of Broadcast Governors, which licensed communications media. He had "recently received a wire from radio regulation inspector B. Monday to stop our broadcasting immediately. I feel that this would be a crime to our local people who have put so much time and effort in this station." Sanders, with some community support, had been running an evening broadcast in Inuktitut that "not only serve[d] our local people but the people in Grise Fiord[,] Arctic Bay and Iglooolik as well. Plus the surrounding camps." He noted that "we have listeners from Alert to Pangnurtung [sic], Spence Bay to Thule Greenland. And we have been operating for one full Year and no damage done so far." Sanders signed his letter as "owner, The Voice of the Arctic, Pond Inlet," and did not make any specific request in this letter, which simply explained the situation and concluded, "relying that You Gentlemen could help us."[42]

His letter was supported by a local petition, addressed to the same individuals and organizations, in the same order, from the same day, and in the same type. The close of each message adopted the same formula. Nevertheless, the petition was signed in syllabics and Roman orthography by an impressive number of local Inuit (at least twenty-five, though so many have faded that there could have been as many as forty). It read (all sic),

> Dear Sirs
> We the people of Pond Inlet, would like to ask you a favor. We have here in Pond Inlet a local Radio station called "The voice of the Arctic" which operates every evening from 8:00 to 11:00 with most of it's programs in Eskimo.

We also know that our station has no license which is requiered for (band) broad casting. We would like to ask if there would be a possibillety to have our station licensed. We feel that it would be a great los to us as well as to Arctic Bay, Grise Fiord and the surrounding camps. If you would close this station down. Hoping you could do something for us.
Yours,
the Pond Inlet, People.[43]

A neatly written syllabic version of the letter was attached. The people of Pond Inlet who signed included Rhoda Opidyooya, Isakey, Sophie, Shirley Bateson, R.W. Matthews, Qamania, Nellie Panipakoocho, Taga, and at least seven syllabic signatures – clearly a range of individuals, most, though not all, Inuit. The petition specifically requested a licence for the station. It referred to some of the same communities as Sanders and like him added "the surrounding camps," a significant concern: the radio likely served as a crucial tool to enable community-based Inuit to send and pass on messages to their land-based relatives.

The letters created a flurry of activity. Alex Stevenson wrote to the director on 1 November, attaching both letters, noting that they had been sent to the ministers, and requesting advice.[44] The director requested advice from an assistant chief of the welfare division, W.F. Shepherd, who, in an extensive letter on 17 November, reviewed the types of licences available, the requirements for broadcast licences, and the problems with Sanders as a licensee (he was a Dutch citizen). Shepherd noted "that, despite the popularity he claims for his broadcasts, there were a number of complaints from other radio license holders (including amateurs) whose transmissions and reception were interfered with." Shepherd also made interesting comments about the wider concerns provoked by the issue:

> Even if we insisted that any costs involved be covered by community residents, it would still be a troublesome responsibility for us – particularly so, since our action might very well constitute a precedent which could trigger similar requests from other communities. For another thing, we believe we are close to success in our joint efforts with the CBC and DOT to work out a system that will enable any small northern settlement such as Pond Inlet to procure and operate its own privately licensed commercial broadcasting station. At this time we see little point in making special arrangements for Pond Inlet outside this system.

That other communities might have similar requests because there was a real need – that is, provoking and meeting such requests might have been one of the concrete ways the department could have served the Inuit for whom it had responsibility – was not a serious consideration. The carefully argued three-page letter from Shepherd ended with "in the meantime, we would recommend that Mr. Sanders should be informed that – as far as the matter of broadcasting is concerned – the Department cannot assist him to continue his operations."[45]

Unfortunately, events had gone beyond the ability of administrators to manage the situation. "The Voice of the Arctic" had captured the interest of media, and its dilemma was reported across the country. *Time* magazine carried a story that led to a letter from a Marion Palmer, of Drayton Valley, to Laing as the minister. His response on 22 November followed the same lines as Shepherd's letter, indicating that the station as it stood could not be licensed but that efforts were under way "to organize a system to assist the twenty-five or thirty small Arctic settlements who need it to establish their own broadcasting stations, properly licensed and operated by volunteers in the community."[46] Two days later Stevenson wrote to the director to report that "our community teacher at Clyde River, Mr. Scullion has for some time been operating a local radio broadcasting station. Mr. Elkin is hesitant to take any action because of the nation-wide publicity given to the Pond Inlet station and as we have no direction on that particular case are unable to advise him." Stevenson again wanted to "know what the present policy is regarding these unlicensed stations." At the outset of his memorandum, he referred to the "alleged pirate radio station at Pond Inlet," the language perhaps betraying some frustration with events.[47]

A memorandum from G. Smith, head of the branch secretariat, to the director of the Arctic Division titled "Pond Inlet – Pirate Radio Station," dated 29 November, noted "that pirate radio stations were operating at Pond Inlet, Cape Dorset and Pangnirtung." Smith later referred to the Clyde River operation as well. Clearly, there was a sense of a widespread problem. Perhaps provoked by the media attention as much as by growing awareness of the extent of the unlicensed radio use, efforts to arrive at a systemic solution seem to have escalated. Smith wrote that "the Interdepartmental Committee of which he is a member, is preparing a draft submission to Council with respect to the establishment of community broadcasting stations in the north. The draft should be ready this week." Meanwhile, all Smith could offer in response to Stevenson was a statement that "broadcasting policy is a matter for the Department of Transport," hardly the guidance or reassurance sought. Smith, however, also wanted "to be kept informed of the existence of unlicensed stations as this would probably strengthen our position when dealing with Council in that the demand for local broadcasting stations could be established."[48] In effect, northern petitions and activities could here be used as leverage to help one group of administrators in the south move another.

The issue caused friction between the DIAND and the CBC. In March 1968, the director of the Arctic Division, writing to his assistant under the title "Radio and Television Services in the North," noted that

Andrew Cowan, Head of the CBC Northern Service, publicly blamed our Department on several occasions for sitting on the proposal to install small radio stations such as at Pond Inlet. I found this very hard to believe because of all the work we had done to bring about the new policy. He was nevertheless quite certain that the head office of our Department was sitting on it and that the proposal had not gone to Treasury Board. Please let me know where this matter stands and also let me know in which communities we hope to install such small stations over the next year or two. For example, are Baker Lake and Igloolik included?

A handwritten note, likely by the assistant director of the Arctic Division, A.B. Yates, in response to the first sentence, which was underlined, reads, "since the CBC has the basic responsibility for the provision of radio services in the north I find this a bit hard to stomach."[49] No doubt the media attention had created some frayed nerves. In response, Yates noted on 29 March that a cabinet submission had been prepared in December but, since it was to go forward under both Laing's and Judy LaMarsh's signatures, had been sent to the CBC, though not until 25 March. The response to the question about where stations were to be placed is interesting because it foregrounds the policy: "The Cabinet submission simply proposes that five stations be established each year for the next five years." In setting out the "broad factors which should be considered in determining priority between competing applications," the approach was that "there will have to be a considerable amount of community 'input' (in terms of community enthusiasm and ability to provide practical support, rather than in financial terms) for any station to be successful. If this input seemed to be lacking no station would be provided."[50] Ironically, it was community input from the Pond Inlet people that had jump-started the whole process. It was not until 19 June that the CBC responded to the cabinet submission. G.F. Davidson wrote to J.A. MacDonald, the DIAND deputy minister, with a redrafted proposal for cabinet indicating that "the Corporation is prepared to purchase and install the radio stations on behalf of your department which would provide the necessary funds" and that "we would be happy to advise you in making applications to licenses on behalf of local communities and would supply technical assistance and certain programming." However, he emphasized that "the CBC would not, of course, be responsible to the CRTC for operating and programming these stations which run counter to our agreements with trade unions. I would also mention that the criterion for allocating the stations is contrary to that used by the CBC for its own coverage planning."[51] Hardly an enthusiastic partnership but enough that locally operated radio stations using Inuktitut could begin to make their official appearance in the Arctic.

Meanwhile, to alleviate the situation at Pond Inlet, the ministers had been provoked to act in advance of the cabinet submission. On 18 April 1968,

Paul Hellyer, the minister of transport, wrote to Arthur Laing, the minister of Indian affairs and northern development, stating that "on December 22 1967 I announced that arrangements were being made with your Department to provide temporary radio broadcasting service for the community of Pond Inlet," while at the same time a deputy minister of DIAND had "requested authority for your Department to operate a broadcasting station at Pond Inlet, N.W.T." The CBC had provided a transmitter, and the Department of Transport had "reconditioned the equipment" to operate on a specific frequency. That is, officials from three departments had moved quickly to ensure that the closing of Sanders' station was matched with equipment and authority for a replacement. Hellyer added that, "in the circumstances, this letter may be considered as this Department's concurrence for your Department to establish and operate the above noted transmitter at Pond Inlet on an experimental basis provided that the residents of the Community will operate the station on a non-commercial basis as a public service."[52] Effectively, the department was to act as a radio licence holder for the people of Pond Inlet, who were also provided with equipment.

Although the specific request for a licence for Sanders' station was not adhered to, the general request of both his letter and the petition were ultimately met. The initial, more unfavourable, response could not be sustained in the face of public pressure: hence, this Pond Inlet petition marked a new phase in Inuit politics. The petition was addressed to federal ministers, further raising the political stakes, as compared to earlier petitions. But it also became a trigger for a public or media campaign that galvanized popular support, which in turn put pressure on the politicians. In spite of the serious administrative hurdles, administrators were provoked by their superiors to quickly find a solution, and they did so. While the solution may not have satisfied Sanders, it certainly would have met the needs of the people of Pond Inlet. It also led to support for similar initiatives in communities across the Arctic. "The Voice of the Arctic" would grow in the variety of forms it could deploy as well as in its strength.

Iglulik: "The Young People Are Not Going to Frobisher Bay"
In a letter to Jean Chrétien, then DIAND minister, on 18 December 1968, Donald Marsh, Anglican bishop of the Arctic, wrote to express a variety of concerns related to several communities and several distinct issues. Under the heading "Igloolik," he attached a letter and a petition. The letter was from "the Rev. Noah Nasook, our Eskimo priest at Igloolik, who is also very much a leader at that point," while the petition was "from Kadlutsiak, the President of the Community Association." Marsh's other concerns will be discussed in due course; for the moment, our attention is directed to the letter and petition. It is worth noting, though, that Marsh added, "may I assure you, Mr. Minister, that when the Eskimos take to writing petitions,

then they feel very, very deeply indeed regarding the subject about which they are writing."[53] In this case, the subject was residential schooling.

The letter from Nasook was dated 19 November and addressed to "Dear Bishop" from Igloolik via Montreal (all sic):

Dear Bishop,

Here I am writing again about the young people. We want you to understand about the big school in Frobisher Bay, before they build it. We heard about it. The people in Igloolik and Hall Beach want to be heard that they don't want the young people to go. You'll be receiving list of names of people, which they don't want the young people go. Maybe most of the people's name will be on it.

The Community Consuil doesn't like the idea of having young people in Frobisher Bay. If we have school in Igloolik. We *don't* want them to go to school in Frobisher Bay. Even the'll be looked after well. The young people are *not* going to Frobisher Bay. Most people understand about the people in Frobisher Bay.

People from Aritic Bay and Pond Inlet want the young people to go to school in Igloolik.

The'll talk about it in Ottawa.

Let God help us about our words.

  Nasook.[54]

The inarticulate eloquence of this letter conveys an encyclopedic volume of information. The exasperation and frustration in the repetition of "we don't" and "they are not" and "the people in Igloolik and Hall Beach want to be heard" are visceral. The note that "we want you to understand ... before they build it" indicates that this time the people knew enough in advance so they would not be faced with yet another fait accompli and another shrug and *ayunarmut* ("it can't be helped"). The matter of sending the young people away was too important.

Nasook did not sign himself as a priest or leader but simply as Nasook. His letter was addressed to the bishop and referred to signatures being gathered: "Maybe most of the people's name will be on it." It appears that the signatures had actually been gathered already: an impressive list of sixty-seven names was attached to a letter dated 13 November 1968 and signed by J. Kadlutsiak as president of the community association, Igloolik, NWT. Kadlutsiak's signature, in Roman orthography, was first on the list, which included "Rev Noah Nasook" and the others, each name in its place in a carefully lined, double-column sheet, most in syllabics, some in Roman orthography, and some in both forms. At least six *Qallunaat* signed on, including the principal John Wayne and Doug Wilkinson. The letter was not addressed to any specific recipient and in full reads,

The Community Council held a meeting including all of the people of Igloolik. The council was trying to find out how the people of Igloolik think
of sending their children to Frobisher Bay. Almost all of them disagreed to
sen[d] their children to Frobisher Bay. The life of the children would change
if they were gathered from many different places and if they were not with
their parents. After the children were in school they will not care what their
parents say. The people of Igloolik want their children to grow up in their
own home. The people of Igloolik think if there were too many children
from many different places, some of them would forget what their parents
have taught them about home life. This doesn't mean that we are against
school. What we think is that, if there was a big school in Frobisher Bay
and many children from many different places or settlements, the children
would not get any better. What we think would be better is if the[re] were
smaller high schools in various places where the children are much closer to
their own people. The idea of having high schools i[n] some places is hard
for there are no landing strips in these places.

   We know that our suggestions will not work out, but we like you to know
that some of the people are against the high school in Frobisher Bay. We
want your help to let the government know these. We are just trying out to
see what answer we would get. We are not against the government plans.
The people were not being asked whether they want high school in Frobisher
Bay or not. The[y] probably had just picked the place and plan it there. The
letter to us would be much appreciated. The people who do not want the
high school had signed their names.[55]

The letter is prescient in its concern for the social impacts of sending children away from the influence of their parents and proposes what in effect
would become the educational system many years later: having as many high
schools as possible in the communities and, where not possible, sending the
children to schools in nearby communities. The final paragraph is curious,
beginning as it does "we know that our suggestions will not work out." It
is as if the people see the government as responsible for doing exactly what
the Inuit do not want, certainly reflective of their historical experience.
But they still want to register their opposition – "but we like you to know
that some of the people are against" – to have it on record, to ensure that
"you know" how opposed they are. Simply letting "the government know"
is the letter's stated intent. They do not oppose the building of a school in
Iqaluit (Frobisher Bay), though they appear to be mystified as to why that
location was chosen: the government "probably had just picked the place
and plan it there." There is a sense of uncertainty about the effect of the
petition. Would anyone respond? They write that a "letter to us would be
much" appreciated. And they sign their names, committing those names

to an uncertain destiny, doing whatever they could that might help them to protect their children.

A letter of 10 January 1969 from Assistant Director of Education D.W. Simpson to Director of Operations G. Smith contains a paragraph that was to be included in the official response to Marsh. Simpson notes that he "already replied to a similar letter and petition which [Kadlutsiak] sent to me last month." In his reply to Kadlutsiak, he "pointed out that it is not possible to construct large occupational and secondary schools in smaller communities such as Igloolik where supporting services and hospital facilities do not exist." He also "mentioned that it is our policy to educate children up to the grade VIII level in local communities wherever this is possible," adding that a new school – "educational construction project" – for that purpose was being built in Igloolik and that "it will not be necessary for a pupil to leave home to further his education until he is at least 14 years of age." One wonders if Simpson himself would have been consoled by that news if his own children had to finish their education in a foreign environment. In any event, "education beyond the grade VIII level requires a variety of high school and occupational opportunities in other northern communities as well as elsewhere in Canada. This variety of courses cannot be provided in communities having a small high school enrolment."[56]

The people of Igloolik got a response and could perhaps derive some satisfaction from knowing that their concern had at least been registered. In effect, they had learned something – if they did not already know it – about how that strange creature "the government" could be addressed in a manner that would provoke a response, an explanation, at the minimum some communication. Their painfully sincere address on behalf of their children was not enough to create empathy among the administrators who received it; their bishop at least could be moved by their pleas and could see beyond the narrow scope of the next memorandum.

The limited objectives of this petition, and the manner in which it almost appears to anticipate its own failure, are themselves testaments to a political dynamic where the people, targets of so many policies and programs and plans for their betterment, knew they were addressing a machinery that preferred to ignore their views. They struggled to find new ways to address the state, to find new tools to regain a measure of control. In their faltering half-steps, they did indeed move far enough to allow those who followed to lead the charge, in minor moves and major victories, to enshrine Inuit rights.

1969: Back to the Land

The July 1969 issue of the *Keewatin Echo*, a monthly newsletter produced by adult educators working for the department, contains a lengthy article from Ipeelee Kilabuk of Pangnirtung called "Ipeelee Kilabuk Seeks Improvement between Enuit and Kabloona." Kilabuk would go on to serve a term with the territorial council but was writing as a local community leader and expressing views circulating at the grassroots level. Ironically, the cover of the issue cites E.A. Ballentyne, the centennial director general, in a speech at Yellowknife saying, "the thing you must think of is unity, the holding of hands, the working together to build our own future." But the phrases were hollow in a context where in the name of equality rights were being trampled. Kilabuk, writing out of the community context, refers to a whole host of issues, from co-operatives, to missionaries, to education, to housing, to government consultation. Among many striking statements is the following: "We must be able to handle our own affairs in our land because it belongs to us. This land of ours should be compensated. It seems the land has never been compensated in the past and it just should not be taken away from us for nothing."[57] The views that circulated in the petition of 1953 were not isolated to one community. More Inuit were finding a greater variety of ways to express their views on Inuit rights. More Inuit were questioning the basic presuppositions of a policy trajectory that seemed not to take their views into account. More Inuit were wondering how the government had come to take control of a land and to establish management regimes for animals that had been occupied and used "since time immemorial" by Inuit.

The petitions, taken as a whole, indicate that there was a wellspring of sentiment among Inuit concerning their affairs, some thoughtful response to the new conditions being created around them, and some frustration over the fact that they were not in a position to influence the policies and practices that governed their lives. As with their actions and their deliberations in meetings, a reading of the petitions tells us that Inuit found ways to resist the totalizing power of the state. They also tell us that an alternative paradigm regarding policy development was available to any sensitive observers who cared to look. A consultative approach would have generated quite a different set of ideas and might even have led to a stronger respect for a notion of Inuit rights as one foundation for policy. The petitions also mark a liminal initiation of Inuit into one aspect of Western democratic forms, "writing back" as a way of talking back, compiling signatures as a way of indicating community support, inventing Inuit ways of deploying Western political techniques. Rather than see these as statements of informed Inuit perspectives on their problems, administrators tended to view the petitions as problems to be contained; instead of receiving encouragement, petitioners more often than not found that their efforts produced resentment. Even where policies were changed as a result of petitions, it was rare that petitioners were informed. As with the concept of Inuit rights that periodically exploded amid the policy paradigms and practices of the time, the state attempted to "keep a lid on" the emerging Inuit adoption of Western-style democratic impulses.

Conclusion: Contested Ground

This book is very much about struggle: a complex web of contests across cultures, time, and space. In constructing the web, we have paid particular attention to the threads of science and policy making, justice and law, as well as resistance and community development. This is ground contested from every angle. *Qallunaat,* who were state agents, were ultimately charged with welding what they saw as the Arctic colonial frontier and its inhabitants to the Canadian polity and addressing the problems – and it is not inappropriate to call some of them tragedies – that arose in the process. Challenges to these agendas came not only from Inuit but also from *Qallunaat* within the state apparatus as well as the public domain. One focus for us has been on attempts to manage Arctic game, an appropriate focus given the degree to which Inuit constructed a hunting culture. The establishment of settlement life and the new demands involved as a result – including an increasing need for cash, access to education (a motor for further cultural change), new forms of social organization, and so on – both challenged this hunting culture and suggested new forms (the petition) and forums (the Baker Lake Settlement Council) for resistance. These forms and forums became an additional focus for our work. While we take both the material and the immaterial presence of capitalist relations of production seriously (after all, who can ignore the interests of the Hudson's Bay Company, game laws intended to preserve caribou and to minimize the likelihood of Inuit dependence on government coffers, and the denial of Inuit title to ensure that potential resources were accessible to prospectors and corporate interests?), we cannot ignore the human dimensions of contests that were not simply between state actors and Inuit protagonists.

It is easy to forget, amid the machinations of academic debate and lofty theoretical reason, that this book is about people. Many of the civil servants, administrators, officials discussed in the text gave the better part of their professional lives to their Arctic careers. In the 1930s, the Arctic branch was a backwater of government. But the Arctic administration that exploded in size and occupied centre stage in the 1950s and 1960s – the decades to which we devote most of our script – counted among its number some of the brightest, most committed, and most passionate men and women Canada could offer. We recall the late Ben Sivertz, former head of the Arctic Division and commissioner of the Northwest Territories, describing how he and other public servants thought nothing of returning to work during the cold evenings of an Ottawa winter to deal with matters demanding attention. There was energy in the air surrounded by a sense of purpose. And while we have questioned many of those purposes, we have no wish to deny the honourable intentions, frozen as they were within the logic of high modernism that characterized the 1950s and 1960s, of many of the state's agents.

What has since emerged is fundamentally different, the impersonal soullessness of many bureaucrats – a species that Horkheimer and Adorno (1944) knew and identified only too well. In this earlier period, the Arctic administration was headed by a deputy minister, Gordon Robertson, who had a lengthy and well-recognized career as a key civil servant, not only in the period in question, but also subsequently for much of the Trudeau era, in the most senior reaches of government. Others are household names to those of us studying this unique period in Canadian – and dare we say international – history. Few people in the world have undergone the transition from principally hunting (and gathering) societies to what some would call "modern" or even "postmodern" culture so late in the development of capitalist enterprise – in a period that can be described as "high modernism." The role of these men (and the leaders were all men) consequently deserves our closest attention, including civil servants such as Ben Sivertz, Graham Rowley, R.A.J. Phillips, Alex Stevenson, Walter Rudnicki, as well as field officers who included John Houston, Bob Williamson, and Doug Wilkinson. This was an exceptional group of public servants who did not always agree with each other and who earned and deserved widespread respect not only as administrators but also as artists, filmmakers, ethnographers, and writers.

Hence, the *Qallunaat* involved in these transformations were not all of the same cloth. Their most firm public critic – Farley Mowat – at this stage in his career did his country a great service in pleading for what, in our view, would have been a better approach to issues regarding Inuit. We have paid more attention to another ally of the Inuit, Justice Sissons. His role in articulating, within Canadian jurisprudence, what has since been recognized as a critical foundation for Aboriginal rights deserves more attention. His reputation in the world is, in our view, not as large as it ought to be. His personal history is worth noting as it casts back on all of us questions about who we are, what motivates us, and the genesis of our commitments. All of these men, whose practices and policies we have variously condemned and saluted, were part of a significant undertaking in the history of the Canadian state. The generation of officialdom that followed them and that dominates affairs in our own time exhibits too little of their passion and commitment, develops totalizing structures so abstracted from everyday life that the term "soulless" only begins to describe their practice.

Nevertheless, we believe that the ultimate results of the efforts of these highly skilled and compassionate men were *tammarniit* ("mistakes"). They moved quickly from the early period of benign neglect when it came to Arctic affairs (Inuit were not commonly charged or arrested in the 1920s and 1930s for hunting violations) and then responded to changing conditions and traumatic disasters such as those we documented in our first book – Henik and Garry Lakes – by moving to "take over" Inuit societies and to "modernize" Inuit communities (see Tester and Kulchyski 1994). What they did not do with conviction was look for ways to actively support the hunting economy. In the late 1960s, some attempts were made to support Inuit outposts (a subject worthy of future examination), but these efforts came too late. The disruptions caused by earlier interventions had already taken their toll. In southern Canada, it was – particularly in the 1950s and 1960s – common for governments to support the family farm because it was the bedrock of communities essential to Canadian culture, social life, and economy. The loss of the family farm is the loss of a sensibility with tremendous social, cultural, and environmental implications – alienation from nature and ourselves – that we are only starting to acknowledge.

Hunting families, who occupy a comparable position in the North, were not accorded anywhere near the same respect as that afforded farm families in the 1950s and 1960s. And their loss has similar implications. The misnamed subsistence economy – a sustainable relationship to land, resources, and the future if there ever was one – is nowhere part of official economic calculations. Subsistence contributes little to the GDP, and to this day countries with large proportions of their populations engaged in subsistence activities are subsequently seen as "poor" and in need of "development." Even the current Nunavut government would need to make significant changes if it were to place the hunting economy closer to the centre of its considerations.

In the 1950s, one could have constructed a mobile infrastructure of support for camp-based Inuit. One could have provided radio access, material support for hunters through access to tools, material support of the same sort for the sewing and manufacturing talents of Inuit women. One could have established a mobile corps of medical personnel, educators, social workers, and justice officials to service and support those living on the land. As noted, thought was not given to this until the late 1960s, though by the time Hugh Brody published *The People's Land* in 1975 critiques of modernization and the importance of preserving alternative and productive human/environment relations were in the public domain.

One reason such insightful and talented people could not respond adequately to the problems that faced them was because their socialization and subsequent orientation to "science" would not let them. The role of science in the development of public policy for the Arctic emerges as an essential theme in the web of relations we have explored. This generation consolidated the notion of a social scientific base for the making of public policy, hiring anthropologists and other social scientists to assist in "pointing the way." Natural science held an even more pre-eminent position: enter Colonel Frank Banfield, John Kelsall, and their critic, Bob Ruttan. What subsequently unfolded makes a strong case for interdisciplinary critique. The scientists involved in problems of Arctic game management during the period under examination appear to have lacked even the most basic understanding of other cultures. As J. Alexander Burnett acknowledges with the title of his book *A Passion for Wildlife* (2003), Canadian Wildlife Service researchers certainly had a singular focus. The methods at hand seemed to be a vast improvement from what previous generations had done: aerial surveying had a certain glamour to it, and being in the bush – miles from anywhere – was certainly a drawing point for anyone disenchanted with the perils of civilization and the foolish comings and goings of the human species. The certainty and faith placed in their methods, stripped of critical insights into the cultural contexts within which they were operating (something that would have demanded a different educational experience), contributed to the undoing of all in the Arctic.

The conflict that emerged in the 1950s and 1960s was, in the final instance, between two arms of the state: the scientific community and the legal community. One deployed a residual and at the same time emerging legal doctrine. That doctrine, Aboriginal rights, was used to resist the impacts felt by Inuit as a result of the pronouncements of the former. The civil servants, who had to adjudicate this debate, rejected the legal arguments and firmly supported policy founded on what appeared to be the solid ground of science – with tragic consequences for Inuit.

The particular failing of some of the officials was not to take adequate account of what was going on in the world around them. The worldwide movement of the 1950s and 1960s to decolonize, which developed enormous energies and enthusiasms, was a call for the self-government of previously colonized peoples. Ironically, it was colonialism that was largely imposed on the Canadian Arctic in this period – a particular colonialism, as we have been at pains to point out, because of its imposition in the period of high modernism, where the state operated with a massively expanded machinery of surveillance and calculation, inducement and enforcement. Talking with the colonizers – learning whom to talk to and how to talk to them, including public officials and particularly the RCMP, as noted by many whom we

interviewed – was a great accomplishment for many Inuit from this generation. As we have discovered, Inuit moved to occupy the consultative void
with written words, with recorded utterances, with actions and gestures that
defied the imposed logic and law. In their own time, these efforts were not
given due attention, except in the most dismissive manner, as in the case of
the Kugluktuk petition. We have only recently begun to learn how to listen
to and document what is now called traditional ecological knowledge, so
intensely prized by a new generation of researchers. The historical record
makes the reasons for doing so compelling.

To our way of thinking, understanding this particular historical record
requires a sense of the material impacts of the policies developed by state
agents, on which we can construct a political sense of where policies and
practices stand in relation to the colonial divide, in relation to the machinery
of totalization. Broad structures established by the totalizing movements
of capital had to condition and circumscribe the activities of planners. We
acknowledge the extent to which these efforts succeed or fail. Doug Wilkinson, for one, succeeded in doing something unexpected: contributing to the
development of a forum that – along with similar forums – in some measure
undid the state's claim to Inuit land. He also resigned in frustration over
the comings and goings of his bureaucratic masters. Most of the individuals
we have named above were themselves complex, and their activities often
had multifaceted, unpredictable results, for better or for worse. We readily
acknowledge that our particular analyses and judgments will not constitute
a "last word" in the debates over this period. We do wish, however, to emphasize that the best debates are rich, not only by virtue of the more grand
policy pronouncements and obvious material circumstances they must study
and encompass, but also by the details and peculiarities of human behaviour
and history they ignore at their peril.

History really is, as Fredric Jameson (1991) said, "what hurts." And it is
often not difficult to see, among the responses of Inuit we interviewed, what
hurts. Totalization announces itself, constructs triumphal monuments to its
victories. It is possible, however, to miss the humour and twinkle of the eye
found amid that which hurts – as in feeding swans to unsuspecting RCMP
officers. The record of resistance is often subtle and frequently needs to be
teased out of documents and stories. We need to recall a long and impressive
history of Inuit who have contributed to our understanding of what hurts as
well as our appreciation of the humour and goodwill required to deal with
historical circumstances. The early generation of strong female leaders –
including the influential interpreter for whalers, Nivisiniaq/Shoofly, and the
informant of Diamond Jenness, Higilaq/Taqtu, through to contemporary
Inuit *arnaq* of the stature of Kenojuak Asheva, or Mary Simon, or Rosemarie
Kuptana – recalls for us that there was, and is, a strong human resource

largely ignored when not completely repressed in the period in question. An early generation of male leaders, their names still resonating in regions of the Arctic (including Angmarlik, Angulalik, Ayaruak, Pootoogoo), also left their traces in the archives we consulted. These are voices whose echoes can still be heard. The leadership of a unique later generation of men – including Tagak Curley, Simonie Michael, John Amagoalik, Jack Anawak, and Peter Irniq – who seized their time to forge a new politics in the Arctic deserves special recognition, their efforts made all the more fruitful by many from past generations whose struggles are part of our text.

Our histories also allow us to join the call made by Hugh Brody in his most recent work, *The Other Side of Eden* (2000): it is time for Canada to start giving hunting people, as hunters, their due. This means recognizing the value of Aboriginal rights rather than treating them as an obstacle to "development." It means cherishing treaty rights, following the logic of the Supreme Court of Canada that treaties should be interpreted in a generous and liberal manner rather than with the mean-spirited approach currently deployed. In the North – both Arctic and sub-Arctic – it means looking with fresh eyes at the "environment" and seeing it as the basis for a modest but critical sustainable economy: that of hunters. It means not assuming that the next oil and gas find, the next mineral "discovery," the next hydroelectric project, or the next clear-cut is the newest, biggest, and best thing. It similarly means not presuming that the northern environment is an unpeopled wilderness. Neither resource frontier nor vacant wilderness but, as Thomas Berger characterized it some years ago (1991), a homeland. Nunavut, in our view, resonates with the possibility of creating a dramatically different approach to lands and resources for the hunting people whose lives demand it.

Notes

Chapter 1: Trapping and Trading

1 The recognition that preservation and conservation were present and often contradictory themes in the early history of Canadian environmental management has recently received some attention. See Altmeyer (1995).

2 The term *Qalluṇaat* is used in the southern Baffin region and in northern Quebec in reference to anyone who is white skinned. The term *Qabloonaat* is commonly used in the Kivalliq region (the west coast of Hudson Bay) and in the central Arctic (Kitikmeot) region. Someone who is East Indian, for example, would be described as *Qallunaat* (*Qabloonaat*) but with a darker skin.

3 Library and Archives Canada [hereafter LAC], RG 109, CWS, vol. A, file "Lewis – History of CWS."

4 The three prairie provinces had control over wildlife and could pass hunting and trapping regulations but did not have control over other natural resources until passage in 1930 of the Natural Resources Transfer Act.

5 According to Diubaldo (1998, 135-36), although he was initially alarmed by the impact that civilization had upon the traditional hunting practices of Inuit, Stefansson was later convinced that contact was inevitable and that the domestication of caribou – and especially musk-ox – was one way of preserving traditional culture and of introducing Inuit to modernity.

6 The same cannot be said for Indian populations of the Northwest Territories who were prohibited from killing buffalo by an Ordinance for the Protection of the Buffalo passed in 1877. The significance of the law was short lived, as by 1882 there were no buffalo left on the Prairies to worry about. See McCandless (1985).

7 Ordinances of the Northwest Territories, Passed by the Lieutenant-Governor in Council, in the Session begun and holden [sic] at Regina, on the Fourteenth day of October and closed on the Nineteenth day of November, 1887, no. 2 of 1887.

8 Ibid., An Ordinance to Amend and Consolidate as Amended "The Game Ordinance" and Amendments Thereto, assented to 31 December 1892, no. 19 of 1892.

9 Ibid., An Ordinance for the Protection of Game, s. 3, c. 29, Assented to 21 November 1903.

10 The game laws for the Yukon and the Northwest Territories were different, as was the responsibility of the territorial council in each jurisdiction. The different laws had different implications for Aboriginal people. For a history of legislation in the Yukon, see McCandless (1985); in the Yukon, Aboriginal people were exempt from game laws until 1920 (36).

11 An Act Respecting Game in the Northwest Territories of Canada, 7-8 George V, s. 3, c. 36, Assented to 20 September 1917.

12 This interpretation of the act runs contrary to that suggested by Foster (1998, 176), who claims that "Indians and Eskimos continued to be exempt from most of the new restrictions (except those applying to wood buffalo, musk-ox, and white pelicans)." The wording of

the clause cited above, as well as subsequent attempts both to exempt Aboriginal people from these provisions and to strengthen and enforce them – particularly after World War II – suggest otherwise.

13 For a detailed account of the exploration of the Thelon and the intrigue surrounding its creation, see Pelly (1996).

14 James A. Lougheed, Report of Sub-Committee of Council on the Commission of Conservation, Appendix (comments relevant to the Department of Marine and Fisheries), LAC, RG 22, vol. 6, file 30, 21-25.

15 Departmental Solicitor, Department of the Interior, Memo to R.A. Gibson, 13 October 1932, LAC, RG 22, vol. 6, file 29.

16 For a more complete discussion of the administration of the Northwest Territories at this time, see Tester and Kulchyski 1994, Chapter 2.

17 Northwest Territories Council, Minutes of the Twelfth Session, 11 December 1929, LAC, RG 85, vol. 2266, file 500-2, vol. 1 (1921-30), 3-4.

18 J.F. Moran to O.S. Finnie, 8 May 1923, LAC, RG 85, vol. 127, file 250-1-1, part 1A.

19 Minutes of the Meeting of the Northwest Territories Council, Ottawa, 1 May 1925, LAC, RG 85, vol. 2266, file 500-2, vol. 1 (1921-30), 2.

20 Report to Mr. O.S. Finnie, Department of the Interior, Northwest Territories and Yukon Branch, Ottawa, from F.G. Banting, University of Toronto, 14 September 1927, NAC, RG 85, vol. 1012-4, part 3A.

21 Privy Council Order 878, 6 June 1928, LAC, RG 85, vol. 2266, file 500-2, vol. 1 (1921-30), 2.

22 Northwest Territories Council, Minutes of the Twenty-First Session, 10 December 1930, LAC, RG 85, vol. 2266, file 500-2, part 1A, 4.

23 "Eskimo Can Laugh at Fate," *Seattle Times,* 24 December 1928, LAC, RG 85, vol. 2266, file 500-2, vol. 1 (1921-30).

24 Minutes of the Twelfth Session of the Northwest Territories Council, 11 December 1929, LAC, RG 85, vol. 2266, file 500-2, vol. 1 (1921-30), 2.

25 Public Notice, Ottawa, 20 June 1935, Northwest Territories Council general file, 1933-37, LAC, RG 85, vol. 2266, file 500-2, vol. 2.

26 Northwest Territories Council, Minutes of the Tenth Session, 22 October 1929, LAC, RG 85, vol. 2266, file 500-2, vol. 1 (1921-30), 2-3.

27 Northwest Territories Council, Minutes of the Twenty-Third Session, 4 February 1931, LAC, RG 85, vol. 2266, file 500-2, part 1A, 2.

28 This is an odd comment since it is hard to imagine that restaurants existed in the territories at the time. Yellowknife was not yet a mining camp, let alone a town, and the only other possibilities were at Norman Wells or Aklavik in the Mackenzie Delta. There were likely more restaurants in the Yukon. The proper reference may also have been to restaurateurs – those running the cookhouses in mining exploration camps.

29 Council of the Northwest Territories, General File, 1933-37, Minutes of the Forty-Seventh Session, 18 December 1933, LAC, RG 85, vol. 2266, file 500-2, vol. 2, 6.

30 Northwest Territories Council, Minutes of the Thirty-Seventh Session, 9 November 1932, LAC, RG 85, vol. 2266, file 500-2, part 1A, 6.

31 Northwest Territories Council, Minutes of the Twenty-Sixth Session, 24 June 1931, LAC, RG 85, vol. 2266, file 500-2, part 1A, 3.

32 Northwest Territories Council, Minutes of the Seventy-Ninth Session, 8 April 1938, LAC, RG 85, vol. 2266, file 500-2, part 2A, 5-6; Northwest Territories Council, Draft, Minutes of the Eighty-Second Session, 20 September 1938, LAC, RG 85, vol. 2266, file 500-2, part 2A, 6-8.

33 First established as a Roman Catholic mission in 1912; a Catholic hospital was built in the community in 1939.

34 Northwest Territories Council, Minutes of the Eightieth Session, 19 April 1938, LAC, RG 85, vol. 2266, file 500-2, part 2A, 8.

35 In the 1950s, Angulalik was charged with murder following an incident that took place at a party on New Year's Eve 1957. The story is told in Eber (1997). Following this event, Angulalik, who had been a thorn in the side of the venerable Hudson's Bay Company

for many decades, asked the company to manage his post. Subsequently, he finished his trading career as a post servant and moved to Ikaluktutiak (Cambridge Bay) in 1967. He died there in 1980.

36 Northwest Territories Council, General File, 1933-37, Minutes of the Forty-Seventh Session, 18 December 1933, LAC, RG 85, vol. 2266, file 500-2, vol. 2, 4.

37 Northwest Territories Council, General File, 1933-37, Minutes of the Sixty-Seventh Session, 28 April 1937, LAC, RG 85, vol. 2266, file 500-2, vol. 2, 6. Underneath this item was a handwritten note that the supply of wooden houses to Inuit by the Canalaska Trading Company was to stand until the Supreme Court ruled on the status of Eskimos.

38 Northwest Territories Council, General File, 1933-37, Minutes of the Fifty-Ninth Session, 8 July 1935, LAC, RG 85, vol. 2266, file 500-2, vol. 2, 4.

39 Northwest Territories Council, General File, 1933-37, Minutes of the Fifty-First Session, 15 March 1934, LAC, RG 85, vol. 2266, file 500-2, vol. 2, 7.

40 Northwest Territories Council, General File, 1933-37, Minutes of the Fifty-Ninth Session, 8 July 1935, LAC, RG 85, vol. 2266, file 500-2, vol. 2, 2-3.

41 Northwest Territories Council, General File, 1933-37, Minutes of the Sixty-First Session, 9 March 1936, LAC, RG 85, vol. 2266, file 500-2, vol. 2, 9.

42 Ibid.

43 Northwest Territories Council, General File, 1933-37, Minutes of the Sixty-Second Session, 6 May 1936, LAC, RG 85, vol. 2266, file 500-2, vol. 2, 4.

44 Northwest Territories Council, General File, 1933-37, Minutes of the Seventy-First Session, 8 November 1937, LAC, RG 85, vol. 2266, file 500-2, vol. 2, 6.

45 Northwest Territories Council, General File, 1933-37, Minutes of the Sixty-First Session, 9 March 1936, LAC, RG 85, vol. 2266, file 500-2, vol. 2, 10.

46 At a council meeting in March 1934, it was noted that "Reference has been made to an incident where Indians had brought meat thirty miles by dog team and had to accept 10¢ per pound, because they had been informed by the restaurateurs and mining companies that if they did not take it, employees would be sent out to get caribou." Northwest Territories Council, General File, 1933-37, Minutes of the Fifty-First Session, 15 March 1934, LAC, RG 85, vol. 2266, file 500-2, vol. 2, 6. The going rate for meat at the time was reported to be twenty-five to thirty cents a pound.

Chapter 2: *Sagluniit* ("Lies")

1 Northwest Territories Council, Minutes of the Eighty-Second Session, 20 September 1938, LAC, RG 85, vol. 2266, file 500-2, part 2A, 13.

2 According to Burnett (1999, 15), writing about the formation of the Dominion Wildlife Service, it came about as a result of the reorganization of the Department of Resources and Development. However, that department was not created out of the Department of Mines and Resources until 1950.

3 Quoted by Harrison Lewis, "Lively: A History of the Canadian Wildlife Service," n.d., LAC, RG 109, vol. 1, 265.

4 Minutes of the 121st Session of the Northwest Territories Council, 23 January 1941, Northwest Territories Archives, G79-042, 2-3.

5 Minutes of the 122nd Session of the Northwest Territories Council, 11 February 1941, Northwest Territories Archives, G79-042, 2.

6 In his well-known and controversial book *Never Cry Wolf,* Farley Mowat (1968) does anything but endear himself to the wildlife biologists and administrators with whom he dealt while studying wolves for the Dominion Wildlife Service in 1948. In setting the scene, he makes considerable fun of the military titles used to address people within the administration: "All memos were signed Captain-this or Lieutenant-that if they originated from the lower echelons; or Colonel-this or Brigadier-that if they came down from on high" (7). The humour is deliberately disrespectful, but Mowat has a point. The operations undertaken to survey caribou and the attempt to manage Inuit hunting were carried out by an administration with a military hangover. The outcome was predictable. The results and so-called science that ensued were impervious to criticism, the scientists were indignant that anyone would

question their conclusions, and the penalties for doing so, if they could have been dished out, would have been no less severe than those handed out to deserters from the Canadian Armed Forces.

7   The school was heavily influenced by the ideas of Aldo Leopold, who pioneered the scientific management of game. He declared that "*Scientific Training* should prepare men for professional research and teaching work. It should take graduate biologists and teach them how to use their biology in solving game management problems. Graduate biologists are already turned out by many universities. What needs to be developed is the second and vital step of application. The School of Forestry and Conservation at the University of Michigan has undertaken to cover this omission" (1933, 416-17).

8   Personal communication, Dr. John Kelsall (son of John Kelsall), Vancouver, 4 November 2003.

9   Aircraft had been used to a limited extent and without much success in the 1930s in attempts to count birds. Smaller aircraft were needed for this kind of work. They were a product of the technology and innovation of World War II and were used extensively for survey work thereafter.

10   Similar observations have been made by Harvey Feit (1982) in regard to attempts by provincial game officials in the Province of Quebec to impose provincial game laws on Cree hunters in response to wildlife conservation and management problems.

11   Minutes of the 179th Session of the Northwest Territories Council, 18 February 1948, Northwest Territories Archives, G79-042, 3.

12   Harrison Lewis, Memo on Wolf Control, 157th Session of the Northwest Territories Council, 2 November 1944, Northwest Territories Archives, G79-042, 1.

13   Minutes of the 169th Session of the Northwest Territories Council, 14 January 1947, Northwest Territories Archives, G79-042, 5.

14   Cubes of buffalo meat laced with strychnine were either air dropped or deposited on the tundra in an attempt to reduce the wolf population.

15   Duncan C. Scott to H.H. Rowatt, Commissioner, Northwest Territories and Yukon, 16 February 1932, Northwest Territories Archives, G79-042, box 22, 3.

16   Ralph Parsons, Fur Trade Commissioner, Hudson's Bay Company, to H.H. Rowatt, Department of the Interior, 25 February 1932, Northwest Territories Archives, G79-042, box 22, 1.

17   The copy in the CWS collection is a draft, as changes have been pencilled in.

18   Kelsall's warnings are those of a cautious scientist. We understand these cautions, like those about limiting Inuit and Indian hunting (noted later in the text), as fragments making clear the observations of Horkheimer and Adorno (1944, 39) that within any totalizing discourse there remains a consciousness that cannot be completely colonized: "This illusion (that the rationality of the rational society is obsolete), in which a wholly enlightened mankind has lost itself, cannot be dissolved by a philosophy which, as the organ of domination, has to choose between command and obedience. Without being able to escape the confusion which still ensnares it in prehistory, it is nevertheless able to recognize the logic of either-or, of consequence and antimony, with which it radically emancipated itself from nature, as this very nature, unredeemed and self-alienated."

19   John P. Kelsall, "Baffin Island Caribou Survey" (with population estimates and recommendations), 1949, LAC, RG 109, vol. 399, file WLU 228-2 (part 1), 12-13.

20   Ibid., 12.

21   Writing in 1964, Kelsall uses a figure of 14 percent as the average for the calf crop in the same period, suggesting that the numbers were more than a little imprecise. A difference of almost 2 percent in the recruitment rate has very significant implications over time for the estimated size of the herd.

22   This would amount to 60,000 caribou per year, enough to keep the wolf population of the Northwest Territories busy twenty-four hours a day, including holidays!

23   While it is not possible to review the extensive literature on aerial survey techniques here, the methods and calculations used by Banfield and Kelsall at the time have since been shown to be very unreliable. In general, aerial surveys underestimate herd sizes, but the factors contributing to these underestimates would be exacerbated in Arctic conditions and

particularly where counting is done on herds wintering in the treed areas of the southwestern territories or the northern prairie provinces. Some researchers have since shown that the visibility bias of aerial surveys leads to a situation where 30-50 percent of animals are usually missed. This being the case, there is every reason to seriously doubt the accuracy of both Banfield's and Kelsall's surveys from the late 1940s and early 1950s, when counting techniques and the extrapolations from them were at their crudest. See Caughley (1974); Pollock and Kendall (1987); and Van Ballenberghe (1985). Even under "ideal" conditions of flat and open terrain, some researchers have found that aerial surveys have not detected 12-17 percent of animals known to be present. See Otten et al. (1993).

24 For example, surveys of the Bluenose caribou herd (a subherd of the barren ground herd) between 1974 and 1981 produced results that ranged, with a 95 percent confidence level, from a possible maximum of 168,000 animals in 1974 to a low of 18,000 animals in 1978. Despite these phenomenal differences in population estimates, the authors of this 1981 report still state with confidence that the numbers of the Bluenose herd are estimated at 39,000 plus or minus 10,000 animals (Carruthers and Jakimchuk 1981). This calculation puts the Bluenose herd as large as 49,000 animals or as low as 29,000 – a phenomenal range. The problem is further illustrated by Kelsall's (1968) estimates of population for the 1950s. Between 1952-53 and 1954-55, he estimated a change from 36,500 to 5,000 animals, a figure that increased to 10,600 in 1955-56 – a logical impossibility. Given calving rates, natural mortality, mortality from hunting, wolves, and other causes, if the herd was 49,000 animals, the implications for its long-term survival would be very different than if the "real" number was 29,000. Slight changes in assumptions about these factors can have dramatic impacts on predictions about the fate of a population. The authors of the study of the Bluenose herd cited above are at their most honest when they state, "in view of the considerable variation in population estimates it is very difficult to provide a definitive estimate of the Bluenose population" (40) (something, as noted, they do anyway).

25 John P. Kelsall, "Baffin Island Caribou Survey" (with population estimates and recommendations), 1949, LAC, RG 109, vol. 399, file WLU 228-2 (part 1), 5.

26 Ibid.

27 Ibid., 6.

28 Ibid., 8-10. Crude – in fact extremely crude – is the only way to describe his guesstimates. Kelsall arbitrarily decides that 900 of the 3,000 survey miles flown were over terrain not suitable for winter habitat. Why is not explained. He notes that large sections of the remaining 2,100 miles contained no caribou, but he says that from the air they appeared to be potential winter ranges. How such a thing could be determined at 1,000 feet, in an aircraft flying at least 100 miles an hour, by a single spotter whose expertise was the administration of family allowances, is anyone's guess. Kelsall then decides that half of Baffin Island as a whole is likely suitable winter range for caribou – a complete guess backed by no rationale whatsoever.

29 The term "do-loop," used in the early days of computer programming, refers to a program whereby the results achieved by a particular calculation are fed back into the system and a recalculation occurs with the result that the output (a number) grows or declines, depending on the assumptions built into the program.

30 Interestingly, Nadasdy writes of our own era, "First Nation elders and hunters, for example, tended to view the biologists' approach as self-serving; several of them told me that they felt the biologists were more concerned with maintaining their jobs (by generating another series of scientific studies) than with saving the sheep" (2003, 159).

31 The reader might recall Charles Dickens in *A Christmas Carol* attempting to point out the human costs of treating everything – including time – within the logic of saving and extracting every advantage from any resource over which one has control.

32 Information about this trip and the photograph was supplied by Delores MacFarlane, Edmonton, who was interviewed by phone by Frank Tester on 18 March 2003.

33 The story of this relocation and its disastrous aftermath is found in Bussidor and Bilgen-Reinart (1997).

34 Many authors have documented Inuit hunting and meat-sharing practices; see, for example, Birket-Smith (1959); Briggs (1967); Brody (1987); and Fienup-Riordan (1990).

Chapter 3: *Sugsaunngittugulli* **("We Are Useless")**

1 This phrase captures how many Inuit came to feel about themselves, having been told that they were "useless" and treated by many *Qallunaat* in the employ of the RCMP, the Hudson's Bay Company, the churches, and the government as if they knew nothing about their own land and the animals on which they had depended for centuries. However, it might be taken as a "play on words" and seen to aptly describe *Qallunaat* attempts to manage Arctic wildlife scientifically during this period. The title was suggested by André Tautu of Igluligaarjuk (Chesterfield Inlet) and Peter Irniq of Iqaluit.

2 The adaptation of Aboriginal hunting practices to new and emerging situations and opportunities of their own making, and resistance to the use of Euro-Canadian legal and administrative means in an attempt to achieve these ends, have been focuses of the work of Harvey Feit (1986).

3 Dr. H.F. Lewis, Chief, Canadian Wildlife Service, to Roy Gibson, 26 June 1950, LAC, RG 109, vol. 58, WLU 3-1, 1.

4 J.P. Richards, Memo to Dr. H.F. Lewis, Chief, Canadian Wildlife Service, Re: Enforcement of Game Laws in the Arctic Regions, 29 December 1949, LAC, RG 109, vol. 32, WLU 300 (2), 1.

5 Ibid., 2.

6 For a detailed and critical examination of the content and style of the *Book of Wisdom for Eskimo,* see McNicoll, Tester, and Kulchyski (1999).

7 C.K. Le Capelain, Chief, MacKenzie River Division, memo to Dr. H.F. Lewis, Chief, Canadian Wildlife Service, 10 August 1950, LAC, RG 109, vol. 25, WLT 200 – Musk-ox (part 1).

8 John Kelsall, Memo to Dr. H.F. Lewis, Chief, Canadian Wildlife Service, 25 September 1950, LAC, RG 109, vol. 25, WCT 200 – Musk-ox (part 1), 2.

9 Ibid.

10 Ibid., 3.

11 Ibid., 4.

12 J.G. Wright, Memo to Dr. H.F. Lewis, Director, Canadian Wildlife Service, Re: Wildlife Conditions – Bathurst Inlet Area, 5 October 1950, LAC, RG 109, vol. 25, WLT 200 – Musk-ox (part 1).

13 Henry Larson, Memo to the Commissioner, RCMP, Re: Game Conditions (Caribou, Musk-Oxen, etc.), Coppermine, Tree River, Hood River, and Bathurst Inlet, 25 October 1950, LAC, RG 109, vol. 25, WLT 200 – Musk-ox (part 1), 1.

14 Nevertheless, Larson seems to have had some impact on Kelsall. A year later Kelsall was writing to John Tener of the Canadian Wildlife Service and stating that, in addition to using every scrap of the musk-ox they killed, all kills had been reported to the RCMP and that the situation in the Bathurst region was not serious. This was a different tune from that he was playing a year earlier. John Kelsall to John Tener, Department of Zoology, University of British Columbia, 3 November 1951, LAC, RG 109, vol. 23, WLT 200 – Musk-ox (part 1).

15 John Kelsall, Memo to Dr. H.F. Lewis, Chief, Canadian Wildlife Service, Re: Recent RCMP Memoranda on Caribou and Musk-Ox, 7 November 1950, LAC, RG 109, vol. 25, WLT 200 – Musk-ox (part 1), 2.

16 Ibid., 3.

17 Ibid.

18 J.P. Richards, "Conditions Affecting the Welfare of the Eskimos," 18 January 1951, LAC, RG 109, WLT 300, box 10 (part 3), 2.

19 James and Alma Houston, Memo to the Chief, Wildlife Investigations – Eastern Arctic, 19 March 1953, LAC, RG 109, vol. 399, WLU 228-2 (part 1), 1.

20 Ibid., 2.

21 At various times in the 1950s and early 1960s, proposals were also put forward for the domestication and ranching of caribou.

22 J.S. Tener, Memo to the Chief, Canadian Wildlife Service, 30 December 1955, LAC, RG 109, vol. 23, WLT 200 – Musk-ox (part 3).

23 Winston Mair, Chief, Canadian Wildlife Service, Memo to James Cantley, Chief, Arctic Division, 3 February 1956, LAC, RG 109, vol. 444, WLU 300-50-1 (part 1), 2.

24 W.E. Stevens, Assistant District Administrator, Fort Smith, NWT, to Dr. A.W.F. Banfield, 10 December 1956, LAC, RG 109, vol. 33, WLT 300 (part 9).

25 J.S. Tener, Memo to the Chief of the Canadian Wildlife Service, Re: Eastern Arctic Research Program, 8 February 1956, LAC, RG 109, vol. 444, WLU 800-50 (part 1), 1.

26 Ibid., 2.

27 J.S. Tener, Memo to the Chief of the Canadian Wildlife Service, Re: Establishment of Eskimo Communities on High Arctic Islands, 15 June 1956, LAC, RG 109, vol. 444, WLU 300-50 (part 1).

28 E.H. McEwen, Biologist, Eastern Arctic, Memo to the Chief, Canadian Wildlife Service, Re: Establishment of Eskimo Families on the East Coast of Banks Island, 7 November 1956, LAC, RG 109, vol. 444, WLU 300-50 (part 1), 4.

29 See also the discussion of the importance of hunted food to culture among the Kluane First Nation in Nadasdy (2003, 78-79).

30 Corporal E.E. Jones, Cambridge Bay Detachment, RCMP, "Musk-Oxen – Protection of: NWT Game Ordinance, Daniel Moore Bay Area, NWT," 5 October 1956, LAC, RG 109, vol. 23, WLT 200 – Musk-ox (part 4).

31 Corporal E.E. Jones, Cambridge Bay Detachment, RCMP, "Musk-Oxen – Protection of: NWT Game Ordinance, Daniel Moore Bay Area, NWT November 22nd," 1956, LAC, RG 109, vol. 23, WLT 200 – Musk-ox (part 4), 1.

32 Ibid., 1-2.

33 Ibid., 2.

34 H.A. Larson, Supart Officer Commanding, "G" Division, RCMP, to the Chief, Canadian Wildlife Service, Re: Musk-Oxen – Protection of: NWT Game Ordinance – Daniel Moore Bay Area, NWT, 12 January 1957, LAC, RG 109, vol. 23, WLT 200 – Musk-ox (part 4).

35 H.A. Larson, Supart Officer Commanding, "G" Division, RCMP, to the Chief, Canadian Wildlife Service, Re: Musk-Oxen – Protection of: NWT Game Ordinance – Daniel Moore Bay Area, NWT, 28 February 1957, LAC, RG 109, vol. 23, WLT 200 – Musk-ox (part 4).

36 Jameson Bond, Northern Service Officer, Cambridge Bay, NWT, Memo to the Administrator of the Arctic, Re: Musk-Ox – Cambridge Bay Area, 9 March 1959, LAC, RG 109, vol. 24, WLT 200 – Musk-ox (part 6).

37 A.G. Loughrey, Predator Control Officer, Memo to W.W. Mair, Chief, Canadian Wildlife Service, 18 March 1959, LAC, RG 109, vol. 24, WLT 200 – Musk-ox (part 6).

38 A.G. Loughrey, Canadian Wildlife Service, to Jameson Bond, Northern Service Officer, Department of Northern Affairs, Cambridge Bay, NWT, 13 March 1959, LAC, RG 109, vol. 24, WLT 200 – Musk-ox (part 6).

39 There is a discrepancy in the dates associated with the offence. In his book *Judge of the Far North: The Memoirs of Jack Sissons* (1968), Sissons notes that the offence occurred on or about 25 September 1959. In her book *Images of Justice* (1997), Dorothy Eber gives the date as 26 February 1959. The latter is the correct date.

40 W.G. Fraser, Q/Supart, O.C. "G" Division, Report to Dr. W.E. Stevens, Chief, Canadian Wildlife Service, Re: Shooting of Musk-Ox, Devon Island, NWT, 2 August 1960, LAC, RG 109, vol. 24, WLT 200 – Musk-ox (part 6).

41 An Ordinance to Amend the Game Ordinance, assented to 23 January 1957, made it clear that there were, strictly, no circumstances under which anyone hunting in the Northwest Territories could shoot a musk-ox (section 1[3][a]). However, a section of the legislation in force at the time did recognize the possible need to violate the law in order to prevent starvation and put the onus of proof that this violation was necessary on the offender. In this case, it may have been argued that, if the dogs had died of starvation, a similar fate may have awaited the RCMP officer and the special constable with whom he was travelling. The 1957 amendment also included a section that was the source of controversy in the Kogogolak case. Section 1(3) prohibited the killing of musk-ox and caribou in any area where it was restricted by regulation or in sanctuaries outlined in an accompanying schedule.

42 This case is outlined by Sissons (1968, 178-79) and by Eber (1997, 90-91).

43 Corporal D.F. Friesen, Coppermine Detachment, RCMP, Report, 8 November 1963, LAC, RG 109, vol. 24, WLT 200 – Musk-ox (part 7).

44 Corporal G.B. Warner, Cambridge Bay Detachment, RCMP, Report, 7 December 63, LAC, RG 109, vol. 24, WLT 200 – Musk-ox (part 7).

45 L.G. Douglas, Administrator of the Mackenzie District, Fort Smith, Memo to the Director, 22 January 1964, LAC, RG 109, vol. 24, WLT 200 – Musk-ox (part 7).

46 C.B. Macdonell, Chief Superintendent, "G" Division, to Deputy Minister, Department of Northern Affairs and National Resources, 14 February 1964, LAC, RG 109, vol. 24, WLT 200 – Musk-ox (part 7).

47 J.R.B. Coleman, Memo to Gordon Robertson, Deputy Minister of Northern Affairs, 27 March 1958, LAC, RG 109, vol. 28, WLT 200 (part 3), 4-5.

48 "Arctic Division Views on Walrus Management," 7 January 1959, LAC, RG 109, vol. 28, WLT 200 (part 3), 1.

49 Regulations for the Protection of Walruses, LAC, RG 109, vol. 28, WLT 200 (part 3).

50 It is interesting to note that historically the Inuktitut language provided only indications of the general size of things (as in "big" or "very big"). Asking – in fact insisting – that Inuit keep track of the number of animals killed, creating settlements with numbered houses (all in rows), and asking individual opinions rather than group opinions all helped to reinforce the idea that individuals and exact numbers were important.

51 The Distant Early Warning (DEW) Line was a string of radar stations stretching across the Arctic. It was part of a North American defence system initiated by the Americans in relation to Cold War fears of Russian bombers or missiles attacking North America from over the pole. Construction, which resulted in the presence of a large Canadian and American workforce, started in 1956.

52 "Polar Bear Utilization," LAC, RG 109, vol. 18, WLT 200-1 (part 1). No date is attached to this document, but from the content it appears to be a summary report compiled in 1957.

53 Minutes of Meeting to Discuss Polar Bear, 3 December 1956, LAC, RG 109, vol. 18, WLT 200-1 (part 1), 1.

54 Ibid., 2.

55 Ibid.

56 Minutes of Meeting to Discuss Polar Bear, 3 December 1956, LAC, RG 109, vol. 18, WLT 200-1 (part 1), 3.

57 Ibid., 4.

58 Ibid.

59 Ibid., 5.

60 Norman K. Luxton to A.W. Banfield, Canadian Wildlife Service, 12 August 1957, LAC, RG 109, vol. 18, WLT 200-1 (part 1).

61 R.N. Milmine, Cambridge Bay Detachment, RCMP, "Conservation of Polar Bear," 14 November 1957, LAC, RG 109, vol. 18, WLT 200-1 (part 1).

62 A.J. Reeve, Chief, Forests and Game, Memo to W.G. Brown, Re: Polar Bears, 3 December 1957, LAC, RG 109, vol. 18, WLT 200-1 (part 1), 2.

63 Ibid.

64 Royal Canadian Mounted Police, "Passage of Greenland Eskimos through Canadian Territory – NWT," Division File No. TP-125-1, 19 May 1957, LAC, RG 109, vol. 18, WLT 200-1 (part 1), 1.

65 W.J. Fitzsimmons, "G" Division, RCMP, Memo to Director, Northern Administration and Lands Branch, Re: Passage of Greenland Eskimos through Canadian Territory – NWT, 20 August 1957, file TP-125-1, LAC, RG 109, vol. 18, WLT 212-2, 3.

66 J.R.B. Coleman, Memo to Winston Mair, Director, Canadian Wildlife Service, Re: Hunting of Polar Bears by Greenlanders, 8 June 1960, LAC, RG 85, vol. 1952, file A-1000/174, 2.

67 B.G. Sivertz, Director, to Eske Brun, Undersecretary of State for Greenland Affairs, Copenhagen, 11 July 1960, LAC, RG 85, vol. 1952, file A-1000/192, 1.

68 Eske Brun, Departementachef, Copenhagen, to B.G. Sivertz, Director, Department of Northern Affairs and National Resources, 6 September 1960, LAC, RG 85, vol. 1952, file A-1000/174.

69 J.A. MacDonald, Assistant Deputy Minister, Memo to R.A. Gibson, Re: Endangered Mammals of the Northwest Territories, 31 July 1964, LAC, RG 109, box 17, WLT 300 (part 4), 2.

70   Corporal R.C. Knights, Rankin Inlet Detachment, RCMP, "Jaki Nanordlux et al. – Game Or-
      dinance, Repulse Bay, N.W.T.," November 1963, LAC, RG 109, vol. 19, WLT 200 (part 3).

71   Hugh Brody notes this classification of knowing or of knowledge in his book *The People's
      Land* (1983), where he cites an elderly man who was loath to talk about life in a settlement
      because he did not have direct knowledge of it: "Between 1944 and now I have been in
      Ikpiarjuk and so I cannot talk much about life here in the settlement; I want to talk of only
      things I know. I am not involved in things happening here." Not being involved implies
      not having any direct knowledge and therefore no knowledge to convey. For a discussion
      of different forms of indigenous knowledge, see Brody (2000).

72   E.R. Lysyk, Criminal Investigation Branch, RCMP, to Dr. D.A. Munro, Chief, Canadian
      Wildlife Service, 4 June 1965, LAC, RG 109, vol. 19, WLT 200 (part 3).

73   Corporal M.J. McPhee, Pangnirtung Detachment, Report to the Officer in Charge, Eastern
      Arctic Sub/Division, Frobisher Bay, Pangnirtung, 7 June 1965, LAC, RG 109, vol. 19, WST
      200 (part 3).

74   Constable G.D. Lucko, Resolute Bay Detachment, RCMP, "Polar Bear Conservation – NWT
      Game Ordinance," 7 June 1965, LAC, RG 109, vol. 19, WLT 200 (part 3).

75   Constable G.J. Jared, Cape Christian Detachment, RCMP, Memo to the Office in Charge,
      Eastern Arctic Sub/Division, RCMP Frobisher Bay, NWT, Re: Polar Bear Conservation, LAC,
      RG 109, WLT 200 (part 3).

76   Constable L.B. Schollar, Grise Fiord Detachment, RCMP, Memo to the Officer Commanding,
      Eastern Arctic Sub/Division, Frobisher Bay, Re: Polar Bear Conservation – Threat to – Grise
      Fiord Detachment Area, NWT, 13 July 1965, LAC, RG 109, vol. 19, WLT 200 (part 3).

77   Corporal D.R. Andrews, Rankin Inlet Detachment, RCMP, Memo to the Officer Command-
      ing, Central Arctic Sub/Division, Fort Churchill, MB, 2 July 1965, LAC, RG 109, vol. 19,
      WLT 200 (part 3).

78   Unofficial Minutes of the First International Meeting on the Polar Bear, 6 September 1965,
      College, AK, LAC, RG 109, vol. 19, WLT 200 (part 3).

79   Statement of Accord, Doc/16, 10 September 1965, LAC, RG 109, vol. 19, WLT 200 (part
      4), 1.

80   A.G. Loughrey, Superintendent, Eastern Region, Memo to Dr. D.A. Munro, Chief, Canadian
      Wildlife Service, Re: Polar Bear Questionnaire, 19 October 1965, LAC, RG 109, vol. 19, WLT
      200 (part 4). Draft of letter signed by Arthur Laing attached.

81   C.B. Macdonell, Chief Superintendent, Commanding Officer Division "G," RCMP, to Dr.
      D.A. Munro, Chief, Canadian Wildlife Service, 17 December 1965, with attachment from
      Corporal D.R. Andrews, Rankin Inlet Detachment, 29 November 1965, LAC, RG 109, vol.
      19, WLT 200 (part 4).

82   A.G. Loughrey, Superintendent, Eastern Region, Memo to Dr. D.A. Munro, Chief, Canadian
      Wildlife Service, Re: Polar Bear Management in Canada, 23 December 1965, LAC, RG 109,
      vol. 19, WLT 200 (part 4).

83   Ibid., 1.

84   Ibid.

85   Ibid., 4-7.

86   D. Davidson, Director, Department of Northern Affairs and National Resources, Northern
      Administration Branch, Memo to Chief, Canadian Wildlife Service, Re: Polar Bears, 23
      March 1966, LAC, RG 109, vol. 19, WLT 200 (part 4), Attachment.

87   Constable L.B. Schollar, Grise Fiord Detachment, RCMP, Memo to the Officer Commanding,
      Eastern Arctic Sub/Division, Frobisher Bay, Re: Polar Bear Conservation – Threat to, Grise
      Fiord Detachment Area, 8 July 1966, LAC, RG 109, vol. 19, WLT 200 (part 5), 1.

88   Ibid.

89   For a detailed discussion of the evolution of the Government of the Northwest Territories
      and the territorial administration at this time, see Dickerson (1992).

90   Constable A.D. Kirbyson, Resolute Bay Detachment, RCMP, Division "G" Eastern Arctic,
      Report, 20 July 1966, LAC, RG 109, vol. 19, WLT 200 (part 5), 2.

91   Jean Chrétien, Minister of Indian Affairs and Northern Development, to Commissioner
      S.M. Hodgson, Government of the Northwest Territories, 18 October 1968, LAC, RG 109,
      vol. 20, WLT 200 (part 7), 1.

Chapter 4: Who Counts?

1 James Scott (1985, 317) criticizes the concept of hegemony as commonly used for ignoring "the extent to which most subordinate classes are able, on the basis of their daily material experience, to penetrate and demystify the prevailing ideology," hence resistance, of which counterhegemony is but one form.

2 The relationship between a land-based life and the need for cash not only to deal with the costs of living in a settlement but increasingly to enjoy a land-based life is succinctly outlined by Hugh Brody in *The People's Land* (1975, 174-75): "Without a cash income of some sort, no one could buy his family's needs – including what they need to go hunting. It follows that Eskimos who do wish to devote much or all of their time to hunting and trapping are forced into some sort of dependence on those who are able and willing to work at low-level clerical or labouring jobs. Because such dependence is unwelcome and is not always reliable, even the most devoted hunters among the older men periodically welcome a chance to earn cash."

3 Subsistence hunting in the Arctic and sub-Arctic has been thoroughly analyzed in relationship to the maintenance of Aboriginal culture and its contribution to the economies of northern settlements (Condon et al. 1995; Wenzel 1991; Wolf and Walker 1987). Other studies have examined closely the relationship between commercial trapping and subsistence hunting (Asch 1982; Knight 1965). Asch argues that the northern fur trade was a mercantile form of capitalist enterprise that did not interfere with traditional production methods, and "traders still relied primarily on price and choice of goods as inducements to increase production. Hence, no external pressure was placed on the Dene to reorient their economy away from its bush subsistence rationality" (363). With the exception of a paper by George Wenzel (2005), little research has been done on sport hunting and its potential role in redefining Aboriginal relations to game, possibly away from those documented by Brody (2000).

4 J.A. MacDonald, Assistant Deputy Minister, draft document prepared for R.A. Gibson, 21 July 1964, LAC, RG 109, vol. 42, WLT 300 (part 13), 6.

5 Ibid.

6 Director, Northern Administration Branch, Report to Director, Canadian Wildlife Service, Re: Sport Hunting of Musk-Ox, 5 May 1966, LAC, RG 109, vol. 25, WLT 200 – Musk-ox (part 9), 2. The difficulties included guaranteeing that only non-herd bulls would be killed and, more significantly, the impossibility of policing such an arrangement.

7 Paul Kwaterowsky, Superintendent of Game, NWT, "Musk-Ox Hunting – Queen Elizabeth Islands," LAC, RG 109, vol. 24, WLT 200 – Musk-ox (part 7), 2. It is clear from the context of the information that follows that Inuit offered to voluntarily restrict their hunting of polar bears, in the same manner that they had been restricted by the state from hunting musk-ox, if the hunting of polar bears for sport could be conducted in a manner similar to the proposed hunting of musk-ox. The suggestion was declined on the basis that not enough was known about polar bear biology.

8 Paul Kwaterowsky, Superintendent of Game, NWT, "Musk-Ox Hunting – Queen Elizabeth Islands," LAC, RG 109, vol. 25, WLT 200 – Musk-ox (part 9), 1.

9 Director, Northern Administration Branch, Report to Director, Canadian Wildlife Service, Re: Sport Hunting of Musk-Ox, 5 May 1966, LAC, RG 109, vol. 25, WLT 200 – Musk-ox (part 9), 5.

10 David A. Munro, Director, Canadian Wildlife Service, Memo to Mr. Carter, Director, Northern Administration, Re: Sport Hunting – Musk-Oxen, 12 May 1966, LAC, RG 109, vol. 25, WLT 200 – Musk-ox (part 9).

11 David A. Munro, Director, Canadian Wildlife Service, to Mr. Carter, Director, Northern Administration Branch, Re: Arctic Islands Preserve, 11 May 1966, LAC, RG 109, WLT 300 – Musk-ox (part 4).

12 "Arctic Caribou, Musk-Ox: Sport Hunting Proposal Deplored," *Ottawa Journal*, 19 May 1966.

13 R.J. Wall, Central Arctic Sub-Division, RCMP, Report to the Administrator of the Arctic, "G" Division, Fort Churchill, MB, Re: Ivor Agak, W1-34 – Game Ordinance – Anderson Bay, NWT – September 1965, 26 August 1966, LAC, RG 109, vol. 25, WLT 200 – Musk-ox (part 9).

14 Milton M.R. Freeman, Department of Biology, Memorial University, to John Parker, Deputy Commissioner, NWT, 18 August 1967, LAC, RG 109, vol. 25, WLT 200 – Musk-ox (part 9), 3.

15 Council Committee of Musk-Oxen, Report of Meetings with the Residents of Resolute Bay and Grise Fiord, LAC, RG 109, Box 10, 9250-52/197 (part 1), 2. (The meeting at Grise Fiord was held 22 April 1968.)

16 "Recommendation to Council: Sport Hunting of Musk-Oxen Queen Elizabeth Islands," LAC, RG 109, vol. 25, WLT 200 – Musk-ox (part 9).

17 Canadian Press, "Musk-Ox Hunt Opposed," LAC, RG 109, vol. 25, WLT 200 – Musk-ox (part 9).

18 Patrick Hardy, Managing Director, Canadian Audubon Society, to Dr. David Munro, Director, Canadian Wildlife Service, 3 August 1967, LAC, RG 109, vol. 25, WLT 200 – Musk-ox (part 9). The society enjoyed a good relationship with the service. For years, a representative of the society had attended the regular meetings of federal and provincial wildlife officials held to discuss matters of mutual concern.

19 C.H.D. Clarke, Chief, Fish and Wildlife Branch, Government of Ontario, to Patrick A. Hardy, Managing Director, Canadian Audubon Society, and Editor, *Canadian Audubon*, 21 November 1967, LAC, RG 109, vol. 25, WLT 200 – Musk-ox (part 9).

20 "Eskimos Line Up with Government in Debate over Hunting Musk-Oxen," *Ottawa Journal*, 18 May 1968: 16.

21 Milton M.R. Freeman, Department of Biology, Memorial University, to John Parker, Deputy Commissioner, NWT, 18 August 1967, LAC, RG 109, vol. 25, WLT 200 – Musk-ox (part 9), 4-5.

22 Dr. D.B. Sparling, President, and Mrs. G. Prior, Secretary, Victoria Natural History Society, to David Groos, Commissioner, Northwest Territories, and Director, Northern Administration Branch, LAC, RG 109, vol. 25, WLT 200 – Musk-ox (part 9).

23 Olive Mazuq, Toronto, to Minister, Lands and Forests Branch, LAC, RG 109, vol. 25, WLT 200 – Musk-ox (part 9).

24 Jean Trapton, Royston, British Columbia, to Mr. A. Laing, Minister of Northern Affairs, 15 May 1968, LAC, RG 109, vol. 25, WLT 200 – Musk-ox (part 9).

25 John S. Tener, Deputy Director, Canadian Wildlife Service, Memo to Minister, Indian Affairs and Northern Development, 3 June 1968, LAC, RG 109, vol. 25, WLT 200 – Musk-ox (part 9).

26 Arthur Laing, Minister of Indian Affairs and Northern Development, to Jean Trapton, Rayston [sic], BC, LAC, RG 109, vol. 25, WLT 200 – Musk-ox (part 9).

27 The impact of environmentalists on the market for seal pelts was phenomenal and created incredible hardship for Inuit, even though the seals hunted by polar Inuit were a different species – ringed or jar seals – and there was no evidence that populations of these seals were in any way endangered. On eastern Baffin Island, young ringed seal pelts sold for $4 each in 1957, a price that had increased to $17.50 in 1963. The contribution to local economies was considerable. But in 1964, the Society for the Prevention of Cruelty to Animals, particularly in Quebec and New Brunswick, started a campaign against the hunting of harp seals off the coast of Newfoundland. By 1967, the market had collapsed almost entirely. The anger directed at one NWT councillor's remarks needs to be understood in this context. It was evident that, given the absolutely essential nature of a land-based economy to Inuit culture and well-being, ongoing attempts to regulate wildlife in ways that defied Inuit needs and experiences would be met with increasing anger (not an emotion easily expressed in Inuit culture) and resistance. See Foote (1971).

28 Milton M.R. Freeman, Department of Biology, Memorial University, to John Parker, Deputy Commissioner, NWT, 18 August 1967, LAC, RG 109, vol. 25, WLT 200 – Musk-ox (part 9), 4.

29 Ibid., 3.

30 Phyllis Thatcher, Ottawa, to Jean Chrétien, Minister, Department of Indian Affairs and Northern Development, 14 February 1969, LAC, RG 109, box 10, vol. 9250-52/197 (part 1).

31 Jean Chrétien, Minister of Indian Affairs and Northern Development, to Mrs. R.G. Thatcher, Ottawa, 3 March 1969, LAC, RG 109, vol. 383, WLU 200 – Musk-ox (part 2).

32 Jack Davis, Minister, Environment Canada, to Miss Elisabeth N. Bell, Vancouver, 10 March 1972, LAC, RG 109, box 10, 9250-52/197 (part 2).

33 Paul Kwaterowsky, quoted by Gorde Sinclair, "A Population Explosion," *Edmonton Journal,* 27 October 1973, LAC, RG 109, box 10, 9250-52/Musk-ox-7 (part 3).

34 The classic text *Never in Anger* (Briggs 1967) is still an invaluable read in understanding the values and behaviours characteristic of Inuit culture: values still intact as the move to settlement life was developing between the mid-1950s and 1960s.

35 H.A. Johnson, Pangnirtung Detachment, RCMP, Report to the Officer Commanding, "G" Division, Re: Annual Report – Game Conditions, Pangnirtung District – Season 1954-55, 30 June 1955, LAC, RG 109, vol. 33, WLT 300 (part 7), 1-3.

36 Constable R.D.S. Ward, Eskimo Point Detachment, RCMP, Report Re: Game Conditions – Eskimo Point, NWT, for the Year Ending 30 June 1959, 5 July 1959, LAC, RG 109, vol. 35, WLT 300-5 (part 1).

37 Resolute Bay Detachment, RCMP, Report to the Officer Commanding, "G" Division, Re: Annual Game Report 1959-60, Resolute Bay, NWT, 4 July 1960, LAC, RG 109, vol. 35, WLT 300-5 (part 1), 2.

38 Constable T. Kushniruk, Pond Inlet Detachment, RCMP, Report to the Officer Commanding, "G" Division, Re: Game Conditions General – Pond Inlet Detachment Area, Year Ending 30 June 1960, 20 July 1960, LAC, RG 109, vol. 35, WLT 300-5 (part 1), 1-4.

39 Constable R.C. Currie, Eskimo Point Detachment, RCMP, Report to Corporal R.D.S. Ward, Re: Game Conditions – Eskimo Point, NWT, for the Year Ending 30 June 1961, LAC, RG 109, vol. 35, WLT 300-5 (part 1), 1.

40 Corporal R.D. Minion, Eskimo Point Detachment, RCMP, Report to the Officer Commanding, Fort Churchill, Re: Game Conditions Eskimo Point, Year Ending 30 July 1965, 26 July 1965, LAC, RG 109, box 17, WLT 300-5 (part 1), 1.

41 J.A. MacDonald, Assistant Deputy Minister, Northern Affairs and National Resources, Memo to R.A. Gibson, Re: Endangered Mammals of the Northwest Territories, 31 July 1964, LAC, RG 109, box 17, WLT 300 (part 4), 5.

42 "Polar Bear, Caribou Facing Extinction," *New Westminster British Columbian,* 22 February 1958.

43 Ibid.

44 Fairclough was first elected in a Hamilton by-election in 1950. She was the first female cabinet minister in the history of the country, being appointed minister of citizenship and immigration in 1958. In 1962, she became postmaster general and was defeated in the federal election of 1963.

45 Canadian Wildlife Service, "The Current Barren-Ground Caribou Situation," Sessional Paper 7, 1961, LAC, RG 109, vol. 24, file 12, WLT 300, 1. Elsewhere in the document, the authors claim that 7,000 caribou were taken in northern Saskatchewan by 170 hunters, emphasizing once again that the numbers used in official documents were, at best, "guesstimates" and that different ones could be found in different – and sometimes the same – documents.

46 Department of Citizenship and Immigration, Memo to Cabinet Re: Proposed Amendments to the First, Second, and Third Schedules of the BNA Act, 1930, and the Indian Act, 8 September 1961, LAC, RG 109, vol. 400, file 228-3 WLU 228 (part 1).

47 David A. Munro, Director, Canadian Wildlife Service, Memo to Director, National Parks Branch, 12 December 1963, LAC, RG 109, vol. 34, file 12, WLT 300.

48 Canadian Wildlife Service, Sessional Paper for the Northwest Territories Council Re: Caribou Preservation, 8 January 1965, LAC, RG 109, vol. 381, file 22, WLU 200.

49 Dinsdale, born in 1916, replaced Alvin Hamilton as minister in 1960 and served in the position until the Diefenbaker government was defeated by the Liberals in 1963. Dinsdale was a social worker from Manitoba and sat in the House of Commons from 1951 to 1980. He died in 1982.

50 Canadian Wildlife Service, "Welfare of Indians and Eskimos Endangered by Caribou Decline," Draft Press Release, 11 December 1962, LAC, RG 109, vol. 380, file 20, WLU 200.

51 Ibid.

52 H.M. Jones, Director, Indian Affairs Branch, Department of Citizenship and Immigration, to J.R.B. Coleman, Director, National Parks Branch, Department of Northern Affairs and National Resources, 7 January 1963, LAC, RG 109, vol. 380, file 22, WLU 200.

53 Inspector E.R. Lysyk, Coppermine Detachment, RCMP, Report Re: Eskimo Conditions – General – Contwoyto Lake, NWT, 14 March 1961, LAC, RG 85, vol. 1347, file 1000/145 (part 6), 1-2.

54 The relationship between caribou and the move to settlements in the eastern Arctic has typically been expressed in terms of the decimation of caribou herds, starvation, and the inability of Inuit to continue to live on the land and depend on caribou for subsistence living. Their move to settlements was often articulated as "necessary" because of these changing material circumstances. See Vallee (1967). While there were starvations in the 1950s among camp-based Inuit, elsewhere we have seriously questioned the claim that they were simply due to a shortage of caribou (Tester and Kulchyski 1994).

55 Constable M. Dwernichuk, Coppermine Detachment, RCMP, Report Re: Eskimo Conditions – General – Contwoyto Lake, NWT, 7 June 1961, LAC, RG 85, vol. 1347, file 1000/145 (part 7), 1, 3.

56 A. Macpherson, Biologist, Memo to Chief, Canadian Wildlife Service, Re: Infraction of Game Regulations by Departmental Employee at Baker Lake, 24 August 1960, LAC, RG 109, vol. 59, WLU 3-1 (part 2).

57 W. Winston Mair, Chief, Canadian Wildlife Service, to B.G. Sivertz, Director, Northern Administration Branch, Re: Infraction of Game Regulations by Departmental Employee at Baker Lake, 25 August 1960, LAC, RG 109, vol. 59, WLU 3-1 (part 2), 2.

58 Inspector E.R. Lysyk, RCMP, to Dr. D.A. Munro, Chief, Canadian Wildlife Service, 13 October 1964, LAC, RG 109, vol. 381, file 21, WLU 200.

59 These reports are too numerous to detail here, and those that follow are only illustrative. However, field reports by northern service officers, game managers, and the RCMP – of which there are many – do not support the claims by the Canadian Wildlife Service that there was a caribou crisis or that Inuit were at risk from starvation.

60 D.E. Wilkinson, Northern Service Officer, Baker Lake, Monthly Report, 1 August 1957, LAC, RG 85, vol. 623, file A205-4/159 (part 1), 1.

61 Don Bissett, DEW Line Northern Service Officer, Extracts from Report (Eastern Section) for Period April and May 1961, LAC, RG 85, vol. 1360, file A207-6 (part 2), 2.

62 J.R. Malfair, Assistant Superintendent of Game, Report Re: Game Management, Keewatin Patrol, 26-30 November 1963, 5 December 1963, LAC, RG 109, vol. 34, file 12, WLT 300.

63 For a detailed account of these tragedies, see Tester and Kulchyski (1994).

64 C.H. Witney, Minister of Mines and Natural Resources, Government of Manitoba, to Arthur Laing, Minister of Northern Affairs and National Resources, 29 May 1963, LAC, RG 109, vol. 380, file 22, WLU 200.

65 J.R.B. Coleman, Director, Parks Branch, Confidential Memo to the Director, Northern Administration Branch, 11 December 1964, LAC, RG 109, vol. 484, file 6735 (part 1).

66 R.A. Ruttan, Technical Committee for Caribou Preservation, Memo to Dr. John Tener, Secretary, Administrative Committee for Caribou Preservation, Re: "A Co-Ordinated Survey of Barren Ground Caribou Herd Composition and Human Utilization," 1 March 1963, LAC, RG 109, vol. 380, file 22, WLT 200, 2.

67 R.A. Ruttan, Technical Committee for Caribou Preservation, Memo to Dr. John Tener, Secretary, Administrative Committee for Caribou Preservation, Re: "Aerial Census of Barren Ground Caribou," 4 March 1963, LAC, RG 109, vol. 380, file 22, WLT 200.

68 D.A. Benson, Memo to Chief, Canadian Wildlife Service, Re: Review of the Barren Ground Caribou Program, 14 August 1963, LAC, RG 109, vol. 380, file 22, WLU 200.

69 Ibid., 7-8.

70 Ibid., 10.

71 Dr. W.E. Stevens, Regional Superintendent, Memo to the Chief, Canadian Wildlife Service, 15 April 1964, LAC, RG 109, vol. 381, file 21, WLU 200.

72 Ruttan recalls that he met Munsternjelm in a bar in Churchill where he told him how Farley Mowat had spent a lot of time in the same bar while writing *Never Cry Wolf*. According to

Ruttan, Mowat's account of eating lemmings – which Mowat called "mouse ragout" – was a tall tale told to him by barren ground prospectors. It was a joke that subsequently found its way into the book. Bob Ruttan, Personal Communication, November 2002.

73 Eric Munsternjelm, Sudbury, to R.A. Ruttan, Management Biologist, Edmonton, 26 November 1964, LAC, RG 109, vol. 381, file 22, WLU 200.

74 R.A. Ruttan, Sessional Paper for the Northwest Territories Council Re: Caribou Preservation, 8 January 1965, LAC, RG 109, vol. 381, file 22, WLU 200. Ruttan maintains that this wording was for the benefit of council and that his terms of reference, in fact, made no mention of "ameliorating the social problems of caribou-dependent people" (2). He claims that any terms of reference he had involved establishing the status of the caribou and developing management techniques. Bob Ruttan, Personal Communication, November 2002.

75 Ibid., 2.

76 A.L. Look, Assistant Superintendent of Game, Churchill, Report on Keewatin Caribou Herds, 28 July 1965, LAC, RG 109, vol. 381, file 22, WLU 200. The results of Look's study seem to have gone missing. The archival records of the Canadian Wildlife Service contain correspondence from Look and a report of what he did and where he was located in the spring and summer of 1965. The notes refer to population data attached to the report; however, the charts to which Look refers in his text were not attached to copies found in the National Archives of Canada. Similarly, they appear to be missing from the historical records of the Canadian Wildlife Service, located in the Environment Canada library in Hull. That the data are missing from the historical record is suspicious given the extent to which they apparently contradicted official wisdom at the time. Ruttan reported in an article he published in September 1966 that he estimated the total herd size for barren ground caribou at about 700,000 animals.

77 John S. Tener, Staff Mammalogist, to Dr. D.A. Munro, Chief, Canadian Wildlife Service, 17 November 1965, LAC, RG 109, vol. 381, file 22, WLU 200.

78 Canadian Wildlife Service/Department of Northern Affairs and National Resources, Notice Signed by A.H. Macpherson, Project Leader, Baker Lake, NWT, 6 June 1966, LAC, RG 109, vol. 381, file 24, WLU 200.

79 David A. Munro, Director, Canadian Wildlife Service, Memo to Mr. Carter, Ottawa, 26 May 1966, LAC, RG 109, vol. 381, file 23, WLU 200.

80 Canadian Wildlife Service/Department of Northern Affairs and National Resources, Notice Signed by A.H. Macpherson, Project Leader, Baker Lake, NWT, 6 June 1966, LAC, RG 109, vol. 381, file 24, WLU 200.

81 "Caribou on Increase, Need Control: Biologist," *Globe and Mail,* 8 August 1966, LAC, RG 109, vol. 381, file 24, WLU 200.

82 *Weekend Mazazine* 16, 31 (30 July 1966): 14-15.

83 B.G. Sivertz, Commissioner of Northwest Territories, to Dr. David Munro, Director, Canadian Wildlife Service, 8 August 1966, LAC, RG 109, vol. 381, file 23, WLU 200.

84 John S. Tener, Deputy Director, Canadian Wildlife Service, to B.G. Sivertz, Commissioner of the Northwest Territories, 22 August 1966, LAC, RG 109, vol. 381, file 23, WLU 200.

85 Robert A. Ruttan, "New Crisis for Barren-Ground Caribou," *Country Guide,* September 1966, LAC, RG 109, vol. 381, file 24, WLU 200.

86 Dr. David A. Munro, Director, Canadian Wildlife Service, "Current Barren-Ground Caribou Situation, Canadian Wildlife Service," Report to B.G. Sivertz, Commissioner of Northwest Territories, 9 October 1966, LAC, RG 109, vol. 381, file 24, WLU 200.

87 G.W. Malaher, Director of Wildlife, Department of Mines and Natural Resources, Province of Manitoba, to Dr. David A. Munro, Chief, Canadian Wildlife Service, 8 December 1966, LAC, RG 109, vol. 381, file 24, WLU 200.

88 The Department of Northern Affairs and National Resources was renamed the Department of Indian Affairs and Northern Development following a reorganization in 1966 that saw responsibility for Indian affairs moved from Citizenship and Immigration to the newly constituted department.

89 Arthur Laing, Minister of Indian Affairs and Northern Development, Statement Re: Barren Ground Caribou of the Northern Canadian Mainland, 16 December 1966, LAC, RG 109, vol. 3, file 9250-52, C1-10 (part 2).

90 J.B. Gollop, Summary of Discussion on Caribou, University of Saskatchewan, 14 December 1966, 15 December 1966, LAC, RG 109, vol. 381, file 24, WLU 200.

91 J.B. Gollop, Research Supervisor, Ornithology, Saskatoon, Memo to the Regional Superintendent, Canadian Wildlife Service, 20 December 1966, LAC, RG 109, vol. 381, file 24, WLU 200. Gollop was a keen ornithologist indeed. In his first report on this meeting, he referred to caribou as travelling in flocks!

92 John P. Kelsall, Memo to David A. Munro, Director, Canadian Wildlife Service, Re: "Mush-Brush and the Caribou (Continued)," 14 February 1968, LAC, RG 109, vol. 382, file 25, WLU 200.

93 John P. Kelsall to the Editor, the *Drum*, Inuvik, and the Editor, *News of the North*, Yellowknife, 23 April 1968, LAC, RG 109, vol. 382, file 25, WLU 200.

94 Northwest Territories Council, List of Motions Passed at the Thirty-Third Session, Resolute Bay, November 1967, LAC, RG 109, vol. 35, WLT 300 – Game Management (part 14).

95 J.E. Bryant, Director, Eastern Region, Canadian Wildlife Service, Memo to Dr. John Tener, Administrative Committee for Caribou Preservation, Edmonton, 30 July 1969, LAC, RG 109, vol. 382, file 25, WLU 200, 2.

96 Dr. David A. Munro, Director, Canadian Wildlife Service, to B.G. Sivertz, Commissioner of the Northwest Territories, 6 October 1966, LAC, RG 109, vol. 35, WLT 300 (part 14).

97 For Kayakjuak's account of whaling in the region of Fullerton Harbour, see Eber (1989, 111-14).

Chapter 5: Inuit Rights and Government Policy

1   This is a common view, argued for example in Cumming and Mickenberg (1971, 13), though for an opposing opinion that suggests Aboriginal rights are not exhausted or founded on Aboriginal title see Asch (1984, 7) and Kulchyski (1994).

2   For an extensive discussion, see Berger (1991) and Henderson (1997).

3   An excellent discussion of the proclamation can be found in Culhane (1998, 54-56), and a detailed historical account can be found in Hall (2003).

4   A key article by Brian Slattery (1987) was partly inspired by the *Guerin* decision, which can be found in Kulchyski (1994).

5   Two of the better short studies of early Indian policy and legislation are Milloy (1991) and Tobias (1991). Olive Dickason (2002) provides a more detailed, comprehensive overview. More recent work by Robin Brownlee (2003) and Hugh Shewell (2004) indicates the interesting directions that newer scholarship is taking and provides invaluable additional historical material.

6   An invaluable source on the particular history of Indian policy and the struggle around land rights in British Columbia is Tennant (1990). There are many studies of treaties in Canada. The starting point is Morris (1991 [1880]). Recent studies of particular treaties include Fumoleau (1973); Price (1999); Treaty 7 Elders and Tribal Council (1996); and Ray, Miller, and Tough (2000).

7   The indispensable study of the white paper is Weaver (1981); see also Cardinal (1999 [1969]). Daniel Raunet (1984) provides a history of the Nisga'a land claim through to the *Calder* decision.

8   Regarding his views on Aboriginal policy, see Kulchyski (1993).

9   Farley Mowat to Henry Larson, Commissioner, RCMP, 6 January 1958, LAC, RG 22, box 33, file 250-34-1 (part 1).

10 As well as the sources on the history of the Indian Act and Indian policy, the various revisions of the Indian Act have been published, and the amendments pertaining to the sun dance and the potlatch can be found in *Indian Acts and Amendments*, volume 1. Christopher Bracken's *The Potlatch Papers* (1997) deals with the ban on the potlatch, though several other studies include material pertaining to it.

11 Frank Cunningham, Director, Arctic Affairs, to R.H. Chesshire, Hudson's Bay Company, 11 June 1956, LAC, N92-023, 17-7.

12 The discussion in Eber, which refers to the case as "the decision of the century," ignores the strongly detrimental implication of the case to a doctrine of Aboriginal rights. The case itself can be found in Kulchyski (1994).

13 Ben Sivertz, Director, Northern Administration and Lands Branch, Memo to Gordon Robertson, Deputy Minister, Re: "Eskimos and Liquor," 5 November 1958, LAC, RG 22, vol. 857, 40-2-13 (F)1, 1.
14 Ibid., 3.
15 Ibid., 5.
16 Ibid.
17 D.F. Brown, Deputy Commissioner, NWT, Memo to Gordon Robertson, Commissioner, 21 February 1958, LAC, RG 22, vol. 857, 40-2-13 (F)1, 2.
18 C.K. LeCapelain, Chief, Mining and Lands Division, to R.A.J. Phillips, Chief, Arctic Division, 29 August 1957, LAC, RG 85, vol. 1266, file 1000/167 (part A).
19 Commander Henry Larson, RCMP, Memo Re: "Rights of Eskimos, Employed by Prospectors and Others in the North," 12 September 1957, LAC, RG 85, vol. 1266, file 1000/167 (part 4).
20 R.A.J. Phillips, Chief, Arctic Division, Memo to Ben Sivertz, Director, Northern Administration and Lands Branch, 24 September 1957, LAC, RG 85, vol. 1266, file 1000/167 (part 4).
21 Ibid.
22 R.A.J. Phillips, Chief, Arctic Division, to Commander Henry Larson, RCMP, 31 October 1957, LAC, RG 85, vol. 1266, file 1000/167 (part 4).
23 Percy Moore, Director, Indian and Northern Health Services, Memo to Ben Sivertz, Director, Northern Administration and Lands Branch, 29 October 1957, LAC, RG 85, vol. 1348, file 1000/150 (part 2).
24 Walter Rudnicki, Chief, Welfare Section, "Eskimo Welfare," 21/24 March 1958, LAC, N92-023 18-6.
25 Bill Willmott to Graham Rowley, Secretary, Advisory Committee on Northern Development, 17 January 1959, LAC, RG 85, vol. 1655, file NR 2/3-17 (part 1); see 1-2 of attached document.
26 Ibid., 2.
27 Ibid.
28 Government of the Northwest Territories Archives, N92-023 23-3, 1.
29 Ibid.
30 Ibid., 2.
31 Ibid., 8.
32 Ibid.
33 *Edmonton Journal* (n.d.) 1959, LAC RG 109, vol. 24, file WLT 200 (part 6).
34 Notes of Meeting, 18 June 1959, LAC, RG 109, vol. 24, file WLT 200 – Musk-ox (part 6).
35 Ibid.
36 Alvin Hamilton, Minister, Northern Affairs and Natural Resources, to Ellen Fairclough, Minister, Citizenship and Immigration, 19 June 1959, LAC, RG 109, vol. 484, file 735 (part 1), 1.
37 Ibid., 3.
38 Alex Stevenson, Arctic Division, to John J. Navin, Secretary and Counsel, Federal Electric Corporation, 13 January 1960, LAC, N92-023 312-6, 9.
39 Ibid., 10.
40 Committee on Social Adjustment, Minutes of Meeting, 27 December 1961, LAC, RG 29, vol. 903, file 437-1-2 (part 1).
41 Ibid., 3.
42 Ibid.
43 Ibid., 3-4.
44 Ibid., 4.
45 Association on American Indian Affairs, "The Eskimos Speak," Newsletter 44 (December 1961), LAC, RG 85, vol. 1356, A1012-1 (part 8), 1.
46 Ibid., 2.
47 Ibid., 4.
48 Gordon Robertson, Deputy Minister, Northern Affairs and Natural Resources, Memo to Graham Rowley, Secretary, Advisory Committee on Northern Development, 29 January 1962, LAC, RG 85, vol. 1356, A1012-1 (part 8).

49 Vic Valentine, Research Officer, to Graham Rowley, Secretary, Advisory Committee on Northern Development, 26 January 1962, LAC, RG 85, vol. 1661, part of file NR 4, 13-12.
50 Ben Sivertz, Director, Northern Administration and Lands Branch, to Professor F.C. Toombs, Ontario Hospital Department of Psychiatry, 20 February 1962, LAC, RG 85, vol. 1356, H1012-1 (part 8), 1.
51 Ibid., 2.
52 Ibid., 2-3.
53 Ibid., 3.
54 Association on American Indian Affairs, "The Eskimos Speak," Newsletter 44 (December 1961), LAC, RG 85, vol. 1356, A1012-1 (part 8), 3.
55 J.R.B. Coleman, Director, Indian Affairs, to Deputy Minister, Indian Affairs, 11 December 1964, LAC, RG 109, vol. 484, file 735 (part 1), 1.
56 Ibid., 2.
57 Ibid., 3.
58 Northern Policy Co-Ordinating Committee, Minutes of 18 January 1965 Meeting, LAC, RG 85, vol. 74, file 1009-32 (part 2), Acc 1995-96/310.
59 Minister of Citizenship and Immigration, Memo to Cabinet, 11 February 1965, LAC, RG 22, vol. 293 1-11-3 (part 11c), 3.
60 Ibid.
61 Indian-Eskimo Association of Canada, Brief, July 1967, LAC, RG 109, vol. 484, file 735 (part 3), 2. For a comprehensive review of the work of the association, see Shewell (2004).
62 Ibid., 14.
63 Ibid., 13.
64 Executive Director, Canadian Wildlife Federation, to Voting Delegates, 10 November 1967, LAC, RG 109, vol. 484, file 735 (part 3).
65 Arthur Laing, Minister, Indian Affairs and Northern Development, to President, Quebec Wildlife Federation, 20 March 1968, LAC, RG 109, vol. 484, file 735 (part 4), 1.
66 Ibid., 2.
67 David Munro, Chief, Canadian Wildlife Service, to Deputy Minister, Indian Affairs and Northern Development, 25 June 1968, LAC, RG 109, vol. 484, file 735 (part 4), 1.
68 Ibid., 2.
69 Ibid., 1.
70 "The Constitutional Position of Eskimos," Draft Report, 13 May 1968, LAC, RG 85, vol. 1898 file 1003-32, box 187 (part 3), 1.
71 A.B. Yates, Assistant Director, Territorial Relations Branch, Memo to Administrator of the Arctic, Spring 1968, LAC, RG 85, vol. 19, file 1012-1 (part 3).
72 Ibid.
73 Hugo Fischer to D.A. Davidson, 23 September 1969, LAC, RG 85, 95-96/310, vol. 52, 163-1-1, vol. 10.
74 D.A. Davidson, Acting Director, Territorial Relations Branch, to Hugo Fischer, 15 October 1969, LAC, RG 85, 95-96/310 251-1 166, vol. 1.
75 Ibid.
76 Northwest Territories Council, Debates, Thirty-Eighth Session, 1 February 1969, 1035, LAC, RG 85, vol. 1667, file A300-2-1 (part 3).
77 Ibid.

Chapter 6: Baker Lake, 1957

1 On the question of democratic forms, see Macpherson (1965). On the question of Inuit traditional governance, an extensive literature exists primarily in an anthropological vein. The earliest anthropological studies of Franz Boas (1964), Diamond Jenness (1930), and Knut Rasmussen (1999) provide important material, as does the more recent work of Asen Balicki (1970), Jean Briggs (1967), Hugh Brody (1975), and Marc Stevenson (1997). See also Damas (1978) for more references.
2 Brody's (1983) discussion of northern community dynamics in *The People's Land* presents an intricate analysis that would certainly suggest reluctance among Inuit to participate with *Qallunaat* in a community council.

3   Representatives from the Anglican and Catholic Churches vied with each other for souls; government agents were also in conflict, with the RCMP divided from the teacher, the nurse, and the northern service officer (and at times this being a three-way split); and HBC officials had their share of difficulties with church and state. While conflicts between these agencies were not uncommon in the North (and could be found among their superiors in the south), in the late 1950s in Baker Lake they were in an aggravated condition.

4   For an extensive discussion of the creation of the position, see Tester and Kulchyski (1994).

5   Doug Wilkinson, personal correspondence, 20 December 2002, 6.

6   Ibid., 3-4.

7   On the face-to-face dimension of Inuit culture, see Kulchyski (2005).

8   Doug Wilkinson to Chief, Arctic Division, Re: "Baker Lake Eskimo Council," 27 February 1957, LAC, RG 85, vol. 515, file 250-5-159, 1.

9   Ibid.

10   Ibid.

11   Doug Wilkinson, personal correspondence, 20 December 2002, 10.

12   Compare Briggs (1967) and Jenness (1930): Briggs argues that women were clearly in a subordinate position, while Jenness stresses their prominence and social power. Interestingly, Brody's view on the matter appears to have evolved. In *The People's Land* (1983, 194-98), he argues for a notion of the traditional subservience of women, while in his more recent *The Other Side of Eden* (2000, 261-64) he argues firmly for considering genders as roughly egalitarian. See also Kotierk (2001).

13   Doug Wilkinson to Chief, Arctic Division, Re: "Baker Lake Eskimo Council," 27 February 1957, LAC, RG 85, vol. 515, file 250-5-159, 1.

14   Ibid., 2.

15   Ibid.

16   Ibid.

17   Ibid., 2-3.

18   Ibid., 3.

19   Ibid.

20   Baker Lake Eskimo Council, Minutes of Meeting, 26 February 1957, LAC, RG 85, vol. 515, file 250-5-159, 1.

21   Ibid.

22   Ibid., 2.

23   See also the distinction drawn by Brody (1975, 135): "Southerners who try to learn the Eskimo language are encouraged by their teachers to get beyond *surusirtitut,* beyond 'talking as children do,' to *inuttitummarik,* 'the way real Eskimos talk.'" Inuit leaders in Baker Lake in the late 1950s were gently encouraging the state to talk to them properly.

24   Baker Lake Eskimo Council, Minutes of Meeting, 26 February 1957, LAC, RG 85, vol. 515, file 250-5-159, 2.

25   Ibid.

26   Ibid., 3.

27   Ibid.

28   Ibid.

29   Ibid., 4.

30   Ibid. The Hudson's Bay Company was, at the time, the only commercial operation in fledgling Inuit communities. It acted as the settlement's bank. Inuit who needed cash or who had credits with the venerable company had to deal with the manager to get the cash required to place an order with a mail order business in southern Canada. In the 1950s, cash was often sent by Inuit through the mail, accompanying their orders. This situation gave the HBC manager de facto control over the finances of Inuit. It is not hard to understand why the manager would be reluctant to give Inuit cash for the credits they had earned by trading their fox pelts at his store, thus making it possible for them to do business elsewhere.

31   Ibid.

32   Ibid., 5.

33 Ibid., 6.
34 Ibid.
35 Ibid.
36 Baker Lake Eskimo Council, Minutes of Meeting, 5 March 1957, LAC, RG 85, vol. 515, file 250-5-159, 3.
37 Ibid. Such declarations of enthusiasm should be treated with some suspicion since Inuit attempted to please *Qallunaat* and likely would have shown at least deference (or enthusiasm as a form of deference). However, genuine enthusiasm does seem to have appeared over the longer term and may well have been there from the beginning.
38 Ibid.
39 Doug Wilkinson, personal correspondence, 20 December 2002, 12.
40 Baker Lake Eskimo Council, Minutes of Meeting, 5 March 1957, LAC, RG 85, vol. 515, file 250-5-159, 3.
41 Ibid., 3-4.
42 Ibid., 4.
43 Ibid.
44 There is no way of knowing for certain, of course, that this was the case. However, that Inuit hunters at Baker Lake were willing some twenty years later to contradict the science of wildlife biologist George Califf in hearings held into the social, economic, and environmental impacts of the proposed polar gas pipeline suggests that at the time there was likely considerable doubt about the prognostications of *Qallunaat* officials regarding caribou, their numbers, and their fate. See Tester (1979).
45 Baker Lake Eskimo Council, Minutes of Meeting, 5 March 1957, LAC, RG 85, vol. 515, file 250-5-159, 4.
46 Doug Wilkinson, personal correspondence, 20 December 2002, 12.
47 Baker Lake Eskimo Council, Minutes of Meeting, 12 March 1957, LAC, RG 85, vol. 515, file 250-5-159, 1.
48 Ibid., 2.
49 Ibid., 3.
50 Ibid.
51 Ibid.
52 Ibid., 4.
53 Ibid. See also Tester and Kulchyski (1994, 91-94).
54 Ibid.
55 Ibid.
56 "Canned meat" likely meant at the time only one kind stocked by the Hudson's Bay Company, luncheon meat called SPAM. It is not difficult to understand why Inuit regarded this as a poor substitute for caribou meat.
57 Baker Lake Eskimo Council, Minutes of Meeting, 19 March 1957, LAC, RG 85, vol. 515, file 250-5-159, 2.
58 Ibid.
59 Ibid., 3.
60 Ibid.
61 Ibid.
62 Ibid.
63 Ibid., 4.
64 Ibid.
65 Ibid.
66 Ibid., 5.
67 Ibid.
68 Ibid.
69 Baker Lake Eskimo Council, Minutes of Meeting, 26 March 1957, LAC, RG 85, vol. 515, file 250-5-159, 2.
70 Ibid., 1.
71 Baker Lake Eskimo Council, Minutes of Meeting, 2 April 1957, LAC, RG 85, vol. 515, file 250-5-159, 2.

72 Baker Lake Eskimo Council, Minutes of Meeting, 9 April 1957, LAC, RG 85, vol. 515, file 250-5-159, 1.

73 Ibid., 2.

74 Baker Lake Eskimo Council, Minutes of Meeting, 16 April 1957, LAC, RG 85, vol. 515, file 250-5-159, 1.

75 Ibid., 2. The Parker referred to here was an ex-RCMP special constable who was retired and living in Baker Lake.

76 Ibid.

77 Ibid., 3-4.

78 Ibid., 4-5. "High-powered" is a bit misleading here. Wilkinson was mainly referring to the .222, a .22 size bullet with a larger load of shot, which may have been more suited to Arctic conditions. Doug Wilkinson, personal correspondence, 20 December 2002.

79 Baker Lake Eskimo Council, Minutes of Meeting, 7 May 1957, LAC, RG 85, vol. 515, file 250-5-159, 2. Angulalik's trial, a case of self-defence, is recounted in Eber (1997, 47-55).

80 Ibid., Minutes.

81 Ibid., 2-3.

82 Ibid., 3.

83 Ibid., 4.

84 Ibid., 5.

85 R.A.J. Phillips, Chief, Arctic Division, Memo to D.E. Wilkinson, Northern Service Officer, 22 May 1957, LAC, RG 85, vol. 515, file 250-5-159.

86 D.E. Wilkinson, Northern Service Officer, Memo to R.A.J. Phillips, Chief, Arctic Division, 26 June 1957, LAC, RG 85, vol. 515, file 250-5-159, 1. See Tester and Kulchyski (1994, 351-53).

87 Ibid., Letter.

88 Baker Lake Eskimo Council, Minutes of Meeting, 25 June 1957, LAC, RG 85, vol. 515, file 250-5-159, 1.

89 It is not clear what was meant by diseased in this instance, but in the archival records dealing with barren ground caribou the only significant attention paid to disease is in reference to the events outlined in Chapter 4 regarding what was most likely an outbreak of brucellosis. The reader will recall that Kelsall, writing about caribou biology in 1966, mentions three outbreaks of unidentified disease between 1948 and 1959. The timing fits. The enquiry recorded here is likely in relation to one of these outbreaks. It is further evidence of the timid and half-hearted manner in which officials of the Canadian Wildlife Service sought opinions and observations at the time. Rather than coming to Baker Lake to meet with Inuit on a matter of such potential importance, they submitted a "mild" request via the northern service officer. In fact, the lack of attention in CWS correspondence to diseases affecting caribou is notable. Despite the apparent unwillingness of the service to take reports of the disease seriously – reports that might have affected its assessment of the conditions and circumstances affecting caribou herds in this part of the eastern Arctic – perhaps its curiosity was aroused enough to find out if Inuit had any reports similar to those the service had received some years earlier.

90 Ibid., 3.

91 Baker Lake Eskimo Council, Minutes of Meeting, 30 July 1957, LAC, RG 85, vol. 515, file 250-5-159, 2.

92 Ibid.

93 Ibid.

94 Baker Lake Eskimo Council, Minutes of Meeting, 8 April 1958, LAC, RG 85, vol. 515, file 250-5-159. As noted earlier, Wilkinson was away for the summer and fall of 1957; when he returned, conflicts among *Qallunaat* in the community had escalated, and he found it difficult to give the council as much attention. Doug Wilkinson, personal correspondence, 20 December 2002, 16.

95 Baker Lake Residents Association, Report, 22 March 1962, LAC, RG 22, vol. 34, file 250-49-1 (part 1), 1.

96 J.M. Saulnier, Superintendent of Welfare, Report to Alex Stevenson Re: 25 January 1963 Meeting of the Baker Lake Eskimo Council, 29 May 1963, LAC, RG 85, vol. 675, file A250-5/159, 1.

97 P.J. Green, Area Administrator, Baker Lake, Report to Regional Administrator, Churchill, 3 November 1966, LAC, RG 85, vol. 8, file A250-1 (vol. 1), 1.
98 *Ayunarmut* translates roughly as "it can't be helped" and is discussed as evidence of Inuit existential fatalism or stoicism by Brody (1975) and by Wilkinson (1955) as *iyonamut*.

Chapter 7: Inuit Petition for Their Rights

1 Jacques Derrida (1976) argues that there is no society without writing; all forms of socious engage in forms of marking that produce meaning, leave traces open to interpretation. Anthropologist Pierre Clastres (1983) argues that forms of writing "on the body" may indicate a "writing against the state," a non-alienated inscription that defies the creation of alien power. While what follows in this chapter does not depend on these theories and speculations, they do open an evocative space for reflection on this material. Clastres also offers strong evidence for the notion that gathering and hunting peoples had deeply democratic decision-making structures, but on this topic see also the essays in Leacock and Lee (1982).
2 In such a vast archival record whose parameters and depths are still to be plumbed, we hesitate to definitively position it as the first time.
3 Eskimos of Coppermine, Petition, 7 February 1953, LAC, RG 85, vol. 41, file R-1875-2-4, Acc. 95-96/310. A version of the document in Inuktitut beginning "Atanek" is attached.
4 See, for example, the speech of Chief Sweet Grass, cited in Ray (1974, 228).
5 R.A. Bishop, Mining Recorder, Northern Administration and Lands Branch, to C.K. LeCapelain, Chief, Lands Division, 23 February 1953, LAC, RG 85, vol. 41, file R-1875-2-4, Acc. 95-96/310.
6 C.K. LeCapelain, Chief, Lands Division, to R.A. Bishop, Mining Recorder, Northern Administration and Lands Branch, 27 February 1953, LAC, RG 85, vol. 41, file R-1875-2-4, Acc. 95-96/310.
7 Frank Cunningham, Deputy Commissioner, NWT, Memo to Hugh Young, Deputy Minister, Department of Resources and Development, 4 March 1953, LAC, RG 85, vol. 41, file R-1875-2-4, Acc. 95-96/310.
8 Ibid.
9 C.K. LeCapelain, Chief, Lands Division, to R.A. Bishop, Mining Recorder, Northern Administration and Lands Branch, 9 March 1953, LAC, RG 85, vol. 41, file 1875-2-4, Acc. 95-96/310.
10 C.K. LeCapelain, Chief, Lands Division, to R.A. Bishop, Mining Recorder, Northern Administration and Lands Branch, 25 March 1953, LAC, RG 85, vol. 41, file 1875-2-4, Acc. 95-96/310.
11 C.K. LeCapelain, Chief, Lands Division, to Paulette Anerodluk, 25 March 1953, LAC, RG 85, vol. 41, file 1875-2-4, Acc. 95-96/310.
12 Paulette Anerodluk to C.K. LeCapelain, Chief, Lands Division, 13 April 1953, LAC, RG 85, vol. 41, file 1875-2-4, Acc. 95-96/310.
13 Ibid.
14 Ibid.
15 See the discussions in *R. v. Sparrow,* [1990] 1 SCR, 1075, SCC; *R. v. Gladstone,* [1996] 2 SCR 723, SCC; *R. v. Smokehouse,* [1996] 2 SCR 672, SCC; and *R. v. Van Der Peet,* [1996] 2 SCR 507, SCC.
16 Paulette Anerodluk to C.K. LeCapelain, Chief, Lands Division, 13 April 1953, LAC, RG 85, vol. 41, file 1875-2-4, Acc. 95-96/310.
17 C.K. LeCapelain, Chief, Lands Division, to Frank Cunningham, Deputy Commissioner, NWT, April 1953, LAC, RG 85, vol. 41, file 1875-2-4, Acc. 95-96/310.
18 Frank Cunningham, Deputy Commissioner, NWT, to C.K. LeCapelain, Chief, Lands Division, April 1953, LAC, RG 85, vol. 41, file 1875-2-4, Acc. 95-96/310.
19 C.K. LeCapelain, Chief, Lands Division, to Frank Cunningham, Deputy Commissioner, NWT, April 1953, LAC, RG 85, vol. 41, file 1875-2-4, Acc. 95-96/310.
20 Frank Cunningham, Deputy Commissioner, NWT, Note to C.K. LeCapelain, Chief, Lands Division, 22 April 1953, LAC, RG 85, vol. 41, file 1875-2-4, Acc. 95-96/310.
21 C.K. LeCapelain, Chief, Lands Division, to Paulette Anerodluk, 24 April 1953, LAC, RG 85, vol. 41, file 1875-2-4, Acc. 95-96/310.

22 James Cantley, 29 June 1953, LAC, RG 85, vol. 41, file 1875-2-4, Acc. 95-96/310.
23 R.A.J. Phillips, Chief, Arctic Division, Memo to Gordon Robertson, Deputy Minister, Northern Affairs and Natural Resources, 25 October 1957, LAC, N92-023 49-4.
24 C.L. Merrill, Administrator, Mackenzie District, Memo to Director, Arctic Division, 9 November 1962, LAC, RG 85, vol. 1347, file 1000/145 (part 7).
25 For a copy of this petition and a brief discussion, see Tester and Kulchyski (1994, 250).
26 See the 1992 National Film Board of Canada documentary *Coppermine* for more on this history.
27 R.A.J. Phillips, Acting Director, Arctic Division, Memo to Gordon Robertson, Deputy Minister, Northern Affairs and Natural Resources, 25 October 1957, LAC, N92-023 49-4.
28 Ibid.
29 Ibid.
30 Evidence of the pattern is found in both global and local contexts, from President Reagan's famous assertions in the 1980s that Cuban infiltrators were responsible for dissent in Nicaragua and El Salvador to the federal mediator's protestations (in conversation with Kulchyski) that "radical activists" were responsible for Dene opposition to the Norman Wells pipeline project in the same period.
31 Ibid.
32 Ibid.
33 Ibid.
34 C.L. Merrill, Administrator, Mackenzie District, to P. Templeton, Regional Administrator, February 1962, LAC, RG 85, vol. 1347, file 1000/145 (part 7).
35 Ibid.
36 C.L. Merrill, Administrator, Mackenzie District, Memo to Director, Arctic Division, 9 November 1962, LAC, RG 85, vol. 1347, file 1000/145 (part 7).
37 Mothers of Cape Dorset, Petition to Commissioner and Council, NWT, 31 July 1962, LAC, RG 22, vol. 871 40-10-1A (part 25).
38 Ibid.
39 Men of Cape Dorset, Petition to Commissioner and Council, NWT, 31 July 1962, LAC, RG 22, vol. 871 40-10-1A (part 25).
40 Ibid.
41 Ibid.
42 Joop Sanders to Arthur Laing, Minister, Department of Indian Affairs and Northern Development, and Jack Pickersgill, Secretary of State, 12 October 1967, LAC, RG 85, vol. 1894, file 340-2 (part 1).
43 People of Pond Inlet, Petition, 12 October 1967, LAC, RG 85, vol. 1894, file 340-2 (part 1).
44 Alex Stevenson, Administrator of the Arctic, Memo to Director, Arctic Division, 1 November 1967, LAC, RG 85, vol. 1894, file 340-2 (part 1).
45 W.F. Shepherd, Assistant Chief, Welfare Division, Memo to Director, Arctic Division, 17 November 1967, LAC, RG 85, vol. 1894, file 340-2 (part 1).
46 Arthur Laing, Minister, Department of Indian Affairs and Northern Development, to Marion Palmer, 22 November 1967, LAC, RG 85, vol. 1894, file 340-2 (part 1).
47 Alex Stevenson, Administrator of the Arctic, to Director, Arctic Division, 24 November 1967, LAC, RG 85, vol. 1894, file 340-2 (part 1).
48 G. Smith, Head, Branch Secretariat, Memo to Director, Arctic Division, Re: "Pond Inlet – Pirate Radio Station," 29 November 1967, LAC, RG 85, vol. 1894, file 340-2 (part 1).
49 Director, Arctic Division, Memo to A.B. Yates, Assistant Director, Arctic Division, Re: "Radio and Television Services in the North," March 1968, LAC, RG 85, vol. 1894, file 340-2 (part 1).
50 A.B. Yates, Assistant Director, Arctic Division, Memo to Director, Arctic Division, 29 March 1968, LAC, RG 85, vol. 1894, file 340-2 (part 1).
51 G.F. Davidson, CBC, to J.A. MacDonald, Deputy Minister, Department of Indian Affairs and Northern Development, 19 June 1968, LAC, RG 85, vol. 1894, file 340-2 (part 1).
52 Paul Hellyer, Minister of Transport, to Arthur Laing, Minister of Indian Affairs and Northern Development, 18 April 1968, LAC, RG 85, vol. 1894, file 340-2 (part 1).

53 Donald Marsh, Anglican Bishop of the Arctic, to Jean Chrétien, Minister, Department of Indian Affairs and Northern Development, 18 December 1968, LAC, RG 85, vol. 18, file 1010-8 I, box 232.
54 Nasook to Donald Marsh, Anglican Bishop of the Arctic, 19 November 1968, LAC, RG 85, vol. 18, file 1010-8 I, box 232.
55 J. Kadlutsiak, President, Community Association, Igloolik, 13 November 1968, LAC, RG 85, vol. 18, file 1010-8 I, box 232.
56 D.W. Simpson, Assistant Director, Education Branch, to G. Smith, Director of Operations, 10 January 1969, LAC, RG 85, vol. 18, file 1010-8 I, box 232.
57 Ipeelee Kilabuk, "Ipeelee Kilabuk Seeks Improvement between Enuit and Kabloona," *Keewatin Echo,* July 1969, LAC, RG 85, vol. 14, file A-690-1/500, Acc. 1985-86/220.

Bibliography

Adams, Howard. 1975. *Prison of Grass*. Toronto: General Publishing.

Agamben, Giorgio. 1998. *Homo Sacer*. Trans. Daniel Heller-Roazen. Stanford: Stanford University Press.

Alia, Valerie. 1994. *Names, Numbers, and Northern Policy*. Halifax: Fernwood.

Althusser, Louis. 1971. *Lenin and Philosophy*. Trans. Ben Brewster. New York: Monthly Review Press.

Altmeyer, George. 1995. "Three Ideas of Nature in Canada, 1893-1914." In Pam Gaffield and Chad Gaffield, eds., *Consuming Canada: Readings in Environmental History*, 384-405. Toronto: Copp Clark.

Arendt, Hannah. 1973. *The Origins of Totalitarianism*. New York: Harcourt Brace Jovanovich.

Asch, Michael. 1982. "Dene Self-Determination and the Study of Hunter-Gatherers in the Modern World." In Eleanor Leacock and Richard Lee, eds., *Politics and History in Band Societies*, 347-71. Cambridge, UK: Cambridge University Press.

–. 1984. *Home and Native Land*. Toronto: Methuen.

Balicki, Asen. 1970. *The Netsilik Eskimo*. Garden City, NY: Natural History Press.

Banfield, A.W.F. 1951a. *The Barren-Ground Caribou*. Ottawa: Department of Resources and Development, Northern Administration and Lands Branch.

–. 1951b. "The Status, Ecology, and Utilization of the Continental Barren-Ground Caribou (*Rangifer arcticus aarcticus*)." PhD diss., University of Michigan. (Document 267, Canadian Wildlife Service Collection, Environment Canada Library, Hull, QC.)

–. 1954. "Preliminary Investigation of the Barren-Ground Caribou." Canadian Wildlife Service, Wildlife Management Bulletin, Series 1, 10A and 10B.

–. 1956. "The Caribou Crisis." *Beaver* (Spring): 3-7.

Bannerji, Himani. 1995. *Thinking Through*. Toronto: Women's Press.

Baudrillard, Jean. 1981. *For a Critique of the Political Economy of the Sign*. Trans. Charles Levin. St Louis: Telos.

Benjamin, Walter. 1978. *Illuminations*. Trans. Harry Zohn. New York: Schocken.

Bennett, John, and Susan Rowley, eds. 2004. *Uqalurait: An Oral History of Nunavut*. Montreal: McGill-Queen's University Press.

Berger, Thomas. 1991. *A Long and Terrible Shadow*. Vancouver: Douglas and McIntyre.

Berkes, Fikret. 1999. *Sacred Ecology*. Philadelphia: Taylor and Francis.

Berman, Marshall. 1988. *All that Is Solid Melts into Air*. Markham, ON: Penguin.

Berman, Morris. 1981. *The Reenchantment of the World*. Ithaca, NY: Cornell University Press.

Bhabha, Homi. 1994. *The Location of Culture*. New York: Routledge.

Birket-Smith, Kaj. 1959. *The Eskimos*. London: Methuen.

Blaser, Mario, Harvey Feit, and Glenn McRae, eds. 2004. *In the Way of Development*. London: Zed Books.

Boas, Franz. 1964. *The Central Eskimo*. Lincoln: University of Nebraska Press.

Borrows, John. 2002. *Recovering Canada.* Toronto: University of Toronto Press.

Bracken, Christopher. 1997. *The Potlatch Papers.* Chicago: University of Chicago Press.

Briggs, Jean. 1967. *Never in Anger.* Cambridge, MA: Harvard University Press.

Brody, Hugh. 1983 [1975]. *The People's Land.* Markham, ON: Penguin Books.

–. 1987. *Living Arctic: Hunters of the Canadian North.* Seattle: University of Washington Press.

–. 2000. *The Other Side of Eden.* Vancouver: Douglas and McIntyre.

Brownlee, Robin (Jarvis). 2003. *A Fatherly Eye: Indian Agents, Government Power, and Aboriginal Resistance in Ontario, 1918-1939.* Toronto: Oxford University Press.

Burnett, J.A. 1999. "A Passion for Wildlife: A History of the Canadian Wildlife Service, 1947-1997." *Canadian Field Naturalist* 113, 1: 140-44.

–. 2003. *A Passion for Wildlife: The History of the Canadian Wildlife Service.* Vancouver: UBC Press.

Bussidor, I., and U. Bilgen-Reinart. 1997. *Night Spirits: The Story of the Relocation of the Sayisi Dene.* Winnipeg: University of Manitoba Press.

Canada. *Indian Acts and Amendments.* Vol. 1. Ottawa: Queen's Printer.

Canada. Department of Resources and Development. Northern Administration and Lands Branch. 1949. An Ordinance Respecting the Preservation of Game in the Northwest Territories. Assented to 21 April.

Cardinal, Harold. 1999 [1969]. *The Unjust Society.* Vancouver: Douglas and McIntyre.

Carruthers, D.R., and R.D. Jakimchuk. 1981. *The Distribution, Numbers, and Movements of Caribou and Muskoxen North of Great Bear Lake, Northwest Territories.* Sidney, BC: Renewable Resources Consulting Services.

Caughley, G. 1974. "Bias in Aerial Survey." *Journal of Wildlife Management* 38, 4: 921-33.

Clancy, J.P.I. 1985. "Caribou, Fur, and the Resource Frontier: A Political Economy of the Northwest Territories to 1967." PhD diss., Queen's University.

Clarke, C.H.D. 1940. "A Biological Investigation of the Thelon Game Sanctuary." Bulletin 36, Natural Museum of Canada.

Clastres, Pierre. 1983. *Society against the State.* New York: Zone Books.

Clifford, James, and George Marcus, eds. 1986. *Writing Culture.* Berkeley: University of California Press.

Coates, Kenneth S., and William R. Morrison, eds. 1989. *Interpreting Canada's North: Selected Readings.* Mississauga: Copp Pitman Clark.

Comaroff, Jean, and John Comaroff. 1991. *Of Revelation and Revolution.* Chicago: University of Chicago Press.

Condon, Richard, et al. 1995. "The Best Part of Life: Subsistence Hunting, Ethnicity, and Economic Adaptation among Young Inuit Males." *Arctic* 48, 1: 31-46.

Cruikshank, Julie. 1998. *The Social Life of Stories.* Vancouver: UBC Press.

Culhane, Dara. 1998. *The Pleasure of the Crown.* Burnaby, BC: Talon.

Cumming, Peter A., and Neil H. Mickenberg. 1971. *Native Rights in Canada.* 2nd ed. Toronto: General Publishing.

Damas, David, ed. 1978. *Arctic.* Vol. 5 of *The Handbook of North American Indians.* Washington: Smithsonian Institution.

Derrida, Jacques. 1976. *Of Grammatology.* Trans. Gayatri Spivak. Baltimore: Johns Hopkins University Press.

Dickason, Olive. 2002. *Canada's First Nations.* Toronto: Oxford University Press.

Dickerson, Mark. 1992. *Whose North?: Political Change, Political Development, and Self-Government in the Northwest Territories.* Vancouver: UBC Press.

Diubaldo, Richard. 1985. *The Government of Canada and the Inuit: 1900-1967.* Ottawa: Research Branch, Corporate Policy, Indian and Northern Affairs Canada.

–. 1998. *Stefansson and the Canadian Arctic.* Montreal: McGill-Queen's University Press.

Eber, Dorothy. 1989. *When the Whalers Were up North.* Montreal: McGill-Queen's University Press.

–. 1997. *Images of Justice.* Montreal: McGill-Queen's University Press.

Fanon, Franz. 1966. *The Wretched of the Earth.* Trans. Constance Farrington. New York: Grove.

Feit, Harvey. 1982. "The Future of Hunters within Nation-States." In Richard Lee and Eleanor Leacock, eds., *Politics and History in Band Societies,* 373-411. London: Cambridge University Press.

–. 1986. "Hunting and the Quest for Power: The James Bay Cree and Whitemen in the Twentieth Century." In R. Bruce Morrison and C. Roderick Wilson, eds., *Native Peoples: The Canadian Experience,* 171-207. Toronto: McClelland and Stewart.

Fienup-Riordan, Ann. 1990. "Original Ecologists? The Relationship between Yup'ik Eskimos and Animals." In *Eskimo Essays: Yup'ik Lives and How We See Them,* 167-91. New Brunswick: Rutgers University Press.

Finnie, Richard. 1940. *Lure of the North.* Philadelphia: David McKay.

Foote, D.C. 1971. "Remarks on Eskimo Sealing and the Harp Seal Controversy." In William Wonders, ed., *Canada's Changing North,* 230-34. Toronto: McClelland and Stewart.

Foster, J. 1998. *Working for Wildlife: The Beginnings of Preservation in Canada.* 2nd ed. Toronto: University of Toronto Press.

Foucault, Michel. 1979. *Discipline and Punish.* Trans. Alan Sheridan. New York: Vintage.

Freeman, Milton. 1992. *Recovering Rights.* Edmonton: Canadian Circumpolar Institute.

Freeman, Minnie Aodla. 1978. *Life among the Qallunaat.* Edmonton: Hurtig.

Fumoleau, Rene. 1973. *As Long as This Land Shall Last.* Toronto: McClelland and Stewart.

Geertz, Clifford. 1988. *Work and Lives.* Stanford: Stanford University Press.

Giddens, Anthony. 1987. *The Nation State and Violence.* Berkeley: University of California Press.

Gillies, Ross W. 1989. "Whaling, Inuit, and the Arctic Islands." In Kenneth S. Coates and William R. Morrison, eds., *Interpreting Canada's North: Selected Readings,* 235-51. Mississauga: Copp Pitman Clark.

Grace, Sherrill. 2001. *Canada and the Idea of North.* Montreal: McGill-Queen's University Press.

Gramsci, Antonio. 1971. *Selections from the Prison Notebooks.* Ed. and trans. Quinten Hoare and Geoffrey Nowell Smith. London: Lawrence and Wishart.

Grant, Shelagh. 1988. *Sovereignty or Security.* Vancouver: UBC Press.

Hall, Anthony. 2003. *The American Empire and the Fourth World.* Montreal: McGill-Queen's University Press.

Hall, D.J. 1985. *Clifford Sifton.* Volume 2: *The Lonely Eminence 1901-1929.* Vancouver UBC Press.

Hall, Ed, ed. 1989. *People and Caribou in the Northwest Territories.* Yellowknife: Government of the Northwest Territories, Department of Renewable Resources.

Hardt, Michael, and Antonio Negri. 2001. *Empire.* Cambridge, MA: Harvard University Press.

Harvey, David. 1990. *The Condition of Postmodernity.* London: Blackwell.

Hays, Samuel P. 1969. *Conservation and the Gospel of Efficiency: The Progressive Conservation Movement, 1890-1920.* New York: Atheneum.

Heard, Doug. 1989. "Research." In Ed Hall, ed., *People and Caribou in the Northwest Territories,* 81-87. Yellowknife: Government of the Northwest Territories, Department of Renewable Resources.

Henderson, Sakej. 1997. *The Mi'kmaw Concordat.* Halifax: Fernwood.

Horkheimer, Max, and Theodore Adorno. 1944. *The Dialectic of Enlightenment.* London: Allen Lane.

Huget, A. 1967. "The Role of the Royal Canadian Mounted Police in Canada's National Wildlife Policy and Program." In *Transactions of the 31st Federal-Provincial Wildlife Conference.* Ottawa: Canadian Wildlife Service.

Innis, Harold. 1962. *The Fur Trade in Canada.* New Haven: Yale University Press.

Jameson, Fredric. 1991. *Postmodernism: Or, The Cultural Logic of Late Capitalism,* Durham: Duke University Press.

Jenness, Diamond. 1930. *The Indians of Canada.* Toronto: University of Toronto Press.

Keenleyside, Hugh L. 1981. *On the Bridge of Time.* Vol. 2 of *Memoirs of Hugh L. Keenleyside.* Toronto: McClelland and Stewart.

Kelsall, J.P. 1964. "The Decline of the Caribou." *Oryx* 7, 5: 240-45.

–. 1968. *The Migratory Barren-Ground Caribou of Canada*. Ottawa: Department of Indian and Northern Affairs, Canadian Wildlife Service.

Kelsall, J.P., and A.C. Loughrey. 1955. "Barren-Ground Caribou Resurvey, 1955." CWS collection, Environment Canada Library, Hull, QC.

Kilabuk, Ipeelee. 1969. "Ipeelee Kilabuk Seeks Improvement between Enuit and Kabloona." *Keewatin Echo*, July: n.p.

King, James. 2002. *Farley: The Life of Farley Mowat*. Toronto: HarperCollins.

Knight, Rolf. 1965. "A Re-Examination of Hunting, Trapping, and Territoriality among the Northeastern Algonkian Indians." In Anthony Leeds and Andrew P. Vayda, eds., *Man, Culture, and Animals: The Role of Animals in Human Ecological Adjustments*, 27-42. Publication 78. Washington, DC: American Association for the Advancement of Science.

Kotierk (Rojas), Aluki. 2001. "Inuit Isumatait." Master's thesis, Trent University, Peterborough, ON.

Kulchyski, Peter. 1993. "Anthropology at the Service of the State." *Journal of Canadian Studies* 28, 2 (Summer): 21-50.

–. 1994. "Theses on Aboriginal Rights." In Peter Kulchyski, ed., *Unjust Relations*, 1-20. Toronto: Oxford University Press.

–. 2006. "Six Gestures." In Pamela Stern and Lisa Stevenson, eds., *Critical Inuit Studies: An Anthology of Contemporary Arctic Ethnography*, 155-67. Lincoln: University of Nebraska Press.

LaRocque, Emma. 1975. *Defeathering the Indian*. Agincourt, ON: Book Society of Canada.

Leacock, Eleanor, and Richard Lee, eds. 1982. *Politics and History in Band Societies*. London: Cambridge University Press.

Leopold, A. 1933. *Game Management*. New York: Charles Scribner's Sons.

Lewis, Harrison. N.d. *Lively: A History of the Canadian Wildlife Service*. Vol. 1. Unpublished ms, Canadian Wildlife Service, Ottawa, ref. R653-207-8-E.

Livingston, John. 1981. *The Fallacy of Wildlife Conservation*. Toronto: McClelland and Stewart.

Lukacs, George. 1981. *History and Class Consciousness*. Trans. Rodney Livingstone. Cambridge, MA: MIT Press.

Macklem, Patrick. 2001. *Indigenous Difference and the Constitution of Canada*. Toronto: University of Toronto Press.

Macpherson, C.B. 1965. *The Real World of Democracy*. Toronto: CBC.

McCandless, Robert G. 1985. *Yukon Wildlife: A Social History*. Edmonton: University of Alberta Press.

McCauley, J.H. 1960. "Contwoyto Lake Report." Ottawa: Department of Northern Affairs and National Resources, Territorial Game Warden Service.

McNicoll, Paule, Frank Tester, and Peter Kulchyski. 1999. "Arctic Abstersion: *The Book of Wisdom for Eskimos:* Modernism and Inuit Assimilation." *Inuit Studies* 23, 1-2: 199-220.

Memmi, Albert. 1972. *The Colonizer and the Colonized*. Trans. Howard Greenfeld. Boston: Beacon.

Milloy, John. 1991. "The Early Indian Acts." In J.R. Miller, ed., *Sweet Promises*, 145-54. Toronto: University of Toronto Press.

–. 1999. *A National Crime*. Winnipeg: University of Manitoba Press.

Morris, Alexander. 1991 [1880]. *The Treaties of Canada*. Saskatoon: Fifth House.

Morrison, R. Bruce, and C. Roderick Wilson, eds. 1986. *Native Peoples: The Canadian Experience*. Toronto: McClelland and Stewart.

Mowat, Farley. 1968. *Never Cry Wolf*. Toronto: McClelland and Stewart.

Nadasdy, Paul. 2003. *Hunters and Bureaucrats: Power, Knowledge, and Aboriginal-State Relations in the Southwest Yukon*. Vancouver: UBC Press.

Netherlands Commission for UNESCO and the Roosevelt Study Center. 1990. *Human Rights in a Pluralist World: Individuals and Collectivities*. Westport, CT: Mekler.

Otten, M.R.M., J.B. Haufler, S.R. Winterstein, and L.C. Bender. 1993. "An Aerial Censing Procedure for Elk in Michigan." *Wildlife Society Bulletin* 21: 73-80.

Pelly, David. 1996. *Thelon: A River Sanctuary*. Merrickville, ON: Canadian Recreational Canoeing Association.

Pike, W.M. 1892. *The Barren-Ground Caribou of Northern Canada.* New York: Macmillan.

Pollock, K.H., and W.L. Kendall. 1987. "Visibility Bias in Aerial Surveys: A Review of Estimation Procedures." *Journal of Wildlife Management* 51, 2: 502-10.

Poulantzas, Nicos. 1980. *State. Power. Socialism.* Trans. Patrick Camiller. London: Verso.

Price, Richard, ed. 1999. *The Spirit of the Alberta Indian Treaties.* Edmonton: University of Alberta Press.

Rasmussen, Knut. 1999. *Across Arctic America.* Fairbanks: University of Alaska Press.

Raunet, Daniel. 1984. *Without Surrender. Without Consent.* Vancouver: Douglas and McIntyre.

Ray, Arthur. 1974. *Indians in the Fur Trade.* Toronto: University of Toronto Press.

Ray, Arthur, Jim Miller, and Frank Tough. 2000. *Bounty and Benevolence.* Montreal: McGill-Queen's University Press.

Riddington, Robin. 1990. *Little Bit Know Something.* Vancouver: Douglas and McIntyre.

Robertson, Gordon. 2000. *Memoirs of a Very Civil Servant.* Toronto: University of Toronto Press.

Rollason, Heather. 1994. "Studying under the Influence." Master's thesis, Trent University, Peterborough.

Ross, W. Gillies. 1989. "Whaling, Inuit, and the Arctic Islands." In Kenneth S. Coates and William R. Morrison, eds., *Interpreting Canada's North: Selected Readings,* 235-51. Mississauga: Copp Pitman Clark.

Rousseau, Jean-Jacques. 1973. *The Social Contract and Discourses.* Trans. G.D.H. Cole. Toronto: J.M. Dent and Sons.

Rowley, Graham. 1996. *Cold Comfort: My Love Affair with the Arctic.* Montreal: McGill-Queen's University Press.

Ruttan, R.A. "New Crisis for Barren-Ground Caribou." 1966. *Country Guide,* November: 24-25.

Sahlins, Marshall. 1972. *Stone Age Economics.* New York: Aldine Atherton.

Said, Edward. 1979. *Orientalism.* New York: Vintage Books.

Sartre, Jean-Paul. 1991. *Critique of Dialectical Reason.* Vol. 2. Trans. Quintin Hoare. London: Verso.

Scott, James. 1985. *Weapons of the Weak: Everyday Forms of Peasant Resistance.* New Haven: Yale University Press.

Seton, E.T. 1911. *The Arctic Prairie: A Canoe Journey of 2000 Miles in Search of the Caribou.* Toronto: William Briggs.

Shewell, Hugh. 2004. *Enough to Keep Them Alive.* Toronto: University of Toronto Press.

Sissons, Jack. 1968. *Judge of the Far North: The Memoirs of Jack Sissons.* Toronto: McClelland and Stewart.

Slattery, Brian. 1987. "Understanding Aboriginal Rights." *Canadian Bar Review* 66: 727-83.

Spivak, Gayatri Chakravorty. 1999. *A Critique of Postcolonial Reason.* Cambridge, MA: Harvard University Press.

Stern, Pamela, and Lisa Stevenson, eds. 2006. *Critical Inuit Studies.* Lincoln: University of Nebraska Press.

Stevenson, Marc. 1997. *Inuit, Whalers, and Cultural Persistence.* Toronto: Oxford University Press.

Taussig, Michael. 1997. *Shamanism, Colonialism, and the Wild Man.* Chicago: University of Chicago Press.

Tener, J.S. 1965. *Musk-Oxen in Canada.* Ottawa: Queen's Printer.

Tennant, Paul. 1990. *Aboriginal Peoples and Politics.* Vancouver: UBC Press.

Tester, F.J. 1979. *The Potential Social, Economic, and Environmental Impacts of the Proposed Gas Pipeline on the District of Keewatin Northwest Territories.* 2 vols. Ottawa: Queen's Printer.

Tester, Frank James, and Peter Kulchyski. 1994. *Tammarniit: Inuit Relocation in the Eastern Arctic, 1939-63.* Vancouver: UBC Press.

Thomas, D. 1960. "Caribou Tagging at Contwoyto Lake, August 1960." Canadian Wildlife Service Report, Library of Canadian Wildlife Service, Ottawa C 858.

Thomas, Nicolas. 1994. *Colonialism's Culture: Anthropology, Travel, and Government.* Princeton: Princeton University Press.

Tobias, John. 1991. "Protection, Civilization, Assimilation." In J.R. Miller, ed., *Sweet Promises,* 127-44. Toronto: University of Toronto Press.

Tough, Frank. 1996. *"As Their Natural Resources Fail: Native Peoples and the Economic History of Northern Manitoba, 1870-1930."* Vancouver: UBC Press.

Treaty 7 Elders and Tribal Council. 1996. *The True Spirit and Original Intent of Treaty 7.* Montreal: McGill-Queen's University Press.

Urquhart, D. 1989. "History of Research." In Ed Hall, ed., *People and Caribou in the Northwest Territories,* 95-102. Yellowknife: Government of the Northwest Territories, Department of Renewable Resources.

Vallee, Frank. 1967. *Kabloona and Eskimo in the Central Keewatin.* Ottawa: Canadian Research Centre for Anthropology, Saint Paul University.

Van Ballenberghe, V. 1985. "Wolf Predation on Caribou: The Nelchina Herd Case History." *Journal of Wildlife Management* 49, 3: 711-20.

VanderWal, Koo. 1990. "Collective Human Rights: A Western View." In Netherlands Commission for UNESCO and the Roosevelt Study Center 1990, 83-107. Westport, CT: Mekler.

Weaver, Sally. 1981. *Making Canadian Indian Policy.* Toronto: University of Toronto Press.

Wenzel, George. 1991. *Animal Rights, Human Rights.* Toronto: University of Toronto Press.

-. 2005. "Nunavut Inuit and Polar Bear: The Cultural Politics of the Sport Hunt." In N. Kishigami and J. Savelle, eds., *Indigenous Use and Management of Marine Resources,* 363-88. Senri Ethnological Series. Osaka: National Museum of Ethnology.

Wilkinson, Doug. 1955. *Land of the Long Day.* Toronto: Clarke Irwin.

Wolf, R.J., and R.J. Walker. 1987. "Subsistence Economies in Alaska: Productivity, Geography, and Developmental Impacts." *Arctic Anthropology* 24, 2: 56-81.

Zaslow, Morris. 1988. *The Northward Expansion of Canada: 1914-1967.* Toronto: McClelland and Stewart.

Index

Aberdeen Lake, 146, 148, 235

Aboriginal rights, 13, 15, 17, 24, 85, 100, 102, 142, 161, 165-67, 169, 170, 172, 174, 179, 181-84, 186-90, 192-95, 197, 201, 244, 250, 274, 276, 278, 293n1

Aboriginal title, 16, 165, 166, 193, 194, 201, 248, 273, 293n1

Adam, Father, 240, 242, 245, 253

Adams, Howard, 18

Adjuk, Monica, 60

Adorno, Theodor, 9, 10, 11, 13, 274, 282n18

Advisory Board on Wild Life Protection, 31, 51

aerial surveying, 11, 65-66, 69, 81, 98-99, 104, 150-51, 154, 156, 157, 276, 282n23

Africa, 81, 92, 207

Agak, Ivor, 131

Agamben, Giorgio, 12

Ahegona, Aime, 172-73

Aklavik, 42, 222, 280n28

Alaska, 38, 48, 55, 63, 116, 186, 187, 202, 219

Albany, 53

Alberta, 141

Alexandra Fiord, 110

Alia, Valerie, 201

Alikut, Guy, 168

Aliuk, 207

Alonak, Jack, 138

Althusser, Louis, 14

Amagoalik, John, 253, 278

Ameetenak, 224

Anarak, Paul, 102

Anawak, Jack, 253

Anderson, Rudolph, 29, 31

Anderson Bay, 131

Anderson River, 62, 97

Andrews, D.R., 115, 116

Anerodluk, Paulette, 244, 247, 249-53

Anglican church, 25, 44, 296n3

Angmarlik, 278

Angnaryouweega, 224-25

Angoojuk, 44

Angotee, 206

Angulalik, 12, 39, 42-45, 48, 96, 232, 233, 234, 278, 280n35, 298n79

Animal Rights, Human Rights, 19

archive, x, xii, 170, 278

Arctic Bay, 140, 264, 265

Arctic Division, 93-94, 104, 110, 111, 118, 148, 208, 254, 266, 267

Arctic exiles, ix, 6, 118, 251

Arctic Islands Game Preserve, 35, 37, 43, 130

Arendt, Hannah, 10

Arnalukjuak, John, 198

Arviat, 15, 56, 140, 141, 154, 167-68, 169, 191, 198, 203

Asch, Michael, 19, 288n3

Asheva, Kenojuak, 277

assimilation, 37, 54, 59, 75, 79, 172, 185, 188, 196, 253

Attungala, N., 221, 224, 236

Auchterlonie, Sergeant, 146

Australia, 8

Ausuittuq, 100, 110, 114-16, 119, 129, 131, 132, 134-36, 264, 265, 289n15

Avadluk, 145

Ayaruak, John, 254, 278

Back River, 94, 148, 174

Baffin Island, 25, 36, 61, 62, 66, 67, 91, 95, 207(fig), 279n2, 283n28, 289n27

Bailey, J.S., 67, 91

Baker Lake, 15, 34, 51, 57, 60, 101, 121, 141, 146, 147, 148, 151, 152, 154, 158,

167, 201, 204-38, 239, 267. *See also*
Qamani'tuaq
Balicki, Asen, 19
Ballentyne, E.A., 272
Banff, 109
Banfield, A.W.F., 13, 54-56, 57, 59, 63-66,
68, 77, 88, 90, 93, 109, 157, 276, 282n23
Banks Island, 94, 118, 137
Bannerji, Himani, 18
Banting, Frederick, 37
Bathurst Inlet. *See* Kingauk
Baudrillard, Jean, 14
Baychimo, 44
Beaufort Sea, 26, 30, 32, 34
Beaver, The, 77
Benjamin, Walter, 9
Bennett, John, 72
Bennett, R.B., 34
Benson, D.A., 150
Berger, Thomas, 5, 278
Berkes, Fikret, 19
Berman, Marshall, 13
Bhabha, Homi, 9
Bilgen-Reinart, U., 75, 282n33
Bishop, R.A., 245-47
Bissett, Don, 148
Blaser, Mario, 19
Bolt, Ikey, 45, 45(fig)
Bond, Jameson, 98-99, 225, 226
Book of Wisdom for Eskimos, The, 83, 88,
122, 123, 125 284n6
Borden, Robert, 27, 28
Borden Island, 158
Borrows, John, 13, 17, 165
Boxer, A.J., 92
Breyant, Gabriel, 39
Briggs, Jean, 19, 290n34, 296n12
British Columbia, 34, 53, 81, 166
Brochet, 75
Brody, Hugh, 13, 18, 19, 172, 275, 278,
287n71, 288nn2,3, 295n2, 296nn12,23,
299n98
Broughton Island. *See* Qikitarjuak
Brown, D.F., 173
Brown, W.G., 107
Brownlee, Robin, 204, 293n5
Bryant, J.E., 159
Burnet, J. Alexander, 24, 35, 36, 52, 53,
69, 276, 281n2
Bussidor, Ila, 75, 283n33

Calder, 166, 192, 293n7
California, 77
Cambridge Bay. *See* Ikaluktutiak
Camsell, Charles, 36-37
Canada and the Idea of North, 9

Canadian Audubon, 133, 134, 157
Canadian Broadcasting Corporation,
265-68
Canadian Wildlife Service, 24, 26, 52, 53,
56, 57, 59, 71, 83, 84, 86, 87, 90-94, 100,
103, 104, 106-8, 110-14, 116-18, 120,
121, 124(fig), 129-31, 133, 135, 137,
139-41, 143-44, 146, 148-50, 153-54,
156-61, 196, 215(fig), 216(fig), 229, 232,
276, 282n17, 298n89
Canalaska Trading Company, 39, 42-45,
281n37
Cantley, James, 93-94, 106, 251
Cape Christian, 107, 115,
Cape Dorset, 16, 233, 244, 254, 260-64
Cape Smith, 254
Carrothers Commission, 119-20
Chesshire, R.H., 170
Chesterfield Inlet. *See* Igluligaarjuk
Chrétien, Jean, 121, 136, 268
Churchill, 75, 77, 291n72
Clarke, 43
Clarke, Bill, 112
Clarke, C.H.D., 52
Clarke, Douglas, 134
Clyde River, 266
Coats Island, 14, 160-61
Coleman, J.R.B., 111, 192
colonialism, xi, xii, 7-9, 14, 16-17, 20, 24,
83, 98, 109, 125, 138, 185, 189, 208,
248, 256, 276-77, 282n18
Colonialism's Culture, 24
Comaroff, Jean, 14
Comaroff, John, 14
Commission of Conservation, 27-28
community councils, 14, 15-16, 138, 154,
205-6, 208, 210, 213, 219, 233, 235-37,
239, 252, 270, 295n2
community development, ix, 6, 20, 50,
127, 187, 200, 205, 208, 237, 263, 273
Contwoyto Lake, 78-79, 78(tab), 146
Coombs, Sergeant, 185
Copenhagen, 29, 111
Coppermine. *See* Kugluktuk
Coppermine River, 242
Coral Harbour. *See* Salliq
Coronation Gulf, 30, 34, 37, 42, 43, 88
Cory, W.W., 36
Country Guide, 156
Cowan, Andrew, 267
Craig Harbour, 36, 107
Cree, 150, 282n10
Critique of Dialectical Reason, The: volume
1, 7, 19; volume 2, 7
Cruikshank, Julie, 19
Cumming, Peter, 17, 293n1

Cunningham, Frank, 170-71, 246-47, 250-51
Curley, Joe. *See* Kayakjuak
Curley, Tagak, 14, 160(fig), 161, 278

Daly, 46
Davidson, D.A., 200-201
Davidson, G.F., 267
Davies, Dr., 256
Dene, 30, 39, 47, 75-77, 79, 85, 143, 150, 192, 288n3, 300n30
Denmark, 110, 111, 116
Dent, Clare, 151
Department of the Interior, 29, 30, 33-36, 40, 46, 58
Department of Justice, 173, 197, 199
Department of Northern Affairs, 77, 99, 106, 141, 143, 167, 172, 179, 183, 213, 292n88
Derrida, Jacques, 12, 16, 299n1
De Vitoria, Francisco, 165
Devon Island, 100, 115, 116
Dialectic of Enlightenment, The, 13
Dick, Inspector, 106
Diefenbaker Government, 143, 290n49
Dinsdale, Walter, 144, 290n49
Discipline and Punish, 9
Distant Early Warning Line, 96, 105, 108, 109, 110, 124, 148, 176, 225, 286n55
Diubaldo, Richard, 29, 30, 33, 36, 279n5
dog teams, 30, 39, 41, 62, 100, 115, 145, 146, 148, 153
Dominion Law Review, xii
Dominion Research Council, 35
Dominion Wildlife Service, 19, 25, 35, 49, 50, 51, 52, 54, 55, 281n6
Drum, The, 158
Drybones, 171
Duck Lake, 75-77, 76(fig), 79
Dwernichuk, M, 145

Eber, Dorothy, 12, 15, 101, 171, 172, 184, 192, 280n35, 285n39, 293nn97, 293n12, 298n79
Edmonton, 81, 283n32
Edmonton Journal, 181
Edwards, Bill, 228
Ekpukuwuk, David, 131·
Elatiak, Joseph, 131
Elkin, Mr., 266
Ellesmere Island, 36, 100, 105, 110, 111, 112, 137
Elton, Charles, 51
Empire, 10

enlightenment, 8, 11,12, 13, 27, 48, 61, 62, 282n18
Ennadai Lake, 67, 141
e-numbers, 197-201, 221
Eskimo Councils, 15, 154, 204-6, 208, 210, 213, 219, 233, 235-37, 239
Eskimo Point. *See* Arviat
Etegoyak, Harold, 219-20

Fairclough, Ellen, 143, 183, 290n44
Falconer, Dr., 256
famine. *See* starvation
Fanon, Franz, 9, 18
Favreau, Guy, 149
Feit, Harvey, 19, 282nn10,2
Finnie, O.S., 30, 32-33, 34, 36, 39, 47
Finnie, Richard, 30, 31, 44
First Nations, 19, 26, 38, 53, 58, 59, 64, 71, 84, 85, 141-43, 181, 177, 191, 204
Fischer, Hugo, 200
Fitzgerald, Dr., 235
Fitzsimmons, W.J., 111
Flagstaff Island, 44, 46
Flaherty, Robert, 38
Flint, S., 46
Fort Macpherson, 32
Fort Smith, 118
Foster, Janet, 24, 29, 31, 34, 279n12
Foucault, Michel, 8-9, 12, 14
Foxe Basin, 140, 237
Franklin expedition, 5, 44
Fraser River, 34
Freeman, Milton, 19, 131, 134, 135
Freeman, Minnie Aodla, 18
Friesen, D.F., 102
Frobisher Bay. *See* Iqaluit
Fullerton Harbour, 32, 36, 161, 292n97
Fur Trade in Canada, The, 28

Gallagher, Bill, 168, 191
game management, 6, 7, 10, 12, 13, 15, 16, 17, 18, 19, 23, 29, 30, 39, 41, 48, 49, 50, 51, 52, 54, 55, 56, 59-61, 74, 75, 77, 90, 96, 118, 127, 134-35, 139, 159, 165, 204, 222, 226-27, 276, 282n7
Garry Lake, 60, 94, 219, 236, 275
Geological Survey of Canada, 29, 31
Germany, 133
Gibson, Gordon, 141
Gibson, Roy, 36, 40, 44, 46, 47, 52, 86
Giddens, Anthony, 10
Gillies, Ross W, 30
Gjoa Haven, 47, 50, 82, 127, 128, 138, 174
Globe and Mail, 155

Gollop, J.B., 157-58, 293n91
Gorlick, NSO, 255, 256
Grace, Sherrill, 9
Graham, Maxwell, 28
Gramsci, Antonio, 122
Grant, Madison, 28
Grant, Shelagh, 12
Great Bear Lake, 25, 40, 62
Great Slave Lake, 25, 39, 47, 62, 66
Green, Donald, 255-56
Green, P.J., 236
Greenland, 105, 110-12, 171, 219, 231, 264
Greenway, John, 37
Grise Fiord. *See* Ausuittuq
Gunn, NSO, 236

Hall, D.J., 27
Hall, Emmett, 192
Hall Beach, 269
Halvana, Connie, 255
Halvana, John, 255
Hamilton, Alvin, 183, 290n49
Hardt, Michael, 10
Hardy, Patrick, 133-34
Harington, C.R., 117, 120
Harkin, James, 24
Harrington, Richard, 131
Harvey, David, 8, 9, 10
Hayes, Samuel P., 25, 74
Heard, Doug, 65
Hearne, Samuel, 77
Hellyer, Paul, 268
Henderson, Sakej (James Youngblood), 17, 293n2
Henik Lake, 148, 236, 275
Hershel Island, 29, 30, 31, 32, 34
Hewitt, C. Gordon, 24, 28
Higilaq/Taqtu, 277
Hikok, Nellie, 242
Hoare, W.H.B. (Billy), 36
Hodgson, Stuart, 120, 121
Holman Island, 87, 110
Horkheimer, Max, 9, 10, 11, 13, 274, 282n18
Houston, Alma, 91, 233
Houston, James, 91, 233, 274
Howe, C.D., 201-2
Hudson Bay, 25, 32, 36, 37, 42, 65, 67, 68, 152, 279n2
Hudson's Bay Company, 25, 39, 40, 42, 43, 44, 45, 46, 58, 79, 92, 93, 98, 101-2, 106, 110, 113, 114, 116, 118, 141, 151, 170, 214, 218, 228, 231, 273, 280n35, 284n1, 296n3, 296n30

Huget, A, 36
Hunters and Bureaucrats, 9

Idlout, Joseph, 123, 129, 207
Igluligaarjuk, 25, 37, 41, 151, 154, 210, 222, 284n1
Iglulik, 88, 106, 140, 154, 198, 254, 264, 267, 268-71
Ikaluktutiak, 33, 42, 43, 44, 45, 96-97, 99, 102, 110, 122, 170, 225, 280n35
Illinois, 64
Images of Justice, 15, 285n39
Immaroitok, Emik, 106, 107(fig)
Imperial Oil, 47
India, 207
Indian Act, 36, 46, 84, 86, 143, 166, 169, 170-73, 177, 181, 193, 197, 293n10
Indian Affairs Branch, 28, 36, 37, 135, 136, 143, 144, 183, 192-95, 264, 268
Indian-Eskimo Association, 194
Indians, 23, 26, 32, 34, 36, 38, 39, 46, 48, 52, 53, 58, 69, 75, 79, 80, 81, 87, 90, 94, 99, 100, 143, 144, 155, 165-66, 169, 170-74, 176, 177, 178, 180, 183, 184, 188, 192-97, 202, 245, 246, 250, 279n12, 281n46
Innis, Harold, 28
In the Way of Development, 19
Inuit culture, xi, 9, 11, 13, 14, 16, 19, 25, 29, 60, 67, 80, 82, 84, 86, 88, 90, 95, 96, 98, 107, 109, 113, 118, 123, 127, 137, 147, 153, 161, 167, 169, 180, 188, 202, 204, 207, 209, 221, 230, 253, 263, 273, 289n27, 290n34, 296n7
Inuit hunting, 6, 11, 12, 13, 14, 15, 17, 19, 23, 24, 30, 32, 38, 46, 48, 55, 56, 59, 62, 63, 71, 77, 82, 83, 84, 87, 88, 90, 91, 92, 96, 99, 100, 102-6, 108, 110, 111, 114, 115, 116, 119, 120, 121, 123-5, 129, 131, 133, 137-39, 141, 144, 146, 151, 153, 154, 161, 169, 178, 183, 229, 273, 275, 281n6, 283n34, 297n44
Inuit Land Use and Occupancy Study, 134
Inuit rights, 6, 11, 15, 17, 24, 28, 54, 85, 96, 99-100, 130, 147, 161, 165, 166, 167, 169, 170, 175, 177, 179-80, 182, 183, 202, 204, 208, 252-53, 271, 272
Inuit Tapiriit Kanatami, 17, 99, 134
Inuit Tapirisat of Canada. *See* Inuit Tapiriit Kanatami
Inuit women, 16, 72, 86, 209, 242, 252, 254, 260-61, 264, 275, 296n12
Inuktitut, xi, xii, 15, 20, 71, 88, 120, 177, 201, 209, 223, 224, 231, 242, 244, 253, 255, 264, 267, 286n50, 299n3

Inupiat, 186-87
Inuvialuit, 6
Inuvik, 112, 158, 185
Iqaluit, 51, 68, 71, 72, 161, 168-69, 173, 186, 202, 204, 206, 207(fig), 219, 220, 227, 228, 253, 254, 269-70, 284n1
Irniq, Peter, 71-72, 73(fig), 278, 284n1
Iyago, Francis, 213, 230-31, 234, 236

Jackson, A.Y., 37
James, Canon, 210, 223
Jameson, Fredric, 9, 277
Jenness, Diamond, 24, 166, 277, 296n12
Jones, E.E., 96-98
Jones, H.M., 144

Kadluk, 207
Kadlutisiaq, Josiah, 88, 268-69, 271
Kadlutqiaq, J., 268-69, 271
Kallooar, Frances, 101, 147
Kanayuk, 211, 213
Kangiqliniq, 113, 115, 116, 117, 120, 141, 154, 233
Kanoyaoyak, 96-98
Kassingwak, 110
Katokra, Peter, 113
Kaunak, 113
Kayakjuak, 161, 293n97
Kazan River, 101, 147, 148, 232
Keenleyside, Hugh, 52
Keewatin, ix, 6, 39, 40, 55, 68, 88, 105, 120, 148, 150, 151, 152, 156, 157, 159, 254, 279n2
Keewatin Echo, 271
Kelly, Dr., 256
Kelsall, John, 9, 13, 14, 54, 54(fig), 55, 57, 59, 61-69, 71, 73-81, 88-92, 96, 97, 98, 103, 141, 150, 151, 152, 155, 156, 157, 158-59, 276, 282nn18,21,23, 283nn24,28, 284n14, 298n89
Kilabuk, Ipeelee, 271-72
King, James, 132
Kingauk, 43, 75, 88-90, 92, 96-98, 102, 140, 145, 150, 155, 159, 284n14
Kingston, 131
King William Island, 45
Kinngait. *See* Cape Dorset
Kirbyson, A.D., 120
Kiumajut, x, 6, 7, 8, 10, 14
Kivalliq. *See* Keewatin
Knights, R.C., 113
Kogogolak, 99, 180, 190, 285n41
Kohoktak, John, 102
Koihok, Moses, 33(fig)
Komak, Archie, 96

Kugluktuk, 16, 26, 43, 91, 94, 102, 138, 173, 240, 241(fig), 242, 244, 245, 251, 252-54, 257, 258, 258(fig), 259, 260, 277
Kulchyski, Peter, x, xii, 15, 17, 20, 32, 34, 36, 39, 60, 68, 83, 85, 166, 170, 181, 205, 224, 236, 251, 275, 280n16, 284n6, 291n63, 293nn4,8, 296n4
Kulutingwak, 110
Kunangnaq, 101
Kuptana, John, 102
Kuptana, Rosmarie, 277
Kwaterowsky, Paul, 118, 129-30, 133, 137

Labrador, 196, 200; duck, 57; icebreaker, 225
Laing, Arthur, 116, 121, 135, 149, 175, 195, 264, 266-68
Laing, Walter, 141
LaMarsh, Judy, 267
Land of the Long Day, 206-7
Larocque, Emma, 18
Larsen, Henry, 83, 87-88, 90-91, 97-98, 108, 148, 175, 251-52, 255, 256, 284n14
Laurier, Wilfred, 27, 28
LeCapelain, C.K., 174-75, 245-47, 249-51
Leopold, Aldo, 24, 282n7
Levinas, Emmanuel, 203
Lewis, Harrison, 26, 35, 52-53, 55-56, 86, 88, 91
Livingston, Dr., 41
Livingston, John, 24
Lloyd, Hoyes, 35, 52, 53
Look, Art, 153-54, 292n76
Los Angeles County Museum, 100
Loughrey, Alan, 61, 62, 83, 99, 103-4, 106-7, 117, 182
Lukacs, George, 9
Lunen, Sandy, 151, 223
Luxton, Norman, 109-10
Lyall, John, 122-3
Lysyk, E.R., 114, 147

Mablik, Anthonase, 113
MacBrien, James, 40, 46
MacDonald, J.A., 267
Macdonell, C.B., 103
MacFarlane, Delores, 75-77, 283n32
Mackenzie district, 32, 34, 39, 52, 78, 85, 88, 93, 103, 118, 259
Mackenzie River, 30, 35, 39, 42, 66, 112, 280n28
Macklem, Patrick, 17, 165
Macpherson, A.H., 154
MacPherson, C.B., 16, 295n1

Mair, Winston, 53, 56, 92, 93, 98, 99, 108, 109, 111, 147
Malaher, G.W., 156
Malfair, J.R., 148
Manitoba, 27, 28, 39, 40, 75, 76, 79, 141, 142, 143, 149, 150, 156, 157, 290n49
Manning, Leo, 254-56
Maritimes, 34, 35
Marsh, Donald, 268, 271
Marxism, 9
Mazuk, Olive, 135
McCauley, J.H., 78
McDougall, Corporal, 256
McGill, H.W., 47, 53
McIntosh, A.B., 110
McKeand, Major, 46
McNicoll, Paule, 83
McPhee, M.J., 114
McRae, Glenn, 19
Meighen, Arthur, 34
Melling, Thomas, 41
Memmi, Albert, 9
Menez, Father, 96
Merrill, C.L., 256, 259-60
Métis, xii, 26, 84, 191, 202, 246, 250
Mexico, 52, 187
Michael, Simonie, 102, 173, 201-2, 278
Mickenberg, Neil, 17, 293n1
migratory birds, 26, 35, 52, 86, 194-95, 196; Convention Act, 35, 46, 47, 122, 143, 194, 196; protection, 28, 32, 35, 36, 87; treaty, 24, 26, 28, 187
Miller, R.S., 157
Milmine, R.N., 110
Miok, Jack, 96
Mittimatalik. *See* Pond Inlet
modernization, 6, 8, 12, 25, 51, 59, 81, 126(fig), 191, 203, 216(fig), 274, 275, 276, 279n5
Mohawk, 188
Monday, B., 264
Montreal, 188, 269
Mooney, Doctor, 184-85
Moore, Percy, 176-77, 257
Morrow, William, 101
Mowat, Farley, 55, 56, 57, 57(fig), 91, 132, 144, 167, 274, 281n6, 291n72
Muir, John, 24
Munro, David, 114, 116, 117, 130, 133, 147, 150, 153-54, 156-58, 161, 196
Munsternjelm, Eric, 151-52, 291n72
Murphy, T.G., 38

Nadasdy, Paul, 9, 14, 65, 132, 283n30, 285n29, 289n15

Nanook of the North, 38
Nanordluk, Jaki, 113
Nargyak, Moses, 50, 127-28, 138, 174
Nasook, Noah, 268-69
National Archives of Canada, x, 240, 292n76
Nation State and Violence, The, 10
Native Rights in Canada, 17
Naujaat, 41, 72, 113, 115, 154
Navin, John J., 183
Negri, Antonio, 10
Netsilik, 174
Never Cry Wolf, 57, 91, 132, 144, 281n6, 291n72
Neville, Bill, 184-85
Newfoundland, 133, 134, 200, 289n27
News of the North, 158
New York, 26, 28, 51
Niago, 219
Nichols, P.A.C., 110
Nivisiniaq/Shoofly, 277
Norman Wells, 35, 47, 280n28, 300n30
Northwest Game Act, 32, 35, 36, 39-40, 46, 47, 52
Northwest Mounted Police, 32, 35
Northwest Territories, 6, 13, 23, 24, 28, 31-41, 44, 47, 50, 51, 53, 55, 56, 58, 59, 63-65, 67, 75, 84, 85, 87, 95, 99-101, 104, 107, 110, 113, 116, 118-20, 129, 131, 133, 134-37, 141-42, 153, 156-59, 170-72, 177, 180, 181-84, 193, 200, 201, 202, 246, 248, 260, 261, 269, 274, 279nn6,10, 280n16, 282n22
Norway, 116
Nunavut, ix, x, xi, 6, 18, 19, 71, 72, 205, 264, 275, 278

O'Brien, NSO, 259
Okpik, Abraham, 102
Ontario, xi, 34, 35, 53, 134, 187
Ookowleaga, M., 236
Ookpuga, 232-33
oral history, ix, x, 15
Orange, R.J. "Bud," 194-95
Oryx, 80
Other Side of Eden, The, 13, 278, 296n12
Ottawa, 34, 37, 44, 91, 116, 118, 120, 139, 160, 195, 206, 225, 249, 269, 274

Palmer, Marion, 266
Pangnirtung, 25, 36, 107, 114, 140, 266, 271
Parker, 231, 234
Parker, John, 131, 159
Parker, P.B., 101

Parsons, Ralph, 40, 58-59
Passion for Wildlife, A, 24, 276
Peace River District, 39
Pearson, Lester, 52, 141, 149
Pederson, Mrs. J.R., 260-61
People's Land, The, 275
Perouar, 146
Perry River, 42-45, 60
Phillips, R.A.J., 112, 174-76, 182, 184, 191, 192, 233, 234, 254-57, 274
Pickersgill, Jack, 264
Pike, W.M., 77
Pinchot, Gifford, 27
Piruyeq, Barnabas, 57, 121, 223, 229, 237
Pitseolak, Peter, 263
Point Barrow, 186, 188, 190
Pond Inlet, 46, 107, 140, 254, 264-69
Pootoogoo, 278
Pope Paul III, 165
Porter, George, 47
postcolonial, xii, 9
Poulantzas, Nicos, 10, 14
Prince of Wales Heritage Centre, x
progress, 5, 7, 136, 138, 185, 195, 207
Pruden, Don, 146-47
Pryde, Duncan, 158
Pueblo, 187

Qajaarjuaq, Joanasie, 72
Qamani'tuaq, 15, 34, 101, 121, 146-47, 151, 153
Qausuittuq, 100, 114-17, 120, 129, 132, 134, 135, 136, 140, 159, 161, 202
Qikitarjuak, 114
Qilippalik, Mangitak, 243-44, 243(fig)
Quebec, 6, 35, 195, 200, 279n2, 282n10, 289n27
Queen Elizabeth Islands, 128, 130, 158

racism, 18, 24, 77, 80, 93, 135, 189
Rankin Inlet. *See* Kangiqliniq
Rasmussen, Knud, 37, 295n1
RCMP, 35-36, 38, 40, 41, 44, 46-47, 50, 52, 56, 74, 81-83, 85, 87-88, 90, 93, 95-100, 102-3, 105, 106, 108, 110-14, 116-20, 122, 125-28, 137-39, 141, 144, 146-48, 150, 151, 153, 167-69, 175, 198, 201, 210, 213, 222, 224-25, 227-29, 251, 254-57, 262, 276, 277, 284nn1,14, 285n41, 291n59, 296n3, 298n75
Re: Eskimos case, xii, 6, 170, 180
Reeve, A.J., 108, 110
relocation, 5-6, 20, 67, 68, 75, 95, 116, 127, 168, 251, 283n33
Repulse Bay. *See* Naujaat

residential schools, 53, 54, 85, 88, 104, 233, 253, 254, 269-70
resistance, 6, 8-11, 13-19, 42, 44, 48-49, 52, 54, 81-84, 86, 90, 95-96, 102, 116, 122-23, 125, 136, 138-39, 176, 202-3, 214, 226-28, 231, 239-40, 252-54, 259, 270, 272, 273, 276, 277, 284n2, 288n1, 289n27
Resolute Bay. *See* Qausuittuq
Révillon Frères Trading Company, 39
Richards, J.P., 87, 91, 108
Riddington, Robin, 19
Ritcey, Ralph, 160
Robertson, Gordon, 9, 68, 99-100, 103, 110, 142, 143, 149, 172-73, 182, 184, 187, 191, 274
Rollason, Heather, 77
Roman Catholic Church, 25, 41, 44, 53, 113, 245, 280n33, 296n3
Roosevelt, Theodore, 23, 26-27
Rousseau, Jean-Jacques, 16
Rowatt, H.H., 58
Rowley, Graham, 46-47, 134, 179, 187, 274
Rowley, Susan, 72
Rowley Island, 140
Royal Proclamation of 1763, 99, 101-2, 149, 165, 167, 180-81, 184, 250
Royston, 135
Rudnicki, Walter, 177, 182, 274
Rupert's Land, 46, 166, 243
Ruttan, Robert, xii, 14, 141, 149, 150-59, 276, 291n72, 292n76

Sachs Harbour, 95
Sahlins, Marshall, 9, 14, 59, 81
Said, Edward, 9
Salliq, 107, 115, 116, 160-61
Sanders, Joop, 264-68
Sartre, Jean-Paul, 7-10, 19
Saskatchewan, 75, 141-43, 149, 150, 153, 154, 157, 290n45
Saskatoon, 143, 157
Sateena, Sandy, 160-61
Saulnier, J.M., 236
Savile, D.B., 131
Schiott, Julius, 29
Schollar, L.B., 115, 119
Scott, Duncan Campbell, 28, 36-39, 58
Scott, James, 14-15, 288n1
Scullion, Mr., 266
Searle, David, 101
Seattle Times, 38
Seeteenak, T., 234, 236
Serkoak, David, 67-71, 168-69
Serkoak, Mickey, 168